ACTING

IMAGING

AND THE

UNCONSCIOUS

ALSO BY ERIC MORRIS

No Acting Please
Being & Doing
Irreverent Acting
Acting from the Ultimate Consciousness

AUDIO TAPES

The Craft of Acting
The MegApproaches
Imaging for Acting

THE ERIC MORRIS ACTORS WORKSHOP IS LOCATED AT:
1540 N. Cahuenga Blvd., Los Angeles, CA 90028 (213) 466-9250

Internet Web Site
www.bookmasters.com/ericmorris

ACTING

IMAGING

AND THE

UNCONSCIOUS

ERIC MORRIS

ERMOR ENTERPRISES

Published by:
Ermor Enterprises
8004 Fareholm Drive
Los Angeles, CA 90046

Library of Congress Cataloging-in-Publication Data

Morris, Eric, 1931–
    Acting, imaging, and the unconscious / Eric Morris.
       p.   cm.
    Includes bibliographical references and index.
    ISBN 0-9629709-4-8
    1. Acting. 2. Imagery (Psychology) 3. Visualization.   I. Title.
PN2061.M589   1998
792'.028--dc21   98-19463
                                                              CIP

This book is dedicated to the memory of
Shaun McNamara
Ker Michaels
and Brandon Lee
all students and friends who left this earth much too young.
I truly hope that they are in a much better place.

Acknowledgements

I wish to thank Scarlett Gani for her editing of all my books and for her research work on this book.
And Ed Zajac for his cover design.
My sincere appreciation to Hal and Sidra Stone for their inspiration, support, and knowledge over the years.
And to all the students, past and present, who have challenged me and kept me reaching.
To Susana, my wife, for her support and encouragement.

CONTENTS

Contents

Contents

"Images are the language of the unconscious."
C.G. Jung

INTRODUCTION

For years in my classes and in the work, we have been using the process of imaging as a tool for acting. One of the choice approaches, Creative Visualization, is a pure imaging technique, while many of the other approach techniques and processes use visualization and imaging as a base of creativity. Nonetheless, I had never thought that there was any necessity to explore this tool any further than I had until I read a small article in *USA Today*. I was returning from teaching a weekend workshop in New York and trying to fight the tedium of a long flight; in such instances I had learned to read anything I could get my hands on. There on the floor was a copy of that paper, and one of the box articles caught my eye. It was about an experiment which had been conducted at a university and in which imaging was used to affect bodily functions. Twenty people had been selected for the experiment; each one was first given a blood test and then shown pictures and drawings of white and red blood cells—what they looked like and how the body created them. For six weeks, twice a day, each of them created an image of his body making more white blood cells. They worked for about an hour each time in a quiet atmosphere with nonintrusive, soothing background music. At the end of the experiment they had another blood test. The results were incredible: all twenty of them had increased the number of their white blood cells by an impressive amount. It had been documented and authenticated and could be proven.

1

I sat staring at the article for a long time thinking how unbelievable this seemed, and even though I was no stranger to the *mind-body* connection, having been exposed to numerous procedures and involvements with holistic healing, the entire concept of what I had just read ignited an excitement and piqued an interest that have been going on for ten years now. I began to read everything I could find that would supply more information on imaging. In 1991, when I started to write this book, I asked my administrator, Scarlett, to begin researching the area and advising me of her discoveries. At first, we found articles, books, and word-of-mouth experiences that dealt with the medical area. I read about the numerous and unbelievable cures of terminal patients who used imaging as a way of sending curative powers to the affected areas of their bodies, miraculous reports of the disappearance of enormous malignant tumors that had been inoperable. I learned that there were many doctors out there who were using the technique with their patients and reporting exciting results.

In *Quantum Healing* the author talks about the natural intelligence of the body and explains how the brain responds to the body's medical needs in case of illness. The *receptor cells* receive the signals from the affected part of the body and send instructions to other parts to manufacture the proper natural "drugs" and send them to the needed areas in just the proper dosages, therefore never creating side effects. By imaging, we do similar things, except that the language is different. The codes and the language of the body are not logically interpretable in verbal terms. The messages are sent to the immune system, and the images are interpreted by that system to create more white blood cells to rush to the defense of the affected area.

For three hundred years Western medicine did not recognize the mind-body connection. It is only quite recently that research has started to accept it on some level, even though there is still a great deal of skepticism surrounding it. However, the interest has been so widespread and the results so formidable that it has spawned a whole new breed of scientists called *psychoneuroimmunologists.*

The use of imaging is growing at an incredible rate. The process is being practiced in a variety of fields and for many reasons. Psychologists are employing imaging techniques to confront various emotional blocks and distortions. In the book *Go See the Movie in Your Head,* Joseph Shorr talks about how he uses imaging in a wide variety of areas to influence the psychological states of his patients. Primarily the imaging gets them to obtain more information about themselves and to change the self-images that keep them in a less-than-healthy psychological state.

Imaging is also being used in self-help areas. There are a number of people out there who believe that you can actually determine the outcome of a situation by imaging it just the way it is going to be, before it happens. You visualize yourself the way you want to be, image yourself to success, create the life you want by imaging the events occurring!

Imaging is becoming, and has become, an important tool in the world of sports. The Olympic skiing team used the technique quite successfully in an experiment which involved the entire group: twenty-five percent of the athletes were instructed to practice one hundred percent of the time on the slopes; another twenty-five percent were told to practice seventy-five percent of the time on the slopes and to image themselves successfully executing the moves the rest of the time; a third group imaged fifty percent of the time while actually practicing for the other fifty percent, and finally the last group were encouraged to image the preparations and the execution of their practice one hundred percent of the time. The last group, the imagers, did best in actual competition!

At Hunter College, sports psychologist Barbara Kolonay, working with basketball players, helped guide them through imaging their free throws, with a fifteen-percent improvement in the results. A Swedish sports psychologist by the name of Unestahl, working with the alpine skiers, had them use imaging very successfully, as they created detailed images of all their movements.

College and professional teams alike have taken to the imaging techniques. Many coaches have realized the power of this tool to influence their athletes to perform well. A basketball player can image himself throwing perfect baskets from various places on the court and moving with flawless accuracy. Baseball players can image the connection of the bat with the ball and actually see the ball flying out of the stadium. It works! It is a way for the brain to influence the performance of the body. The basic premise is that by imaging repeatedly, the mind, from a conscious place, influences the unconscious, which in turn influences the performance of the body.

Over a period of time I experimented with a variety of imaging techniques I had already been using and supplemented them with new thoughts and ideas. With the help of my students and their courage to try this new tool, I made a lot of discoveries about using imaging in acting. There are an enormous number of areas to be addressed with this incredible process and endless ways in which it could be used. While doing this seemingly endless research, I began to see similarities of approach and application among the huge number of people who were using the process. Everyone seems to agree that *relaxation* is the beginning preparation for imaging. Most of the doctors and psychologists start by using a variety of relaxation techniques, usually done in a sitting position and accompanied by deep breathing. Most of the people whose work I read share the feeling that it is best to image with the eyes closed. I don't agree with that approach. However, one might start that way and then open the eyes. It also seems that the technique is largely an inner-eye visualization process, but no one is clearly specific about *how* it is actually done. In the medical area, the imagers create their own images to confront the disease. For example, they visualize an army on horseback dressed in armor, with extended lances, riding to attack ugly demons. The knights in armor represent the white blood cells, and the demons, in the form of dragons or gargoyles, are the cancer cells. Other patients create a horde of Pacmen-type organisms that, like piranhas, devour the bad cells. The images usually come from the imager's imagination, and that approach is encouraged by the doctors. In other areas, such as self-help, the images are less symbolic and more logical. The people see themselves dressed in a certain way, behaving as they would like to behave, and so on.

After digesting the various approaches and techniques, I began to explore imaging on a much more specific level. In all of my work it has always been paramount to define the specificity of a process: How do you do it? What are the specific steps involved in the execution of the technique? Since I have always felt that an intellectual involvement leads an actor to a kind of intellectual and retrospective result, all the techniques in my system are "pragmatized" into some kind of sensorial or outwardly expressive approach. What had excited me and inspired this journey was the realization of the impact and potential yield of the imaging technique. If the mind could effect such miracles on the body, with some adjustment one could program the instrument to experience anything in totally real terms. It is a natural continuation of what we have been working on up to this point. If the actor's responsibility is to fulfill material from a real place, to actually experience the emotions, needs, and impulses of the character, then imaging is a fantastic tool in that it takes the process to a new and deeper level of organic experience.

At first I thought of imaging just as a *choice approach,* but I very quickly found that I had a tiger by the tail! The depth of the imaging process is bottomless, the potential of it staggering. It goes far beyond just a simple acting tool. It crosses over the line into affecting the instrument on conscious and unconscious levels. I found that it could be used in a variety of ways: to prepare the actor to act, to address certain instrumental blocks and obstacles, and, if practiced daily, as a wonderful instrumental-therapy tool for solving living and acting problems. The number of preparations grew with every class. Of course, imaging is a marvelous choice approach. It has joined the ranks of the other choice approaches in my system and become number twenty-six. It can also be used to communicate with the unconscious and, with certain adjustments, to program the unconscious. In my book *Acting from the Ultimate Consciousness,* I talk about conscious-unconscious communication through dream work and other techniques. Imaging can also be a powerful tool in influencing the unconscious in pictures, visual symbols, and so on. If you image a place, an event, or a belief structure indigenous to a character in a play or film just before going to sleep or for that matter at any time and repeatedly, you are on the road to creating an unconscious support and belief system, actually structuring the thoughts, responses, feelings, and prejudices of the character. The influence of ongoing imaging while you are working on a specific part will evidence itself in your dreams and waking thoughts and behavior. In a sense it fulfills the old Stanislavski bromide: *You become the character!* If in your imaging journeys you attach the experience that you are imaging to certain objects or symbols, you can restimulate an entire feeling by using those objects or symbols as triggers for the experience. This whole concept takes acting into an entirely different realm!

The critics of my approach might scream that we are now leaving an art form and treading into parapsychological territory and wonder what that has to do with acting! In a sense they are right—especially if we consider that acting has not come very far in three thousand years! Certainly it has not kept up with man's technological evolution. It was just fifty years ago that actors used gestures to support their fakery. As we have become more sophisticated, our hunger and demand for reality have grown; however, we still accept much less than dimensional reality in our plays and films. Imaging and all that it means take this approach a step further in the direction of making acting a real dimensional experience for both the actor and the audience.

The process of using imaging to "program" the unconscious should have form. The various events and experiences should be structured to build the unconscious background of the character. Using your own parallels, you can image the people and the relationships of the play, the places in which the character functions, his thoughts, hopes and dreams, and the very nature of the impelling forces in his life. Through your imaging involvements you can create an entire parallel life for a character, one that the play never deals with but that underlies and motivates every one of his actions. Sometimes called the *subtext,* this is really much more than just a collection of intellectual facts about the person.

In this book, I am going to explore and discuss imaging in all the ways it relates to acting: as preparation, as a choice approach, and as a way to get down deeper into oneself and to use the unconscious to inspire and "dimensionalize" one's work. Most actors approach a role from a very conscious and technical place. Why not give the necessary information to the unconscious and let it do the work? When an actor establishes that communication between the conscious and the unconscious, it is usually an unforgettable experience for both him and the audience.

Imaging starts as a thought process, moves into pictures and images, affects the body, and stimulates emotions and impulses, as well as creating an unending stream of thoughts. What starts out with a simple thought or picture ends in behavior. If the actor first identifies the nature of the character's inner life, his emotional patterns and his behavior in the play, he can then essentially select the various images that stimulate and create that behavior from very deep places. The results of this type of preparation and process lead to a kind of acting that is extremely rare. If you want to journey to the center of yourself, if you want to experience life and acting on these levels, then read on; if not, this book is not for you. Imaging and all that it means can elevate acting to a level heretofore only visible occasionally in those actors we consider geniuses.

CHAPTER 1

A MICROCOSM
OF THE SYSTEM

At this point I feel it is necessary for me to outline and briefly discuss my system of acting and how imaging fits into it. My other four books, *No Acting Please, Being & Doing, Irreverent Acting,* and *Acting from the Ultimate Consciousness,* detail the system quite well. It is essentially composed of two major parts: **the instrument** and **the craft**. I believe that one cannot create truth from any other place but truth; therefore an actor must strip himself of all the obstacles and inhibitions that block his instrument from impressive impact and expressive reality. The journey to a free and expressive instrument is a large part of his training.

THE INSTRUMENT

The work I do in my classes is equally divided between the instrument and the craft; however, at the beginning of the training process there is an emphasis on the instrument, since it is not practical or possible for anyone to learn a craft until he has reached a place of authenticity in the moment. We do exercises that are designed to confront and eliminate fears in all areas of impression and expression. If, for example, an actor is afraid to be ugly or antisocial and puts a high priority on being socially acceptable, I will ask him to do exercises which address that fear directly: antisocial tirades, antisocial encounters with people in the class, and so on. Once he has done that a few times, his inhibitions and his fear of being antisocial dissipate, and he is free to address another obstacle area. So it is with all of the instrumental blocks: we eliminate them one at a time until the actor is free and comfortable on the stage, doing no more or less than what he feels in the moment. Having reached that state, he can then use the craft organically. It is not possible for an actor to deal with the obligations of material, hoping to authentically create the reality of a character, until he has reached a starting place at his own level of reality. So many actors suppress or sublimate their real impulses and feelings only to impose representational life on top of the reality. When this happens—and it is the rule, not the exception—the audience is deprived of a dimensional and unpredictable reality. Unfortunately, we have become accustomed to that kind of acting and as an audience have learned to supply the missing reality ourselves. It is the actor's responsibility to be real! It is his responsibility to experience the life of the character. Anything less is unacceptable! Therefore, the system starts with an exploration of the actor's obstacles, inhibitions, and dependencies and progressively eliminates them so that he can achieve craft readiness.

There are literally hundreds of instrumental considerations. Eliminating tension is the actor's first responsibility, since tension covers his real emotional life and stops him from functioning honestly. We all grow up in what is essentially a suppressive society; so when we come to the theater, we are usually loaded with all kinds of suppressive conditioning. All actors have obstacles and problems in common, and each has his specific individual blocks. It is therefore dependent on each one and his teacher to collaborate in the elimination of those obstacles, which were developed over a lifetime. Since it has taken twenty or thirty years to build these structures, it will also take some time to dismantle them. In the thirty-seven years in which I have been training actors, I have used in excess of one thousand different instrumental exercises, many of them invented in the moment while I was searching for a viable technique to address a specific block.

The basic preparation of the actor is first to achieve a state of relaxation and then to elevate his sensory accessibility. Once he has done that, he should find out how he feels and get comfortable experiencing and expressing that moment-to-moment life. To help him reach that very necessary first state, I use a group of exercises called *the Relaxation Cluster*, which includes any one of several relaxation techniques followed by Sensitizing and Personal Inventory. Once the actor has accomplished this first preparatory step, he is free to take the following one, which is to determine what he needs to do next. If he is relaxed, sensorially alive and accessible, in touch with what he feels in the moment and freely expressing his impulses, he is then ready to address the material or at least the pre-preparation state leading to the first obligation of the material.

The journey to freeing his instrument is largely related to his specifically confronting his fears by doing exercises that fly in the face of those fears, thus creating a successful antidote to the obstacle. He must then repeat this process as many times as necessary to convince himself that there is nothing to fear by expressing his feelings or impulses. This works somewhat like the domino effect. As soon as he feels he has nothing to be afraid of in one area, other fears dissipate at the same time. If a number of obstacles are addressed progressively, many of the adjacent blocks evaporate simultaneously. The goal is a free and confident actor who likes himself and is ready to *BE* whatever he is and to use himself totally to stimulate the experience of the character in the piece. An actor must become a *professional experiencer,* and in order to accomplish that, he must first be able to authentically experience himself.

The techniques used to free an actor of his obstacles and also to prepare him instrumentally are numerous. Many of them are imaging approaches or incorporate imaging as part of the antidotal involvement. If, for example, the problem is one of low self-esteem and the actor needs to do instrumental work in ego areas, he might create a better image of himself by visualizing himself as he wishes to be, looking a certain way and having the things he has always wanted; or he might image people relating to him in an accepting and complimentary way. Another good ego workout would be for him to list all of his fine qualities, talents, and abilities and then image these very endowments being appreciated by the people in his life. Relaxation can also be achieved if he images a state of well-being and comfort. Almost all of the inhibited areas of the instrument can be addressed through the use of imaging. In fact, any instrumental exercise might be confronted with an imaging approach technique, as chapter 4 will demonstrate.

THE CRAFT

The craft is the process by which the actor addresses dramatic material and fulfills it. *Craft,* unfortunately, is an overused cliché and for that reason has come to mean very little. Actually, artistry and craft are dependent on each other. Craft is process. It is the system through which an actor, or any other artist, creates his product. In acting, craft is the technique the actor uses to stimulate the emotional life of the character; it is the way in which he creates the environment, the relationships of the play, and all the other experiences and realities of his character. Once he has achieved a *being-state* level of personal reality, he begins with the first obligation of the play. He finds out what his responsibility is and creates a "choice" that will stimulate the desired response.

The craft is divided into three sections: *the obligations, the choices,* and *the choice approaches.*

THE OBLIGATIONS

There are seven major obligations related to material:

1. *Time and Place*
2. *Relationship*
3. *Emotional*
4. *Character*
5. *Historic*
6. *Thematic*
7. *Subtextual*

All of these obligations are explored and discussed in great detail in *Irreverent Acting.* Each of them addresses a different element in the material. After reading the script, the actor identifies the obligations that are relevant to the piece and decides on a chronology for approaching them. If, for example, he elects to deal with time and place first, he will select a place from his own life experience that will stimulate the feeling and impact of the environment described by the author of the material. At this point, he will begin to create the place he selected, by using one of the twenty-seven choice approaches (choice approaches will be discussed later in this chapter). Let us suppose that the environment described in the play is a dingy New York apartment replete with the customary cockroaches and peeling wallpaper, with odors to match. The character is a mirror image of his surroundings and is also sorely in need of redecoration. To accommodate the obligation of living in the described environment and being affected by it in the same way as the character, the actor might choose an apartment he lived in at a time when he was financially bereft and in an equally undesirable emotional state. His next responsibility would then be to re-create that place so that he actually achieved the sense of being there again. To do this he would need to select a choice approach that would do the job. It could be any one of six or seven possibilities. He might use Sense Memory or he might image the place, supporting the image sensorially. Once he created the environment, he would move on to the next obligation, which might be a relationship responsibility. Here again he would define the nature of the relationship indicated by the material and select a parallel from his own life, repeating the process of selecting a choice and a choice approach to create the choice.

After identifying the obligation, the actor must look to his own life for a choice. It must come from a knowledge of what has affected him in the past and would now stimulate the desired response. Even if the choice is a fantasy involvement, the actor should know himself and his availabilities well enough to select one that would appeal to him or impact on him in the desired way.

THE CHOICES

A choice is an *object,* person, place, or thing. It can be an odor or a weather condition. A choice is not a decision to do something. In this case it always refers to an object. (I use the word *object* to indicate the various kinds of choices listed below.) The number of choices available to the actor is infinite and usually depends on how in touch he is with his life, his past, and his memories of the events in his life. Actors who recall their childhood well usually have a much larger repertoire of choices to use in their work. However, even if you don't remember specific events and the objects and people involved in them, you can use a number of exercises in the work to open up those memory banks.

Choices are used to address all of the seven major obligations of material. They come directly from the actor's life and are selected with a knowledge of what they mean and how they will affect him. Very often a choice is selected which does not stimulate the desired responses, and it must be discarded for another. The creative purpose of rehearsals is for you to explore the choices and discover where they will take you and whether they fulfill the responsibilities of the character.

A choice can be a person, an animal, a photograph, a letter, an article of clothing, an environment, an odor, food, the rain or the wind, the texture of silk against your body, a piece of music, a relative, someone you love, a dead parent or friend, the ocean, the smell of flowers, a telephone call, footsteps in the dark, snow falling, the seasons, the sound of birds singing, an award, a piece of jewelry, an automobile, a doll, the sound of rain falling, the odor of freshly cut grass, medicinal odors, hospitals, doctors, dentists, a favorite piece of furniture, art, a familiar place, books, and so on. These are just a few examples of the infinite possibilities available. Once the choice has been identified, the actor begins to create it, hoping it will stimulate impulses, feelings, and thoughts that address what is going on in the scene.

➤ *Example*

Let us say that the obligation of the character in the scene is to feel nostalgic and a little sad about the loss of "the good old days." The action revolves around three men sitting at a table, looking at old photographs and talking about the old days and how wonderful they were. The actor might elect to explore a number of choices from his own life. He might in fact work to re-create his own photographs—pictures that relate to a time in his life which stimulates similar feelings—or he could create his real friends in relation to the other actors, or select a specific environment—a place out of his past that makes him feel nostalgic and sad. He could use a combination of all three choices to approach the obligation of the scene.

The three possible choices then would be

1. real photographs;
2. real people from a time in his life that would parallel the circumstances of the scene;
3. a place from his life that would affect him similarly.

To make these choices real the actor would have to create them, and that process involves the *choice approach*.

THE CHOICE APPROACHES

There are twenty-seven choice approaches in my system at the present time, Imaging being the twenty-sixth. The first twenty-five are discussed in great detail in my other books, while Imaging is explored totally in this one. So I will mainly talk about what a choice approach is and how it works as part of the system.

The choice approach is the approach to the choice—the way in which the actor creates the choice, makes it real for himself. It is necessary that the object be real for him no matter what it is. It will not have a significant impact on him if it is intellectual or suggested. It must be created so that he can see it, feel it, hear it, and so on. Therefore the process involved in creating it has to be effective enough so that it actually exists for the actor. If the obligation relates to time and place, for example, the place and the time of day or year must be created so that the actor really believes that he is in that place at that time. The reason why there are so many different choice approaches is that some work better in some instances than others. It is the actor's responsibility to select the one that will best create the choice in a particular scene structure. If, for example, the character is angry about something that was just said to him in the scene, the actor would not have to use a complex Sense Memory approach to stimulate that anger when he might just do a simple inner monologue, saying things to himself that would stimulate what he wanted to feel. That would be simpler and take much less time. In a sense, doing the other would be like killing a fly with a cannon. Selecting the proper choice approach is a result of experience. An actor selects the wrong choice approach many times before he learns to discriminate and know when to use what.

Basically the craft breaks down very simply to:

What do I want to experience? **The obligation**.
What will promote or stimulate that experience? **The choice**.
How do I create the what that will stimulate the experience? **The choice approach**.

Identifying the OBLIGATION and selecting the proper CHOICE are largely intellectual processes. The actual pragmatic work of the actor is done with the CHOICE APPROACH.

While working in a scene or in a rehearsal for that scene, the actor should be involved in the process of creating the choice selected to fulfill the obligation he is addressing. He does this work while saying the lines of the play and also includes everything else he feels, even distractions, thoughts, and impulses that might not seem reverent to the material. If the actor were using a sensory choice approach, he would then ask the sensorial questions in between the lines of the scene. If he were using Evocative Words, he would be saying words or short phrases as an inner monologue, under and in between the lines. Available Stimulus as a choice approach would mean that he would be relating to that part of the other actor or of the environment that affected him. Whichever one of the twenty-seven approaches he would use would be worked with while he was doing the scene. Very often he will begin to work before the scene starts, either on a preparation or to get the emotional life flowing before the first line. In those cases the process is the same, except that there aren't any lines to contend with. It is up to the actor to select the proper choice approach, and if he does so intelligently, it will be one that works well with the choice and that expediently creates the reality.

The instrumental journey is the actor's first responsibility. He must reach his own truth before being able to create truth on the stage. Mastering the craft is the work of a *lifetime* and a never-ending quest to reach further and higher. Imaging is another incredible tool that the actor can use in both the instrumental and craft areas. Its potential is limitless. In this book I will outline all of the imaging exercises and techniques and discuss their use and application. For more in-depth information about the system, however, please refer to my other books.

CHAPTER 2

IMAGING: WHAT, HOW, AND WHY

Every once in a while I get a fleeting image of my mother changing my diaper. It comes to me quite unexpectedly. I see her smiling and looking down at my anatomy, sprinkling talcum powder all over the irritated lower part of me; I see my own tiny feet convulsing with a mixture of excitement and warmth, and suddenly, over half a century after the event, I am flooded with warmth and security, and I experience an overwhelming feeling of being loved. What is that? Why do I remember so vividly an event that happened so long ago? Why does it still have such an effect on me? I am a grown man with grown children of my own, and yet that feeling of protection and motherly love still surfaces from the deep recesses of my being. Obviously, it burned an indelible mark on my mind. It affected me so strongly and with such importance that it remains lodged in the depths of my memory with tens of thousands of other important and impacting events and stimuli.

This experience starts as a mental image. I see with my inner eye the place, my mother, and myself. As the image progresses, I smell the talcum powder, feel my mother's warm hands on my body, and hear sounds, some of which are identifiable and others not. This whole experience is an involuntary imaging event. When it occurs, I do not think or decide to make it happen. It just does. I am sure that something precipitates it, but I don't know what that something is. I am sure that it has a definable pattern. I most likely get it when I am insecure or feel the need for that kind of love or nurturing. Whatever it is that stimulates the image, it definitely impacts on me, causing me to think and feel a certain way.

I have worked with this same image, exploring its component parts through the use of Sense Memory with very exciting results. By asking sensorial questions related to the event, I have been able to create richer and fuller tangible realities. I see my mother much more specifically as she was over sixty years ago; I feel her touch very distinctly; I see more of the room and the table I am on. At first, the image was like those created in a film to communicate memories of past events: it was blurred, and only the very center of it was clear enough for me to make out the objects in it. As I used the sensory process, my image became clearer and clearer until I had a real sense of being there.

Imaging is something that we have all been doing since infancy. Before we learned a language, we experienced preverbal imaging. It is natural for us to image. Every day we have fleeting images of past or future events, fragmented images that occur so rapidly that it is difficult to hold on to them. Daydreaming, fantasizing, wishing, and imagining are all comprised of visualizing.

WHAT IS AN IMAGE?

An image is a mental picture. It can be a still picture or a moving picture. It is something we see in our mind's eye. You may have a complete imaging experience while looking out at the ocean or staring at a blank wall. It is as if your outer eyes are seeing the view in front of you while your inner eye sees what you are imaging. When the inner image gets stronger, the outer one appears to fade, and you seem to be looking without really seeing what you are looking at. How often in the middle of a conversation has someone asked you where you had just gone? It is obvious that you lost involvement in the conversation and "tuned out." Well, where did you go? It could have been a series of thoughts that suddenly preoccupied you, and then again it could also have been an imaging journey to another time and place. Whatever it was, you left the place you were in and the person you were speaking to and became involved in another dynamic. Sometimes that happens involuntarily, and at other times you purposely run to something more interesting. These occurrences are natural and happen all the time. We image every day. Our dreams are full of images; in fact, a dream is an imaging experience. Imaging affects our moods and thoughts and stimulates emotional responses. It affects our bodily functions and can even change our vital signs. With a tool this powerful, a process that is being used in the medical area and is the fulcrum between life and death, imagine what power you can unleash and harness to create life on the stage or in front of the camera!

Our images include all kinds of people, experiences and events. There are literally no restrictions that should be placed on the kinds of images we experience. Anything that we can imagine can be imaged. One has to wonder what early science-fiction writers imagined and what they saw in their images. There is absolutely no limit to what we can and should explore with our imagination, and imaging is the transportation of the imagination.

How do you start on the imaging journey? What are the first steps to take? Begin with the realization that you are already imaging and have been all your life! Therefore, beginning would involve becoming conscious of what, how, and why you image. What kind of imaging do you mostly do? What does it deal with? When do you do it? How do you do it? Is there a particular pattern to it? Asking all of those questions will start you on the road to awareness about you and the imaging process.

THE KINDS OF IMAGING WE DO

Whether we do it consciously or unconsciously, our imaging takes on several different forms. The following is a list of the seven imaging techniques I have identified in my system.

Involuntary Imaging consists of thoughts and images that jump into our consciousness. While driving in heavy traffic, you see a carousel replete with music or someone you know walking down the street and laughing. The picture—the image—occurs without any prior thought of that place or person. These involuntary images come to us in large numbers every day. Sometimes they are not even well developed but are incomplete images of people, places, or events.

Symbolic Imaging usually occurs in sleep-wake states or in dreams but can also be brought about by letting the imagination have free rein. Suggest something to yourself and let the images come. Recently, just before dropping off to sleep, I experienced myself negotiating my way

17

through some sort of maze that turned out to be a cornucopia made of beehive material. Startled back to wakefulness, I was amazed at the image and wondered what it meant and what the symbolism was. Symbolic Imaging can be very useful to you as an actor. Once you become facile with imaging as a process and an acting tool, you might encourage yourself to image symbolically in relation to the character you are working on. The images can stimulate very imaginative responses to the person in the play, as well as pique nonverbal, nonintellectual unconscious involvement with the character.

Fragmented Imaging can be done with a theme or impulsively. You can, for instance, decide where you are and what the event is and from that point encourage yourself to supply an unending stream of fragmented images related to the experience. For example, you choose to be on the beach with an exciting and beautiful woman who is lying at your side. From this point on, you fragment images of the actions that follow: Her hand on my thigh…kissing her…the breeze…her blue eyes…love in them…my hand on her breast…smells of the ocean…under the sheets in a different environment…etc. The images do not have to connect chronologically or even make sense.

Free-Association Imaging, unlike Involuntary Imaging, is done by design. You sit or lie down and choose to image free associatively, blanking out all thoughts, working to relax, and encouraging whatever images pop into your head. A number of psychotherapists use this technique to help their clients. Interpreting the images allows the therapist to understand some of the patient's obstacles and problems. As an acting tool, the technique can be used in a variety of ways and for a number of reasons. As a preparation, it can stimulate the imagination and at the same time work as an involvement exercise. It also starts the actor off into imaging, and with very little adjustment he can then move into a more organized form of it.

Story Imaging is the more conventional kind of imaging that we do. Either consciously with leadership or less than consciously and without leadership, we follow a story and usually a logical sequence of events to carry us through an experience. We daydream using Story Imaging as well as other kinds of imaging. We fantasize through Story Imaging. We entertain ourselves in a variety of ways using Story Imaging.

Verbalized Imaging involves making the process audible—imaging out loud. Usually this technique is used in Story Imaging: "I am walking down the path. I smell the pine trees. I feel the air. It's cold. I see a clearing ahead of me. What am I feeling? How tall are the trees around me? I see the density of the forest. It looks foreboding. How far into the forest can I see? How many trees are in front of me?" and so on. The value of Verbalized Imaging is that you also hear your images. It encourages you to use the auditory sense as well as the visual. Having to verbalize is also very good discipline. It keeps you from wandering.

Guided Imaging, sometimes called *Facilitated Imaging,* can be done two ways: by yourself acting as your own guide or with another person doing the facilitating. It is simply a process of being led through an experience where the facilitator suggests elements of the event or asks questions about the experience, to which the person being facilitated responds sensorially.

All of the various types and ways of imaging will be discussed and explored in great detail in the next chapter. They all share a common process: seeing, visualizing, picturing vividly and sensorially an event, a place, a relationship, or a desired state or goal consciously until, after being held or repeated frequently and over long periods of time, the image sinks into the unconscious and ignites a power to heal, to believe or to accomplish whatever one wants to. "As you see yourself, so you shall become!"

Succeeding in any endeavor is predicated upon believing in what you are doing. Besides having a growing consciousness of what, how, and why you image, you must believe in the outcome. It is the same as with any of the other choice approaches.

HOW TO IMAGE

It may seem strange to write a section telling you how to do something that you have been doing all of your life, but it really isn't. We do a lot of things automatically and without plan, purpose, or design, and that is fine except when we need to repeat a process specifically; then we find that our intuition and the less-than-conscious way in which we have been doing things are not specifically available to us in a way we can count on. An actor who doesn't have a craft or process won't be able to tell you what he does when he acts. It is extremely important to know *how* to do anything you do! The form, structure, and technique not only supply you with a sense of security in your involvement but also lead you dependably to your goal.

There are literally dozens of books about imaging, or that refer to it in conjunction with other involvements, but they are not very specific on the actual execution of the process. Mostly they talk about "seeing" objects or events as if on a screen inside the head. Some of them do mention smelling or feeling the objects that are part of the image, but none of the ones I have read tell you how to create an image sensorially so that it leaves that inner screen and becomes a living experience that surrounds you.

All of the practitioners of imaging, however, suggest that you start by relaxing. Since tension acts as a distraction and a block to your real feelings, it must be eliminated. The bottom line in all acting craft is relaxation. It is not just coincidence that Stanislavski started his journey to his system with the exploration of tension and how it affected the actor. Whenever you want to create anything, you start with a relaxation process. In creative terms, how you image depends on what you are imaging, why you are imaging and what your goal is. As an actor using imaging as a tool to reach a certain emotional state, you might structure the process differently than if you were doing it as a preparation to get ready to act. The various kinds of imaging call for slightly different adjustments in the process. If, for example, you are obligated to a particular emotional point of view in a scene, and you select a choice—an event or object to create through imaging—only a part of which is meaningful or impelling, you would use a process called Selective Emphasis in conjunction with your imaging. There are many variables in the process. The way imaging is generally approached is that the person is simply told to see or picture images of his body—to see, for example, where in his body the tension is, to look at it, see what it looks like, then see it melting away. That is very abstract! It is also very imaginative, since it calls on the imager to imagine and create what the "demon" tension looks like. Seeing that demon melt away can be very creative, almost like the job of a cartoon animator. Please understand that I am not in any way diminishing this kind of mental imaging. It is possible that it is sufficient to create a mind-body connection and accomplish the desired physical responses. *It works!* I just want to contrast it with what I believe is a more specific *how* to image. After thirty-seven years of working to get the acting process out of the head and make it more practically impelling, I am inclined to think that combining mental imaging with the sensory process will take imaging to new and exciting heights.

As we get further into the book, I will explore and define the various approaches to imaging. For now, I want to start with basically outlining the process. When you begin to image, to see a place or a person, image yourself as part of that place or with that person. Avoid doing it as if the image were on a screen that you were watching. Unless otherwise indicated, it is very important for you to become a part of all your images. If you detach yourself from them, they will have a very different effect on you. It will be like remembering an experience as opposed to reexperiencing it.

Start imaging by visualizing the environment. *See* the place. If you want to start the process with your eyes closed, that is all right; however, shortly after you begin, you should open your eyes and image the place with your outer eyes. Even though the word *imaging* conjures up visual activity, you can start by using one of your other senses. If, for example, you were going to image a day at the circus, you might start with *I smell the popcorn and cotton candy...I hear the circus music ...I feel the crunching of the sawdust under my feet as I walk...*By starting this way, you are involving your whole being in the image, making it a greater reality from the start. As you continue, begin to involve your visual sense, and go back and forth between the senses to establish and experience the impact of the entire place. Life experiences and events affect the total instrument, not just the eyes. If you went back into your life right at this moment and remembered a group of experiences you had while you were at school, for example, you would recall them through all your senses. You might remember how your girlfriend smelled or felt, or how peculiar Joe's laugh was, or the awful sound of the bell signaling your first class and how beautiful that same bell sounded when it was time to go home, or the taste of the special "George's hot dogs" in the hangout across from the school. All of those memories are not visual but involve the other senses. Imaging is a process that must involve all of the senses. You can begin with *I see. Where am I? I am at the corner standing under the street light. What am I experiencing? How do I feel in this place? How does it affect me?* or any other way you can imagine to get a feeling of being in a specific place or event. The most important element in all the imaging you do is that *you must involve your senses!* The specific use of the senses takes the entire process to a more dimensional level. It is quite natural for all the senses to become involved in any image automatically. Even a person without any orientation or knowledge of how to use all five senses creatively will have sensorial responses. However, these will usually not be full or complete and will definitely be undependable.

It is important here to discuss the use of imaging on various levels— for pleasure or fantasy, as a motivational tool, or as a process for creating emotional life on the stage. The difference between these various uses is like that between finger-painting in a classroom for the purpose of exploring colors and feelings or for the pure fun of getting messy while attempting to express some abstract inner feeling, and being a serious, trained artist mixing colors to create a painting on canvas.

Imaging is a tool, a process that the actor can use to create environments, objects, people, and experiences that will transport him into the reality of a play; therefore, it needs to be defined and structured. Unfortunately, acting techniques have historically been vague and fragmentary, and actors have been left to their own devices without much craft process or structure. Imaging is a process, just as Sense Memory is a process. There is a definite *how* to approaching each of these techniques. Combining both into a way of imaging dimensionalizes that process and elevates it into an area of structured involvement that not only facets the experience but makes the whole process of imaging a technique that can be counted on.

Sense Memory is explored thoroughly in my other books. There is an entire chapter devoted to it in *No Acting Please*. The process is detailed with great specificity, so if you need more information than I will supply in this text or if you want to delve deeper into it, refer to the other books.

IMAGING WITH SENSE MEMORY

Start by doing a relaxation exercise. Clear your mind of intrusive thoughts. Start with an *inner vision* of a place or an event, and try to see the environment by "sketching in" the overall elements. If, for example, you are up in the mountains above a lake, see the trees and the lake, the mountains behind the lake, the strip of sand that makes up the small beach, the sky surrounding the whole picture. See these elements with your inner eye to begin with. As you continue, begin asking sensorial questions that *must* be responded to with the specific sense involved. In effect, begin to fill in the inner-vision sketch with specifics. Sense Memory is a process designed to memorize the impact of stimuli on the senses. The common mistake often made in approaching it is to assume or supply the sensorial responses intellectually or verbally. The responses to the sensory questions are made by the senses—by each sense in the area at which the question is specifically aimed. For example, *What does the air smell like?* is directly answered by the olfactory sense. The odor is experienced in the nose! *How many different odors can I smell?*—a supplementary question—is responded to in the part of the nose that determines odors, and so on with each sense. By combining imaging with Sense Memory, you create a definitive process rather than being general and fragmentary. The combination makes the experience a hundred times richer. With practice and repetition, the actor, or imager, will learn how to start, how long to image before involving the sensorial process, and in what percentage to use Sense Memory in conjunction with imaging. If the purpose for imaging, in all the areas where it is employed, is to affect the body and to pique unconscious support and belief, then it would seem that the entire goal would be reached with greater speed and efficiency if one created a dimensional and overall experience. If all the other senses were involved on the same level as the visual, it would be reasonable to expect that the reality being imaged would be greater and more fulfilling, while at the same time the un-conscious would be encouraged to believe and respond.

> ### Imaging Examples

Going back to the example of the mountain lake, create the image at first with your inner eye or inner vision; then quickly transfer that image to your outer eyes or outer vision. Sketch in the overall elements as stated above, and then begin to involve the other senses in some kind of suggested chronology:

It's very blue...I see the variations in the colors of the water as my eyes move across the lake...The mountain behind rises in levels and layers above the lake and blends into the blue of the sky...I feel the gentle breeze on my face and at the same time smell the pines...I am surrounded on all sides by the beauty of this natural paradise...I hear the wind high above me rustling the trees, and that sound has a haunting feeling to it...I can almost taste the minty sap from the pines...I feel the sun on my forehead. It's warm and comforting, and the combination of that warmth and the slight crispness of the wind gives a wonderful sense of bittersweet chocolate...

I am alone...My eyes follow the shoreline as it traces the shape of the lake...There is a mist that lies on the water and takes ghostly shapes, like pictures that one might see in the clouds...I feel the wind moving the hair on my head, first one way and then another...

None of the images are actually verbalized or described. They are experienced through the instrument! At this point, being well into the images, you can begin to support them and the sensorial responses by a deeper exploration of all the sensations.

As I look across the lake, how does the water look? (The response to this sensory question is a continuation of the visual involvement; only now, you begin to demand a greater degree of specificity in the visual area.) *Is it still or is it moving?* (Again, your eyes search for the response by seeing the texture and currents of the water in the lake.) *How does the sun reflect off the surface of the lake?* (Sensorial response.) *How many colors do I see in the water?...How do the colors blend into each other?...Are there any whitecaps?...How high are they?...What is the contrast between the white and the blue of the water?...*(All the while you are responding to the sensory questions and allowing the image to run free and become more dimensional.) *Where on my face do I feel the breeze?...*(Respond tactilely in that part of your face where you feel the sensation of the wind.) *What does it feel like?...How is the temperature of the breeze different from my own body temperature?... How does the sun feel on my forehead?...*(Respond sensorially while at the same time including all the other sensations of the image already established.) *What do I smell?...What is that exact odor?...What other odors are mixed with it?...Where in my nose do I detect the odor?... Does it get stronger?...How many different odors am I aware of?...Can I taste any of the odors?...Where is that sensation of taste taking place in my mouth?...As I look across the lake, what is the first thing I see?... How tall is that tree?...What is its shape?...How many trees surround that one?...Do they touch each other?* (All the time, intersperse images between the sensorial quest.) *I feel the enormity of nature caressing my entire body. I feel small and insignificant, and at the same moment I feel at one with God!...What are the sensations of that in my body and how do they manifest themselves?...*(Respond sensorially at the very points in your body where you experience any of those feelings and sensations.) *I feel as if I could jump up and fly across the water...and all at once I feel like crying, not with sadness but with joy, the joy of being alive!...*

The process is balanced by sensorial exploration and support of the existing images, at the same time creatively leading the imager to new explorations. Adding the sensory process enlarges the image. It encourages the imager not to stay with the immediate feelings stimulated in the first moments but to include those responses and go further with the exploration, on a more courageous and imaginative imaging journey. In addition, it forces him to use the other four senses equally with the visual. It encourages the image to leave the "screen" and helps the imager to become a three-dimensional object in it.

The combination of imaging and sensory support will establish a greater conscious and unconscious reality, thereby fulfilling one of the goals of imaging, which is to truly experience the image as a reality. If, for example, imaging as it is used in the healing arts could be supplemented with sensorial responses, those "armored knights" on white horses massed to attack the demonic cancer cells in the body could do so with the support of the imager's feeling those miniature horses galloping through his veins and arteries, actually *feeling* their movement through his body, feeling the attack and the battle wherever the malignant cells were lodged. As this battle took place, the imager might even hear the sounds of the cells being slaughtered and dying and feel the corpses of these demons being carried out of his body as dead waste. If this entire process could thus have the support of all the other physical sensations, is it not possible that the results would be faster and more formidable?

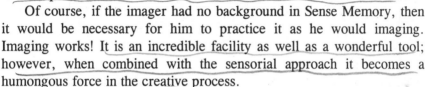

Of course, if the imager had no background in Sense Memory, then it would be necessary for him to practice it as he would imaging. Imaging works! It is an incredible facility as well as a wonderful tool; however, when combined with the sensorial approach it becomes a humongous force in the creative process.

Imaging anything can also start with the sensory process and then move into imaging. Sense Memory itself is a form of imaging. When imaging an actual event of your life, you may not have to re-create the entire experience in order to have a meaningful emotional response. If the image in this case were to begin as a sensorial expedition, it would do so with the first sensory question:

What is this place?...(Sensorially respond—visually—with the first thing you see.) *What is it I see in front of me?*...(Respond visually—see it.) *How tall is that object?*...(Respond sensorially.) *What is the shape of the object?*...*What is the overall color of the object?*...*How many colors do I see from here?*...*What is the most noticeable sound in this place?*...(Respond in the auditory area.) *Where is that sound coming from?*...*With which of my ears do I hear it the most?*...*Are there any other sounds involved with that one?*...(All of these questions are aimed at the auditory sense and should be responded to in that sense. You should attempt to hear the sounds.) *As I turn my head what do I see?*...*How far away is it?*...*If I touched the object, what is the first thing I might feel?*...(Respond tactilely.) *Where in each finger do I feel the texture of the object?*...*What does it feel like to the palm of my hand?*...*As I move my hand across the object, how does the texture change?*...*How high is the wall that the object hangs on?*...*Where do the ceiling and the wall meet?*...*What does the molding look like?*...*How wide is it?*...*What are the differences in the colors of the wall, the ceiling, and the molding?...*(All of the above questions are aimed at the visual sense and should be responded to in that sense.)

The sensorial process might continue for several hundred questions before you begin mixing the imaging techniques specifically with it. At the point where imaging becomes part of the involvement, you should go back and forth between sensorial queries and imaging: *I see the painting and feel that I could enter it...What is the subject of the picture?...It looks so deep, as if it continued into infinity...I feel as if I were having a religious experience...How does the bench feel on my backside?...What is the essence of this place?...How do I know that this is an art museum?...What tells me that?...I look at Van Gogh's self-portrait. I see his eyes, his beard, and the texture of his ruddy skin, and I feel his pain...What do I see in his eyes?...What is the shape of his nose?...his hat?...What are the main colors of the painting?...Do I see the brush strokes?...I know how he felt. I can hear his voice!...What does that sound like?...What are the specific sounds in his voice?...Do I hear what he feels?...I see him looking in the mirror as he paints himself ...I can see a half-eaten banana next to his easel...What does that smell like?...I feel alone in this place with Van Gogh...Should I dare call him Vincent?...He might enjoy that...If he only knew how many of us love him and what a wonderful legacy he gave to the world!...I feel vulnerable, sad...How has the light changed as I have been sitting here? ...Is there anyone else here?* (Continue to image and ask sensorial questions. The image itself will suggest the sensorial investigation.)

I see people milling around, passing the paintings and just glancing at them. I look at the floor and see textures and designs, creatures and activity in the marble veins...I feel as if Vincent were looking back at me. I once saw a movie where the subject of the painting was alive, trapped in the canvas, and saw and experienced everything around him ...What if that were true for Van Gogh?...I'm letting my imagination run away with me...I really see his pain and disappointment. I hear people whispering in corners, discussing that painting over there. What does it smell like here?...How many different odors do I smell?...I think I can see his studio...his clothes draped over his bed...There are tubes of paint everywhere...How many other paintings do I see around this one? ...How far away is the one hanging in the background?...How large is it?...What can I see of it from here?...What is the subject of the piece? ...What are the colors?...How do they blend and contrast with each other?...(All of these sensory questions are responded to and included in the entire imaging event.) *I feel hungry, and I remember reading that*

Van Gogh's brother, Theo, would send him money for food and that he would buy paints instead...I feel sad. He must have spent many a night going to sleep hungry!...It makes me wonder about life—whether there is justice or logic to any of it. I recently read that one of Vincent's paintings had sold for fifty-eight million dollars, while in his entire life he only sold one painting—and that was to his brother Theo. How could a talent and a passion like his go unnoticed and unrewarded?...As I sit here in this museum, I feel so many different things! I am inspired by his work, sad because of his life and the pain I see in his face, and disturbed by the seeming lack of appreciation of these Sunday museum goers. I'm confused about life...his life, my life...What is the purpose? And yet I feel exhilarated by all of it, hungry to ingest it, excited by all of it!

The experience was the re-creation of a time I had spent at the Metropolitan Museum of Art in New York. The imaging was combined with Sense Memory to re-create the event as I had experienced it several years before. In this example I started the process sensorially. I could, however, have begun by imaging and supported my images with sensorial questions. It is optional. You can start with either approach, except at those times when you feel the need to establish the environment sensorially first in order to feel that you are in a specific place. As I re-created the museum experience and as I sat at the typewriter recording it, I went through many of the same feelings I had felt at the time. If I were obligated to stimulate that kind of emotional life for a piece of material, that would be a very good *choice* and the imaging process would be a very good *choice approach*.

Quite often, I am asked: "What is the difference between Sense Memory and imaging? They seem very similar." They are! Imaging is a sensorial process; that is, when one images, one sees, hears, feels, tastes, and smells. However, when doing a Sense Memory exercise or using Sense Memory as a choice approach, the actor responds to each sensorial question specifically in the part of the sense at which that question is aimed. For example, if the sensorial question is, *Where in my fingertip do I feel the temperature?* the response is totally isolated in that part of the fingertip. On the other hand, in an imaging framework, even though the actor also responds directly to the query, he does so with all five of his senses *simultaneously*. He is seeing, hearing, and feeling all at the same time. The emphasis and specificity are quite different. Once again, while in both cases the sensorial response to each question is specifically the same, the major difference is that, when the actor uses Sense Memory in tandem with imaging, while the emphasis is in one sense, all five senses are responding simultaneously with equal involvement. The reason an actor uses the conventional Sense Memory approach in imaging at all is that sometimes it is necessary for clarity, specificity, and discipline.

IMAGING SENSATIONS

There are a number of imaging processes that the imager can use, but basically they are variations of just two approaches: the sensorial-and-imaging combination, and something I call *Imaging Sensations*. While in the first approach the imager asks sensorial questions and responds with each sense involved, in the second the senses function without the question-and-response process. The actor images the choice or event without involving the intellect.

The word *imaging* immediately conjures up visions, the visual sense, a visual image. Try for a moment to expand your thinking, and let us redefine the word *imaging* to include all of the other senses. What if they could all image? What if they could all *see* by hearing, or feeling, or tasting? What if an image meant a smelling image or a hearing image? By consciously expanding our concept of the process, we might, for example, think of having a complete auditory image! Start by believing that all of your senses have equal value and equal power to experience and create images. You can restimulate an entire event by reexperiencing the taste of some food you had as a child. Just getting a sense of that taste can flood you with feelings and thoughts related to another time in your life. If one of your senses has the power to take you on that kind of trip, imagine what all five would do if they were working together! The sensory involvement and response should be as large in each sensory area. Imaging Sensations are achieved if the imager allows each sense to function as a total and integral part of the imaging process. *I see the rain falling...*Here the eyes see the rain falling to the pavement. *I hear the drops of rain hit the sidewalk...*The same sensorial value, involvement, and emphasis are placed in the auditory area as were in the visual. *I smell the rain, the dampness, the cement...*The entire consciousness of the imager goes into the nose at this moment, and the image is an olfactory one. It is as if each sense had a "brain" of its own. As the emphasis jumps from one sense to another, the senses combine to create a total image. While, for example, the imager is imaging tactilely, the visual, the auditory, and the other senses are still receiving images. It just becomes a matter of shifting the moment-to-moment emphasis from one sensory image to another.

Like any other ability or facility, sensorial involvement and success are dependent on practice and repetition. It is like working a muscle. If you work it, it grows bigger. Practicing Imaging Sensations begins with consciously involving all five senses equally. We are conditioned to put more emphasis in the visual area, since it is one of our strongest and most literal senses. To accomplish Imaging Sensations, you will have to consciously allow yourself at first to respond with each sense, taking an imaging journey with all five.

It might be helpful for you to practice Imaging Sensations by using all the other senses first and with greater emphasis than the visual just to create a habit of equal time! In the beginning you may have to isolate each sense to work with it specifically; however, as you become more facile with each one, it will be necessary to combine all of them in the manner in which they normally function. To successfully image, all of your senses must function simultaneously. The image is an entire experience, and if it is to become a reality, you must feel it and believe it with your entire instrument.

> ➤ *Example, Using Imaging Sensations*

For this example, I am going to create a fantasy image. Even though it is not an experience I have actually had, all the sensory elements are things I have encountered in my life. I start with a relaxation exercise and achieve a state of readiness to image. Then I begin the process: *I am in a strange place...The ground is bright red with orange veins running in kaleidoscopic patterns.* (My emphasis is visual, and I attempt to really see the place and the colors of the ground.) *There is a peculiar odor in the air, which is light blue. I smell familiar yet strange combinations of odors...It is something like being inside a bakery, and yet there is a distinct odor of flowers. I smell gardenias and roses mixed with freshly baked bread and cookies. I am beginning to salivate. I can feel the hot bread on my lips and tongue. I feel its heat in my mouth, and I taste the freshness of the grain and wheat used to bake it.* (The olfactory and gustatory senses are working as fully as the visual, and each sense seems to have its own computer responding to the plethora of sensory stimulations.) *I feel very large, mainly because everything around me seems small...Looking ahead of me, I see a forest, a strange kind of forest. The ground is bright red and orange, and the trees have all the colors of the rainbow—not just the leaves, but the bark too. I see colors that seem new to me, and the shapes of the trees are unique and different, as if there were not two that were alike. I'm walking towards the trees. I feel my feet sink into the ground. It seems spongy, and at the same time I have the feeling of walking on a trampoline.* (With each sensorial image I respond directly and totally with that sense.) *I hear what seems to be a kind of music—only it is different from the music I am familiar with. I listen, but there doesn't seem to be a melody that I can identify. As I get closer to the forest, the sounds and the music become more distinct. It isn't music created by musical instruments, but the sounds of all the elements of the natural environment. I hear a cacophony of birds and the sound of the trees moving with a distinct rhythm that seems to harmonize with all the other sounds…This is an orchestra of nature…I am among the trees, and the ground is covered with the most brilliant, almost psychedelic blanket of fallen leaves…I hear the wind singing in unison with a variety of animals, and it seems like an enchanted forest. I smell cotton candy, popcorn, and candied apples, and I feel the cotton candy melting in my mouth…The taste is brilliant as it explodes with incredible flavors in my mouth…The tastes are overwhelming!…The air is sky blue, and the sky is a light pink with billowy white clouds. I feel a sense of well-being and peacefulness I have rarely experienced. I sit down against a bright yellow, green, and chartreuse tree and immediately sink into the softness of it…The texture feels like a kind of elephant skin, yet softer and definitely alive…It embraces me lovingly. At first, I am startled, but soon I feel the loving energy course through my body, and I instinctively know that it is love and benevolence that I feel. This is truly an Alice-in-Wonderland world, and I feel fortunate to be here. I drift off to sleep, but I am suddenly awakened by the feeling of being gently massaged all over my body at once…I am surrounded by the most incredible collection of strange-looking creatures, the likes of which I have never seen before…except that somehow they are familiar…I look to see what is massaging my face and body, but I see nothing at all…I try to feel what it might be but feel nothing except my own skin…when suddenly a little voice that sounds as if it were coming from a very articulate child says, "Don't be frightened. It's the Light People and you cannot see or touch them, but they are here to watch over you and keep you from harm."* (All of the sounds, feelings, and visual elements are responded to fully with each sense, and as I go on with the fantasy image, they begin to blend with each other.) *I wonder who said that. I am looking from creature to creature and don't know where that sound came from…They are all different. Some look like birds, others like little humanoid creatures...They are all brightly colored, and some are translucent.*

"Who said that?" I ask.

"We all did! We speak with a single voice, the voice of Truth!"

I look at what seems to be the mouth of one of the creatures, but it didn't move when I heard the words. "Where does the sound of your voices come from?" I see their eyes dart back and forth from each other. They are obviously confused by my question..."From the atmospheric vibrations of our thoughts, of course!"

Suddenly, a foxlike creature approaches me and touches my hand as if investigating...I involuntarily pull my hand away, at which point the creature jumps back several feet..."I am sorry," I say. "You startled me!" He cautiously returns to my hand and takes it in his...His odor is magnificent. He smells like soap and talcum powder and everything that is clean and innocent. He looks into my eyes, and I hear the voice say: "There is no need to be afraid here. There is no danger, no violence—only joy, freedom and love!" I am touched by what I hear and begin to cry, at which point they all gather in closer to observe my tears running down my face...I feel them wiping the tears away. These take on a prism effect, move slowly through the air, and become part of the bark of the trees and the fur of the creatures and melt into the ground, becoming brilliant prismatic crystals...

"What was it that just happened?" I ask, and again the soft melodic childlike voice responds, "Your tears and all the tears shed in your world are what has created our world. We take the sadness and misery of your world and transform them into the beauty, joy, and love of our world!" Again, I cry...I weep with joy and amazement...My tears fly on the wings of the Light People and begin to create new life in this place. My whole body vibrates with physical strength and well-being...I feel clean inside, and I experience love for myself and for everything around me...

"It feels as if I were dreaming and none of this were real!"

"You are dreaming! But it is nonetheless real...Your reality is the dream. This is truly reality, and when your world becomes too much for you to tolerate you can come back to this reality...In fact, we all wish that you would take this back with you!"

At this point I feel myself flying in what seems to be a tunnel of whirling air currents, and all of a sudden I am on the beach in Malibu with the sun and the sea spray in my face and the smell of the ocean in my nostrils, and I suddenly and completely realize that I can have that other world right here in my own just by looking for the beauty and seeing it, feeling the love and sharing it with everyone around me.

Having completed the fantasy image, I am left with all the impact of well-being—a feeling of joy and love resulting from my journey. It was a complete sensorial adventure. My senses, one by one and collectively, responded to and totally experienced all the sensory elements of each image. The emotional impact was extremely pleasurable. The experience could be used as a preparation to get ready to act or as a choice to fulfill the obligation of a scene.

Imaging Sensations is the alternate approach technique that can be used in combination with imaging. You must be wondering, Why not just use Imaging Sensations instead of going through all those sensory questions? It certainly seems easier! They are different techniques used for different purposes. It is like having two screwdrivers, one with a Phillips head and the other with a conventional blade. They are both screwdrivers; they both put screws into wood and take them out—but different kinds of screws! You need both techniques. Using the conventional sensory approach with imaging will help you create a very tangible reality. It will solidify and dimensionalize the place, the objects, and the experience you are imaging. It might take a little more time, but it is definitely worth it if you are attempting to use imaging as a tool to approach an Affective Memory experience. As with other choice approaches, such as Affective Memory, it is very necessary here to create a state of reality that will be believable enough to pique unconscious responses. The conventional sensory approach is also necessary when it is important for you to be concerned with the details of an object, when you must create that object as fully as possible in order to establish the sensorial reality. Imaging Sensations is not a shortcut to the process. It is a different approach. As an analogy, consider, for example, Sense Memory and Sensory Suggestion. They are likewise two separate choice approaches that are used in different circumstances. Sensory Suggestion is a sensory process that is employed in a scene when the actor doesn't have enough time to do a full-blown Sense Memory exercise. It takes much less time and can be effectively used for quick emotional transitions as well as to go from one relationship to another. And so it is with the two imaging techniques: Imaging Sensations would be used in circumstances where the actor would not want the process to be intrusive to the flow of the image. For example, if he were doing some sleep-wake-state work with imaging, he would be in a somewhat altered state of consciousness, and asking sensorial questions would interfere with that conscious-unconscious connection. Free-Association Imaging would also call for a less intrusive process. Asking questions would interrupt the flow of the actor who was programming the unconscious with an uninterrupted story-telling kind of imaging. It would be wise to experiment with both techniques to determine where and when one is better than the other. Imaging is an incredible tool for living as well as acting and should be explored and investigated daily.

It is very important to note here that anything one does should be done with some kind of process or approach. There are many people out there experimenting with imaging, and that is wonderful. It is like the "hundredth monkey" phenomenon. We are reaching a universal consciousness. All over the planet, people are becoming aware that there is a connection between the mind, the body, the psyche, and the emotions. The reality is that imaging is such an incredible tool that it works even when the practitioners are general about it and the clients are not instructed in a specific process or in how to image specifically. If the unconscious is so responsive to general and suggestive imaging—no matter how imaginative the images or symbols might be—then it stands to reason that if people are taught to make those images more real and more dimensional and to create a greater reality in a conscious state, the images will have a quicker impact on the unconscious and will be more fully absorbed. The most important reality of all is that, if done properly, imaging would work where it now fails. Wouldn't the percentages of miraculous cures be much higher if the technique were more specific and led to results that were more tangible? Only time and proper orientation with a method will determine if it is so! However, for the actor the time is at hand. The other techniques of my system have proven that being specific and having crystal-clear approaches do work and make it possible for the actor to be more organic, more authentic, and better able to repeat emotional life successfully over and over again.

The same level of specificity is needed with imaging. There is a *how* to all of it, a technique for successfully doing imaging, mental imaging, visualization, mind pictures, or whatever else the process may be called.

GUIDELINES FOR IMAGING

First, imaging must be taken out of the head and become a sensorial experience. To do this, see the images with your outer eyes, then use all the other senses to make it a living, happening reality.

You must then combine the sensorial exploration with imaging so as to promote the actual seeing, hearing, feeling, tasting, and smelling experience.

Train your instrument to understand and use all the senses equally—not just the visual—and create an ability for each sense to become its own imager, almost as if it had a mind of its own (Imaging Sensations).

To learn how to image, take the knowledge and instructions on the preceding pages, and then practice the process consistently.

WHY WE IMAGE

We image because it is natural! Pictures may be the preverbal language of infants. After experiencing your mother's breast a number of times, you must have lain in your crib and pictured your next feeding many times and long before you knew intellectually what breast-feeding was. I don't know when imagination develops in a human being. It may be an innate and instinctive ability, but as soon as we begin to imagine anything, we begin to image. We dream every night—in symbolic images. Dreams are our greatest teachers, as well as a very necessary release of accumulated anxieties, pressures, and tension. They are often difficult to understand because the unconscious has its own language. Freud, Jung, and a number of other important psychologists devoted a good part of their lives to attempting to understand and interpret dreams. Clinical tests have been conducted which studied the effects of interrupting or completely stopping people from dreaming. The researchers could see by the subjects' rapid eye movements (REM) when they were beginning to dream. Each time the sleepers would go into a REM state the researchers would wake them up, depriving them of the ability to dream. After just a few days, the subjects became disoriented, irritable, and insecure. The obvious conclusion was that the process of dreaming was very necessary to mental health.

Daydreaming, also considered to be therapeutic, is full of images. We see our daydreams inside our heads in the form of pictures. We tell stories using these pictures, usually as some kind of fantasy and wish fulfillment. Before any event, we usually have some kind of image about what may happen or what we would like to have happen. Often, we see some object that we would like to own, and we image having it or driving it. We do a lot of *what if* imaging—sometimes in little fleeting images that hardly register in our awareness. We image the outcome of things. We see ourselves going to a party, a picnic, the school prom, a first date with an important person. Such images are automatic, and we have had them all of our lives. Some are foreboding and frightening—the expression of our anxieties and fears. Things go wrong: We see ourselves tripping the waiter in a restaurant or doing some equally clumsy thing. At other times, imaging is a very pleasurable activity. It enhances much of our daily routine. Often, when I am sitting in traffic inching along the freeway, I use the time imaging what is to come later in the day. I see myself having a wonderful dinner with someone; I image her responses and the way she relates to me; I experience a wonderful restaurant with attentive waiters and fine cuisine. We go somewhere to listen to good music and have after-dinner drinks. The tastes and odors are delectable. The entire evening is one to be remembered, and I experience it all sitting on a smoggy freeway waiting to reach my off ramp.

A great deal of sexuality is made up of what we image. We stimulate and excite ourselves prior to making love by imaging a variety of activities in and out of bed. Even during the act we take the available stimuli and enhance feelings, odors, and sounds. All of this makes sex even more pleasurable than it already is. A good part of our lives is spent consciously imaging or less than consciously living in images. It is like having another life that exists in parallel to our real one. We daydream in a sense to achieve and have the things we want in our lives. While a daydream might begin with a thought, it usually moves into pictures. We image the involvement or experience and "see" it unfold episodically. Daydreaming is often an escape from a dreary job or a boring life. *The Secret Life of Walter Mitty* gives a perfect example of a man who wasn't what he wanted to be and who therefore created an elaborate daydream life in which he actually experienced himself being all the things he wasn't. A certain amount of daydreaming is healthy, but if it substitutes for living, then one must deal with it psychologically—get to the bottom of the problem and eliminate it. Daydreaming can activate the imagination and elevate it to a very creative state. It may impel a person to take action, to change his job or his relationships. If he repeatedly sees himself in a certain way, his manner of dress may begin to change; the way he talks, walks, or relates will be influenced by the images he repeats in his daydreams. Essentially, imaging is an ability that has been with us from the beginnings of mankind, and I would venture a guess that it was much more developed and frequently used before language evolved to the level it has.

Most of the imaging I have discussed in this section is automatic. It is not designed or structured but is something we do innately. When we plan an image, it is usually to create a reality or cause something to happen. As a society, as a result of decades of media bombardment, we have become sophisticated to the technique of imaging for success and to the various other uses of imaging; consequently, a lot of it is done with some knowledge that it has an effect on the outcome of certain events. Most often people who image without any orientation to or training in imaging techniques do so generally and without process. *I am going to ask my boss for a raise! I can see his face. At first he thinks, No, not now, and then he looks at me, thinks how efficient and valuable I have been, and gives me the raise.* We do that kind of imaging all the time, often without thinking about it.

Fantasy Imaging is more outrageous. It usually goes into areas of improbability. We fantasize for a lot of the same reasons we daydream: for pleasure, for wish fulfillment, to aggrandize ourselves, and so on. Fantasies can be a lot of fun and very rewarding. They sometimes supply the excitement and adventure that are lacking in a person's life and at other times supplement an already active and exciting existence. Whatever the case, when a person fantasizes, he uses imaging as the approach to creating the fantasy.

➢ *Example*

Almost every actor I have ever spoken to has had the fantasy of receiving an Oscar, an Emmy, or a Tony. These fantasies take the shape of full-blown images: *I see myself arriving at the theater. I feel excited. I am dressed in formal clothes. I feel the stiffness of the collar against my neck and the perspiration running down the side of my face. I can smell the flowers that the women have on their evening gowns. The theater is full of celebrities, and there is an excitement you can almost reach out and touch. It begins. I hear the opening music and feel the butterflies in my stomach. There is a buzz all around me. They are announcing the first award. I hear the applause. The excitement in my body is building...Now they are at the category I have been nominated in. I can hardly stand the suspense. I see the faces of the people at the podium. Time seems to have slowed into an endless collage of slow motion choreography, and then I hear my name as if from the other side of a long tunnel, and everyone is smiling at me and applauding. I stand shakily and begin that long walk to the stage. I feel as if all my joints were floating in water. I finally reach the podium and look out at that sea of faceless people applauding, and I feel the tears welling up in my eyes. I have rehearsed this speech a thousand times over the years and have had fantasies of this moment since I first became an actor, and at this very moment I can't think of a thing to say. My mouth and throat are dry and I am blank. Time seems to have stopped, and it all seems like a dream. I can feel a tear running down my right cheek as I begin to speak. I thank everyone, while at the same time I am able to express the profound feelings I have for my art and profession. I leave the stage with the award in my hand, and I feel as if I could fly, leave the ground, and in that moment I understand what everyone in the world must have felt in the realization of the greatest moment in his life.*

The award experience is a fantasy imaging involvement. Most actors do it for pleasure and wish fulfillment. Whatever the reason for imaging, it is a fantastic tool for stimulating emotional life.

For centuries, Shamans, witch doctors, and ritual healers have used imagery to cure diseases. In modern medicine, there are many doctors who use imagery to cure the ills of mankind. I imagine there are endless reasons why we image, beyond what has already been discussed.

WHY AN ACTOR IMAGES

An actor images for a lot of the same reasons anyone else does— except that for him there is a creative goal, a result in mind. Imaging is a tool, a process that he uses to prepare the instrument to act and to address the responsibilities of material and fulfill the emotional obligations. For the actor the *why* is extremely important. Imaging affects the instrument in a variety of very important ways. It elevates the imagination, it stimulates a willingness to believe, and it intensifies the gullibility of the actor. Imaging is probably the most commonly used technique in acting. Even untrained and non-Method actors have been known to say that they "pictured" an event or person in order to feel what they wanted to feel. It is natural to image, so actors do it intuitively. Unfortunately, it is usually approached very generally, starting and staying in the head; whereas, like all the other approaches in this system of acting, it has a specific process of exploration and execution. If it is not done properly, the results will be less than exciting or creative.

There are twenty-six other choice approaches in my system, and almost all of them use imaging as part of the process. At this point you may be wondering, If that is true, why spend time writing a whole book on something that you have been using all along? The answer is that since the core of the work involves imaging and since imaging is a central element of the imagination and creative process, it must be specifically explored and defined in all of its uses and applications. There are five of what I call MEGAPPROACHES. Imaging is the fifth, and it could probably be called a SUPERMEGAPPROACH. It is a tool so powerful that it defies the imagination.

Later in this book, I will get into all of the techniques of imaging and all the areas in which to use this incredible tool. For now it is important to have some idea of why an actor images—**to become more emotionally accessible, to elevate his vulnerability, to believe in the circumstance, to stimulate the desired emotional life and the relationships of the material, to pique unconscious responses, and to address all of his responsibilities to the play.**

There are many ways in which the actor can use imaging in his work: as a daily exercise to work his creative muscles, as a preparation to get ready to act, as a way of communicating with or programming the unconscious, and as a choice approach to deal directly with the obligations of a scene. Once he has identified his obligations to a piece of material, he then decides what his choices will be. To create a choice or event, he can structure an imaging approach to take him in the direction of the material. If, for example, he wanted to feel exactly what the above Academy Award fantasy stimulated for him, he could image that entire experience to produce those results.

One of the most important reasons for imaging is how effective it is in communicating with the unconscious. The impact is incredible! If a person repeatedly images something, it will become a part of his unconscious and will ventilate itself into his dreams and conscious actions. The potential power of this phenomenon for the actor is indescribable. If he can use images to create the life of a character in parallel to his own by programming his unconscious, the results will elevate the art of acting to a height never before dreamed of! To acquire this ability, the actor must first understand and master his capacity to image.

As I have said in my other books, there is nothing about this process that is alien to life, to the natural functions of life. Imaging is a process that starts at the beginning of our life and stays with us to the end. It then becomes a matter of harnessing and structuring this ability so that it works the way we want it to in a creative framework.

CHAPTER 3

THE VARIOUS
IMAGING TECHNIQUES

THE SEVEN IMAGING TECHNIQUES

At the moment in my classes, we use seven different ways of imaging. Each has its own structure and, like the various choice approaches, each would fit certain material circumstances better than others. Why have so many? Why not? The more tools an actor has available to him, the better a craftsman he can be. Each of these techniques requires a specific discipline, but they all lead to the same destination. Selecting the *right* one depends on experimentation and experience. If you ask an auto mechanic about his work, he will tell you that selecting the right tool for the job is everything; the work becomes simple when the proper tool is used. That is also true about acting. If an approach or technique is cumbersome and intrusive, it gets in the way of the flow of the impulses.

I have already briefly discussed some of these techniques in the previous chapter, but in this section I intend to get much deeper into the exploration of each of them and to suggest their various applications to acting.

INVOLUNTARY IMAGING

You might say that *Involuntary Imaging* is kind of automatic since it occurs without premeditation. Often we image involuntarily when we get bored or distracted or when we are idly waiting for someone. A conscious or less-than-conscious thought or experience might spark a group of involuntary images; it could be something you see which you may not even be aware of, a sound, an odor, the remnants of last night's dreams, a film you recently saw, a thought or series of thoughts, your brain looking for some activity, boredom, anxiety, unfulfilled desires, desperation, needs of all kinds—whatever might be floating around in your mind. Daydreaming is filled with involuntary images. I remember that as a boy in grade school I was often admonished by my teacher for staring dreamily out the window during a lecture or demonstration. Whether it was boredom or disinterest in the academics of grade school, I am not sure. I know that it was a pleasant escape from the imprisonment of the classroom. Even though a good number of years have passed since then, I can still recall the warmth and comfort of those little journeys. Depending on what was outside the window, my daydreams and images would jump from one thing to another. They usually involved heroic activity. I would often be able to fly and therefore went to many different places. The teacher finally moved me away from the window to the other side of the room near the wall, which made it difficult for me to see anything but the sky through the windows. It slowed me down a bit, but it didn't stop me! There were clouds and airplanes and birds of all kinds out there, and so my Involuntary Imaging was now influenced by different stimuli.

I remember in those days desperately wanting to be a "patrol boy," a street-crossing guard who put his arms out to stop the children from running into the street and into the path of oncoming traffic. Those boys wore a white shoulder belt that went across the waist and a school badge that seemed like the mark of great accomplishment. I wanted to be one of them, but I was too small at the time, and I could only dream about it. My imaging, in and out of school, therefore involved heroic patrol-boy deeds! I would experience myself snatching a young and helpless kindergarten girl from the path of an eighteen-wheeler just before she would have been crushed by its front wheels. I saw myself standing in front of huge tanker trucks, forcing them to stop on my command while

40

a stream of innocent children walked gratefully past me. I was Superman—or rather Superboy!

This kind of Involuntary Fantasy Imaging is natural and healthy. It exercises the imagination while at the same time fulfilling whatever needs trigger it in the first place. I imagine that the content of our involuntary images might have something to do with where we are and what we are doing at the time. An activity that requires concentration and mental involvement is probably not conducive to Involuntary Imaging. If we take note of the images, become aware of them after the fact, much as when remembering a dream, they will also tell us a lot about what is going on inside. With that information we can take steps to change or improve our lives, discover what is important and what kinds of things stimulate our emotions; we may even find out how we feel about certain things and people. If there are discernible patterns to our images, there is certainly some kind of message for us to interpret. I think that our most important responsibility in the journey through life is the elevation of our consciousness. Anything we do to know, to understand, and to elevate that knowledge and understanding helps us to fulfill the purpose of our existence on this earth.

For the actor Involuntary Imaging has many facets. As I have already mentioned, learning more about how he functions and what makes him feel and discovering the many emotional points of view that he has incubated are all important to his growing knowledge of himself and his instrument. Involuntary Imaging also helps him discover new and exciting choices that can be used in his future work. It can function as a device to explore a character in a play. If during a rehearsal the actor encourages himself to relax, finds a quiet place backstage, clears his brain of any background noise, and promotes the natural process of Involuntary Imaging, he might make many exciting discoveries about the play and the characters in it, including his own! Since he is already addressing the material, working for choices which are designed to create impulses that parallel the life of the character, it seems quite logical that these forces and stimuli would affect his unconscious and promote involuntary images that would come from those specific areas. In other words, the actor is enlisting help from his unconscious through his involuntary images, and these, in addition to yielding knowledge about the character and the play, also stimulate emotional support for him in the piece.

> ### *Example of Involuntary Imaging*

This technique is a tough one to illustrate. How do you voluntarily promote an involuntary image? I start by relaxing and clearing my brain as much as possible. I am trying to avoid any leadership. I see someone water-skiing on the lake, the wake of the boat pulling the skier. I remember my one and only water-skiing experience many years ago. I feel that place on my body...smell that lake...I feel my heart beginning to pound harder. An image flashes across my eyes...*I see my report card from sixth grade...Mrs. Anderson's face as she hands it to me...She looks at me disapprovingly...I'm in the water. It's cold. I can feel it all over me...I want to get out, but I am embarrassed...I'm in Fish Creek, Wisconsin...I'm sitting on the rocks at the edge of the lake...I'm sad...I don't know why...I'm afraid of water when I can't see the bottom...I see that water-skier again, and I feel that handle in my hand and the pull of the boat in front of me...I'm scared...I feel myself beginning to come out of the water into a standing position. I see the lake in front of me. I feel excited and scared at the same time. I want to let go of the rope...I see faces on the shore...smiling...cheering me on...I can't let go. It would be humiliating...I get an image of people reading this...what they look like generically...I hear someone in the kitchen...pots...dishes...I see Robert Morley dressed as a chef in a big white hat...He's stirring some gigantic caldron in a huge restaurant kitchen...Everyone is scurrying around him...I feel like I'm standing outside looking in...I remember that's from a film I saw once...I am sitting at a makeup table on a soundstage being made up...I smell that pancake makeup...I feel the cold pad as the girl applies it to my forehead. I feel excitement about acting...I don't know what I'm acting in!...That feels strange and frightening!...*

All of the images in this example really happened moment to moment as I explored Involuntary Imaging. It is difficult to re-create something that happens so naturally. However, it will give you an idea of what comes up when you allow yourself to image without any direction or leadership. I am sure that there are other ways to use Involuntary Imaging in your process, and I am confident that with practice you will discover how and where to employ this particular technique. The first priority is to become aware and conscious. Once you know that something exists, and particularly how it works or functions, you can use it and even enjoy it! We are continually bombarded by impulses, thoughts, and *images,* moment to moment. They fleet through our instrument so rapidly sometimes that many are not even noticed. Some are subliminal—meaning that we seldom experience them consciously—but our moods are very often affected and even controlled by them. How many times has your mood dramatically changed without warning or understandable justification? That happens all the time and to everyone. Those mysterious mood swings can almost always be attributed to some thought or image that fleeted through your less-than-conscious state.

If this is a normal phenomenon and it happens to all people, then it must also happen to characters in plays, right? Is it uncontrollable? Are we just victims of our unconscious or subliminal images? Let us suppose that a character in a play experiences a number of emotional changes within a ten-minute scene. Some of these can be directly traced to the action in that scene, the way he is affected by the other characters in it, and so forth. However, as it is for anyone in life or on the stage, a great deal of the fabric of the character's emotional life is created by an internal flow of impulses, which in turn give rise to moods and other impulses that are not directly stimulated by the action of the scene or the impact of the other actors' behavior but are the manifestations of the unique and individual makeup of a particular actor. In other words, these internal dynamics, stimulated by what might be *involuntary images,* are actually the expression of a single actor's personal fabric and cannot be duplicated by anyone else in the universe. Before you think that I am being carried away by some kind of supernatural force or possibly that I have been sitting at this typewriter for too long, let me assure you that all of what I am saying is true! If an actor evolves to the level of master craftsman and is close to becoming a professional experiencer, it is then possible for him to be affected by all those wonderful thoughts, impulses, and involuntary images. If, on the other hand, he is "acting," imposing behavior, premeditating expression, or being representational, it is impossible for him to be an open vessel through which impulses can flow. What I have described above is a natural result of being organic. It is not, however, uncontrollable!

In this context the word *control* may seem like a contradiction in terms. If the desired state is to be real, organic, and to discover the next impulse in the next moment and at the very same time as the audience, then what is meant by *control?* It is not that one should interrupt or interfere with the authentic flow of impulses or short-circuit feelings that would otherwise be naturally expressed, but simply that it is possible that with work an actor can become increasingly aware of how involuntary images are stimulated, how they can be elevated from his unconscious to conscious awareness and be "directed" by him so as to enrich his emotional life on stage.

Let us break it down into some kind of routine or involvement so that we might come up with a way of becoming aware of how our instrument creates and processes these thoughts and pictures. As I said earlier, Involuntary Imaging goes on all the time. It happens when we are bored or mentally idle or when something stimulates a rush of images. On the way to an audition, for example, an actor feels the gnawing insecurity of the unknown or a fear of failure, which in turn may stimulate a flow of either negative or positive images. He might see himself waiting for hours before getting to read, or his images might go in the direction of great theatrical success as he experiences the audition as some kind of tour de force that completely astounds his audience. Recently, I saw *The Secret Life of Walter Mitty* for the fifteenth time on television. I watched it again with the same delight I had experienced the first time. As I mentioned before, the character, Walter Mitty, is a mild-mannered, somewhat inept man, who is unable to do many of the things he wished he could. People take advantage of his openness and naiveté. As a result of feeling insecure and inadequate in any given situation, he has these flights of fantasy where he experiences himself as a great fighter pilot and world-war ace, or as a cool and self-assured Mississippi gambler humiliating his real-life opponent. It would seem that he actually *decides* to have these daydreams, and it is certainly true that he promotes them; however, it is also possible, if we consider the phenomenon from a different perspective, that his journeys into fantasy actually begin with a rush of involuntary images. It really does not matter whether that is what the author, James Thurber, had in mind or not! For the sake of making a point, let us just conjecture that each time Walter Mitty goes into this fantasy state, some event precipitates it! He always slips into his fantasies as a result of some insecurity he is suffering from: his rival is criticizing him in some way or poking fun at him for some faux pas he has just committed, or he has done something clumsy in front of a woman he is attracted to, and so on. Imagine that you were playing this character. Every time the scene called for you to go off into fantasy, you could use a choice that impelled you to *image* yourself in a particular situation that would actually produce *involuntary fantasy images*. What it all means is that you, the actor, would actually be paralleling the impetus, the need of the character to escape into fantasy. In addition, your own personal images would create a response that was real for you. That reality is what we strive for.

In the film Mitty's fantasy life is portrayed. We see him being the character he is fantasizing; so you might ask, If the visuals are supplied, why must an actor create the impetus? Why indeed? Because nothing takes the place of reality! If the actor *needed* to escape into fantasy and relished it while it was happening, then he would truly be fulfilling the organic demands of the role. The difference between really being impelled to fantasize and enjoy the fantasy, and imposing the need and the enjoyment, that is the difference between creation and imitation.

Suppose an actor could identify in each of the other characters in a play or film the impelling stimuli that caused his character to act, respond, and behave in certain ways, wouldn't it then be possible for him to stimulate involuntary images which would enrich the fabric of every performance? If indeed the choices he selected promoted images that affected him and stimulated other kinds of emotions and moods indigenous to his character, his behavior would certainly become more dimensional. In addition, the images would surely stimulate even more impulses than his original choices might have.

In my classes we have been exploring and experimenting with the various imaging techniques for quite some time. Recently, I suggested an exercise involving Involuntary Imaging. In the first part of the experiment, I asked my students to address a single obligation from a piece of material they were working on at present or had worked on in the past. I told them to make the obligation very specific and to work for a choice that would hopefully stimulate the desired emotional life. They could use any kind of choice and any of the choice approaches, and it was even suggested that they might explore more than one choice. They were also to take inventory of the number, nature, and kinds of involuntary images that would flash through their consciousness while they were working for their choices.

They worked for about fifteen minutes, being very aware of all the images that were produced in the interim. In the second part of the exercise, I asked them to recall the involuntary images that they had experienced—no matter how abstract or seemingly unrelated they were to the obligation or the choice—and to re-create them using Imaging as their choice approach. When they finished, we discussed their experiences and the kinds of images that had been produced in the first part of the exercise. What was amazing to me was that, for almost all of the actors, working for the involuntary images had stimulated impulses and emotional life that addressed the original obligations, even though some of those images were abstract and fragmented pictures of objects and places that did not logically have anything to do with either the obligation or the choice. Everyone felt that the emotional life that came out of re-creating those images was more impacting and dimensional than what their original choices had produced. My theory is that the involuntary images generated by their choices were actually unconscious connections with the obligations and the choices. If what Jung believed is true, that consciousness and the unconscious speak two separate languages— consciousness being more "rational" and verbal while the unconscious speaks in images—then it is possible that the actors' choices stimulated image responses that were somehow related to the experiences involved with their obligations. If this theory is valid, then the far-reaching implications could boggle the mind!

Bear with me while I hypothesize on this phenomenon. Let us imagine that our brain works very much like a computer. Something is "entered" either as a verbal suggestion or accidentally, as possibly a sound would be or a piece of music barely audible in the distance. The unconscious part of the brain, or "computer," produces an *image* response to that entry, thereby generating an involuntary image or a group of them, which in some way are understood only by the unconscious. The entry and the response are totally related to each other. If that is true, the images are extremely valuable to us. In the first place, they come from an unconscious source and therefore constitute fuller and deeper responses; secondly, they carry messages to us that, if interpreted properly, can be of great significance in learning about ourselves; and thirdly, they help us as actors to create a direct conduit to the unconscious, which will not only pique deeper emotional responses but shorten our work process as well.

For example, an actor who has been in rehearsal for three weeks, having identified his specific responsibility in each scene and explored a variety of choices, might have inventoried many of the involuntary images he experienced during the rehearsal period. Let us suppose that he decides to re-create those images rather than working for the separate choices. Is it not possible that he might be able to stimulate the desired results in every area of the play? I think that it is not only possible but very probable, and that this technique would produce experiences far richer than the original approach to the scene. It is in this way that the actor can use and *control* his involuntary images. If every actor would use charts and journals during the rehearsal period, he would not only be able to follow the course of the obligations, choices, and different choice approaches he explored, but would also be able to record all of his involuntary images along the way.

MATERIAL EXAMPLE USING INVOLUNTARY IMAGING

A while ago, two actors in my advanced class were working on a scene from *Hatful of Rain,* the scene where Johnny returns to the apartment after having been out all night looking for a "fix." His brother Polo is in the room. The scene deals with the brothers' conflicts and the realities of being a heroin addict. The two argue about money. Johnny needs "twenty bucks" for a fix, and Polo, who has supported Johnny's addiction for a very long time, refuses to give him the money. He tries to appeal to Johnny, telling him that all of the money has already gone for drugs and that he even had to refuse giving their father money when the latter wanted to go into business, because there was nothing left. Johnny understands the truth in all of these accusations, but he is desperate, as he feels the effects of withdrawal. There are other elements that must be dealt with in the scene. The two are brothers and love each other; Johnny has a wife who is at work, and Polo has fallen in love with her—information that Johnny doesn't have. In addition, some "guys" are coming over to get eight hundred dollars that Johnny owes them—or they will "kick his ribs in"! As you can see, both actors are responsible for a number of obligations, but—as is true in all of my classes—they are encouraged to deal with them only one at a time.

The first time they did the scene in class, the actor playing Johnny obligated himself to the physical symptoms and desperation of withdrawal. He wanted to stimulate an intense need for a fix. In addition, he wanted to experience the ambivalence and helplessness of his addiction and the tragedy it was producing in his life. At first, the actor worked sensorially to create the physical symptoms of withdrawing from a drug. This did stimulate some of the need and desperation he wanted to pique, but it was not dimensional enough to deal with the relationship elements of the scene. In this particular instance the actor had had a drug problem a number of years before. It was with a different substance, but the symptoms were very similar. He could identify with many of the character's feelings: his need for the drug, his guilt and self-hatred for being in this position, and his awareness of what this addiction was doing to the people in his life.

While he was working to re-create the symptoms of withdrawal, many images were stimulated, a number of them related to that time in his life and to the places and experiences that surrounded his addiction.

47

Many of the images were *involuntary* and hard to understand. Some fleeted through his consciousness too quickly for him to hold on to them; however, one very strong one kept repeating itself. It related to a rehab center where he had finally gone for help. These were his images:

I see colors...mostly whites and grays and various shades of those. There is a smell of antiseptic mixed with floor wax. I see a long, dimly lit corridor with closed doors on each side, naked light bulbs hanging from the ceiling, faces—some of which I recognize and others not. There is a large window with frosted glass that has a wire-mesh gate in front of it. I hear or feel a moaning sensation coming from inside of me, while at the same time it seems to be coming from outside. I have a metallic taste in my mouth, and I feel like I shouldn't swallow. I see people moving away from me. They have no faces, only the backs of their heads. They are moving very slowly. I see the reception desk. It looks large and foreboding. It is tall, and I can't see the top of it. It's just like the teacher's desk when I was in kindergarten. There are echoes everywhere. I hear people talking at the end of the corridor, and their voices sound as if they were coming through a long dark tunnel. My body feels prickly all over, as when my foot falls asleep.

All of those images manifested themselves as a result of the actor's re-creation of the physical state he was in at that time. By working sensorially to create the feelings of withdrawal, Jerry (I am giving the actor that name arbitrarily to protect his privacy) obviously accessed unconscious memories connected to the physical, sensory state he had created through Sense Memory. No matter how the unconscious mind categorizes or stores its responses to conscious experience, when we push a particular "button," it belches up images into our consciousness. It is those images—whatever they mean unconsciously—that we can use to create life on the stage, the kind of life that is extremely rich with complex and often unexplainable impulses.

By working to re-create some of those images, Jerry was able to get a strong sense of being in that place at that time in his life. He felt the frustration and helplessness he had experienced then, all of which fit *Hatful of Rain* perfectly. By using some of those involuntary images, Jerry experienced impulses and feelings on a much deeper level than when he worked only for the withdrawal symptoms. In addition, he established a strong connection with his unconscious. If ninety-five percent of our talent truly lives in the unconscious, then it is clear that we must make reaching it our goal! If Jerry were doing this play eight times a week and had to access that life in each performance, he could do so by re-creating the involuntary images that originated from his unconscious.

SYMBOLIC IMAGING

Symbolic Imaging is also automatic and natural. It is very unpredictable and often hard to interpret. It comes largely from the unconscious, usually in dreams or sleep-wake states. The reason dreams often need to be interpreted is that many of them contain symbols or symbolic actions that are not clear. Some people feel that the unconscious codes its messages so as to make it harder for us to understand them, but I don't think that that theory has any validity. The unconscious functions differently from the conscious mind, and its language is different. **"Images are the language of the unconscious!"** And those images are specific to it!

Symbolic images also happen when we are fully awake and in a conscious state. Quite often, while experiencing an involuntary or a fragmented image, you will have some kind of symbolic image that attaches itself to it. For example, you might get a flow of images about someone you are about to meet for dinner, and in the middle of that a large tuba appears. What that means, or how it relates to the person you are imaging, is up for interpretation and endless discussion. Is the tuba representative of the person in some way? Is that the way you symbolically see her? Or does it mean something else? Possibly it is a suggestion that you should go listen to some music after dinner; or maybe it relates to where you should have dinner! Who knows? I don't think anyone really completely understands the workings of the unconscious. *I* certainly don't! I do, however, know that for our purposes it is not important to delve deeply into the scientific explanation of how and why it does what it does. What is really important is that we know how to use its power for creative purposes.

Let us for a moment return to the image of the tuba. Suppose that while you were waiting for your dinner companion to arrive, you deliberately attempted to re-create that tuba, using Sense Memory or Imaging to do so. Create it in a variety of visual perspectives: the front, the side, and the rear of the instrument. After spending some time doing that, see where it takes you.

This activity can be repeated a number of times each day. At the very least you will have some fun doing it! What you can learn from involving yourself with re-creating those images is how they affect you. If by working to re-create the tuba you are affected in a particular way and that emotional response maintains itself every time you repeat the image, that could mean that it is connected with an unconscious personal point of view related to the person you were waiting for or to your relationship to her. If we were to carry this further and apply it to craft, we could assume that every time you wanted to feel a certain way about that person or your experiences with her, you could just re-create the symbolic image.

Suppose that every time you remembered being in Hawaii, you experienced this almost blinding flash of bright yellow—everything turned a bright and beautiful yellow, the richest hue of yellow you had ever experienced. It is fairly simple to understand the image: the sun is yellow, Hawaii is mostly very bright and sunny, and so on; but for the sake of making an important point, let me ask again: What if you did get that image every time you thought of Hawaii or something reminded you of it? To access your feelings about that place, all you would have to do is work to create this incredible color. If, for example, you were addressing a time-and-place obligation in a scene, and you wanted to feel the same way as when you are sitting on the beach in Waikiki, you might simply re-create the symbol. If this indeed works, and in my personal experience it does, then it is possible to collect hundreds of symbolic images and to use them as needed. This would be an incredible shortcut in the process—not to mention the depth and wealth of the image itself: Where does it come from? What does it mean? What are its components? How deeply rooted is its origin? When we experience the emotional life produced by this image, what are the dimensions and colors embodied in our resulting behavior?

As I said before, every actor should keep a journal, or in fact a number of journals: a daily record of his experiences and sensory involvement in those experiences; a choice journal, including all the images he receives each day; and a dream journal with a complete record and description of all his dreams and the symbols in them. To record our dreams is to keep them intact to use in our lives and our work. Underline all the symbols and symbolic objects in each of your dreams. Interpret them if you want to. Try to understand what they mean or what the message is. Make a note of what you felt during the dream and how those feelings changed throughout and after you woke up. When you were in a conscious state, did the objects in the dream have a different impact on you? By recording your feelings, you can follow and chart how a particular dream affected you, as well as the patterns and repetition of symbols in a series of dreams. If a symbol reappears several times, you might be able to trace it to some real object or event in your conscious life. In addition, your continued involvement with your dreams establishes a greater connection with your unconscious. If after a while you become familiar with dream work, you might be able to access various areas of your unconscious simply by finding the "triggers" in the form of symbolic images.

THE SPECIFIC USES OF SYMBOLIC IMAGING

There are many ways in which an actor can use Symbolic Imaging:

1. As a learning tool, to understand more about how we function and what people, events, and objects shape and affect our lives
2. To discover many new and impacting choices
3. As another way of using the imagination to support the creative process
4. As a way of discovering new areas of affectability
5. To reach emotional places not accessible to more conscious and conventional approaches
6. As a technique for reaching and communicating with the unconscious (later in the book, I will explore conscious-unconscious programming in much greater depth)

While working on a specific role, as an actor you should be particularly aware of all the images that occur in either your conscious or your sleep state. Since your concentration is focused on the structure of the character you are attempting to create in relation to yourself, much unconscious activity is generated. Images of all kinds will be produced by the conscious process of working for choices. While sleeping, you will automatically turn over that responsibility to your unconscious, which in turn will create dreams filled with all kinds of images and symbolism. It is very necessary to pay close attention to those images in either state of consciousness. Symbolic images culled from your dreams can be converted into choices and possibly access an entire emotional life that addresses more than one character element.

Last night I had a nightmare that was really terrifying. It was one of those episodic kinds, where you wake up scared and go back to sleep only to have it continue where it left off. That happened twice. Finally, I accepted its persistence and surrendered to its conclusion. It was about vampires, although I cannot recall any part of it where anyone actually sucked anybody else's blood; but nonetheless, somehow I knew they were vampires! People were getting killed by them, and I vividly remember feeling incredibly helpless. What was funny about it was that the vampires were all frail, emaciated, unattractive women. No one

51

seemed to be able to do anything about the situation. I was terrified all through the nightmare. I think that is why I woke up twice. The places are rather vague now. They seemed to be interiors. A very interesting thing was that there weren't any colors; everything was in various shades of gray. At one point, I was lying next to one of those vampires and with my right hand was strangling her. I felt my fingers dig deeply into her throat, and I felt powerful, even though I was not sure that I could really go through with killing her. She remained motionless, just looking at me while I did this. I specifically recall her face. She looked dead already. I remember thinking, during one of the times when I awoke, that as soon as it would start to get light outside, I would be safe from the vampires.

That was a very complete dream, and I remember a good deal of it. I am sure that it was entirely symbolic and filled with things that could be re-created and used to pique unconscious impulses. I know that while writing about it, I reexperienced some of that hollow feeling I had last night. Communication with the source and origin of dreams is an important connection, which grows stronger as you work with it.

I came up with a couple of interpretations of the vampire dream: I have had a couple of unsuccessful marriages and one or two not-too-successful romantic relationships. I have felt victimized by women at various times in my life, either because of a lack of communication or an ugly split up. Possibly, I have felt that my life's blood was being drained by those women. Whether that is objectively what happened or not, it is one possible explanation of the dream. In it I felt helpless and unable to do anything to stop the "vampires." The fact that all of them were unattractive and frail was perhaps an indication that internally I felt more powerful than they. In the part where I was lying next to one and attempting to strangle her, I see two elements: first, a reference to a romantic or sexual relationship, and second, an indication that I wanted to put an end to her power over me. The thought that I might not be able to kill her alludes to my insecurity in giving up the victim role.

Of course, this is only one possible interpretation. I am sure that there are other plausible ones. However, I am going to use this dream, and whatever symbolism exists in it, to promote an understanding of Symbolic Imaging and how it might serve as a tool for acting.

Imagine that I am playing the role of a man in a relationship where he feels trapped and helpless, unable to change things. He loves his mate but has become an unwilling victim in the relationship. There aren't any alternatives for him but to go on with life as it has been. As the play progresses, he becomes weaker and weaker in his resolve to change anything. Even his physical state seems to degenerate. He gets pale and thinner and loses any zest he may have had for life. From time to time, however, we still see a small spark of fight in him as he stands up to his wife.

This description closely parallels that of a character in a forties film called *The Big Street,* with Henry Fonda and Lucille Ball. The character described was played by Henry Fonda. The female lead was one of the very few dramatic roles Lucy ever had, and she was wonderful in it.

So where do I begin? The interpretation of my vampire dream certainly seems to fit the character and the dynamics of the relationship between the two protagonists. There are numerous alternative approaches I could use: I could go back in my own life and pick one of the relationships I have had—the one that most closely resembles that in the film; I could use Endowments as a choice approach, do Affective Memory to re-create specific events which parallel the piece—or possibly Inner Imaginary Monologues with my former mate; or I could evoke images related to experiences which directly parallel the material. It is wonderful to have a full box of tools from which to choose! There are a number of possible approaches to any piece of material, and the actor must be craftsman enough to select the most expedient and important for the circumstance. O.K., I have decided to use the nightmare as the choice, because of the multiple elements that exist in it—all the various feelings I experienced while asleep and also when I was awake recalling it. It seems to me that the unconscious components are many and very complex, so much so that I feel the dream actually cuts down to the core of who I am in this framework. It uncovers how the facets of my personality are layered with lifelong conditioning, which may find its origin in my relationship to my mother. It possibly discloses my entire profile when it comes to men-women relationships. Because I feel so convinced that this choice is linked to unconscious "gold," I elect to use it above all others.

➢ *Symbolic Imaging Example*

I start the exploration with the imaging process, choosing Imaging Sensations as the approach technique. With my eyes closed, I attempt to re-create the sleep state. (I could also approach this in a fully awake state but decide to do the former so as to closely parallel the original dream.) The first feeling is of being cold.

I feel cold all over. It is very quiet. There is an unusual stillness to everything. I don't know where I am—what this place is. I see only blacks and grays. It is lit like a Frankenstein movie, filled with darkness and shadows. I feel afraid. (At all times I am trying to stay very loyal to the elements of the dream and to avoid embellishments.) *I see one of those creatures coming out of the darkness. She is moving slowly towards me. Her face is thin and pale, and her eyes are lifeless. There is a hard mean line that frames her mouth, and her expression is deathlike. She is draped in something black and flowing. I don't recognize the face, yet there is something familiar about her—I don't know what. The odors are strong and not identifiable, although I am familiar with them. I see another creature coming out of the darkness. She too is moving towards me. She looks different and yet the same as the other. I don't know how I know that they are vampires, but I do! Without seeing blood I sense the presence of it. I can feel my heart beginning to pound harder. I feel afraid and helpless. They are smaller than I am but in some way much more powerful. I want to back away; I feel like running, but I can't move! Another one emerges from the shadows. All three of them are staring at me...I try to back away slowly but can only move a few inches in any direction. All of a sudden I feel as if I have been in this situation before. It seems like some kind of déjà vu. As they come closer, I begin to identify the odor as a combination of various perfumes that sour each other. Instead of a single sweet odor, it is a repulsive mixture. The first vampire comes closer and is within arm's reach of me. I can't move away, and a part of me doesn't want to. She comes closer. I see her gray, lifeless eyes, and they seem to be accusing me. I reach out and touch her, only to feel an awful icy coldness—of what doesn't even feel like flesh. She pulls me down on what seems to be a bed...I feel the softness beneath me, and suddenly I feel as if I were being set up for something...I am all at once filled with terror, and I respond almost instinctively by grabbing her throat, sinking my fingers deep into the rubbery flesh, which seems not to yield to the pressure I am applying. I want to kill this beast! I feel ambivalent about my violent urges, but I want to kill her! I feel the strength in my hand, and I squeeze harder and harder. Suddenly, I feel very sorry for whatever or whoever this being is. I release my grip on her throat, and for the first time I feel my own power. I am looking deeply into her eyes, and I can see my face in the reflection looking back at me, as if I were someone other than myself. I am feeling confused and helpless. I don't know what to do or to whom I can turn. My overall feeling is one of depression, but what is frightening to me is that it seems familiar!*

After the experience I feel the residual of all the emotions I went through while in the process of imaging. I am still depressed and helpless. I have an overall sense of defeat. I feel angry without knowing how to express it. This is all-too-familiar a conglomeration of emotions. I feel as though I have lived here before. It is exactly that combination of impulses and feelings which convinces me that I am in the right area for the obligations. My feelings seem to be coming from the bottom of a deep well.

In that example the symbolism existed in the environment, the colors, and the vampires—the way they looked and smelled, as well as their behavior. All my actions and feelings when I was re-creating the dream were a result of many of those symbols. If it is possible for an actor to access elements in his unconscious which reflect the entire profile of who he is, then what he accomplishes by using these imaging approaches is to bring to the stage the depth and dimension of his entire life. To do this kind of work, to be ready to *experience* life on this level, an actor must be willing to explore the depth of his very soul. He must be willing to discover and face things about himself that are not always pleasant or positive and to expose the dark sides of his being for the world to see and possibly judge.

Symbols that present themselves to us either when we are awake or in other states of consciousness are usable in our present or future work. There is no guarantee that all the images you experience in the realm of symbolism will work for you, but you should assign them a place in your repertoire of possible choices and, when the time comes, explore them to see where they lead.

FRAGMENTED IMAGING

Unlike Involuntary or Symbolic Imaging, the third technique, *Fragmented Imaging,* is done completely by design. The actor decides how he wants to use it and encourages his senses to experience images. He clears his mind and begins the process. If he starts with a visual image, he should immediately encourage the other four senses to support it. This is a multifaceted tool. It can be used in many different ways and for many purposes, as a tool for preparing to act or as a choice approach in a film or play. It contrasts with some of the other imaging techniques in that it can be done quite quickly. You needn't construct an entire scenario as you would in Story Imaging; you can just evoke short images connected to or disconnected from each other. The process can be used to address all or any of the seven major obligations. When using it for preparation, you might just allow yourself to impulsively encourage a stream of fragmented images to stimulate involvement or affectability, to excite your imagination, or just to begin the creative process. When imaging to stimulate a specific state of life, you would creatively manipulate the images by suggesting certain things and allowing the images to springboard from there. As a choice approach, Fragmented Imaging is directed to the choice itself. The actor decides on the choice, knowing what its components are, and suggests the first images. It can be used when the material calls for speedy transitions or when there is very little time to use a more elaborate choice approach that demands more concentration. Fragmented Imaging is to Imaging what Sensory Suggestion is to Sense Memory.

➤ *Example*

Let us suppose that I wanted to elevate my level of vulnerability as a preparation. I would start with a theme, an idea about what event, objects, or people might affect me and raise my vulnerability level.

I see my mother as she was on the last day before she died...(Using all five senses.) *She looks ill and resigned...I know she knows and has accepted her death...I smell the flowers around her casket and hear all the people mumbling in soft voices...I feel this place. It is somber...I hear Beethoven's Ninth Symphony...It is magnificent!...It builds...the crescendo...I hear my sister crying...I feel her pain...*(At this point I create a collage of fragmented images relating to my early life when I was still living at home with my parents.) *My father eating dinner at that funny table in our house in Chicago...He makes unique sounds. I've never heard anyone make sounds like that while eating...I love him!... My mother cooking at that four-legged stove...It's kind of yellow. I smell the food...I love her cooking...She says I'm finicky...Am I?...The radio on the shelf...We all listen to "The Shadow." My father is reading...It feels like Sunday...The carpet is warm...We are all together and I feel secure...I think about endings. Everything ends...I think that's a bad joke...I love them...and now they are both gone...I wonder where?...I feel sad...and lost...Why is it we never outgrow the need for our parents?...My dog Corky...totally crazy dog...I love him. I see him sitting in his place against the wall in the kitchen...He looks at me, growling..."O.K., Corky, I won't look at you." Crazy dog!...My brother just came home...He looks tired...Works hard...unhappy...Wants to be*

*in New York...in theater...What does he have for me?...He always has
something!...Love him...He smiles when he sees me...He loves me too...*

As you see, this example had a specific theme, which was encouraged throughout the entire exercise. All or most of the images
elicited meaningful responses and certainly elevated my vulnerability
level! At times, while typing this example, I had difficulty seeing the
keyboard through my tears.

The process could have served as a choice approach. In that case,
the choice would have been the content of the images, and the obligation
possibly to experience sadness and nostalgia for things that are gone or
have been lost in my life. Fragmented Imaging would have been the
choice approach.

This technique can also be used for pleasure and be a lot of fun.
When you incorporate this work into your daily life, the entire imaging
involvement can become a very good habit. It stretches the imagination
while sharpening the senses.

FREE-ASSOCIATION IMAGING

Another of the imaging techniques, somewhat similar in form and
structure to Fragmented Imaging, is *Free-Association Imaging*. It is different enough, however, to warrant some space in this book to delineate
it separately.

Unlike Involuntary Imaging, but very much like Fragmented
Imaging, Free-Association Imaging is initiated voluntarily. One *decides*
to do it. Usually in a relaxed state, the actor will sit or lie down, clear
his head, and begin to create images free associatively. Without any
preconceived ideas or design, he will just allow and encourage whatever
may occur. There are many purposes to this type of imaging, and the
rewards are multiple. As an involvement preparation it really gets the
actor away from his concerns with performing, as it eliminates any obligations and self-consciousness. It piques the imagination and encourages
the taking of very creative journeys. Because there aren't any expectations from the outset, the actor is free to go wherever it takes him. It
will usually create the flow of various impulses and emotional life,
which act as a preparation to get ready to act. By stimulating a higher
degree of emotional energy, one who comes out of a free-association
preparation is then ready to encounter his first choice for the scene.

When engaged in Free-Association Imaging, you will experience
many kinds of images, some of which are so completely unrelated that it
staggers the understanding. While you are encouraged to creatively

manipulate Fragmented Imaging in the direction where you want to go, you should not do so with Free-Association Imaging. The minute you try to lead yourself in a particular direction, you interrupt the flow of what is free association. The difference between Free-Association Imaging and Fragmented Imaging is analogous to that between doing Evocative Words without an experience or belief structure—just saying words as they pop into your head—and using it to re-create a specific experience.

Fragmented Imaging and Free-Association Imaging often look very similar, for the simple reason that their content and expression are the same. In both techniques the images are *fragmented*. When an actor decides to stimulate images free associatively, those images are produced in fragments and may jump around and include many elements. Even if he decides to encourage himself to free-associate in relation to a theme or choice, it is an open-ended process; that is to say that there isn't any direction to the images or manipulation of them. He might just suggest to himself that he wants to stimulate images related to a particular time or place in his life. He would then encourage a stream of disconnected free-association images and accept anything that might come up. In Fragmented Imaging, on the other hand, while he also selects a theme, time and place, or experience, he is much more involved in *creatively manipulating* the images in the direction in which he wants to go. He may employ Selective Emphasis or creative leadership and even comment on the images he receives. In a word, Free-Association Imaging is a *hands off* involvement, while Fragmented Imaging involves direction and steering of the content to achieve a certain desired goal.

Probably one of the most important dividends of Free-Association Imaging is what we learn about ourselves from it. If done daily, it is a bottomless well of information. Whatever liberates itself from the regions of the unconscious and whatever is locked in the recesses and convolutions of our complex brains may float to the surface of our awareness and open doors that were bolted for most of our lives. I am not suggesting that we become our own psychotherapists or try to analyze ourselves with this technique, but merely saying that, with practice, we can learn, discover, and use much of the information that makes itself available to us.

> ➤ *Example*

I am using myself to explore this technique, and since it is not possible to free-associate and type at the same time, I have a tape recorder to capture the moment-to-moment images that occur to me.

"I am lying on the couch...just about to explore and experiment with Free-Association Imaging...I am breathing deeply...trying to relax... clear my mind...no thoughts...I want this to work...I want to get a good example for the book...My eyes are closed...Relaxing...I'm not seeing anything at the moment...Spots in front of my eyes...I hear cars going by...down the road...It's very quiet here...I'm at my house in Lake Arrowhead, and it's very quiet here...no sirens, no horns...Feel tired... Feel more tired now that I am relaxing...Been writing all day...Don't see anything...Hear an airplane in the distance...Don't hear anything... Don't feel anything...Relaxing...I get a thought and then I get an image ...I thought about a pencil and then I saw an eraser...I don't know whether I'm leading myself or looking for something or whether this is really Free-Association Imaging or not...I see a dog...I saw a dog earlier...when I took my walk...Saw a Doberman earlier...It scared me ...locked up...Heard his barking...I'm afraid of dogs...got bitten when I was young teasing a dog...Still have the scar...(I chuckle.) I see where I lived...the street I lived on...no, the street I played on...I didn't live on that street...I see a little girl...curls...The name that comes to me—I don't know if it is her name or not—Lucille...cute...blond curls. Breathing, trying to relax...I remember that day when the dog bit me... We were out in front of the house...See the house...the front yard... Everything looks big...probably because I'm little...I'm playing with Lucille and this dog, and the dog is jumping up...I see it's a light-colored, pale dog...not large...Smell that dog...I like that smell...He smells doggy...Gasoline...Like that smell too...Just got a whiff of gasoline...Valerian...lived on Fillmore Street...Used to play with Valerian ...She had twin sisters...Cheryl and somebody else...I see them...I forget the guy's name who beat me up...Marshall...See him too...(Chuckling again.) It's funny...How I wish I could meet him now and beat the shit out of him...That was over fifty years ago...Why would I want to beat him now?...I see his smug expression...Punch him right in the mouth. Punch his lights out...I see Boy Scouts...Mr. Nemec...Ah, Mr. Nemec!...Nice man, false teeth...His teeth are the falsest-looking teeth I've ever seen...Mr. Nemec...nice man...I liked him...Troop 370...See Morty Levin...Ah, Morty has got black curly hair...He's short and fat ...and we're both in the Boy Scouts...I remember that church...down in the basement...I see it, the hallway and the tile floor with all the scuff marks...I'm in the Lion Patrol...Red Kerchiefs...John Graff is there too ...See John Graff's father and mother...(Blowing out air.) They look old to me...They're not old, but they look old to me...Mayfield Street... They lived on Mayfield Street...Roosevelt Road...the Town Theatre... See that...Ohhh, I just got an image of that guy with no arms...Only saw him in the movies...There he is, sitting there...short hair...He's got no arms...They let him in free, because how could he get money out of his pockets?...I don't know...I mean I see him walk in, so...so he sits and watches the movies...How does he scratch?...I see his face...He doesn't look unhappy...laughs at the movies...I'm watching him a little bit...hmm...Pa...(I laugh.) "Did you lock the locks, Freddy?" (Inside joke, experience between my father and me. Laugh some more.) My daddy...my pa...loved him. See his face...My uncle Abe...see his face too...Cemeteries, tombstones, see them...all the old people...see them... smell flowers...sweet smell...Squirrels chasing each other in the trees... My eyes are still closed...They are all internal images...I'm opening my eyes...see the ceiling of my house...It is way up there...hmm...My mother...standing at the sink, I see her...Monitor Avenue...Wow!... (Short pause.) Thinking now...close my eyes again...hear a car...motorcycle—it's not a car...See a motorcycle...a Harley-Davidson...Phew!... School...Key Clark branch...Visited there recently...Mrs. Lane...I see her sitting at her desk...didn't like her...She didn't like me...See the backs of the heads of all the people in my class sitting in front of me... bored...school...Looking out the window...see houses across the street ...It's winter...Not so bad being here...awful in the spring and summer ...School yard...summer school...different school...hmm...Where was that?...Which school was Ed Tyrell at?...See his face...Where did I know them from?...Hmm, Austin High School...Vuchavich...football player...See him standing there...Campus school...See my forty-seven Dodge...visor nice...brand-new blue...The seat covers are awful...plaid seat covers?...Ooh, plastic...shock...used to get shocked all the time. Hated it...Playing...Walgreens drugstore...Standing behind the counter ...Look at my uniform...Ha...the manager...What was his name?...See his face...as if it were right here today...attitude...company man...He's really into it—I see it...this is his life...He's going all the way. I don't give a shit about this place...I'm good...People I work with...flashes of faces...Boy, that woman is a bitch...See her face...unhappy...redhead, behind the cash register...What is her name?...Mr. Solomon, pharmacist and the manager of the store...nice man...See his face...his smock...

mustache...little man...Nice feeling about him...He likes me...Looking around. See the store...Smell the odors...ah...Walgreens smells like... Walgreens...The moment I walk on all those boards behind the fountain ...I smell all those smells...ice cream, syrups, bananas, the counter, malted-milk powder...See it, dispense it...Phew!...(Deep sigh.) God... trip...trip through my life...I'm not...(pause) I'm just following what comes...Looking at the furniture in this room...Feel nostalgic...feel a little sad...feel that most of my life has gone by already...I see old people...people getting old...Think maybe it's going to happen to me?... Looking at that glass duck...cookie jar...table...See an image of a duck ...beautiful living duck in the water down by the lake...Feel tired...See an airplane...in my imaging...Don't really see one...Have to fly soon...I don't know what any of this means...don't know if it means anything... It's just truly what's coming to me...Cobwebs in the eaves near the windows...Why are they called cobwebs?...See corn cobs piled high in a field...see corn-cob pipes...Walter Brennen...What's he doin'? I don't know!...Sucking on a corn cob...Did he ever suck on a corn cob?...See him though...He's got that funny hat on, the one in *The Beverly Hillbillies*. Only he wasn't in *The Beverly Hillbillies*...O.K., I think this is enough of an example...I'm going to stop."

This Free-Association Imaging example was recorded and transcribed verbatim. It is purposely unedited so that it can be totally authentic. Because I had to verbalize my free-association images, I also included my responses to them. I don't know why the exercise went in that direction or what precipitated it. I just allowed it to take me wherever it did. I am sure that when it is done silently, there is a greater flow of uninterrupted images. However, it can be done either way.

When I finished the exercise, I felt a number of things: I was relaxed and a little tired; I felt very nostalgic, a little sad, contemplative, and a little resigned. My vulnerability level was certainly elevated! When I played the tape back, I realized my voice was filled with many kinds of emotional life, which unfortunately cannot be translated to paper. I heard the subtleties of all the feelings I described above and many more. So what did I learn from it? How did it affect me, and how was it a usable acting exercise? Well, first of all, I was definitely very affected by the images! During and after, I had a multitude of feelings and impulses. Having gone back to a specific period in my life, I experienced that time and many of the feelings I had then. Why did the exercise go to that time and those places? I don't know! I certainly was ready to act when it was over. I felt vulnerable and very affectable. If I had introduced a choice at that moment, I feel that it would have really taken me somewhere. Immediately after I finished free-associating and when I listened to the tape, I experienced an underlife of feelings that seemed very elusive. They appeared to be coming from a very deep place. It was so powerful that I had to wait an hour before going back to the typewriter. Last night, my dreams were filled with objects, people, and events related to that time in my life!

Secondly, the experience yielded many insights about myself that could explain the way I am now. I have listened to the tape and read the transcription several times, and with each repetition I understand a little more. In the first place, I think that that time must have been very important to me! I remember saying to people throughout the years that being a Boy Scout was the single best and most exciting experience in my life. It was an adventure filled with discovery, learning, and growth. I feel that I grew up in that troop and discovered many of my role models during that period. Some of the traumas of growing up were also related to those times, particularly when I lived on Fillmore Street and Monitor Avenue. Many of the nightmares that I have to this day are located in that area of Chicago. A thought just occurred to me: I have always disliked that city—almost irrationally. That might be a result of my early experiences as a child on those streets. Most of the rejection and abuse I suffered happened there. A great number of the insecurities I still have can be traced to those places and some of those people. I encountered a great deal of discrimination as a young boy. I am Jewish and always seemed to live in neighborhoods where I was a distinct minority. As a result, I suffered ridicule, abuse, and sometimes physical pain from totally unjustified beatings by my schoolmates! When I started college, and later when I moved to California, the discrimination and prejudice ended, and I am happy to say that they haven't appeared in my life for many years now. In the exercise I also discovered how much I loved my father and how deeply I miss him! The theme of age, cemeteries and old people must mean that I am beginning to experience feelings of my own mortality. The thought that I have already lived more of my life up to now than what I have left is very illuminating!

I am certain that if I continued to study the exercise further, I would extract much more from it. Think about the value of adding all of your Free-Association Imaging experiences to your daily journal! It could become quite an informative document about who you are, how you got to be you, and why you do the things you do.

THE SPECIFIC REWARDS OF FREE-ASSOCIATION IMAGING

There are many rewards to using Free-Association Imaging:

1. You become more facile with the imaging process.
2. It is a very good involvement preparation. It takes you away from yourself and the obligations that the "spot" produces and into a selfless-involvement state.
3. The emotional impact prepares you to act by elevating your affectability.
4. The understanding and insights into yourself are tremendous.
5. It is a wonderful way to discover new choices and unexplored areas of your life.
6. It has a connection to your unconscious impulses and makes it possible for you to enlist the help of your unconscious in approaching a specific role. Since some of the images must emanate from the unconscious, often while you are doing this kind of imaging, a door will open into an incredible area of life that is rich with unconscious dimension.

Free-Association Imaging can be utilized in an important way while you are in rehearsal for a film or play. Since so much of our work is designed to reach and pique facets of our personality that are parallel to the character's, and since the choices we select hopefully stimulate the desired results, wouldn't it make sense if at those times an actor imaged free associatively to see what kinds of images are produced? If your choices create a profile that matches the life of the character in the piece, might it not be possible to liberate images from your unconscious that would support your journey to the fulfillment of the play? I think so! At any rate, you might try it!

STORY IMAGING

Yet another of the seven techniques that are part of the twenty-sixth choice approach, the MEGAPPROACH of Imaging, *Story Imaging* is probably the most commonly used of all. We have been doing it since childhood, and it is natural. The approach is the same as for any of the other involvements: You either use Sense Memory in its conventional structure or Imaging Sensations. The major difference between this technique and Fragmented Imaging is that this one has continuity. There is a plot, a story, that has a beginning, a middle, and an end. It too is initiated by decision, although it quite often occurs involuntarily. People prone to daydreaming and fantasizing will often slip into a full-blown fantasy involving Story Imaging. As I demonstrated in the previous chapter, it happens quite frequently in anticipation of an event: We are waiting for something to happen or someone to arrive and we begin a Story Imaging journey. Quite often we create these stories without being fully conscious that they are taking place. It sometimes starts as a result of boredom or depression. People unhappy with their lives and what they do for a living will often create a story to experience life in a much more fulfilling way. There are cases where the imaging is episodic; in other words, each time it picks up where it had left off the day before. Sometimes it is all a person has to hold on to some kind of hope.

Story Imaging is a very useful tool to the actor. Just as you can't be too rich or too thin, you can't have too many creative tools! Using one of the two ways of imaging, you create a complete story in pictures, sounds, odors, and so on. Essentially that story is the choice. It is selected with a purpose or goal in mind.

➤ *Example*

This imaging involvement is done specifically to stimulate greater accessibility and to elevate the emotional state.

I see the television screen, the people in Somalia...thin, dying...see their skeletal bodies and bulging eyes...babies too sick to do anything but sleep...I hear the crying and see the U.N. volunteers passing out pails of food...I see the flies on the children's faces...crawling into their mouth...(As always, these images are not verbal. The story is a collection of images processed through all the senses.) *A mother is holding a dead baby...She is crying and rocking back and forth...In the background they are carrying the dead to be buried...A doctor is talking to a newsman...I hear him say that it may be "too little too late!" I feel a lump in my throat and tears in my eyes...I feel helpless!*

The choice is intelligently selected to accomplish whatever it is that the actor set out to do. In this case he chose to elevate his vulnerability using a story he saw on television that was obviously very impacting. If he wanted to feel vulnerable but somewhat more uplifted, he could have used another choice or experience. There are an endless number of choices that can be created through Story Imaging.

This technique may also be selected to address an instrumental issue, such as an ego problem. Suppose the actor was suffering from a temporary attack of low self-esteem; he could opt to create a very self-aggrandizing choice and an entire scenario about it.

Story Imaging can be used in all areas of instrumental and craft preparations. It can also work to supply the background of a character in a play when no information is given about his life prior to the action of the piece. In such a case, the actor must cull every bit of information he can from the text, then create the character's entire life from his birth to the first scene, as well as filling in what happens in between the written scenes. I will give examples of how to do this later in the book.

VERBALIZED IMAGING

The sixth technique, *Verbalized Imaging,* can be applied to almost all of the others. It is more of a discipline than a technique, and it helps keep the actor on track. By verbalizing his images, he receives auditory input, which often has a supplementary impact. In addition, this helps him start the imaging process. If you are having difficulty knowing where to begin, you can simply say aloud: "I see...I hear...I smell...I feel...I taste..." and fill in the blanks with specific sensory responses. Be careful, however, not to respond in words. If that happens, it will short-circuit the sensory process; it will cease to be imaging and become a verbal running account of the experience. Once you are well into the imaging involvement, you can stop verbalizing or limit the number of words you use.

Verbalized Imaging has another value: It allows and encourages you to express your emotional responses to the images you are creating. In many cases an actor will be reluctant to express his moment-to-moment impulses for fear that such expression will get in the way of the imaging. This does occur sometimes but is less likely to happen if he starts out verbally.

Another way to use Verbalized Imaging is to bring it into play well into the imaging process. Verbalizing any image or impulse can act as an impetus for the actor to go even deeper into his process. If, for example, he verbalizes some of his involuntary images, his audible description may spark other images. The entire involvement with imaging is so rich and rewarding! There are so many variables and alternatives.

As I said earlier, Verbalized Imaging can be used in relation to any of the other imaging techniques. In other words, the actor could begin to verbalize, for whatever reason, at any point in any imaging area. After spending some time creating a choice, he begins to feel what and where the *triggers* are—what parts of his choice, what specific images, stimulate the greatest flow of impulses and feelings. Knowing this, he can elect to verbalize those images that will create the entire experience through one or two words. It is similar to what can happen when one has been working with Affective Memory for a period of time. An entire experience, which in the beginning took hours to re-create, can be stimulated in seconds! It is important to note that, when evoking an image verbally, the actor must accompany the words with the specific image, and the image must be shared by all of his senses. It is something like using Evocative Words—another of the twenty-seven choice approaches—only in reverse: When using Evocative Words, the actor attempts to re-create an experience by saying words related to it. This, of course, is done to stimulate images connected to the original event. On the other hand, when he is verbalizing images or parts of an imaging experience, the actor is in effect accessing an already created experience by using words as the key to "punch up" the images that were evoked. If he wants to use Verbalized Imaging to access the emotional life engendered by his original imaging involvement, he must experiment with the process to see which words pique a replay of the entire experience. This exploration can be done at home or in rehearsal.

THE VARIOUS USES OF VERBALIZED IMAGING

Verbalized Imaging can be used in the following ways:

1. **As its own approach to accompany any form of imaging**. After selecting the choice, the actor can start to image (create) it, being totally verbal. This can be done with any of the other imaging techniques. He can start to story image, use fragmented images, and so on.

2. **As a discipline to start the process**. There are times when the actor is at a loss as to what is the best choice or is having some difficulty in starting the imaging. At points like these, he can simply begin to verbalize. Starting with a stream of consciousness or a Personal Inventory, he may sneak into his image by simply using words:

   "I feel reluctant to start doing this...I'm looking around the room hoping to find some inspiration...I don't trust the choice ...I feel afraid to find out that it won't work...I'm not sure where to start...At which point in this experience should I begin the process of imaging?...I'm afraid to fail...What if I can't even create the choice?...(Starting with I see...I hear...I feel...) I see...a lot of very tiny newborn babies all lying next to each other in small baskets...(He should immediately encourage sensory responses in the visual area.) They look small and red and wrinkled...I hear them crying...(Auditory response.) The sound is muffled through the glass...I see my own reflection in the glass; it looks transparent...I'm looking for my baby...My heart is beating rapidly...I feel excited...I can smell a mixture of hospital and baby smells...I think I see him...He has a full head of blond hair...I don't believe it..." (All sensory responses.)

By beginning the exploration with the acknowledgment of the obstacles, the actor can move forward into creating the image with Verbalized Imaging.

3. **To stay on track**. The actor can introduce Verbalized Imaging if he begins to wander or allows commentary to interrupt the evolution of a specific imaging involvement. Commentary is a very common trap for actors. It can and does derail us very often, sometimes right at a crucial point in a scene. There is also a tendency for us to be affected by our images and reminded of other events, which may, right in the middle of an experience, introduce impulses or memories that do not service our original goal. It is at these junctures that the actor can use verbalization to get back on track, while acknowledging the commentary or the other impulses, including them in his behavior, and expressing them through the written words.

4. **To supplement the images with sounds**. When we hear the description of something, it often acts as a stimulant to what we see or feel. It can *dimensionalize* all of the individual sensory responses. It is like when two frightened children, huddled close together listening to normal wood creaking in the night, scare themselves by verbalizing imagined terrors, actually creating sounds that do not exist: "Do you hear that?...It sounds like someone slowly coming up the stairs...Do you hear the creaking of the steps?...He's on the top one!...I can hear him coming close to our bedroom door!..."

The innocent settling of the house is blown into a terrifying experience by the use of imagination and verbalization. In the same way, an actor can heighten an imaging experience by creative verbalization. The right words at the right time can authenticate and magnify an imaging experience.

5. **As a device to access parts of already created events or experiences**. In NLP (Neurolinguistic Programming) certain words are used to stimulate responses. Those words are

somehow an integral part of an event or experience or directly relate to some meaningful object; by using one or several of them, a person can create a complete emotional state. Thus, by verbalizing specific images, an actor may be immediately flooded with feelings and impulses that were originally the result of a complete imaging experience. For example, let us say that in one scene, the actor is imaging his drunken mother screaming at him, so close to his face that he experiences all of her disgusting odors and sounds in a very magnified way. After creating this entire imaging experience a number of times, he could just simply verbalize: "I smell her rotten breath...hear the shrill screech of her voice...see her bloodshot vacant eyes!..." That is all it may take to restimulate his entire emotional response to that part of the experience. If that were so, the actor could verbalize those things as an inner monologue during the scene and catapult his life on stage to the highest places.

6. **To stimulate emotional expression.** While verbalizing the images and responding sensorially, the actor experiences emotional responses. Often, these incubate and are not expressed until he feels confident that he is *really feeling* the impact of a particular image. Many important impulses are denied during this journey and never break the surface of an actor's expression in the scene. During the rehearsal process the actor could do a Verbalized Imaging exploration, encouraging the expression of everything he feels on a moment-to-moment basis. By so doing, he would not only promote his emotional point of view in every moment but also allow his imaging process to go forward without any denial of what is happening from one moment to the next. This kind of expression allows the imaging process to unfold without any "short-circuiting" of impulses.

7. **As a way to pique unconscious responses.** By verbalizing images that come to us in our conscious state as well as in our dreams, we can elicit unconscious responses. If we verbalize dream images in a totally conscious state, we may experience feelings, moods, or other responses that are unexplainable. If they stimulate life that can be utilized on the stage or dimensionalize our behavior, then they are definitely worth exploring. The same is true for involuntary images. We can verbalize fragments of those that come to us all through the day. If you record your involuntary images during rehearsal, for instance, it

may even be possible for you to return to a specific state of life by verbalizing some of them. All of this must be explored and experimented with.

TWO-PERSON VERBALIZED IMAGING

As its name indicates, two-person Verbalized Imaging is done by two actors and can be approached in different ways. The actors can verbalize their specific images simultaneously or one at a time. Each approach will accomplish different things. If, for example, both actors were creating the place simultaneously, but each was using his own personal choice, they would not participate in each other's images, but each would be totally involved in creating his or her own place. On the other hand, each of them could listen to the other's process and be inspired to include some of the other's imagery. If they do the imaging one at a time, there are a couple of ways in which they could proceed: The "listening" actor could respond to the Verbalized Imaging of his scene partner by imaging corresponding elements of his *own* place, or he could engage in *Shared Imaging,* which is part of the **Guided Imaging** process and involves imagining specifically what the other actor is creating. By doing the second, he would get more deeply involved with his partner while elevating his own imagination at the same time. Two-person imaging is also a very good way of getting to know another person. Many things are expressed and exposed in the framework of Verbalized Imaging—not only what is explicitly said, but also what comes out during the unspoken spaces.

There are many components to Verbalized Imaging that can be used and explored endlessly.

GUIDED IMAGING

Guided Imaging also requires two or more persons to work together. It has proven to be a very effective tool for creating the realities that exist in a scene. There are three different approaches to this technique: *Guided Imaging, Simultaneous Guided Imaging,* and *Shared Imaging.* All of them require the involvement of two or more people, but each has its own thrust and structure. In some instances one will work better than the others.

Guided Imaging is done by one actor leading or facilitating the other through a complete experience. The guide or facilitator, knowing the components of the experience, leads the "facilitatee" through it by asking sensory imaging questions about the place, the time of day or year, the people who are there, and so on. All of the responses, of course, are silent imaging responses, employing all five senses.

Simultaneous Guided Imaging is done by both actors simultaneously facilitating each other. Each one continues the facilitation where the other left off.

Shared Imaging, already mentioned in the section on Verbalized Imaging, is a process where one actor verbally shares his images with the other. These might be related to an event or be part of an experience. The other actor attempts to image the same things. It is a very creative process, which involves both actors deeply in each other's lives.

Each of these approaches will address the different and varied demands of material. The actor, as a result of his experience with all three of them, will learn how to make the best selection in each case.

GUIDED IMAGING (ORIGINAL TWO-PEOPLE APPROACH)

Guided Imaging is a wonderful relationship preparation as well as a choice approach. The two actors naturally become very involved with each other during the facilitations. The technique usually comes into play after they have been working together for a while, although it probably works just as well in the beginning rehearsals. The advantage of using it later is that the actors know each other better by then, and each can therefore better understand what kinds of things affect the other. Knowing that one's partner is vulnerable and "affectable" in certain areas and responds to particular questions and facilitations with greater "rise-ability" will shorten the process and, at the same time, make the facilitation much more impacting and successful. In the next chapter, I will give a very complete explanation and example of how to do this technique.

How to Use Guided Imaging

Guided Imaging can be used in the following ways:

1. **As an involvement preparation**—involvement with the scene and the circumstances of the material, involvement with the other actor, involvement with the choice.

2. **As a relationship preparation.** Both actors become intensely involved with each other—first, by sharing personal and sometimes intimate details of their lives, and secondly, through the facilitation process itself. The facilitator becomes responsible for leading his partner through a meaningful experience and is usually quite emotionally affected by it. The one who is being

facilitated often develops a creative dependency on the facilitator. This mutual relationship can then be carried directly into the scene.

3. **As a way of exploring a choice**. Quite often an actor anticipates the impact of a particular choice. He knows why he selected it in the first place, so there is almost an unavoidable anticipation involved in his exploration. The kinds of questions and suggestions he uses are often attached to that expectation. On the other hand, when he is being facilitated, he cannot predict the questions the facilitator will ask or the direction in which she will lead him. Therefore the exploration of the choice can be conducted, and its impact determined, without leadership or premeditation.

4. **As an exercise to practice and master the process of imaging**. I have seen actors in my classes achieve a real understanding about how imaging works for them when they were relieved of the responsibility of creating the images by themselves. When allowed to just respond to the facilitation, they were able to really create the images related to the experience. In addition, since everyone has different ideas and perspectives, they learned from their partners new and exciting ways of creating images. Hearing another person supply imaginative suggestions sparks a different perspective on an event or experience, as well as teaching us new ways of producing images.

5. **As a choice approach,** a tool for addressing and fulfilling the obligations of a scene. In this case the actors would facilitate each other to stimulate the desired emotional life or relationship.

In order to facilitate another actor effectively through the process of re-creating an experience or event, the one doing the facilitating must be very familiar with that event. He must know all of the elements comprising it: the time and place—time of day and year, climate, temperature, weather, interior or exterior décor—the objects, people, sounds, odors, and activities involved; the ambience; the clothing, behavior, and attitudes of the "players"; the mood of the person about to be facilitated, as well as what the specific experience stimulated, what the emphasis of the entire involvement was, why the actor selected it as a choice, and what he hopes to accomplish if successful with his images. All of this information is necessary in order for the facilitator to structure his facilitation with accuracy and authenticity.

Usually the facilitation begins with establishing the environment—all of the elements that lead up to the meaningful and impelling parts of the experience. In this way, it resembles the approach to Affective Memory, the logic being that, if you create all of the surrounding realities, by the time you reach the parts of the experience that stimulate the behavior required by the material, you are so involved with *being there* that the emotional life naturally flows out of the already created realities.

When an actor decides to use Guided Imaging as the approach to the material, it should be because it is the best selection for dealing with the circumstances and the obligations. It is especially productive in scenes where the characters have a history together and are intimately involved in the events in each other's lives. Each of the actors in any scene may come to Guided Imaging after having used a variety of other choices and approaches. The facilitation can begin after they have already established an emotional state that acts as a foundation for the obligation being approached through Guided Imaging.

There are quite a number of variables in working with Guided Imaging. The facilitator can go back and forth between sensorially emphasized questions and encouraging the actor to express his emotional responses throughout the entire process. Where in the experience the facilitator starts is usually up to him, but, as I said before, it should be well before the impacting moment. The facilitator should begin with the creation of the environment and as many of the objects and people as are part of the experience. If he sees that the actor is in the throes of an emotional response, he should stop his facilitation and allow his partner to go through the entire experience for as long as it takes. Both actors should take turns facilitating each other with their own respective choices. Ultimately, as the rehearsals near their conclusion, all they might have to do to trigger the experience is to image silently only the igniting parts.

SIMULTANEOUS GUIDED IMAGING

Simultaneous Guided Imaging is done very much in the same way as Guided Imaging, but instead of one actor facilitating another, both are imaging simultaneously. This technique is a shared experience. Both become simultaneously facilitator and facilitatee. Either might start the questioning process, but they both respond, each by imaging his *own* choice. If, for example, the first actor starts with, What kind of place is this? both of them begin to image their respective places using all five senses with Imaging Sensations.

There are a variety of ways in which this can be done, and the approach should be adjusted to fit the specific situation. The actors could alternate asking several questions each, while they both respond with images; or, picking up where the other left off, each can ask one question in turn. It is important to note that both actors are responding *simultaneously* to the facilitation. While they start with creating the place and the elements of the experience that lead up to the actual impact of the event, they must both be cognizant of the ultimate goal of the exercise and creatively manipulate the facilitation to the desired area of impact.

If they are doing a scene together, it would be quite simple for them to promote the realities of the material by using this process. Since they both understand the relationship responsibilities, the conflicts, and the emotional life of their characters, they can select choices from their own lives that not only take them where they want to go emotionally, but also address the dynamics of the action of the scene and the statement of the play.

The major difference between Guided Imaging and Simultaneous Guided Imaging is that in the second technique, each actor facilitates himself, so to speak (out loud, so that the other actor hears the facilitation), and they both respond to that facilitation. The questions asked sound just like a typical Sense Memory exploration. Each of the actors responds to his specific choice by imaging all of his sensory responses to his partner's questions. In other words, if she asked: What do I hear? Where are those sounds coming from? and so on, he would respond within his own choice, his own place. Whatever the questions are, both actors would use them as the facilitation from which to create the event by evoking all the images that comprise it. Later in this book there will be a specific example of how this technique is used in relation to a real piece of material.

SHARED IMAGING

Another of the "sub-techniques" of Guided Imaging, *Shared Imaging* is slightly different in that the emphasis is on one actor sharing an event or a personal experience with the other. The first one describes images of a particular experience, vividly imaging his descriptions in chronological order with all five of his senses, while the other images the *same* events, creating images from his partner's descriptions. This establishes a knowledge of, familiarity with, and affinity for the other's life. It brings the actors closer together and creates a deeper relationship and some history between them. Depending on the nature of the choices they are working with, the level of emotional impact, and the meaningfulness of each of their experiences, their mutual understanding and their involvement with each other can become so dimensional and complete as to add many facets to their performance.

How to Use Shared Imaging

There are many reasons why an actor might use Shared Imaging:

1. As an involvement technique
2. To become familiar with the other actor's life in relation to his own choices—which stimulates a greater understanding of the other
3. As a technique to build a history of sharing the same or similar events together
4. To mutually create the environments, events, and relationship contained in the play
5. For the unconscious programming potential

As a preparation for getting ready to work, either of the actors could create an experience or a place that would hopefully stimulate the character's emotional point of view or his kind of life at the beginning of the scene.

➤ *Shared Imaging Example*

The obligation of the scene might be that the two characters, who are brother and sister, have just been to the cemetery to place flowers on their mother's grave. The emotional obligation is to feel a *bittersweet ambivalence* for a mother whom they loved but by whom they felt neglected. The place carries with it a feeling of somber respectfulness and a sense of introspective quiet. The actress in the scene volunteers to start the Shared Imaging exploration. She selects a place, an old cemetery in the East where most of her ancestors are buried:

"I feel the grass, spongy beneath my feet...As I walk towards her grave, I can feel my feet sink into the sod...It feels comforting in a strange way...I smell flowers and freshly cut grass...and I'm aware of the silence...I see headstones all around me...I walk carefully to avoid stepping on the graves...I stop and read a headstone which is barely readable...It is so old...'Elijah Simmons, born seventeen twenty-eight, died seventeen sixty-nine.' I wonder about him...what he was like...if he had any children...I move on towards my mother's grave...I'm not sure exactly where it is...It's been a while since I've been here...and it has changed somewhat...I feel a little sad...not for the dead, but thinking about us...We all end up in a place like this...What it is all about?... I mean life..."

All of those thoughts and images are shared aloud. The other actor attempts to image everything that is being described. He does not try to substitute or parallel any of his own choices. That is the main difference between Simultaneous Guided Imaging and Shared Imaging. In this case the listening actor tries to sensorially imagine what the other is describing. By doing this, he becomes familiar not only with her experiences but with the way she feels about what she is creating, with her emotional points of view and basic sense of life, with how she felt about her own mother, how she feels about life, death, and so on. She might continue the Shared Imaging experience for ten or fifteen minutes. If they are successful with the process, the actors should both be emotionally affected in such a way as to be able to take the next step towards addressing the scene.

At this point *he* might do a Shared Imaging experience to promote some other element, either related to the scene or which establishes a greater familiarity with each other's lives. By repeating this process over a period of time, the actors create a feeling of having actually shared these experiences in their real life. If these Shared Imaging journeys are re-created in a hypnagogic state, they may sneak into the actors' dreams and stimulate strong unconscious connections to each other and to the shared realities. All of this will creep into their performances and establish a kind of life on stage that is rarely seen or experienced by anyone.

This technique can be used more specifically to address the responsibilities of a play if the actors share images chronologically from scene to scene. In other words, the first actor might share an image related to an event that parallels the first scene in the play, as he creates the environment and action to stimulate the emotional life required by that scene. The actress could then do the same thing for the second scene, and so on through the whole play. With repetition, the potential of this process is incredible.

Shared Imaging can also be used to create experiences and events that do not appear in the play—all of those shared by the characters before the play and in between the scenes, and even the actors' conjecture about what will occur after the action of the play is over. Creating subtextual and "extra-textual" life adds dimension to the relationships between the characters. It is phenomenal how having the history of a relationship and shared experiences pays off when you reach the performance stage of the process. When it is not possible to take the time or have a rehearsal period long enough to actually create the parallel realities, Shared Imaging can be used to do just that.

All of the aforementioned imaging techniques are usable as choice approaches for creating the choices that address and fulfill dramatic material. In the next chapters I will give more examples of how to apply them to instrumental and craft work. As I've said before, the specific use of any of them is dependent on which will most expediently address the nature of the material, the obligation requirements and what exactly the actor is attempting to accomplish. Exploration and experimentation will usually lead to the right decision. Of course, experience with the craft is also a very important factor. That is why an actor has a rehearsal process, to explore the techniques he will use in performing the play. Feel free to experiment with all seven of the imaging techniques. Apply them where they best serve you. Use them in tandem with each other or with other choice approaches. Explore them for practice, for pleasure, or for instrumental therapy. Those that relate directly to the unconscious can be used in your dream work, hypnagogic-state explorations, and so on—in short in all your work with the unconscious. Almost every craftsman in every field has a set of tools with which he works. This craft and all of its component parts are the tools of the actor craftsman.

FANTASY IMAGING

In most of the examples given above, I have used real events or experiences from the actors' actual lives. However, it is also possible to create images that come directly from the imagination and to fashion an elaborate fantasy that will fulfill the purpose at hand. Probably the most fun to do, *Fantasy Imaging* is almost like playing a game. Just like Believability, it hooks directly into the child in us. It is like all of those "pretend games" we used to play when we were children. If only all the parts of this craft could be approached with the same sense of play, acting would cease to seem like work! Like any other type of imaging, Fantasy Imaging is done either with Sense Memory or Imaging Sensations, plus any of the seven imaging techniques outlined above.

There are many reasons for using this approach. It is wonderful for releasing the full power of the imagination. It creates a willingness to believe and to take creative chances with our work. It is tremendous fun and sometimes the only way to create a choice that will address the obligations of the material.

There is a very good example of Fantasy Imaging in chapter 2 of this book in the section where I describe Imaging Sensations. It is a kind of *Gulliver's Travels* fantasy, which describes waking up in some strange place replete with little creatures, incredible odors, and colors which would make psychedelic ones look pale.

Imaging is a familiar involvement, since we have been doing it all of our life. We experience fantasy images every day, whether they come as full-blown stories or as little fleeting images as we walk along the street, window-shopping. One of my standard fantasies occurs while I'm sitting in bumper-to-bumper traffic. I fantasize that I push a button on the dashboard of my car, and, suddenly, like some James Bond invention, wings sprout from the sides of my doors, and the gasoline engine is miraculously converted into a multidirectional jet engine that lifts me straight up like a helicopter over the freeway and with Mach speed thrusts me through the air past all those gridlocked cars below! This fantasy happens quite automatically. I hear the sounds of the wings coming out of the doors; I experience the thrust of the jet engine as it lifts me like a Harrier jet straight into the sky; I see myself flying above all those trapped cars below, and I feel elated by the experience. At other times, I see a Ferrari driving down the boulevard, and suddenly I am behind the wheel of this Red Devil, accelerating at breakneck speed. I feel the soft-leather seats caress me like a hungry woman in lust, and I am washed over by a sense of success and well-being. I also fly a lot—and I don't mean in an airplane. I fly like Superman! That is one of my favorite fantasy images—flying over the city, feeling the breeze blowing through my hair, increasing and decreasing my speed and altitude. We won't explore my sexual fantasies for a variety of reasons! Suffice it to say that they are numerous and frequent and extremely exciting! My fantasy images also include all kinds of heroic activities, such as rescuing people from impossible life-threatening circumstances. In addition, I quite frequently image myself winning a running marathon, as well as being the most valuable player in the Super Bowl. With every movie or television show I watch, I have fleeting fantasies of participating. I know that if you strung all my combat fantasies together, I would have single-handedly won all the wars we have fought in the last fifty years! I have a very long list of what I call "omnipotent" fantasies or "miracle-worker" fantasies, where I heal people with a touch of my hand or in a dream discover the cure for cancer or AIDS! They are always such simple remedies, which I concoct by boiling the leaves of an oak tree and combining them with some herb I discover in my kitchen cabinet. Oh! I almost forgot the invisible-man fantasies. Those are great! I love to image myself invisible in a variety of places where I could never go otherwise, overhearing what people say about me, getting on airplanes and into the movies for free, playing pranks on people, and so on. Mind-reading fantasies are another area that I relish. I fantasize being able to hear people's thoughts and answering them as I pass those people on the street or at a table in a restaurant, leaving them totally amazed! I experience imaging fantasies of time travel, usually where I go back in time, because it puts me on a superior plane instead of having to deal with some smug schmuck who can molecularly disintegrate in front of me and reappear on the other side of the street! Who needs *that*? My time-travel fantasies always put me somewhere where I can save the day. I have been to the Alamo, saved Jim Bowie's life countless times, defeated Santa Anna's entire army by bringing a dozen M60 machine guns to the fight. I have taken care of Sadam Hussein so many times that he has already had three times as many lives as a cat! I have done him in so often because I am still looking for the most spectacular way to exact justice! I have also escaped from prison camps all over Southeast Asia, accomplishing the impossible in every case. I have received the Academy Award so frequently in my fantasies that there isn't any room for furniture in my house!

I think you have a good idea by now of the number and variety of fantasies that we can experience each day. If encouraged, they touch every area of our lives. I fantasize for pleasure and fulfillment, and I get a lot from it.

When you engage in Fantasy Imaging, remember as usual to respond with all of your senses. When an actor trains himself to use Imaging Sensations, his senses begin to respond simultaneously. As he starts a fantasy image, even by suggestion, the senses rally behind the suggestion and begin to experience the components of the fantasy.

For me there is always the question, Why did I select that choice, why that choice approach? And could I have picked a better one? The selections of an accomplished craftsperson should be simple. They should address the obligations of the material with the most expedient technique possible. A master craftsman does not create unnecessary work for himself. He selects the tool that will do the job. He also makes it look as if he weren't doing anything! The reason for selecting Fantasy Imaging as a tool is directly related to what you want to accomplish. If you were doing it for pleasure or to change your state from depression to elation, you would pick a choice that addresses that specific issue. Let us suppose, for example, that you are on your way to the theater after a perfectly terrible day, where everything that could have gone wrong in your life has! The last thing you feel like doing is acting! You would much rather go home, pull the covers over your head and sleep for a week. What do you do then? There are a lot of options: You could work for a number of choices using any one of a dozen different choice approaches, but you decide to address your depression with a fantasy.

➢ *Fantasy Imaging Example*

Searching your memory for an experience, an event, or a topic that could suggest a good fantasy, you go back in time to look for the most pleasurably memorable times in your life. They all lead to the gate of *the circus!* Recalling the many times you were taken to the circus speeds up your heartbeat, so you know that you are in the right arena. Instead of imaging a real experience, you decide to explore a lifelong fantasy— that of being a clown! You were always most affected by the clowns!

Feel the grease paint on my fingertips…Looking down, I see how bright and white the makeup is. (What I am describing in words are in reality sensory imaging responses. You feel the grease paint; you see it. There is no need to say the words or to suggest anything.) *I feel my fingers gently applying the paint to my face, and I see it transform my image into someone else…Looking in the mirror, I see a clown being sculpted…I love the smell of grease paint…It is what theater and circus are all about…I put the bald wig on, with the funny red hair sticking out from the sides, see the funny mouth and eyebrows…My fingers gently squeeze the bulbous red nose making a honking sound as I do it… Putting on the oversized candy-striped shirt that looks like a signpost on the Yellow Brick Road…I feel the shirt on every part of my chest and arms. It seems to move in unison with my skin…I stare at myself in the mirror and see the magic of the circus and the excitement dancing in my eyes…I feel that "tickle" starting in my stomach and rising up into my throat, and it makes me start to laugh…At first, I feel the laughter as a tiny chuckle moving in my throat in the same way as a horse who is beginning to trot…faster and faster the trot, and the chuckle bursts from my throat and out of my mouth and explodes into an uproarious bellow of uncontrolled laughter…I am convulsing with laughter, feeling the tickle inside growing in size and shape…It is going into my lower body like veins of electricity…I begin to jump high into the air totally alive* *with that feeling…that wonderful, all encompassing feeling gripping every part of me…**the enchanted sense of play!*** (Everything that the actor experiences is processed totally in each sense. All of the descriptions of what he sees, hears, feels are all sensorially and emotionally experienced.) *I am clutching the sides of my baggy pants as I waddle back and forth writhing with laughter…I look down at my three-feet-long shoes and take long exaggerated steps forward and then backwards …I feel as I did when I was a child…I smell the sawdust under my feet and look for the shapes created by the footprints…I smell the cotton candy…My mouth waters as I recall the first time I tasted it, when it magically dissolved in my mouth…I taste it now…The music from the arena comes crashing into my dressing room, and I hear the huge bellowing voice of the ringmaster as it echoes off the walls around me… I feel a squadron of butterflies take off in my stomach…and in a moment I am catapulted out of the dressing room and into the arena…I stand there silently, blinded by the lights and feeling as if I were surrounded by a sea of people waiting for me to do something…All of a sudden I understand everything!…What it means to stand in the light…what it means to be there to perform, to create, to want to express every thought, feeling, impulse that I have ever experienced…I begin to see the faces of the people piled up in throngs on top of each other tier by tier…I see the expectant faces of the children with their eyes wide open …and their mouth agape in anticipation of what I am about to do… Suddenly, all those children are me when I was here at the circus. I see how I was…how I still am, and I feel the tears coming down my cheeks …I understand now that these are the important moments in life!…I open my mouth to speak and only a squeak comes out…a high-pitched squeak…They begin to laugh, and the tickle inside again begins to grow …I pull three balls out of my pocket and throw them into the air… reaching for them only to find that they all hit the ground bouncing and rolling in all directions…I missed all three…which sends the audience into raucous laughter…I was really trying to juggle…I wanted to catch the balls but didn't…I begin to chase the balls, as they roll away from me, but trip over my gigantic shoes…falling flat on my face…The people howl with laughter…I retrieve one ball and jump to my feet…Not seeing where the others went, I begin throwing the one ball into the air and catching it…with great satisfaction, and not knowing what else to do I take a bow…which sends the audience into hysterics…I feel elated by their response…and I feel an enormous wave of love and acceptance coming towards me!*

The fantasy may continue for as long as the actor wants it to or as long as time allows. The original purpose for it was to elevate his emotional state. Feeling depressed and stressed, he needed something that would change that and hopefully inspire him to want to act. Very often, the creative juices must be courted and seduced into making an appearance. The "slings and arrows" of daily living often create automatic insulation. In order to survive we must protect ourselves from the noise and the horrifying events that take place every day in the city, but as actors we must also have the tools to antidote the insulation membranes.

USING FANTASY TO ELEVATE THE IMAGINATION

As a tool to excite the imagination, fantasy ranks right up there. The moment an actor begins to use imaginary circumstances, he shifts into the realm of his imagination. There are numerous approaches to enter this area. Just as one can use several choice approaches in tandem with each other, one can also combine imaging techniques. For example, let us suppose that this actor was doing a preparation to stimulate and liberate his imagination; he could combine Fantasy Imaging with Fragmented Imaging or with Free-Association Imaging. The fantasy could be created in the form of a story, as in the example above, and so on. What would be the deciding factor? As usual, whatever works best!

When using fantasy as a preparation to approach a piece of material, the actor could stimulate images that promote the life of the character in the play. He could fill in the information gaps about his own or the other characters. Creating an entire life for his character prior to the first scene could be done totally with Fantasy Imaging.

A WORD ABOUT MENTAL IMAGING

Most of the Fantasy Imaging we do is what I call *mental imaging*. Although I do not include that particular technique as one of the seven we use in this craft, it must be discussed as part of the process, since it is the most common and most natural form of imaging, the kind we do from birth. We *mentally* see the pictures in our mind's eye; we hear not with our ears but with the ears inside our brains, so to speak; we "image-ine" people, places, events, experiences; we "picture" them. It is like having a movie playing in our heads. A baby images his mother coming with his bottle of formula. Does he actually *see* her, or does he see that image in his head? We mentally image eating something wonderful and we salivate—which is a sensorial response; but do we actually *taste* the food—*really taste* its flavor and consistency as when it is really in our mouths? Our sexual fantasies and images are quite stimulating, but do we really feel what it is like to be touching another person's skin?

There is no doubt in my mind that mental imaging stimulates sensory responses or that it affects our behavior and even our bodily functions. As I have said before, I am aware that it yields positive results and that it has effected thousands of cures, and I don't diminish its value; but does it create reality on the level that must exist in order for an actor to be impelled to behave? I think it falls short of that, and that is the reason why I do not include it as one of the recommended imaging techniques. I guess that it is all right to start with a mental image if you very quickly use the sensory responses to support it, but I have always felt that something which starts in the head and is promoted intellectually will stay in the head and not translate into impelling stimuli. It is quite a different story to be in a room full of people and mentally image it catching fire, and to actually create smoke and flames that are beginning to fill that same room. While it is possible that your heart rate might increase with the mental image, your response would be very different for sure if you actually created the *real* smoke and flames. What separates the men from the boys is the ability to create the smoke and flames so that they are *real!* That is what working with the craft is all about! If an actor dedicates his life to becoming a *master* at his craft and uses the techniques and tools inherent in this approach, he will ultimately be able to create anything so that it **really exists for him!**

In the following chapters you will learn in greater detail how to use the different imaging techniques described above to address the instrumental and craft demands of a play or film and to work with your unconscious. The evolution of these techniques came about over a period of time and with the experience of working with actors who were using Imaging as a choice approach. As usually happens with all exploration and experimentation, it started when I discovered another approach to fulfill the responsibilities of material. When one imaging technique didn't work the way I had hoped it would, I began to explore new ones that specifically fitted the circumstances and structure of the particular scene we were addressing. I have always encouraged myself to be open to new discoveries and fortunately been brave enough to try them! The seven imaging techniques, to which we can add Fantasy Imaging, plus the infrequent use of mental imaging, provide you, the actor, with rich and varied approaches to material.

CHAPTER 4

IMAGING AND
PREPARING

IMAGING AS A WAY OF LIFE

If you're an actor, then you're an actor twenty-four hours a day, not just when you are in class or in a play or film! Everything must be of interest to you. In chapter 1 of *Acting from the Ultimate Consciousness,* I discuss the need to elevate consciousness and how necessary that is to being an artist. An actor must have a daily work schedule, exercises he or she does each day to become instrumentally freer, more open and accessible, and a better craftsperson. In *Being & Doing,* there are sections that outline such a schedule—what to do and how to do it. The actor even works in his sleep, participating and ultimately manipulating his dreams. The commitment is total! It all depends on what kind of actor you want to be. If it is your life, it will become *a way of life* to you. Imaging is something that we do already. It is just a matter of becoming conscious of the process and of how to structure it for the variety of ways in which we will use it. We do many things in life without really knowing how or why we do them, and we don't get the most from them because of our lack of knowledge or structure. Imaging is a powerful technique, and it can be used in many ways. It must, however, be specified and structured to become part of our actor's set of tools. Every time you start visualizing or getting pictures in your head, acknowledge what is happening. Try to find out what precipitated the images and how and why you are imaging. It is like taking a personal inventory of your images. At first, this may interrupt the image, but soon you will learn to become aware without disturbing the flow of the process.

The second step is to take the images out of your head and put yourself in the picture. Become a part of them. At the very moment when you begin working consciously with imaging, encourage the fun and enjoyment of your involvement. Make it an adventure, and know that to master the ability to image will give you awesome power as a person and as an artist.

THE USES OF IMAGING

Imaging can be employed in a variety of ways and in many areas:

1. For *physical and mental health:* to heal the body and mind
2. For the pure *pleasure and enjoyment* of it, to enhance all the joys of life—sex, reading, going to the theater or the movies, and so on
3. For *instrumental* therapy and preparations
4. To elevate and pique the *imagination* and to stimulate it to become an innovative part of the actor's talent
5. As a *preparation* to get ready to act
6. As a *choice approach* of its own to create the choice
7. As an *approach process* or as a *craft technique* used in conjunction with other choice approaches
8. To communicate with, influence, and program the *unconscious*

Since this text is devoted to the art and craft of acting, I have limited myself to exploring imaging as it relates to the actor, his instrument and the craft process he uses to fulfill material. In the following pages, I will address these areas and suggest exercises and techniques to be used in each. As is true for any kind of conditioning and mastery, these must be practiced on a daily basis.

Quite often, one of my students will come to me and say, "But Eric, there is so much to this work! How can you practice and use it all?" Well, it is like having an incredible pantry stocked with delectable gourmet foods from all over the world. When you are hungry, you go into that pantry, look around and select only the food you want to taste. You cannot eat it all, and it isn't meant to be consumed all at once or even all the time. It is there so that when you need or desire it, you can choose what you want.

As an acting tool, imaging can be very useful. In the introduction to this book I mentioned that I had "a tiger by the tail." By that I meant that imaging is an incredible well of untapped riches and that its applications and uses have been virtually unexplored.

Since the system is divided into two major parts—instrument and craft—we will begin the journey with **the instrument, removing obstacles to act and preparing the instrument to investigate the craft.** From there we will move into the area of **the imagination: how to elevate and inspire it through imaging;** then I will go into **using imaging as a preparatory tool, dealing with many of the requirements of getting ready to act and addressing the specific responsibilities of the material;** from preparations into **using imaging as a choice approach and as an approach technique;** and finally into dealing with it as **a way of communicating with the unconscious.** The important thing to remember here is that imaging is an incredible technique that is used to influence the unconscious, to create a mind-body connection, as well as to affect behavior from an inner organic place. If it is done repeatedly and with practiced skill, it will stimulate a level of unconscious impetus and reality that will give acting a new dimension.

INSTRUMENTAL IMAGING

The instrument is your mind, your body, your voice, and your emotions. Nature created the instrument to function as an integral unit. All the parts are made to work in harmony with each other. When there is tension or other obstacles to that natural state, the instrument ceases to function normally or with its natural harmony: The voice disconnects from the emotions, the body moves stiffly, and the brain is distracted and disconnected from the rest. At this point the actor is out of control and not functioning organically. That is why all instrumental preparation should begin with *relaxation*. If after taking a *Personal Inventory* the actor discovers that he has tension, he must begin the creative journey with one of the many relaxation exercises. There are many good ones that we do in my classes: Tense and Relax, Logy, Rag Doll, Weight and Gravity, and so on. There is also a very rich cluster of relaxation exercises that use imaging as the approach.

EXERCISES WHICH PROMOTE RELAXATION

Imaging a state of physical relaxation or well-being, imaging places and environments which encourage relaxation, imaging events or relationships that stimulate deeper levels of involvement—all work to eliminate tension and promote a relaxed state.

IMAGING PHYSICAL RELAXATION

This first exercise can be done sitting or lying down, with your eyes open or closed. I suggest starting with your eyes closed and opening them as you get further into the image. Image yourself physically relaxed and comfortable. Actually see yourself relaxed. Go through your entire body, and image yourself loose and relaxed, with an overall feeling of physical well-being. Support the visual image with tactile responses in every part of your body. Tactilely image *(Imaging Sensations)* the feeling of looseness in all the parts of your body where tension exists. Image yourself moving around with this comfortable, relaxed feeling. Use as many of your senses as is applicable in this framework. Image your physical demeanor and posture as you have always wished them to be. See yourself relating to the world from that physical place. At first, it will be difficult to totally translate that complete sense of BEING; however, after repeated involvements with this kind of imaging, your body will slowly be influenced by the images you have created and will begin to comply with them.

Another good imaging technique, which will not only promote relaxation in the moment but also help change the way you function on a day-to-day basis, is to image yourself relaxed in tense circumstances—when meeting people who intimidate you, when going on interviews, in a romantic encounter, and so on. If you image yourself as you would like to be and support the image with all your senses, in a short time it will become your reality instead of your image. A large variety of physical relaxation exercises can be approached through imaging. Feel free to modify those I have suggested or to invent your own. Once you have acquired the basic ability to use imaging successfully, you will become quite inventive with the process.

IMAGING ENVIRONMENTS

In the same way as you promoted physical relaxation, you can also use Story Imaging or Fragmented Imaging to begin creating a beautiful and relaxed environment—either a place that really exists or one that you create through your imagination. It helps for you to know yourself fairly well so that you can select a place that has affected you before. I personally respond to natural environments—the beautiful creations of nature on this planet, such as the ocean, the forest, the desert, a gorgeous sunset, or any natural surrounding that makes me feel at one with God and the world and happy to be alive.

➤ *Example*

This is an exercise that you can do at the beginning of a class or before a rehearsal or even before going on for a performance. With your eyes closed or open, begin to image the place: *I smell the ocean and the mixture of salt and fish and the clean odor of the sea.* (This image, which starts from an olfactory place, must be responded to with that sense.) *I smell the heat on the sand and the wind itself. The sun feels wonderful on my naked body.* (Respond tactilely in all the places that the image suggests.) *I feel the breeze as it dances around my face and slowly moves lower and lower on my body...It feels cooler and then warmer.* (Again, all these sensations are *felt* in the various parts of the body.) *As I open my eyes I see the blue sky straight ahead of me...It is many colors of blue. There are faint, white wisps of clouds sprinkled in undefinable patterns, and if I stare at these designs they become almost hypnotic. I haven't a care in the world. It is as if time had stopped and I were suspended in space.*

Remember that, as you involve each sense—either asking sensory questions or using Imaging Sensations—it is extremely important that you respond sensorially, and not with your intellect or inner eye. The image can go on for however long it takes for you to achieve relaxation. As I said earlier, I respond to natural environments; however, that may not be what relaxes you; so you can image being at the symphony, at a rock concert, or in the intimate environs of your home. Your imagery can take you to any place that promotes relaxation, involvement, and a sense of well-being.

Another good relaxation exercise involving imagery is *floating,* creating a sense of being in water, being buoyant and weightless, and floating. If you have ever had the experience of being in a Shimadi tank, you will instantly relate to what I mean. The Shimadi experience is one of the most incredible ones I have ever had. It consists of lying in an enclosed tank of water which is dark and soundproof. While it is quite shallow (there is no danger of drowning), you nonetheless experience sensations of floating, weightlessness, and solitude that take you into an altered state of consciousness. After about half an hour, your fantasy and free-association journeys are unbelievable! It is probably the most relaxing experience you could ever have! If you have already had it, you can re-create it through the use of imagery; if not, you may sensorially image being in warm water and floating freely in a dark, comfortable place. As you achieve this weightless sense of floating, you will probably also experience other images that freely pop into your consciousness. Go wherever they take you.

Another very relaxing sensation is rocking. Lying on your side, start rocking back and forth, and begin imaging any activity that involves that movement: being in a rocking chair, on a rocking horse, or on a carousel, being rocked by another person—your mother, or someone else you love—and so on. Continue the physical act of rocking until the image takes over and supplies the experience without the actual movement.

RELAXATION-THROUGH-INVOLVEMENT IMAGERY

Since any kind of involvement is the enemy of tension, imaging any event or experience, or for that matter any imaging that takes you off the spot, will work to relax you. You could simply start to free-associate—allowing one image to merge into the next—or you might decide to story image and pick a theme or experience to do it with. Whatever the approach or content might be, you will surely get progressively relaxed as you become more and more involved in the image. Whatever the imaging technique might encompass, it is definitely another way of eliminating tension. It provides you with a cluster of added armaments in the war against tension.

INSTRUMENTAL THERAPY IMAGING

While relaxation is the first step in the instrumental preparatory process, the next involvement must address the specific obstacles the individual actor has. These might be blocks he has had for a long time, they can exist as a result of the "spot," they can be part of where he is at this moment in time, or they can be a combination of all of the above or exist for other reasons. Whatever the case may be, the actor must deal with them and eliminate them in order to proceed towards addressing the responsibility to the material. After relaxing, he must find out where he is, usually through the use of Personal Inventory, and he must then select an instrumental-therapy exercise to eliminate any obstacle that stands in the way of BEING. Obstacles can exist in any area. If he is truly relaxed at this point, he may, for example, discover that a lack of trust or ego is preventing him from confidently beginning to address the first obligation of the piece. If that is the case, he might elect to do some kind of ego exercise to elevate his self-esteem; or the obstacle may be self-consciousness or fear of failure, or the actor may suffer anxiety without knowing the content of the anxiety or the reason for it. There are an endless number of possible obstacles he could encounter on the stage. Whatever the problem, there is certainly an antidote to it. Instrumental-therapy exercises exist in legion numbers, and with the proper experience the actor can become quite adept at selecting the right one and the proper approach technique to execute it, in order to eliminate the obstacle and take the next step in the process of dealing with the play. Imaging has unique advantages over other existing exercises and techniques, however. To prove the point, let us imagine, for example, that the actor is "conflict phobic" and for that reason has a history of avoiding any kind of encounter or confrontation. I could give him a variety of exercises that would encourage him to face the problem head on. He might do a series of Imaginary Monologues expressing his anger and frustration to people in his life who are not really present in the room, or I could have him repeatedly do Virginia Woolf Exercises until he felt much more comfortable in conflict areas, and so on. Of course, these techniques work. I have been using them successfully for years. So why not stick with them? Simply because there are other usable tools as well as new exercises on the instrumental-therapy list which might work better in certain situations. The most important reason for introducing imaging in this area, however, is that, if properly repeated, it has the ability to affect the unconscious and create new images for the actor. If, for example, he works on this obstacle every day, imaging himself as powerful, articulate, and able to decimate any opponent with his razor-sharp tongue, his steel-trap mind, and his confidence in his ability to stand up to anyone, he will eventually begin to see himself that way in life. In a sense, you might say that imaging is a kind of brainwashing, a way to alter consciousness, address lifelong psychological problems and solve them.

Until now the work was based on the concept of dealing with the most serious obstacle first. By discovering that he could confront the problem and successfully survive the ordeal, the actor would progressively gain confidence in his ability to experience and express heretofore-terrifying impulses. So the instrumental-therapy journey consisted in eliminating obstacle after obstacle until he could be comfortable doing no more or less than he felt and could achieve a BEING state every time he got ready to act—and that has been working very well! Imaging is just another way of achieving this goal, possibly more quickly and definitely with the capacity to influence the unconscious. By imaging, you are soliciting the help of the most powerful part of any of us. You are turning your problems over to the genius of the unconscious—which is much like programming a computer. You do this daily in the form of images. The unconscious in turn processes these images and begins to feed the responses back into your conscious behavior. If you do this over a period of time in all the problem areas, lifelong obstacles that have damaged your ability, not only to act but also to function happily and successfully in life, will be eliminated. What makes imaging so powerful and so humongous a discovery and a SUPERMEGAPPROACH is that it is capable of altering consciousness, of changing the way we relate to ourselves and the world, as well as being an acting tool that can create reality and belief on the very deepest unconscious levels. All my life as an actor, I have heard it said that some actors have the natural ability to act and that others do not. I imagine that this ability is somehow an integral part of what talent is. I have also heard many directors say that this or that actor had too many problems to act—he was too screwed up or he was so constipated emotionally that he could only play parts that did not call for heavy emotions. Does that mean that those of us who are lucky enough to have reached maturity with the least amount of damage are the only ones who can act? Or does it point to the necessity for instrumental training and the elimination of those obstacles? Most of the actors I know personally have been in psychotherapy; but most psychotherapy is "talking heads," and the majority of those actors have not been able to solve their emotional and expressive problems that way. So what is the answer? It is not my purpose here to denigrate psychotherapy, which has literally saved the lives of millions of people. What I am trying to communicate is that it takes a very special kind of "therapy" to eliminate blocks and other obstacles so that the person is able not only to function but to do so in a totally expressive way, experiencing all the colors of the emotional spectrum without any inhibitions to block expression.

INSTRUMENTAL OBSTACLES AND IMAGING ANTIDOTES

The most common instrumental obstacles actors suffer from are tension, fears of all kinds—of failure, of ridicule, of looking foolish or untalented, of forgetting lines, of exposure, of intimacy, of violating privacies, of losing control, of conflict; moral or religious fears relating to expression; fear of being antisocial, ugly, improper, vulnerable, or of expressing emotions that society thinks improper for one's gender—ego problems, such as shyness, self-consciousness, self-involvement, a lack of self-esteem or self-worth, or negative self-images; physical, emotional, social conditioning and obligation, and guilt about many things. These instrumental obstacles plague the actor and make it impossible for him to be organically free and impulsive. When addressing any of them, he must first become aware of its existence and then committed to eliminating it. Once he has accomplished this, he can approach it with an antidotal technique.

Using imaging to address any obstacle involves building an antithetical belief structure through the creation of new behaviors and relationships. If the actor becomes intimately familiar with his obstacles, he can create a daily work schedule of imaging to address each of them, progressively building a whole new image of himself in each of these areas. Imaging exercises can also be done right before he acts. If he combines the imaging process with onstage preparations and makes imaging a way of life, he can ultimately expect to achieve his highest goals.

Fears

There are as many kinds of fears as there are people, I imagine. We all experience a wide variety of fears, and normal acting obligations intensify them. All fears, if not dealt with and eliminated, block the actor from organic experience. They exist even when he is not on the spot, so they must be dealt with on a daily basis as part of his instrumental-therapy involvement. All of us have insecurities for which we have learned to compensate at an early age and which we have obscured as a result. When the spot gets hot enough, they surface with a vengeance and strangle our creative abilities. By that time it is often too late to eliminate them, so the compensational activity shifts into a higher gear, and we become "impositionally" relaxed and "cool," while underneath, tension and fear are rampant. This compensational activity becomes a habit that prevents potentially talented actors from ever realizing the truth and dimension of their talent.

There are many exercises that can be done right on the spot. They often work quite well, but just as often, they are only temporary Band-Aids that hardly close the open wound. One of the most successful antidotes to acting obstacles of all kinds is getting involved. That in itself will quite frequently eliminate or lower an actor's fear. It is, however, only a temporary cure for a lifelong problem; but if the actor is serious about his work, he must strive to eliminate that problem permanently! On-the-spot instrumental therapy might include an imaging process that has *benevolent acceptance* as its thrust.

➢ *Example*

First, the fearful actor acknowledges the tension and the specific fear. If in a class or laboratory, he does so out loud; if in an audition or on a job he does it silently:

I am shaking all over...I wonder if they can see my legs trembling... I feel a sinking feeling in my stomach...I am afraid to open my mouth! ...I am afraid to say the first line...I don't want to look scared...but I am...I wonder if they know it—and so on until most of his fear is at least acknowledged to himself.

At this point, he can begin to image all the people in his environment as supportive and benevolently accepting of everything he is about to do: *I see all the people looking at me! I see affection in their eyes. They all seem to be on my side.* He starts the Fragmented Imaging after relating to available realities. In other words, he looks for benevolence wherever it really exists. He may *selectively emphasize* it, *enhance* it, or whatever allows him to believe that he is in an accepting and supportive environment. When he has exhausted the realities, he can sneak into imaging beyond what really exists: *I see friendly faces wherever I look. The lady in the first row is smiling at me and nodding approval. Even the room looks brighter and more colorful. The sounds of silence are comforting, and I feel myself standing tall. I can almost experience the excitement and anticipation of what I am about to do.*

There are other imaging techniques an actor can use on the spot or just before going on stage; for example, he might create an elaborate story image of successfully executing the scene and of the incredible response that follows his work. (This is like the baseball player who images hitting the ball out of the park before he goes up to bat.)

All of these pre-acting instrumental-therapy imaging techniques are valuable, and they work! The real job of the actor is to address the problem at hand—which has most likely been a part of his life since childhood.

Neurolinguistic Programming is a process which deals in part with the negative images we create for ourselves, which get us into the habit of thinking that our lives have been depressing or uneventful. We support those negative beliefs by adding to them consistently. In the book *Using Your Brain for a Change,* Richard Bandler talks about the ways in which we can change these negative thoughts and images. He says that the brain learns things very rapidly and sometimes instantaneously and that "it can take one instantaneous experience for a person to learn something so thoroughly that he'll remember it for the rest of his life." In this way, we all learn to be afraid and insecure. The images we create and implant in our brains often stay there for our entire lives—that is, unless we address and change them! How do we accomplish a task so great that it often takes years of psychotherapy to confront it? Well, the first step is to be totally unconcerned with why we got that way to begin with. Understanding the *why* does nothing to eliminate the problem, though it often takes years of therapy.

For our purposes it is important only to eliminate the fears, and not to concern ourselves with why they are there. Imaging is a powerful tool in this area. Sometimes we do not distinguish a response as coming from a particular image or thought, but very often an involuntary picture flashes in our head so quickly that we hardly notice it, and we immediately become fearful and insecure. It might be a harmless childhood experience, triggered by something or someone in this place at this moment, which could consist of falling off your tricycle with everyone laughing at you. That might have been the basis for an entire life of fearing involvements with mechanical objects—things like riding a bike or a motorcycle or even driving an automobile. The fear started when you were four years old and still exists in your late twenties! Of course, you haven't done anything to change that image of failure or ridicule. Quite the contrary, you have unconsciously supported it!

There are two approaches to eliminating fear, which both involve changing the images that are already there. The first step is to identify the fear or insecurity—to isolate it. Let us take the example of falling off the tricycle at the age of four. Assuming that the fear is that of ridicule, you must go back in your memory and try to recall all of the experiences you had that involved being laughed at or ridiculed. Go over each of them in imaging terms. Allow yourself to feel everything you felt at the time. Make the memory of those images very clear to yourself. After experiencing each event a number of times, using all five of your senses to support the image, begin to *change it!*

➢ *Example (the Tricycle Experience)*

I feel the seat of my tricycle hitting the inside of my thighs, and it feels solid and strong! I see the sidewalk in front of me, and it glistens with the reflection of the diamond sparkles of glass in the cement. It looks like a racetrack waiting for me to run on it! (It is very important in the re-creation and changing of an image to enhance its brightness and color. The vivid brilliance of the event in "glorious Technicolor" makes the images larger and more dimensional.) *I am beginning to pump the pedals, and I can feel the muscles in my legs flex...They feel strong and powerful. As I push down, my tricycle moves forward with speed and thrust...I love the feeling of that movement, and I feel the wind as it touches my face and blows my hair...I see my friends watching me with awe and envy...I push harder and faster. I am moving like a rocket sled ...I hear myself scream with the joy and excitement of my prowess and the speed of movement. All my friends are smiling with encouragement. Some of them are laughing with me! I feel the warm caress of the spring sunlight on my face, and I have a wonderful sense of well-being!...I hit a crack in the cement, and I feel the front wheel of my tricycle twisting to the left...It is falling out from under me...and I am airborne...flying wonderfully through the air without fear! As I fly past my friends, they all cheer me on because I put my hands in front of me and instantly transform into Superman...I feel the air hissing past my ears, and I scream with glee and am met with a chorus of similar sounds from my friends. I arch my body something like a ski jumper about to make a landing, and I hit the pavement standing and running at the same instant. I feel like Superman! All my friends run towards me howling with joy and admiration. I can hear their individual sounds and words proclaiming me the hero that I feel like!*

The entire fantasy story should be structured so that you respond with all five senses. The *Creative Manipulation* that helps to change the original experience should be used over and over again each time you work. You may create subtle differences each time, but remember to stay positive and heroic. You will be able to use this technique with every experience you go back to and in every area of fear and insecurity.

The alternate way in which to approach an obstacle is to identify the fear or insecurity as it exists in this moment or at this time in your life. You need not go back in time and find the origin of the problem. You need only understand that you are insecure about a particular thing or person. Let us suppose, for example, that you have a fear of intimacy. It is hard for you to be close to other people, and it affects your acting. Whenever you have to do a scene where you need to express love or tenderness, you find it very embarrassing and extremely uncomfortable. Touching the other actor or being touched is almost painful. This fear could have originated in a hundred different experiences or result from having unaffectionate parents, who frowned on displays of love or affection. It doesn't matter at this moment where it originated. What is important is that you can structure images that will antidote it.

Your images could start with fantasies; for example, you could image yourself with very attractive members of the opposite sex. At first, the images could involve sharing personal and intimate things about your life. Later, you could both share intimate feelings you have about each other. Create the fantasy image vividly in a specific place. See, hear, feel, taste, and smell all the elements of the environment and the person with whom you are sharing yourself. Start with a fantasy person and image that person being very affectionate physically as well as in words and gestures. Create a nonjudgmental attitude in him or her, and work to feel that way yourself. The image can also be sexual, but it needn't go that far. Practice daily variations of this fantasy image using different people and environments. After a time, begin creating images that are not just fantasy but involve specific individuals in your life. Image successfully relating to people who have been difficult to approach or to be intimate with. Image yourself hugging and touching them and receiving a very positive response from them. Create these images just before meeting with a particular person. Image the appointment being filled with warmth and affectionate touching. Do the same thing with a difficult scene on stage. Image yourself specifically doing the scene just the way you want to. Be careful not to try to repeat any premeditated behavior. The purpose is to antidote a fear, not to plan your behavior.

Shyness

That fear of opening one's mouth to speak, which causes one to remain silent and is often thought of as *stage fright,* is another very common acting obstacle. There are a variety of antidotal images one could create to overcome this concern, all of them involving circumstances where one would normally feel intense shyness.

➤ *Example*

Using Fantasy Story Imaging, create a scene of success in a public place: *I am standing at a podium in front of four thousand people. There is a sea of faces in front of me.* (From the outset of the imaging exercise the actor must actually visualize sensorially the place, the people, and so on.) *There is a deafening silence, and the air is filled with the expectation of what I am about to say. I am full of passion and excitement about what I want to communicate to these people.* (The temperature of the auditorium and all the sounds must be created as part of the image.) *I begin to speak. I hear the words as they come tumbling out of my mouth, filled with conviction and passion. There is thunderous applause in response to what I have just said! People are on their feet applauding and whistling. That response is for me! I go on sharing my feelings about the need to save the planet, to band together and become strong in our numbers, to enlist the help of more and more people, to become conscious about the air, the water, the insecticides, and to hold all life in a state of reverence. I hear my words and feel increasingly inspired by my own beliefs. I feel my body shaking with excitement. All four thousand people are on their feet cheering me! My body feels strong, and I feel powerful in this place and at this moment. I feel as if I could do or say anything and it would be accepted. I feel a sense of enjoyment at being the center of attention. I feel important and that I count as a person in this world!*

The more specifically the image is approached, the greater the reality for the imager. With repetition, this kind of imaging will very quickly antidote a lifelong obstacle such as shyness.

It is important to note that there are many images you can create for this purpose. The example I gave you might have to be worked up to and the imaging done in smaller increments. You might start, for example, by imaging yourself speaking freely to just one person or having a satisfactory telephone conversation. The most important thing to understand is that imaging is a process that must be repeated on a daily basis so as to pique and ultimately seduce the unconscious into believing and supporting your image.

Self-consciousness

Another obstacle most common to all of us is self-consciousness, a result of tension, fear, self-involvement, and obligations of all kinds. The antidote can take many forms: the actor can deal with the tension, elevate his self-esteem, get selflessly involved, or confront the specific fear in the moment. Once he has determined the original cause of the problem by taking personal inventory, he can select an antidotal exercise to confront it. If he chooses to use imaging, he might elect to kill two birds with one stone by structuring an image of well-being, thus creating successful results and at the same time becoming "selflessly involved" through his involvement with the process. In other words, imaging a sense of well-being and success will eliminate the fear and obligation, while the act of imaging itself will take the actor away from any concern with the expectations of the moment. There are two imaging techniques he might use in this case:

- *Story Imaging,* which involves simply structuring his image to parallel the circumstance in the scene or monologue and imaging himself approaching the material with confidence and craft facility, or
- *Fragmented Imaging* of a whole situation or event followed by positive responses to his work, as he feels the full emotional impact of what he is doing and images himself deliciously experiencing the emotional life of the scene.

Low Self-esteem and Lack of Ego

Another very common and plaguing problem is lack of self-esteem. It is very difficult to reach maturity with a healthy ego. Most actors have a very fragile ego and suffer from a multitude of ego afflictions that can stand in the way of their functioning creatively and organically. Most of us are damaged and battered by parents, teachers, peers, or the clergy before we reach puberty. As a result, we grow up fearing that we are not enough. In some areas of performance the situation is even more aggravated. Many of us become actors to prove that we are enough, only to encounter this demon at every turn. Here again, as with many other belief structures, the images and convictions were planted in our brain at an early age, and they are constantly replayed whenever that particular button is pushed. It is your responsibility to identify exactly what your ego obstacle is and to create images that antidote your low self-esteem. In this area it might be wise to go back and recall—reimage—the events that contributed to the problem, then modify that image. You can also build an imaging scenario that progressively heightens your self-esteem.

The story should begin with an appreciation of yourself. Create yourself in an attitude of attractive power, feeling good physically as well as mentally. Even before you bring others into the image, emphasize your admirable qualities and looks. Image yourself as bright, articulate and verbal, able to think quickly and to formulate ideas and theories that are innovative. Allow yourself to be impressed with yourself in your images. By the time you involve others, you will feel that you deserve their admiration and praise. I once heard someone say, while staring at a very overweight, pretty young woman, "Inside that heavy young girl is a beautiful and thin young woman!" That is true about everyone in one way or another. So start your self-esteem imaging with what you look like; see yourself the way you feel you are inside; look in the mirror, and image a beautiful body—and keep doing it.

Self-involvement

The next obstacle you might want to address, self-involvement is not a sign of egotism as most people think. Just the opposite! Usually people who are self-involved are so because they feel the need to look out for themselves, most often as a result of fear and feelings of not being enough, which lead them to preoccupying themselves with their own activities. It is like a prison sentence in a way. Instead of being able to come out into the world and to develop curiosity, consciousness, and pleasurable involvement with this wonderful planet, the self-involved person goes through life holding a mirror and wearing blinders, which block his view of the world. Hopefully, such a person can be paroled. The antidote for him is first, to deal with elevating his ego and convincing himself that it is safe for him to come out and secondly, to help himself become aware of the many wonderful and selflessly involving things that exist in the world. But first, he must become aware that this, like any other instrumental problem, is an obstacle to affectability and expressive freedom. Once he has accomplished that, he can create images that will pique and excite curiosity and selfless involvement. These can be structured on the spot or used in a daily imaging schedule to antidote the obstacle as a life problem.

The Various Emotional Obstacles

One of the most common emotional obstacles is the fear of being emotional at all! Most people grow up in an environment where emotional expression any larger than what is socially acceptable is a symptom of loss of control or of a weakness of some kind. It is not civilized to lose your temper! That kind of conditioning is widespread and insidious and happens without our awareness. There are a great many emotions that are not comfortable to many actors. To some, anything above normal conversation is somewhat awkward—from manifesting disapproval, irritation, sarcasm, hostility or conflict, irrational or critical behavior, to experiencing any of the large expurgating outbursts of violence, anger, or rage and expressing any vulnerability, remorse, extreme grief, bereavement, anxiety, fear, depression, feeling sorry for oneself, and so on—the list could fill this entire page, but you get the idea, don't you? How many of these do you personally have difficulty with? There are literally dozens of instrumental-therapy exercises which deal with emotional liberation in my other books, but the emphasis here is *imaging*, so why not confine our attention to the imaging techniques that address these obstacles? That is not to say that you are limited only to that process; it just means that you would serve yourself well to really explore this incredible MEGAPPROACH.

For example, if you wanted to address your fear of expressing anti-social rage and anger, you could create a story image of yourself righteously expurgating all of the repressed anger you have carried with you since childhood, possibly in the environment where you grew up during the formative years of your life.

➢ *Example*

I see the fireplace in front of me, that one chipped brick that was never repaired. I'm looking into the fireplace at all the blackness of all the wood burned over the years. What do I feel on my back? What is the texture of the material of the sofa where I am sitting? (Respond with the proper sensory response.) *I hear my father yelling at my sister in the other room. What does his voice sound like?* (Respond with the auditory sense.) *He is so unreasonable...so demanding...so unfair!...What is he saying to her? I smell the odors of this room...What are they specifically?...*(Respond sensorially.) *I am standing looking into the mirror on the mantle...What do I see?...*(Respond visually. Ask more questions in this area.) *I'm a little boy, and I'm angry. I feel the anger rising in me ...I want to scream at my father, but I'm afraid!...I'm moving towards the kitchen...The sound of his voice is growing louder and more intimidating...I'm frightened! Where in my body do I feel that fear?...*(Respond in that part of the body.) *What does it feel like? I'm standing looking at my raging father. What do I see? How tall is he? What does he look like? Where do I see the anger in his face?...What does that look like?...How do I feel? I hear myself scream, "Stop! How dare you treat children that way? You take your own frustrations out on us because you cannot deal with your own failures...You are nothing but a bully!" I hear these words coming from my mouth, and it feels as if someone else were speaking, but it is I, and I feel strong and righteous. He looks at me in amazement and shock...I see the anger drain from his face...He walks towards me, not with violence but with shame...What do I see in his eyes? He is kneeling down to me...I smell his particular odor. What is that? He embraces me and begins to cry, telling me how sorry he is. What do I hear in his voice? I feel his strong arms around me and his love pouring out to me. I hear him tell us how sorry he is and how much he loves us both.*

As usual, all of the above imaging should be sensorially supported, and all the senses allowed to create the image. If it helps the image, you can support it by verbalizing out loud. Of course, a little boy would not have the sophistication or knowledge to know any of those things or to say them to his father; however, an image of this kind goes back to a time when these obstacles were created, and that in itself addresses the origin of the inhibition.

Another antidote in the area of anger and rage could involve imaging confrontations with all of the people in your life whom you never confronted before. You could expurgate all of the anger and rage that you have incubated throughout your life. Each image should be structured like the example given above. You should make it as complete an experience as possible.

Another very common obstacle for actors is something I refer to as *conflict phobia,* the fear of getting into any kind of conflict with anyone about anything. It is a peculiar instrumental obstacle to have, particularly if one is an actor, since almost all of dramatic literature must contain some kind of conflict in order to qualify as such. The fear of conflict usually begins at an early age and is often the result of an overbearing or intimidating parent. Sometimes it comes from living in an environment which is filled with conflict and raging emotions.

Whatever the cause, if it exists it is a formidable obstacle. Most actors who are conflict phobic impose or manifest behavior that represents the emotions inherent in a piece of material that requires a conflict. The antidote is instead to recognize the obstacle consciously and to confront it by admitting an aversion to conflict and then choosing material that is loaded with it to explore in a laboratory circumstance. You can do Imaginary Monologues, encountering and confronting the very people who helped create your fear of conflict and going into great expurgatory tirades with them. Whatever the obstacle, you can be sure that the structure which supports the fear is well rooted in your unconscious. Something put it there! It may have been planted by what would now seem like an insignificant event, but it was nourished by other experiences and grew into a full-blown, unconsciously supported reality. Any of the instrumental antidotal exercises will create new confidence in this area and with repetition will unbalance the old habit; however, *imaging* has a much more immediate impact on the unconscious and will probably save you a lot of the time and energy you might otherwise have to expend on the more conventional techniques.

Before designing a specific image to combat your fear in this area, it would be wise first to explore and understand the dynamics of the obstacle. You may be afraid of conflict for a variety of reasons; for example, you may fear losing control and hurting someone, or you may be intimidated by the power of this kind of emotion. Possibly you have always felt that in a conflict situation you could not hold your own. Whatever your specific fear is in this area, you can create an imaging circumstance that is antithetical to how you really feel.

Let us imagine that you are, and have always been, intimidated by people who seem to have the power to be big, loud, and angry and that you have always shied away from such intimidators. You might create a fantasy story image of being imposing, large, and intimidating to others. As part of the fantasy, you could overhear friends of yours discussing your powerful presence. You might create a Clark Kent–Superman situation, even without the need for a telephone booth in which to change!

➢ *Example*

I'm sitting in a crowded outdoor restaurant on the Sunset Strip having lunch. (Create the image in sensorial detail using all five senses with Imaging Sensations.) *It is the middle of the afternoon, and I can feel the warmth of the sun streaking through the louvered windows. I see the endless stream of traffic, but somehow it doesn't bother me. The food tastes particularly good today. I see some familiar faces and am aware of the cacophonous din of conversations, of which I only catch a stray understandable word now and then. I am feeling strong and looking well. I can tell that my presence has an aura of power by the way the waitress relates to me. I feel the energy of the earth through the soles of my shoes. It seems like a primal energy. I am intent on my meal, lost in fleeting thoughts that come and go as through a colander.*

My reverie is suddenly interrupted by a harshly familiar voice, a voice which in the past made me bristle with protective energy. I look up and see what I expected to be there—Jim! Arrogant, smiling, over-bearing, critical Jim! "Hi, how are you?" I say, cheerfully. He looks at me long and hard, not knowing quite what to make of such an open and self-assured approach. He sits...I can tell by the deliberateness of his movements that he intends to intimidate me and make me cower...Oh, boy, is he in for the shock of his life! I have already begun to shed the trappings of my Clark Kent persona, and I am relishing the encounter. He is smiling at me. Under that smile is something I had never noticed before, an insecurity that makes his eyes shift back and forth. Obviously, my self-confidence shook him. I look deep into his being and perceive a frightened and unhappy person who needs to denigrate others in order to feel all right about himself. He isn't quite sure what to make of me and for a few moments hesitates to say anything. I continue to appraise him silently, and it is obvious that he doesn't like this new me at all. He makes a move as if to leave but quickly sees that I have no intention of allowing that to happen. I break the silence: "So, Jim, what have you got to report today?" He looks at me with obvious confusion, not knowing how to respond from a glib place. "What do you mean by that?" he barks! His voice seems a bit loud and forced, and he is aware that some heads have turned to look at him. He responds with a mixture of embarrassment and belligerence. With a very deliberate and confident smile, I say, "Aren't you going to tell me how busy you are and how in demand you have been lately? Aren't you going to blow your horn for ten minutes, only to end up showing no interest in me?" The color drains from his face, his eyes become rimmed with red, and he is unable to say anything. For the first time he is speechless! Finally, he manages to utter in an almost inaudible voice, "What the hell has gotten into you?" Still smiling and feeling an overwhelming sense of victory, I say, "Why, nothing new at all, Jim. I've just begun to realize that you are a little bully, frightened and ineffectual! All my life I have let blowhards like you intimidate me, but no more, Jim! I think you should see a therapist!" I can see his rage. He wants to say something but cannot! It is at those moments that people who feel helpless turn to being physical, and I see the thought of that possibility fleet across his face. He rejects it, possibly because I do not waiver in my intensity or purpose. I am not afraid of him on any level, and he knows it. We sit there looking at each other, and I realize that I have hurt him deeply! I suddenly understand that real power lies not in hurting someone but in understanding him. I reach over and gently put my hand on his, which seems to be resting lifelessly on the table. He is startled by my action, and his first impulse is to pull his hand away. Instead, he places his other hand over mine and smiles, the first genuine smile I have seen on him since I first met him. This is a great victory and possibly the beginning of a real friendship on equal terms.

Creating images like that one can become part of your instrumental involvement. The structure will change, of course, depending on the nature of your fear. Feel free to create as many imaging experiences as you want. With repetition you will soon find that the fear of conflict will disappear entirely. Another good way to approach this kind of imaging is to go back to every conflict experience you can remember and change its nature and outcome.

Taking any of the emotional obstacles, you can also create an image that stimulates a specific emotional response and follow that image all the way into that response. If you are dealing with grief, for example, you could create the funeral of a very dear friend or family member, imaging everything—the coffin, the body, the sounds and odors of the cemetery, the clergyman, the people there, and the sounds of grief around you. You could encourage the grief to happen to you while you image the event, experience the overwhelming public expression of your own grief, and carry the image through to the conclusion of the services.

Several of the examples I gave in the previous chapter can serve well in raising vulnerability and emotional accessibility. Experiment in every obstacle area, and repeat your images until you are free of all your inhibitions. Remember that you are not only creating an image to antidote a specific problem, you are also planting all those images in your unconscious. They affect you in the same way as your inhibiting images did, only in reverse.

Social Conditioning

As a result of the pressures of society and of growing up in a world filled with judgment and taboos, we are all insidiously influenced by social obligations and behavioral proprieties that inhibit free expression. These restrictions become so subtle that they are hardly noticeable sometimes; yet they are formidable obstacles to free and *impulsive* expression. How many times have you heard someone described as a "nice guy"? In itself it sounds like a compliment, and it very well may be one, but if that is the individual's pervasive personality element, it is clear that his persona is a result of conditioning.

The obstacles of social obligation can be addressed in a variety of ways. Some of the techniques already discussed in relation to antisocial behavior, dealing with conflict, standing up for yourself, and so on, will help to alleviate part of the social conditioning. With every obstacle an actor discovers, the first and most important step is for him to become totally conscious of its existence and of the dynamics of how it operates in his life and to see what he can create to antidote it.

Imaging in every one of the obstacle areas with consistent repetition will ultimately antidote the problem. Let us for a moment go back to the use of imaging as a healer to the body, a tool which is capable of curing terminal diseases. The images had to be created over and over again every day and over a long period of time. In a large number of cases the results were startlingly successful. The two major ingredients for making imaging work for you is first, your willingness to believe that it will and secondly, the disciplined repetition of its practice.

If you do some of your imaging before going to sleep or even before taking a nap, preferably in the sleep-wake state, it will get into your unconscious more rapidly. Having done this conscious-unconscious communicating for some time now, I find that it is often difficult for me to distinguish the images I have created from the reality. I have caught myself thinking that a particular image was something that had actually happened in my life, and I had to remind myself that I had structured that image for a specific reason. As with all the elements and techniques of this system, the more you do the work, the less you need to do to believe and to be affected by it. Imaging is a wonderful tool and can be used in any part of the work. As a device for addressing the obstacles that impede the actor from functioning freely, it works consistently.

Unfortunately, most actors do not, or will not, accept that acting is a twenty-four-hour-a-day involvement and that, like any art, it will grow stronger with constant work and practice. In addition to any daily work schedule you may already have, it is important that you identify and catalogue your instrumental obstacles and decide on the order in which you will deal with them, usually depending on the degree of strength each has to stop you from functioning freely. Once you have done that, include an imaging process that will create an antidote to your already existing belief structure. Take the examples I have given, and create your own images. Be adventurous in the exploration of the process. You cannot create the wrong image. If an image is not effective in antidoting a problem, structure another one. Soon you will begin to *see* and think of yourself in a different way. In your imaging journal, record all the images you use in each obstacle area, and repeat the ones that seem to have the greatest impact on your unconscious. After a time you will notice that each of your fears and obstacles has a diminishing impact on your behavior. You will become less shy and more able to express yourself impulsively; conflict areas won't paralyze you the way they had before; confrontations of various kinds will be handled in constructive ways; and so on in every area where you were unable to function comfortably before. **The most important reason for reading this book is to understand that imaging is an incredibly powerful tool because, with practiced repetition, it has the power to affect the unconscious and to change the things we have come to believe by supplanting them with new images and belief structures.** Imaging an event that has occurred in our life for the purpose of reexperiencing it also brings up the colors and textures of that experience, which only the unconscious remembers, and the impact of elements long since forgotten by our conscious memory.

INSTRUMENTAL PREPARATION TO ACT

There is a chronology involved in preparation. While eliminating instrumental obstacles is a daily job, it is also a never-ending responsibility before one gets ready to act. Even if the actor has liberated himself from lifelong blocks, there are always obstacles that manifest themselves when something is expected, when there is a spot or an obligation to perform. These obstacles are always present and must be eliminated in order to free the instrument and reach a BEING state. Once the actor has dealt with the obstacles to freedom of expression, the next step is to make his instrument accessible and expressive. Elevating his affectability is the next logical involvement. For the sake of clarity I am therefore going to separate instrumental preparation into two different categories, the first being the on-the-spot *obstacles* and the second relating to *instrumental accessibility* and readiness to address the specific emotional demands of the material.

In the first category are tension, fear, self-consciousness, self-involvement, the obligation to succeed, and so on. There are a wide variety of exercises that will eliminate these spot blocks. Any imaging involvement would take you out of yourself while at the same time stimulating impulses and emotions to help you achieve a general and overall readiness to take the next step in getting ready to get ready. If getting out of yourself while at the same time getting into yourself is the goal, you might try the I'm Five Years Old imaging workout.

This exercise is done almost exactly as when approached conventionally, except that instead of responding to "I'm five years old and I..." verbally, you allow whatever impulsive image appears to happen, respond emotionally to it, and go on to the next one. You might go from five to eight or nine years old or even beyond. This technique accomplishes a number of things: you get selflessly involved, while at the same time being affected by a large number of impacting and varied images from your childhood; the variety of experiences stretches your emotional state in many directions and also elevates your accessibility. The bonus is that it also piques unconscious involvement. It elicits fragments of unconscious memories and brings them crashing into consciousness, so that while you are eliminating obstacles and elevating your affectability, you are also bringing the unconscious into play—which dimensionalizes your BEING state and makes you readier to act.

Start the process by saying the sentence, "I'm five years old and I..." and allowing whatever the image is to occur. For example, you might immediately see a kindergarten room filled with paper cutouts hanging above the blackboard, other children whose faces you had forgotten, a table covered with clay and finger paints...Encourage all of your senses to respond and get involved. You might do this by asking what the room smells like or what the predominant sounds are. Allow yourself to be affected in whatever way the image impacts on you. Continue at this age for a while: "I'm five years old and I..." This time the image may be your bedroom at night with the shadows of the trees spilling all over the walls. You remember how you used to create pictures out of the shapes of those shadows, sometimes scaring yourself so badly you had to sleep with the light on. You can stay at five for as long as you are getting productive responses. Then go to six and then seven and eight. Complete the exercise when you feel involved, affected, and off the spot.

If this technique succeeds and you are free of spot obstacles, go to the next level of instrumental preparation and the second category: addressing the instrumental demands of the material. Ask yourself, What is the instrumental state I have to reach before dealing with the craft preparations or the obligations of the piece? Let us imagine that the character in this hypothetical scene is very expressive and that during the course of the scene he experiences a gamut of varied theatrical emotions. Then your responsibility would be to achieve an instrumental state of impulsive accessibility. To do this you must first know exactly in what emotional state you are right at this moment. Assuming you are in a BEING state that is not necessarily very vulnerable but is open, you could begin to elevate your accessibility in a variety of ways. If you decided to use imaging, you could try a number of varied techniques, such as Fragmented Imaging, for example, selectively emphasizing images of different kinds of objects that will appeal to your vulnerability:

Puppy...brown eyes...(All of these suggestions come in the form of images. There aren't any words involved.) *Mom crying...Rocking chair ...She's lonely...My girlfriend...smiling...loving me...Dad as he was... Brother...sick...uncommunicative...See his face...blank eyes...My first red wagon...my BB gun...Red Ryder...empty lot...playing...Carmine... Danny...Lucille...school yard...recess...graduation...cap and gown... Mom crying...funeral...casket...sister crying...black veil...*etc., etc.

Other kinds of imaging techniques can also be used and should be chosen according to the circumstance. You might elect to re-create a real experience that had great impact on you, approaching it as an Affective Memory, using Imaging to re-create it; or you could use Story Imaging to create an event—real or imaginary—that would affect you and achieve the desired results. Two actors working on a scene might use Guided Imaging to elevate each other's availability. Whatever the approach or the content of the image, it should be directed towards making the actor more accessible, "rise-able" and expressive.

Besides increasing his vulnerability level, every actor should take a complete inventory in the area of instrumental preparation to determine his individual needs. The goal of such preparation is to get ready to take the next creative step into craft preparations that deal directly with addressing the material. If an instrumental exercise is needed to act as an interim between instrumental availability and craft preparation, the actor should determine that through Personal Inventory. Other instrumental preparations might be needed in specific emotional areas. Even though he may be open, in a BEING state and vulnerable, he might not be instrumentally accessible to a particular emotional state. If that is true, other imaging techniques can be used with specific choices that pique the desired emotional life.

ELEVATING THE IMAGINATION

Some teachers and many actors contend that acting is *all* imagination. If only that were true, all we would need to do would be to imagine that the circumstances of the material were really happening to us and to believe that they were. If every actor could do that, then there would be no need for training, craft, or techniques that stimulate the willingness to believe a hypothetical circumstance. Unfortunately—and this has been my personal experience over a forty-five-year period in this field—most of the actors who rely only on their imagination usually end up assuming reality rather than experiencing it. This leads to presentational acting. Certainly you cannot act without a well-developed and active imagination! It is an absolute necessity to creativity. It is, however, just one of the components—although a mandatory one—of what comprises talent and a creative instrument.

All of the work that I do and all of the exercises that are part of my system are directly related to the imagination. Sense Memory, which is a cornerstone of the Method and a foundation approach in this work, is totally dependent on the imagination. The word *imaging* itself suggests *image-ination*. To see, hear, feel, taste, and smell something that isn't really there employs sensorial imagination.

Imagination is an innate ability. I remember imagining events and happenings when I was very young. No one taught me to do it. I just did it naturally! I have been daydreaming and fantasizing as far back as my memory goes. I think everyone has the ability to imagine. Most people do imagine. The issue then is whether or not most of us have an imagination that is active, innovative and creative enough to supply the necessary thrust that an actor needs to create exciting and believable life on the stage. The problem that exists with most actors who come to the profession is that they are also people who have grown up in this society, which is not nurturing to the development of a healthy and creative imagination. The proof of this statement lies in the comparison between childhood and adulthood. How many of you who are at this moment reading these words are nearly as imaginative as you were as children? Think about it! As we grow older and become more "responsible," we lose our ability to play and pretend, partially because we have less time and our priorities have changed, but especially because it isn't socially encouraged or tolerated, as it was when we were children. That is really unfortunate, since it would certainly be a better world if we retained that ability. So an actor must work to nourish his imagination on a daily basis. Fortunately, it is built into this system. In order for an actor to succeed with the craft, his imagination must carry its share of the load. Practicing the seven imaging techniques daily will strengthen it and give it free reign. If you were a bodybuilder you would have to exercise certain muscle groups on a regular basis: one day you would work on your upper body and the next on your lower body. The same essentially holds true for your instrument. You must allow a certain amount of time to exercise your imagination muscles.

Here are a few suggestions that will give you a good workout:

Object Imaging. Look around the room you are in at this moment, pick an object in it—let us say a lamp—look at it, and allow yourself to imagine (in images) what it was before it was a lamp, where it was created, and what other environments it inhabited before it came here. Imagine what it would say if it could speak. Would it choose another part of the room to be in? What different sounds would emanate from its different parts? If it was a baby lamp before growing into an adult lamp, what did it look like? Was the light that emanated from it different? If it had parents, which one does it most resemble? Does it have a relationship to the other lamps or furniture in the room? What can you see in it that gives you any information about the way all of them relate to each other when no one is around? Imagine what those two lamps would say to each other. Try to hear and understand their language.

What about that painting on the wall—a Paris street in the rain, a bus, people walking with umbrellas? Imagine where each of them is going. What is the woman in the foreground wearing under that raincoat? Imagine the home where she lives. What is it like? What are the colors of the walls? Is she speaking French? To whom is she talking? Is that her husband? her lover? What does he look like? smell like? What is he doing? What are they saying to each other? Is it still raining outside? Can you hear the rain on the roof?

All of these images should be addressed to all the senses. To allow the imagination to really feast on this involvement you must encourage a multidimensional involvement.

Impulsive Object Imaging. Start this second exercise in the same way as Object Imaging, but instead of creating a story or life for the objects around you, simply look at one of them and impulsively allow any image related to it or suggested by it to appear. For example, you might look at the same lamp and abruptly get an image of a sunburst or of a halo of Technicolor light. You might go to another object in the room, such as a rocking chair, and get an immediate image of Grandma Moses rocking back and forth, whistling *Danny Boy.* You should move from object to object very quickly so as to stimulate impulsivity. A number of the images will probably make no sense at all. That is good, because it indicates an absence of logic and the beginnings of an active imagination, which is starting to hook into the unconscious. There are no limitations in Object Imaging. You can be as outrageous as you desire. If your images defy logic, all the better! The purpose is to stretch and elevate your imagination, so keep logic out of it. Open the doors and let your imagination run free. You will notice that soon you won't have to make any suggestions at all. Your imagination will create its own scenario. When that happens, you will know that it is functioning as it should.

Fantasy Imaging. When using imaging in relation to fantasy, you structure an event by imaging all parts of it: the place, the people, the actions involved, what you see, hear, feel, and so on. You live in it, become a part of it. This is not only a very good technique for piquing the imagination; it is also a lot of fun to do. The section on Fantasy Imaging in the previous chapter gives you good examples of the process.

Free-Association Imaging. When using Free-Association Imaging to excite the imagination, don't introduce a subject or theme; just get out of your own way and let the images pop in. You can do so with your eyes open or closed, but somewhere into the exercise open your eyes and use them to image. You may be sitting, lying down, or standing. Start from a relaxed state, and allow the images to come from anywhere. With Imaging Sensations they can emanate from an auditory or tactile source. This can be a very good instrumental preparation before a rehearsal.

➢ *Example*

I feel a wave of heavy air around my body...I see a small boat far out in the ocean...I can't see anyone in it from here...It looks battered... I smell barbecue coming from somewhere...I see an Erté art-deco statue of a woman dressed in green...a dog snarling...barking...laughing at my fear...I hear a xylophone behind me...and Cab Calloway sauntering to the tune...Tuna are jumping high out of the water...barking like cocker spaniels...I feel butterfly wings tapping my forehead and melted butter running into my eyebrows...I see a clown...He has a blue nose...He isn't happy and he isn't sad...He just isn't...I feel my body being tossed from side to side as the cigarette boat I am in hits one hundred and eighty miles per hour...He has a cigar in his mouth...Dumbo has a new family...I feel like a long-distance runner...My leg muscles are vibrating with energy...I see two walruses mating on a rock...Do they know I'm watching?...Water running...dripping onto a dry rock...It makes patterns, pictures, and ultimately I see the rock drowning in it...Cymbals crashing...Lightning and thunder and Mickey Mouse scurrying around in that dunce cap...I see a mouse eating a cat with relish... burping...an old lady out of time cooking something over an open fireplace in a log cabin...Dustin Hoffman in a cap and gown...He smiles ...I wave...

I suddenly feel as if I were that crazy character in *The House of Blue Leaves!* The above example is slightly bizarre, but I really did a Free-Association Imaging exercise so that I could create an authentic example of the process. It was impulsive and stream of consciousness, and I was affected by the experience.

The various examples I have suggested in this section are all designed to stimulate, seduce, and excite your imagination. Feel free to create your own. You will know when a technique is working and when it isn't. Make it an adventure.

CRAFT PREPARATIONS

Preparing actually falls into two categories: the *instrumental* area and the *craft* area. In *Irreverent Acting,* almost all of the instrumental preparations are also listed under craft preparations, because with a slight adjustment an instrumental obstacle or issue can become a craft responsibility. While you may, for example, have self-esteem problems in the instrumental area and need to use instrumental exercises and techniques to address and overcome them in your personal life, you might also need to address a character responsibility in that area and thereby need to use some imaging technique as a *craft* involvement to address the obligation of the material. Eliminating instrumental obstacles allows the actor to move into the next area, which includes *craft preparations* to deal with the responsibilities of the play. Here too, imaging is a powerful tool.

RELATIONSHIP AND RELATING

One of the most important categories of craft preparations has to do with relationship. Almost all drama involves relating to one or more persons. Most scenes on stage or in films take place between two or more people. The relationship between them—who they are to each other and how they feel about and affect each other—is what relating is all about. Just looking at the other actor and saying memorized lines, hoping that the content of the material will communicate all of the relationship elements, is like putting a closed book to your forehead and expecting to digest its entire content that way. Acting is a process which leads to a high form of art! Much work and specificity go into creating the elements of a dimensional relationship—first for yourself and subsequently for the audience. The author of the piece tells you something about who the characters are and what their background is: where they live, how they relate to the environment and are affected by it, what they want, how they feel, how they relate to and affect each other, what the conflict is between them, and so on. Once you understand and assimilate all those facts, your job begins: to turn all of them into reality—not the representation of reality, but *experienced* reality!

There are many relationship preparations listed in *Irreverent Acting* which are very good craft preparations for getting ready to deal with the material. They take the actor into a place of deeper involvement with his acting partner, from which he must then go even further into creating their history together, their shared experiences, their familiarity with each other, the issues between them, and the specific dynamics of the way in which they relate to and affect each other. It is not nearly enough for the actor to substitute memories of his past experiences or his present relationship with someone, unless he knows how to use those parallels specifically and is able to translate them with his craft so that what is hypothetical information becomes real for him. There are numerous ways of arriving at an organic relationship. Since the emphasis of this book is imaging, however, I will focus on imaging techniques and will describe and discuss how to accomplish authentic results. However, I want the reader to remember that this system includes a very rich and almost endless variety of other techniques and approaches, which also address the fulfillment of relationship.

A few years ago at my theater in Hollywood, I directed *'night, Mother,* a play by Marsha Norman. It is a relationship play between a mother and a daughter, a full-length play without intermission and with only two characters. From the moment it begins to its conclusion, it consists of two people relating to each other. In the first five minutes the daughter, Jessie, announces that she is going to kill herself "in a couple of hours." From then on her responsibility is to convince her mother that she is serious about it, to explain why she is doing it, and to take care of all the loose ends so that her mother will know where everything is in the house, how to pay the bills, and how to deal with the milkman, the doctor, and the other people in her life. The mother's responsibility, once she believes her daughter, is to stop her from committing suicide. Essentially, that is the action of the play. The meat of the piece is the multileveled relationship between the two women, which comes out during the course of the play—how they feel about themselves, each other, Jessie's father (who does not appear), her brother Dawson and his wife (who also do not appear), and why Jessie has decided to end her life. The mistake many directors have made when doing this play is to emphasize the suicide. This is not a play about suicide; it is a play about life—about Jessie's inability to realize what she was and wanted to become and about Thelma, the mother, living in an unconscious shell, not knowing, caring about, or realizing any of the realities of her daughter's feelings. The play evolves with the exposure and impacting realization of all of those realities and the communication that takes place between the two characters in the course of an hour and a half.

This is just a thumbnail description of the content of this play, but it is sufficient to set up the structure so that we can discuss some of the relationship techniques I had the actresses explore. The actresses knew each other. They had both studied with me for a considerable period of time, though separately. They shared a creative approach and the language that goes with it. They were both from the Dallas–Fort Worth area, had similar traces of regional accent, had taken drama classes from the same high-school teacher twenty years apart and even had similar body types. So to start with, there were a number of available realities already in place to promote the truth of the relationship and the play. Rachel, who played Thelma, the mother, has in real life a daughter about the same age as Jessie. There were some usable parallels that she did relate to—certainly not the suicide circumstance, but the history, the background, the shared experiences, and so on. Cynthia, who played the daughter, Jessie, identified certain parallels and relationship dynamics she shared with her own mother. These could later be used in the form of choices for addressing the specific obligations of each scene in the play.

We discussed the available realities and agreed to find a specific way to apply them to the rehearsal process. In creating the relationship preparations we started with how the actresses felt about each other. I had them relate on a moment-to-moment level, expressing their own realities to each other, thereby establishing a basic foundation of truth in their communication. Understand that both actresses are fine craftspersons and operate from a place of truth ordinarily, so that it was not difficult to get them to do what I wanted. We did a number of relationship exercises to build a dimensional reality. Since Thelma and Jessie live together in the same house, get up at the same time in the morning, share conversation over coffee at the breakfast table, I suggested to the actresses that they spend some time living together—which they did at Cynthia's house. They woke up at the same time in the morning, discussed their real lives over coffee, shared experiences of all kinds. They took long walks together and became increasingly familiar with each other's colloquialisms, habits, and idiosyncrasies. They got involved in Shared Imaging, thereby establishing a familiarity with each other's lives.

Later in the rehearsal process, the actresses used imaging to endow each other with their own mother or daughter respectively. I asked Cynthia to talk to Rachel as if Rachel were her real mother and Rachel to talk to her own real daughter in relation to Cynthia. They would then both image how the real-life person would respond, and combine that image with the responses they got from each other. In other words, each heard the other actress's response while she was imaging her choice—

the way that choice looked, sounded, moved, and related to her. This technique works to blend one's living reality with those elements that are not real, until the latter become acceptable as truth.

> ➤ *Example (not a verbatim report of what was actually said)*

Cynthia: ([Jessie] talking to Rachel [Thelma] but really relating to her own real mother.) Mother, how come you never took seriously the things I told you I wanted to do with my life? (Using all of her senses [Imaging Sensations], she images her own mother—her expressions, the sound of her voice, her specific mannerisms, and so on. She includes images of the time and place.)

Rachel: (Imaging her own daughter asking that question—her behavior, speech patterns, and so on—in relation to Cynthia, and responding from her own truth.) I always took the things you said seriously. I don't know how you can say such a thing!

Cynthia: (Imaging her own mother responding the way Rachel did.) I told you that I was interested in becoming an actress, and I don't feel you really supported that! (Continuing, through imaging, to create her own mother in relation to Rachel.)

Rachel: You expressed interest in many things. As a matter of fact you kept jumping around from one interest to another. Do you remember?

Cynthia: That was when I was younger. I'm not talking about that. I'm talking about when I was older. You said that acting was foolish and that I should take a long nap and wake up more practical!

Rachel: Oh, I don't remember saying any such thing, and if I did, I was joking! (At this point, Rachel might intersperse images of her daughter as a child—how she looked, sounded, and so on.)

Cynthia: That's exactly what I mean, Mother. You were joking! It's not something to joke about, now is it?

Rachel: (A little uncomfortable from Cynthia's last statement.) Well, I suppose it's not, but you know I love you, and I didn't mean to hurt you or make you feel that I don't consider your feelings. (The imaging process should include parallels of past ways of relating.)

Cynthia: That's just it, mother. I don't think you know who I am. Yes, I know you love me! But I don't think you ever took the time to find out how I really feel about anything. When I got divorced, you felt ashamed that your daughter had an unsuccessful marriage, but you never bothered to find out why I decided to leave, did you? (Cynthia, using all of her senses—either just with Imaging Sensations or with Sense Memory support—could include specific elements that were present at that time.)

Rachel: (At this point experiencing a combination of discomfort and indignation and visibly affected by this encounter.) I didn't think it was any of my business! What would you have had me do? (Continuing the imaging and adding images of her daughter's behavior that might not actually exist in Cynthia's.)

Cynthia: How about showing some compassion, giving me some unconditional love, instead of worrying about what the neighbors thought?

Rachel: I just didn't really know how you felt or what you wanted from me! You know it's a two-way street. You keep a lot of your feelings secret from me!

Cynthia: (A slight realization at the last thing Rachel said.) I guess that's true to some extent, but I think things would have been different if I felt seen by you.

With imaging experience, an actor creates images which she knows or senses will pique unconscious life.

This dialogue could go on for any length of time. Each actress was imaging not only the person she was substituting but also the place where the encounter could or did take place, the time of day, and any other elements of the environment that might support the reality. Besides using selectively emphasized parallels to the play, they were both told that they could include Believability in tandem with the imaging process. Using imaging techniques like this one progressively influences the actors to combine their own realities with the circumstances of the play and, by so doing, to assimilate both into one state of reality. In this instance, the images, in combination with the Believability, are cumulatively absorbed into the unconscious and further support a willingness to believe in the realities of the material. Techniques like this one also stimulate Involuntary Imaging. If one repeats them often enough in preparation and rehearsal, soon one begins to have involuntary images related to the events and scenes in the piece—to the dialogue and the action as well as to the relationship involved.

In addition, I suggested to the actresses that they might do *parallel imaging* on their own. That involves imaging oneself having the life of the character—her experiences, her relationships and conflicts, even with the people who do not appear in the play—creating a specific story image using the actual circumstances of the play and putting oneself in the center of them. I also suggested that while they did this, they might, whenever applicable, use real personal experiences which resembled or paralleled the events in the play, thereby combining reality with un-reality and weaving them together with the hope that it would all meld into reality.

In order to establish a meaningful relationship on the stage, the actor must believe that what the characters are experiencing is real to her. This is accomplished by setting the stage for it to happen, by preparing and creating a foundation of relationship with the other actor involved. As I said earlier, there are many ways to do this, and imaging is one of the best. I am going to suggest other imaging techniques that will help to create that foundation. If you apply them properly, they will accomplish your goal. As with everything we do in our lives, if you become pro-ficient with a technique, then you can expect to succeed with it. As you already know, to master anything, you must practice it daily.

GUIDED IMAGING

As mentioned in the previous chapter, Guided Imaging is a mar-velous relationship preparation. The actors should experience the impact of being both the facilitator and the facilitatee. The exercise can be ap-proached in a variety of ways, with the emphasis varying depending on the purpose at hand. In this instance where the goal is to become more involved with and affected by the other actor, it might be done twice— the first time just to elevate the other's accessibility while becoming more involved and concerned with her, and the second time to select a personal experience that parallels the material and would take both ac-tors closer to experiencing the life and the relationship demanded by the text.

Remember that before beginning the guided journey into the expe-rience, the actor being facilitated should give the facilitator enough information about that experience. The latter should feel free to ask whatever questions he deems necessary to establish his initial approach, questions such as, How were you dressed? How long had you been in this place? How did you feel just before the action started? and so on.

➢ *Example*

Facilitator: Where are you?...Look around. What do you see?...How do you feel in this place?...Where is the light coming from?...

(The other actor responds to all of the facilitator's questions sensorially, imaging the response to each question with all five senses, seeing, hearing, feeling, smelling, and tasting.)

Facilitator: How do you feel?...Continue to look around the room... What is your overall emotional point of view regarding this place?...Specify each object or piece of furniture, and ask yourself how each affects you...Are you standing or are you sitting?...Are you comfortable?...What are the sounds you hear?...How many different sounds are there?...Where are they coming from?...

(The other actor is fully responding to every question that the facilitator puts to her, not limiting herself just to the sensory area at which the question is directed but responding at all times with all five senses, using Imaging Sensations.)

Facilitator: How are the sounds affecting you?...Who else is in the room?...Where is that person in relation to you?...Who is he?...How do you feel about him?...How is he dressed? ...What are the colors of his clothes?...How does he feel in them?...What tells you that?...What is he doing right now? ...Is he relating to you?...in what way?...How do you feel at this moment?...Do you feel the need to do anything?... stand?...sit?...leave?...Do you feel like making contact with that person?...What is that feeling like?...What are you doing now?...Has that person made any moves towards you?...What is he doing?...How do you feel as he approaches you?...What is happening to you right at this moment?...What is your body doing?...What is the temperature in this room?...Has it changed in the last few minutes? ...As the person approaches you, what more do you see in his face?...Can you interpret his intentions or what he feels?...What tells you that?...

(The other actor encourages the full emotional impact of the experience, allowing herself to respond emotionally while continuing to be involved in the complete image.)

Facilitator: As he comes closer, do you experience a greater sense of him?...Can you smell his scent?...What does that smell like?...How close is he now?...What are you experiencing?...Do you want to say anything?...Do you feel like retreating?...What are you experiencing now?...What is he doing?...And is he saying anything?...What?...What is the unique sound of his voice?...What are the peculiarities, and can you hear the emotional content in his voice?...How does what he just said affect you?...How do you feel?...Are you expressing your response truthfully?...What do you say?...How do you feel just before you open your mouth to speak?...What is the first sound you utter?...What does it sound like to your ear?...What do you see in his face?... How is he behaving at this moment?...Are you aware of anything or anyone else in the room?...What do you feel? ...Are you aware of all your feelings?...What are they?... Have your perceptions been affected?...Has the light in this place changed in any way?...(There should be ample time between questions to allow your partner to respond in all sensory areas.) Has your sense of time and place changed? ...If so, how do you see things around you?...Are people in the room moving faster? slower?...How have the sounds around you changed?...What do they sound like now?... What is that person doing? saying?...How has he changed since you last saw him?...Does he look older?...How?... Does he look the way you remember him?...How do you feel about him this minute?...What are you impelled to do? say?...(If the other actor has an impulse to verbally express anything at any time during the facilitation, she is encouraged to do so.) As he reaches out to touch your arm, what do you see?...What do you feel?...Do you want him to touch you?...Do you feel like touching him?...What does that feel like?...Where in your body are you having any kind of feelings?...What are they?...What is your sense of time?...Has it speeded up or slowed down?...What are you most aware of?...

Facilitating someone is like creating an outline for a long novel. The person being facilitated is responding with her images faster than the facilitator can formulate words, and the images are infinitely more dimensional and varied than the amount or quality of the inquiry might warrant. It is a fuller and more dimensional experience than what the questions might indicate.

The above experience as told to the facilitator was that the actress had accidentally run into her ex-husband at a party, and since she had not seen him for two years and was still in love with him, it had been an extremely traumatic, and yet exciting, experience. As a result of this chance meeting, they had started to see each other again and eventually gotten back together. During the Guided Imaging the actress being facilitated reexperienced many of the emotions and sensations she had had at the time of the original event. There is much to be gained in relationship preparation by both these actors as a result of the Guided Imaging workout. First, they both get more involved and more related to each other while taking the journey. They feel that they know more about each other and that they have shared a personal and meaningful experience. It sets them up for the next level of involvement. Secondly, as I explained in the previous chapter, the imaging has the added advantage of being *totally unpredictable* to the actor being facilitated, since she cannot know where the facilitator will go or what the exploration will consist of. It allows her to respond without any premeditation or expectations.

After both actors have facilitated each other, they may want to address the scene they are doing. In that case they would structure an experience that closely parallels the events of the piece. They could do it exactly as they have just done it, or since the piece has a structured event that involves them both in the same environment and experience, they could do Simultaneous Guided Imaging, each selecting an experience that would seem to mirror the material. They should discuss their separate choices with each other, understand all the salient elements of the experience, ask each other any questions they want, then launch into the imaging process.

➤ *Example (Simultaneous Guided Imaging)*

Let us go back to Cynthia and Rachel doing '*night, Mother*. Let us suppose that they have each selected a parallel personal experience for a specific part of the play. The exercise is a shared experience. Either of the actresses could begin.

Rachel: Where am I?...

(They both respond in images to each other's queries, and they do so simultaneously.)

Cynthia: How large is this place?...How high is the ceiling?...What color are the walls?...

(Each actress is imaging her own place, slowly sneaking up on the "meat" of the event.)

Rachel: What is the predominant odor of this place?...How many odors am I aware of?...As I look around what attracts my attention most?...

Cynthia: Why is that object so interesting to me?...Do I remember where it came from?...What is the light like in this place?...

Rachel: How does it illuminate the room?...Are there places I have difficulty seeing?...

(While each of them is responding to the questions, each in turn also picks up the exploration by continuing where the other left off. It is important to do this in order to promote a common reality.)

Cynthia: Who else is in this place?...Where is he?...What is he doing?

Rachel: How far away from me is he?...How is he dressed?...How do I feel about him?...What is he doing?...

Cynthia: What does he sound like when he speaks?...How does he feel about me?...

Rachel: Who else is here?...Where is she?...What is she doing?... saying?...How do I feel about her?...

Since both actresses know the material—the obligations and all of the relationship elements—they would naturally select a good parallel circumstance and would mutually guide each other in the right direction for the material. The actual image hopefully would contain all of the stimuli of the original experience. Each actress, if successful, would create through her imagery a sense of being in her place, hearing all the sounds and voices of the people who were originally there, as well as seeing the place and experiencing all of the component parts of the event as it unfolds.

Another very good imaging technique for promoting relationship preparation is *Relationship Imaging*. This exercise can be done with an actor you are meeting for the first time. Starting with what is real between you, you begin to silently image modifications in the other's real behavior, changing what is there into a variety of relationship dynamics. For example, you begin to image the other actor flirting with you, at first subtly and then more obviously. Two actors can do this process simultaneously, and neither of them needs to know what the other is doing. Their responses are sure to affect each other and to elicit moment-to-moment impulses, thereby promoting the beginnings of a relationship that can be built on.

Imaging on the level at which we are involved goes way beyond what would be considered "mental imaging." Once again, all the techniques in this book are designed to take the actor to the total realization of the image, which essentially means *being there!* If an actor has already elevated his craft to a level of mastery and at the same time increased his gullibility level and his willingness to believe, then imaging will take him to the reality very quickly. If this is not the case, he will need to encourage the cooperation of his senses until he can be transported to other places and other times.

CHAPTER 5

IMAGING AND ACTING

THE CRAFT PROCESS AND IMAGING

The goal in all of this is, of course, to fulfill material. All of the exercises and techniques in my system exist for one purpose only: to enable the actor to create reality on the stage or in front of the camera. Imaging is just another tool in this system of acting—for sure an incredible tool, but just a means to an end. Once I saw a book entitled *The Actor's Art and Job*. The title appealed to me, even though I never read the book. It is a provocative title, and I have often wondered what the author meant by it or how he defined the "art" and what was the "job." To me it seems like a simple distinction. The actor's job is to fulfill all of the obligations of the piece, to create the reality of the character from his own life experiences and to really *be* in the situation that the material describes. The art of the actor is *how* he manages to do that. Notwithstanding his talent—whatever that might be—the art is his process, his approach, the techniques he uses to impel himself to feel, experience, and believe. Without a dependable process an actor has no art! That seems like a harsh statement, doesn't it? Well, it's true! Certainly there are hundreds of wonderful actors who function instinctively and even create work that is moving, inspiring and artistic. That is a natural gift— but it is not given to many. Most great actors are very talented to begin with, but they also have some technique for liberating their talent in just the right ways and the right proportions once they have identified their responsibilities. That is what craft is all about! The greatest antidote for insecurity is knowing what to do. If you trust your knowledge and your process, the rest is based on getting involved in the exploration of your craft and the material.

OBLIGATIONS

The very first step is to read the piece and identify the OBLIGATIONS. What are your responsibilities to the material? Where does the action take place? Who is your character? Where does he live? in what period of history? What kind of person is he? What does he want? How does he behave? express himself? How does he feel about his life, the world he lives in, the people who surround him? How does he evolve from the beginning of the play to the end? How does he grow? What are the forces in his life that impact on him and effect a change? What are the obstacles that impede his evolution? Who are the other characters? What is his relationship to them? What is the conflict? Is there a statement in this piece? Does the character have any responsibility to make that statement? Those are some of the responsibilities every actor must address in any piece of material.

After identifying the obligations—and they could exist in all seven areas—the actor would decide which of them to address first, based on a number of variables. Once he *really knows the play,* he must determine how all of the existing obligations affect each other—how they "fit" together. For example, the time and place may be so impacting on the action of the scene that this obligation would have to be dealt with first. In the film *Alive,* which was released a few years ago, for example, all of the action involves survival. It is about a plane crash high in the icy mountains of South America. In order to stay alive, the characters eat the flesh of those who have died. They have to survive the environment, the cold, and the lack of food—all elements having to do with TIME AND PLACE. It is therefore quite clear where the actor must start to work. In *The Diary of Anne Frank* or *Schindler's List,* on the other hand, everything that happens is influenced by the HISTORICAL obligation—World

124

War II and the horrors of the Holocaust. In *The Defiant Ones* the RELATIONSHIP elements are so powerful that the actors must confront them before moving on to anything else: A black man is handcuffed to a bigoted white man; they are running from the law and have no alternative but to stay together. There are, of course, other very important obligations present, but without the relationship elements everything the characters do might be approached differently.

In a sense, selecting the first obligation to be dealt with is similar to constructing a jigsaw puzzle. The first thing you must do is look at the complete picture on the front of the box; then, you identify colors and shapes, and then you begin to fit the pieces together. You must return to the picture many times to re-familiarize yourself with how it looks. When working with material, you will also have to return to the play many times to cull information that will help you determine your creative "road map." It is very surprising to me how many actors in my classes will attempt to do a scene without first having read the entire play.

All seven obligations rarely exist in a single piece of material. However, there are always a time and a place to be dealt with, there are always relationships, and every character has some kind of emotional life!

Later in this chapter some of the major obligations will be defined briefly and explored using one or more of the imaging techniques that were described in chapter 3, with IMAGING as the choice approach or craft technique. Material examples will be supplied whenever possible. The goal is to create a clear understanding of imaging as an important component of the craft process.

CHOICES

After identifying the obligations, the actor moves on to selecting his CHOICES. As has already been stated, a choice comes from one's living experience and is a *person, place, thing,* or *"object"* of any kind. When selecting a choice, the actor should consider the nature of the obligation and what he wants to accomplish with the choice—where he hopes that it will take him. Some choices are more readily accessible, easier to create and conducive to addressing the composition of a particular obligation; so when addressing an obligation that might be approached in several ways, you might ask yourself what would be the most interesting and enjoyable way to do it. Imaging can be used in relation to almost any

125

kind of choice. It always seems to be fun and to create a very dimensional result. In addition, certain choices lend themselves better to the imaging process; for example, environments, fantasy choices, complete experiences, endowments of various kinds, and so on. Once the actor has decided on a particular choice, for whatever reason, the next step is to adapt it to an Imaging choice approach.

IMAGING AS A CHOICE APPROACH
WITH DIFFERENT OBLIGATIONS

I imagine by now you all know what a choice approach is, right? Well, just in case you are still a little unclear about it, a CHOICE APPROACH is the process you use to create the choice. It is how you "see" what it is that you want to create, how you make the choice real in all the sensory areas. Just like the other twenty-six choice approaches, Imaging is a way to do that.

The way you would explore a choice using Imaging as the choice approach would vary with the obligation. Depending on the desired result, you would creatively manipulate the image by suggesting and asking certain questions that would steer it in the direction in which you wanted to go.

Suppose you wanted to address the first of the obligations, time and place. First, select a choice—a specific place. Now, you want to *be there,* so start to create that place by using Imaging as the choice approach. You are familiar with the place, and the moment you decide to use it as a choice, you get a sense of it, a feeling about it, followed by some kind of emotional response. Allow all of that to happen. It will help to thrust you into the image. Start the imaging by allowing yourself to sensorially perceive anything that comes up. The first response may be an odor, followed by some sounds. Let them in. Continue to image the place, going back and forth between the senses. Put yourself there, and surround yourself with the sensory elements. Use Imaging Sensations to encourage each of your senses to have the same capacity to image as the visual.

The decision on whether to use Imaging with Sense Memory or Imaging Sensations depends on which one will work best, can be applied with ease, and will take you where you want to go. It also has to do with the nature of the choice itself: How vivid or remote is it? Can you stimulate dimensional image responses with Imaging Sensations, or do you need a more specific Sense Memory investigation to remember and liberate the images for yourself? Those and other issues must guide your decision in choosing the right technique. After a while, you will begin to feel which is the right way to go with a particular choice or experience. Nonetheless, you will sometimes make mistakes and have to adjust the technique or change your approach altogether. If, instead of feeling that you did the wrong thing, you approached the work with the sense of being an *explorer* and encouraged yourself to celebrate it as an adventure, you would always be benevolent and accept the dead ends as challenges to embark on a new path.

TIME AND PLACE

The TIME AND PLACE obligation is the first on the list because it is a very good point at which to start to build the realities of the material. It refers to where the action of the play is set and when—whether it is indoors or out, where on earth it is located, and what time of the day, season, or year it is. This obligation often changes from scene to scene, and each change carries with it a responsibility for the actor to address. It is a very important obligation, and the actor *must* always deal with it. The scene is set in a particular environment for a reason. The action is affected by the place, the time of day or year, the weather, and so on. Whether the impact is obvious or subtle, the character is influenced by all of those elements. He has an emotional point of view about them, and his behavior is certainly affected by them. Unless otherwise preempted by the pervasiveness of another obligation that cries out for attention, time and place should be considered first. As I have said so many times before in my other books, working on it stimulates a connection to the place. It impels the behavior of the actor to match that of the character, while at the same time allowing the actor to build an environment that takes him off the stage. We have all seen plays and films where the actor/character seemed to be standing in front of scenery rather than in a place that had a multitude of obvious and subtle effects on him. The relationship to a place even affects and elicits unconscious emotional points of view.

Naturally, the time and place described in the material more often than not have no significance to the actor doing the role; so he must select a place and a time that will mean to him what the environment in the scene means to the character. It is very important that this selection not be made impatiently or hastily, since the place has impact on many levels. The actor should consider the character's history in relation to that place, as well as what it means to him in the present and whether or not it has a direct impact on the way he behaves in the scene. The objects and people in the place, as well as the weather, also play an important part in establishing a personal point of view, one that quite frequently permeates the entire scene or play. So, once again, the selection of the place is extremely important! The choice approaches are many: Sense Memory, Sensory Suggestion, Evocative Words or Evocative Images, Available Stimulus with adjustments, Believability, and so on. Here, however, we will discuss and explore the fulfillment of this obligation using Imaging exclusively.

Besides the two approaches of Imaging with Sense Memory and Imaging Sensations, the actor can also select one of the seven imaging techniques outlined in chapter 3 to address time and place. As usual, it depends on which works best. Often, he might have to try several of the techniques before deciding on the most expedient. Fragmented Imaging with some Creative Manipulation could create the reality of being there for him, or a more complex Story Imaging approach might work better. Whatever he decides to use, it should be for simplicity and success.

THE EXAMPLE OF *MASS APPEAL*

A number of years ago at my theater, I directed a play called *Mass Appeal*. It is a one-set, two-character play, involving an old priest and a young man who is studying to become a priest. The action takes place in the old priest's home office, which is sparsely furnished and has a modest austerity that hangs in the air like leftover smoke. It is totally devoid of creature comforts and makes the statement, "I have taken the vow of poverty." As far as décor is concerned, it is just a few steps above Junipero Serra's cell at the Carmel Mission. The conflict that takes place has its roots in the young seminarian's battle with his sexual identity and his resolve to become a priest, as well as in his clashes with the "Monsignor"—a character who does not appear in the play but is very much present in the dialogue—over his attitude and behavior. The actor playing the young seminarian is affected in a number of ways by the place. The old priest is benevolent, understanding, and sympathetic to him for the most part; so some elements about the place are comforting, while others are not. The office and adjoining living quarters represent strong discipline and the judgment of the church, as well as the young man's internal ambivalence about the austerity and denial that go with this kind of life. So to summarize the components of the place obligation, we could say that this room stimulates a number of ambivalent elements and a varied emotional life. Of course, as the play progresses, the conflicts become more apparent and theatrical. Progressively, coming to that place takes on greater and greater emotional significance, which the actor must address as he is obligated.

For the sake of this example, let us imagine that Tony, the actor playing the part, had been sent to boarding school fairly early in life. He hadn't really wanted to be away from home or his parents, but he had had to go because both his mother and his father were professional people who spent a great deal of time away from home. The headmaster of this institution, though not an unfair man, was an advocate of the old-fashioned school of structure, rules, and discipline. His domain, while certainly not sparse or austere, was filled with oversized furniture and overstuffed leather armchairs, and lined from floor to ceiling with musty books with titles that might only be recognized and understood by an Oxford scholar. The room always seemed dark and had a foreboding ambience that clung to the walls like cobwebs. Mostly, being summoned there was either unpleasant or frightening. There were times when the "old boy" seemed somewhat more understanding and benevolent, but those were rare and unpredictable. During the period when Tony hypothetically attended the school, he constantly wrestled with the conflict he felt toward his parents for sending him away. To him it constituted a rejection that meant that they did not love him.

If we continue with this example, we can assume that when Tony considered all of the elements and issues that existed for him in that time and place, he decided that this would be a perfect choice to use in addressing the time-and-place obligation of *Mass Appeal*. He was twenty-two years old when we did the play but had only been twelve when he attended the boarding school. A decade separated the two experiences, and during that time some of his images and feelings about the place had somewhat faded. Nonetheless, it was too good a parallel to pass up as a choice.

Tony started the imaging process sensorially, asking questions about the room—the height of the ceiling, the light sources, the color, size, and texture of the furniture, the color and texture of the walls and what hung on them. He repeated the sensorial process a number of times, responding with images in all five sensory areas. Along with his images came thoughts and emotional impulses that seemed very right for the play. While the choice approach he had decided to use—Imaging with Sense Memory moving into Imaging Sensations—seemed to affect him and stimulate some of the emotional life experienced by the character, his memories seemed a little too vague to really stimulate a feeling of being in that place. At that point, a lot of actors might have abandoned the choice and sought something more recent, but Tony was convinced that he had the right choice for this obligation, and he decided to do some Free-Association Imaging to start himself off. Lying down with his eyes closed, he suggested to himself that he was in his own room in the school dormitory. After doing so, he was flooded with images from that time and place. These were not necessarily in any order or logical sequence. At that point, he moved into Fragmented Imaging by creatively manipulating his images.

> ### *Fragmented Imaging Example*

Smell...cleaning fluid...the pea-green ceiling...with abstract pictures formed by chipped and peeling paint. Feel the roughness of the pillow on the back of my neck. Sounds of boys in the hallway yelling, playing...It blends into a particular mixture of indistinguishable voices melding into a particular kind of din that echoes only in this place...I hear myself crying inaudibly...feel what that feels like in my chest and throat...feel the bars on the windows. (Although there weren't any bars on the windows, this was a perception Tony had as a result of feeling imprisoned in that place. As a matter of fact, he often dreamed about being at that school and frequently imaged barred doors and windows. His dreams were filled with such symbols of incarceration, even though they had not existed in reality.) *Hear doors closing with the thunder of steel meshing with steel...the tile floors neatly swirled with wax forbidding you to walk on them...the lip of each stair rimmed with metal and worn where it was most used...rain...more rain...angrily trying to get into the room...and pounding on the roof...windows...making a ferocious sound as it beats on the glass...his voice: "Boys, boys, to your rooms now!" That sound ...always filled with threat and judgment...I hear him saying my name: "Anthony! Anthony! Anthony!" Each time the roar of his voice deepens! ...His office...red carpet...deep, almost like blood...the yellow tape line ...see it right in front of his desk where we stood and listened to his reprimands...wide bloodshot eyes with little brown growths surrounding each eye...I look at the marks instead of his pupils...his gray mustache yellowed from the nicotine of his cigars...his crooked teeth...the smell of his tobacco breath as he leans forward to emphasize a point...the bell for changing classes, for lunch and dinner...the same bell for lights out ...sandy oatmeal...brown sugar and cocoa made with water...that taste ...the long wooden dining tables carved with the initials of hundreds of boys just like me...Looking down at "Homer," someone's name, a name he had probably carved with his fork...He must be a hundred by now...*

Kitchen sounds...metal pots clanging...boys talking, laughing, teasing...
Johnny Harrington...looking at me...freckles...separated front teeth...
red hair...nice kid...Like him...

The actor could repeat the process frequently. In Tony's case it really worked to open up his memory banks. It brought that time and place
into specific focus.

Quite often, when an image is cloudy or vague, the actor can jar or
seduce his unconscious into giving up that image. By using Fragmented
Imaging, Story Imaging, or Symbolic Imaging, he can open his memory
banks and release the images locked away by time. Tony was able to reexperience enough images to continue working for the place using
Imaging Sensations. This approach is more logical and sequential in its
exploration. The images are related to all five senses and would follow a
logical line in creating the headmaster's room. As usual, all of the
images are nonverbal. The actor sees, hears, feels, tastes, and smells the
various components of the place he is creating.

In our imaginary scenario, Tony had such a strong agenda related to
this experience that it had inhabited his dreams for many years after it
was over. In a case like that, the actor might want to solicit the help of
his unconscious in creating the choice. As mentioned above, Tony saw
images of bars on the windows and even dreamed of barred doors.
There were probably other symbols that he could have used to promote
dreams and "sleep-wake-state" images. In chapter 7, "Imaging and the
Unconscious," we will explore in much greater detail the techniques we
can use to solicit the help of the unconscious.

THE OBLIGATION: (Time and Place)	The office/living quarters of the priest (from the play *Mass Appeal*)
THE CHOICE:	The headmaster's office in a boarding school that the actor attended from ages twelve to fourteen
THE CHOICE APPROACH:	IMAGING (combination of techniques) Using Imaging Sensations to create the choice

Even though Tony finally approached the choice with a chronological type of Story Imaging, he was unable to recall many of the
objects and elements that comprised the full image of the headmaster's
office. He used Free-Association and Fragmented Imaging to pique the
recollection of the place and the ensuing experiences he had there. The

potential for Symbolic Imaging also existed, and that technique could have been explored in addressing the choice.

When dealing with time and place as an obligation, an actor can use any of the various imaging techniques to create parallel realities. Imaging is the tool that helps you create the experience of being in a place at a specific time and believing that you are really there!

RELATIONSHIP

Also very important, the RELATIONSHIP obligation involves all the other characters in the play—who they are to your character and how he feels about them. Each relationship in the play is different. If there are six characters, and you, the actor playing the leading role, have a relationship with each of the other five, then you have five separate relationship obligations to address. Of course, you would deal with them one at a time.

This obligation has two parts: The first is, Who is this person to my character? What is their relationship? Is she his wife? his mother? his sister? Is she a casual friend or someone he grew up with? The second part of the obligation is, How does my character feel about this person? What is his emotional point of view toward her, and how does it change? The actor must first establish what each relationship in the play involves and then set out to create those realities for himself. If, for example, the most significant relationship in the play is that between a man and his wife—a relationship that has existed for ten years—the actor must select a choice that will allow him to believe that the actress playing his wife *is* indeed his wife or someone with whom he has had a similar relationship. He can do this in a number of creative ways: He can use Available Stimulus (the actress), selectively emphasizing all the features and behaviors that are familiar to him and remind him of a parallel relationship; he can "endow" her with qualities and features that affect him in similar ways; he can create another person in relation to her, using Endowments as a choice approach; or use Imaginary Dialogues, Inner Imaginary Monologues, Believability, and so on. If he elects to use Imaging, there are still many possibilities: He can image the actress behaving and relating in ways that would promote both components of the relationship obligation, or he can use Imaging as a craft technique in relation to any of the above-mentioned choice approaches (this will be explored later in the chapter).

Imaging can also be used in a variety of ways to create a history with someone the actor has just met. Over the rehearsal period, using

Imaging as the approach, he could create an entire background and history between himself and the actress playing his wife. It would, of course, be fictitious but if structured properly, could parallel the history of the characters in the play. This could also be done by programming the unconscious to accept the hypothetical as real (see chapter 8). By creating all of the events and experiences that might have occurred between the characters, the actor is building an experiential reality that, if accepted as real, will feed and dimensionalize his behavior in the play.

Any of the seven imaging techniques can be used to address the relationship obligation, as the following examples will demonstrate.

EXAMPLE USING STORY IMAGING

Story Imaging can be used to accommodate a single scene require-ment or as the major approach to the relationship responsibilities for an entire play. Let us take as an example *The Four Poster*, a two-character piece, which takes place in a bedroom dominated by a four-poster bed. The action of the play spans the entire lifetime of the two characters, from their early twenties into old age. This is definitely a relationship play, I would say—right? Story Imaging could help structure the rela-tionship between the main characters before the events of the play. The actors might construct an elaborate improvisation about how they met, the events that followed, and so on. When dealing with the action of the play itself, they could use the technique to specifically address the obli-gation of each scene. It has been a very long time since I saw this play, so my memory of the specifics are vague; however, I remember that the characters' relationship was very romantic, though sometimes volatile and stormy. If I am just trying to promote an understanding of how Story Imaging is used, however, it does not matter how loyal I am to the play.

The two characters sit in this bedroom and talk about their life to-gether, and as the play continues, their relationship evolves and changes as they age. Let us imagine that in the early scenes they are talking about how they fell in love with each other—their first impressions of each other. From this perspective, his responsibility is *to experience nostalgia and a sense of wonder about how beautiful he thought she was*. The actor doing the imaging therefore decides to actually re-construct the early part of his relationship with the woman he is married to. The entire imaging experience is a re-creation of the first time he saw his wife. They were both at an audition waiting to read. They sat directly across from each other.

I see an incredible face...her hair...color...eyes...deep and blue... She is not even aware of me...She's mouthing the lines of the script... Need to get her attention...Clear my throat...I can smell her perfume from here...She's gorgeous...Her skin's almost translucent...I'm smiling and can't help it...I wonder what she feels like...if I touched her cheek ...She looks at me...our eyes connect...I feel a weakness in my stomach ...Can she see me blush?...I feel my blushing...the heat in my face and neck...She's smiling at me...Should I say something?...I can't move my mouth...I feel like I'm in grade school. I'm suddenly aware of the rest of her body...I feel such an excitement...I can't describe these feelings...

All of the elements of the story must be responded to with all five senses. The thoughts and feelings that come from the sensory responses are automatic and are not verbalized as in the example. It is the actor's responsibility in this instance to re-create that first meeting through Story Imaging. How far he takes the experience is totally dependent on what he is trying to accomplish and how much he has to do to accomplish it. Of course, as always when it comes to choice approaches, the actor has a number of alternatives to choose from. In this example he could have used Available Stimulus (the actress he is working with), Sensory Endowments (endowing the actress with the features, personality and behavior of another woman), Evocative Words, Evocative Images, Inner Monologues of various kinds, Imaginary Monologues (talking to the actress as if she were another person), Affective Memory, and so on. He could also have used one of the other imaging techniques, such as Verbalized Imaging.

EXAMPLE USING VERBALIZED IMAGING

Verbalized Imaging can easily help address the relationship obligation. In the last monologue from the play *I Never Sang for My Father,* the character is speculating about his relationship to his father. He is confused and sad about whether or not they have ever loved each other and about how to deal with the regret and remorse he feels "whenever the word *father* is mentioned." An actor I will call "Gino" did this monologue in my class recently, so I will take the liberty of using him and his process as examples. He selected a real experience from his own life, when he visited his father in the hospital, after the latter had undergone bypass surgery following a heart attack.

(In this case the actor started by expressing his emotions and where he was, before he explored the actual event.)

Gino: I feel afraid to do this...I have so many feelings related to this experience, not to mention all of the ambivalent feelings I have in relation to my father...I feel sad just thinking about this experience...(Using Verbalized Imaging and including all of his emotional responses moment to moment.) I see him lying there...(Imaging response.) He looks pale and weak...I can see all the tubes connected to his body...Hear the sounds of the machines...I feel afraid that he might die...I don't know what to do with that feeling...His eyes are closed...His breathing seems irregular...I can smell the medications...the antiseptics...I feel there are so many things unresolved between us!...I'm afraid that we may never have the chance to really talk...I feel sad...He opened his eyes...He is trying to smile...It seems difficult for him to do...I touch his hand, and all at once I feel the tears coming down my cheeks...He is sick...and I feel sad and afraid...He was always so busy when I was little...he never had time for me...I wanted him to come to my games...he didn't...I resent him...I feel a mixture of resentment and grief, and I don't know how to express them both...I see the white sheets...and the bruises on his arms from where they put the needles...I feel love for him, but at the same time I feel sorry for him...I'm suddenly angry at all of this...I don't want to feel anything...It is just like him to do this...He smokes and doesn't eat right, and now this...I know he didn't do this on purpose, but it sure seems like something he might do!... I wonder if he loves me...I wonder if he has ever loved me...I see him going in and out of sleep...I hear him wheeze as he breathes...What will I do if he dies...dies before I can communicate with him?...He's looking at me...smiling...Does he recognize me?...I know he is heavily sedated...He might not even know it's me...I wish I could talk to him...It has always been that way...I could never say what I felt...I'm frustrated and confused by all of this!

As a preparation, the entire exploration could be done out loud. While actually saying the lines, the actor could do exactly the same thing, but in an inner monologue. While this choice may not have addressed all of the obligations inherent in the play or even in this monologue, there was definitely a very strong relationship parallel involved.

Again, Gino could and probably did use a good variety of approaches while exploring this piece. He also did a great part of his work nonverbally; however, it was the expression of many of the obstacles that allowed him to jump into the creation of the hospital experience.

In a classroom environment, which is used as a laboratory for the actors, a place where they can fail, I always encourage them to express and include all of their impulses verbally. This allows for the elimination of obstacles that might otherwise inhibit their expression. Besides, if these impulses are included, they add facets of life to an actor's behavior, which make him more dimensional and interesting on the stage.

EXAMPLE USING GUIDED IMAGING

For the third example, I will use the relationship circumstances that exist in *Key Exchange,* a play about a man and a woman who are involved in a romantic relationship. For a variety of reasons the male character has difficulty making a commitment to that relationship. Even though the play is complex and includes many other elements, this example will only address the scenes that deal with the conflict surrounding his inability to seriously commit to her and her insistence on his doing so.

The actress decides to use her former marriage to parallel the responsibilities of the play. She tells her scene partner of the many conflicts she faced trying to get her ex-husband to "grow up" and take responsibility for being married—much less for making a commitment to her. She recalls so many incidents that it becomes difficult to determine which of them to use to parallel the specific requirements of the scenes. Picking the closest parallel is important if one does not want to go off in a direction different from that of the material. Having decided to use her former husband as a choice, the actress can also select to endow her scene partner with the features and behavior of her choice, although she must not begin the endowment process prior to the Guided Imaging facilitation, since that might prejudice her responses. In the play, the characters exchange their apartment keys—ergo the title. At this point, however, she asks him to return hers. Running through a series of arguments she had with her former mate, the actress finally finds one particular experience that very closely relates to the scene she is addressing. She recalls a Sunday morning over breakfast when she decided to "call it quits." She remembers the incident very clearly: After almost half an hour of staring at the back of his newspaper, she exploded and asked for a divorce. This incident had been preceded by many discussions and arguments about the relationship. It wasn't that she didn't love him—it was an issue of his lack of commitment to her and the marriage.

She filled her scene partner in on many of the events that had preceded this particular one and then told him everything she could recall about that morning—the time, the room, the furniture, the way they were both dressed, how she felt when she woke up that morning, what they were eating, and so on. He then started the facilitation:

Facilitator: Close your eyes and try to get a sense of being in that place. Listen to all the sounds related to that room...What do you hear?...What is the most obvious sound?...Can you feel the chair you are sitting in?...What does that feel like? ...What do you smell?...How many odors are present?... Which is the most distinctive?...Can you feel this place?... Do you feel that you are there?...What makes you feel this place?...Where do you feel his presence?...Can you hear him chewing his food?...

(All of the facilitator's suggestions and questions are responded to sensorially. All five senses are working in tandem with each other throughout the process. In this example, the facilitator started his partner off with her eyes closed and encouraged her to get an overall sense of being in the place. All of her other senses were inspired to respond to that environment.)

Facilitator: Open your eyes! (She does so.) What do you see?...How do you feel about what you are looking at?...Look around the room. What do you see?...How do you feel about those things?...Ask yourself how you feel!...(The actress does that and discovers that she has a variety of feelings about all of the objects she sees around the room. She remembers the specific time when she acquired that pillow on the sofa and how important that event was. All at once she is over- whelmed with a plethora of emotions related to that time in her life.) Express what you are feeling...(She begins to cry, sobbing deeply. Her emotional response is a retrospective one: She is not yet back in that time and place but is re- sponding from a here-and-now feeling about that time in her life. If that happens, it should not be discouraged, since it sets the stage emotionally for her going back in time to that place.) Look at that table in front of you. What do you see?...Is there a plate there?...What is in the plate?...Can you smell it?...What does it smell like?...Do you taste the remnants of the food in your mouth?...Where?...What do you taste?...How many different foods can you detect in your mouth?...How do they blend with each other?...What other tastes are there?...Do you taste the coffee?...How does that taste?...What does the surface of the table look like?...Feel it!...(She puts her hand out reaching for the tactile response.) How does it feel on the tips of your fingers?...What is the texture?...temperature?...What is the condition of this table top?...Is it new?...Are there any worn spots?...Where did you get this table?...Remember that?...How do you feel about it?...Lift your head up... Look across the table. What do you see?...How far away is he?...Can you see him?...What do you see?...What does the newspaper look like?...Can you read the print?...What does it say?...What are the ads like?...Are there any pictures?...What do they look like?...

(Since the actress is using Imaging Sensations and all her senses are reacting to the various stimuli simultaneously, her sensory responses are far ahead of her facilitator's questions. Not only is that normal, but it should be encouraged.)

Facilitator: How do you feel?...Is he aware of you?...Do you want to get his attention?...What are you feeling in this moment?... Can you hear him behind the newspaper?...What do you hear?...What do you say to him?...Say it!

(At that moment the actress bursts into a furious tirade at her "imaginary" husband.)

Actress: Look at me, you son of a bitch! I am sick of living alone! Don't look so surprised. I'm tired of your selfishness! I want out of this marriage!...I want a divorce...Do you hear me?

Facilitator: What do you see now?...Is he looking at you?...What does he look like?...What do you see in his face?...his eyes?... What is he doing now?...Is he responding to what you just said to him?...What is he saying?...What do you hear?...

(The actress is imaging everything that followed her outburst. She is creating her husband and his response to what she expressed—his features, his skin color, his physical and emotional reactions, his words at that moment, and so on. If in this case she decides to engage in an Imaginary Monologue with her choice, the facilitator should be sensitive enough not to interrupt the flow. He may continue his facilitation when he feels that she is finished with her monologue.)

Actress: Don't look so surprised! I have been telling you how unhappy I've been for a couple of years now! You don't do anything to change things. You are selfish and only get involved with the things that interest you!...I'm surprised that you don't read the sports section while we make love! I mean it! You are the most self-involved human being I have ever known! I want to be with a man who looks at me and wants to know how I feel, what I think, and what I want! You don't even know what my interests are—and that's because you don't care!

Facilitator: How do you feel?...What is he doing?...What is he saying right now?...What do you hear in his voice?...see in his eyes?...How does that make you feel?...What are you most aware of at this moment?...What do you hear?...How has his expression changed?...What do you want?...What are you feeling?...Express it! (She begins to cry again, this time very softly and with a great sense of regret coming through.) What is he doing?...

At this point, the facilitator tells her to begin the written scene and continue the dynamics and emotions of the experience. She turns to him and says the first line, talking to him as if to her husband in the circumstances that she has just created. If she finds it necessary, she could begin to endow the facilitator/actor with the features of her ex-husband while continuing the scene.

He, on the other hand, could select a situation in his life that would complement her choice and have a similar structure. He could pick, for example, a time in his life when he was breaking up with a woman, at that moment when they both realized that what they had wasn't working; or he might select another kind of experience entirely, one that, although not romantic, might still embody many of the components of *Key Exchange*. Whatever his choice, the process would simply be to relate all the facts to his acting partner. They could then launch into a Simultaneous Guided Imaging exploration, facilitating each other until they both felt or experienced that "moment of truth" as a cue for starting the scene.

> ➤ *Simultaneous Guided Imaging Example*

The actress is using the same choice as above, and her partner has selected an experience he had in his ex-girlfriend's living room. In both instances there was a showdown kind of dynamic.

She: Where am I?...How large is this room?...

(They both respond to these questions, using all of their senses to promote the image.)

He: What is the feeling in this room? Where in my body do I feel it?... What do I hear?...How many different sounds are there?...Where are they coming from?...How do I feel about what I hear?...

(Again both actors are relating to the same queries, responding in all sensory areas and allowing other images to form and evolve.)

She: Do I hear his voice?...What does it sound like?...Can I tell what he is feeling in the sound of his voice?...What is he saying?...What do those words sound like?...How does he pronounce particular words?...

(The actor attempts to hear and image his girlfriend in exactly the same areas as are addressed by the actress's questions.)

He: What does she look like?...What do I see in her face?...How has her anger distorted her face?...mouth?...eyes?...What do I see behind her eyes?...What do I love about the way she looks?...What is it that repulses me about her behavior?...When she opens her mouth, how many of her teeth show?...Is that different when she is angry?...What does she smell like?...Can I smell her anger?...

She: How am I feeling in this moment?...Can he see my pain?...Does he care?...He is standing up, walking away...How does that make me feel?...

He: She always walks away when it gets too hot for her!...I see her back...Can I tell how she is feeling from her body language?... What about her body tells me anything?...Is she hurt too?...What do I hear?...Is she crying?...

She: I can't stand it when he is hurt!...I feel guilty, even when I'm not to blame...What is he doing?...thinking?...I can't see his face!... (At this point the actress speaks to her imaginary choice.) Turn around and talk to me! What are you feeling?...What do you want from me?

(The actor responds to his choice as if she had said that to *him*.)

He: What do I want from you?...That's funny...It seems that you're the one doing the asking all the time!

She: How do I feel about what he just said?...What does he look like now?...

When the actors reach a point in the process where they feel ready to start the scene, one of them could go into the lines. Once they begin the scene, they can combine their images with Available Stimulus realities and even use Endowments if they choose to. If any of the questions either of them asks as they create their images comes in conflict with the reality or the logic of the other's choice, an immediate adjustment or substitute response should take place. Sometimes an actor will be derailed by such a question, and it will take him out of the experience. If that occurs, he should immediately reinvest in his imaging process. This will happen much less frequently as he acquires more experience with the craft.

EMOTIONAL

The next obligation, the EMOTIONAL, relates to what the character feels and how that changes from scene to scene and moment to moment. The actor reads the text and determines what the character is experiencing and why—what is causing the emotional life in the scene. It may be a variety of factors, all of which must be identified and understood before the actor can make intelligent selections in attempting to fulfill the emotional obligation. For example, if the character is very angry and is having a tantrum because after a very difficult day he has come home to a house that is in total mayhem, the actor must create his personal reality to accommodate those components. Suppose that after blowing up, the character is treated differently by all the others in the scene and as a result he mellows and becomes quite warm and affectionate, then there would be two identifiable emotions to deal with. It is often the case that the emotional obligation is affected by what happens in a scene and that it changes as a result of new and different stimuli which present themselves as the action of the play moves forward. Often, the actor need not select new choices to accommodate these emotional shifts. If he has created the relationship and the time and place so that they are truly real for him, then the changes in the behavior of the other characters will be accepted in that framework, and the evolution in the reality will affect him accordingly. The emotions of a character in a piece of material may be stimulated by a large variety of things: the relationships, the character profiles and elements, the action of the play, the environment, and so on. In fact, the emotional life of a character could come from any one of the seven obligations or a combination of all of them.

CREATING A PIECE OF MUSIC

Almost any choice can be created through Imaging. Imagine, for example, that our actor is playing the part of a union organizer at a rally. His obligation is to incite and excite a group of workers to unite against their company and strike for better wages and working conditions. The actor selects a particular piece of music as his choice, one that stimulates a feeling of excitement and inspiration and has always made him feel like doing heroic things. Of course, there are a number of other obligations that would need to be addressed first, but for the sake of this example, let us suppose that he has already dealt with them.

The music he has picked is from *The Big Country,* a movie he saw many years ago. He remembers it very well. The specific scene involved a group of horsemen riding triumphantly to a justifiable confrontation. Every time the actor re-creates this music, he feels inspired to "fight windmills."

He might approach his choice in a couple of ways: He could start by imaging the scene from the film, creating the visual images first and then the music, or he could begin by imaging the sounds and the instruments involved through his auditory sense. If he decided to create the visual elements first, he might use Verbalized Imaging to get himself going:

"I see a vast panorama of desert and mesas, beautiful colors. The sky is a deep blue, and there are billowy clouds forming incredible shapes. The shapes seem to support the men riding on gorgeous horses ...They all seem filled with purpose, as they gallop in unison ever faster towards their destination...I can hear the music behind them...It starts with horns...and then I hear the string instruments in the background. It almost seems as if the men and the horses also hear the music and are moving in rhythm with it...I hear it building to heights and climaxes that make me feel as if I were there with them."

As he creates these elements, he must in every instance supply the sensorial response to each of his verbal suggestions. So when he suggests the image of a vast panorama of desert and mesas, he must create that image in detail. Although there are no olfactory responses when one is watching a film, he should also supply those. The more senses an actor responds with, the greater chance he has of creating a dimensional reality. As he creates the images and sounds of the music, he should be affected the way he wants to be. When he begins the lines of the scene, he must continue the music beneath those lines, so as to support the emotional life he wants to create. By using Imaging he will be able to promote and sustain the choice throughout the entire scene, and if it was a proper choice in the first place, it should stimulate the desired life all the way to the end. The approach technique should be Imaging Sensations, unless the actor has difficulty either recalling the images or creating them—in which case he would use Sense Memory.

THE OBLIGATION: (Emotional)	To feel inspired and excited, to feel the impetus to ignite and inspire a group of men to take action
THE CHOICE:	A particular piece of music from the movie *The Big Country*
THE IMAGING TECHNIQUE:	Verbalized Story Imaging
THE CHOICE APPROACH:	Imaging, using Imaging Sensations

CREATING AN EXPERIENCE

For this second example, I am going to use *Hearts,* a play we did a few years ago at my theater in Hollywood, about three lost and unhappy people who are attempting to find answers for their lives. The main character is a man who has just broken both his legs by falling off a bridge he was working on. At the beginning of the play it isn't clear whether he fell or jumped, but he has a recurring feeling of falling from that bridge over and over again. As a matter of fact, the play opens with his having a nightmare about it. Even though the play deals with many elements, including the characters' relationship with one another, I am only going to address here that recurrent feeling and fear of falling that the character experiences a number of times throughout the play.

The obligation, therefore, is a *helpless feeling of falling from a great height and the terror involved as a result.* Having never fallen two hundred feet from a bridge before, the actor intelligently decides to pick something that he really did experience and that could be re-created through the imaging process. After doing a "choice hunt," he remembers a motorcycle accident he had. It could have proved fatal, but by the grace of God he came through it without major injury—just bruises and scratches.

The accident involved rear ending a car that had stopped abruptly in front of him. He was travelling at about thirty miles an hour, when suddenly he became aware that the car ahead was not moving. He was too

143

close to negotiate a stop, and in spite of applying his brakes, he rammed the car at about twenty-five miles an hour. At the very moment of impact, he was catapulted into the air at that speed, becoming airborne for what seemed like an eternity—during which time he imagined hitting an oncoming car, rear ending another stopped car, or falling onto the pavement and being splattered all over it. He had an incredible feeling of helplessness as he was falling. He remembers it vividly and at times has sensations of its happening again, even when he is not riding his motorcycle.

While writing this example of a potential choice, I remembered a very vivid dream I had, which also involved a motorcycle. It was so incredible and shocking that after eight or nine years I still remember every detail as if I had dreamt it last night. It was my custom at the time to ride my "bike" to Carmel at least once a year down Route 1—which is my favorite highway in the world. I had done it several times and at least once with my son riding with me. The road is scenic and incredibly curved, with twists unlike anything I have ever seen. It is a cyclist's dream. At certain points up along the northern coastline, there are drops of a thousand feet or more. In many places there aren't any guardrails, and it would be very easy to understeer a curve and go right over the edge to certain death. That *happened* to me—but fortunately, only in a shocking nightmare that startled me into a waking state full of terror, with an accelerated heartbeat. The dream was so real in every detail that I smelled the burning oil from the engine of my bike. In it, I was going about sixty miles an hour as I entered the curve, slowing slightly. The next thing I knew, I was unable to turn the handlebars enough to stay on the pavement, and I went off onto the shoulder and straight over the cliff! I knew as I became airborne that this was it! I was a dead man! I remember thinking that this was really happening to me. I had heard of other people dying like this but never believed that it could really happen to me! The motorcycle fell out from under me, and I was in the air, falling very fast but in slow motion—if that is understandable! I cannot describe the fear I felt. It was unlike anything I had ever experienced before. It was also unlike any other dream I had ever had. Actually, I had only come down a short distance when I fell onto the top of a lower cliff, which was obviously jutting out from the main rock mass. I landed on the narrow crest, straddling the cliff as if riding bareback on a horse. My sense of relief was incredible, but the fear remained. What I found so amazing about the dream was how vividly real it was and how I was able to remember every last detail, down to my hitting the rocky cliff—

which hurt! I never took that motorcycle trip again, and shortly after I had that dream, I gave up riding completely!

Both the experiences described above could be good choices for an actor to use in relation to the obligation of the play. The decision as to which one to pick would depend on which would produce the most authentic responses, which would stimulate the proper emotional life and have the most impact on the actor. In this case the question is academic, since one of the experiences happened to the actor doing the play and the other to me! So unless we were both playing the part at the same time, there wouldn't be any need to make a choice! But supposing that both experiences had happened to whoever was doing the play, he would then have to make a decision as to which one to use. When deciding on a specific choice, an actor must take several things into consideration: first, is it right for the scene—does it stimulate most, or all, of the requirements? and second, can it be created easily and in the time frame within which he is working? As an actor, I have often had to discard wonderful choices because they were too complex and time-consuming for the frame of a scene, only to select much less impelling ones to do the job. Another consideration is the expediency of the choice approach. The choice may be perfect for the circumstance of the play, but if the actor decides on a cumbersome choice approach, he will again run into the same problem. In this case, where we will be using Imaging as a choice approach, we will select the first experience rather than the second.

➤ *Imaging the Experience (Using Story Imaging with Sense Memory)*

I am riding my bike. I feel the tightness of my leather jacket...Where do I feel that restriction?...(Responding sensorially in that part of his body.) *I see the traffic in front of me...The sky is blue.* (Responding visually to all the images, the actor must attempt to see them with his outer eyes.) *I feel the vibration of my bike between my legs and thighs... The air feels cool on my face...Where do I specifically feel that?...How does it feel?...What is the temperature?...I hear the engine and the sound of traffic...I feel the road as it vibrates through my bike and into my body...Where do I feel those sensations?* (Again the response is sensorial. Remember imaging is a five-sense experience. Each sense has its own ability to "image.")

My hands are gripping the handles. I feel the power of the bike in my hands...I glance at the speedometer...Imagining myself going faster ...I see the scratch on the gas tank from the last time I dumped it...I see the Marlboro billboard...Going by it...My mouth feels dry...I see other motorcycles going in the opposite direction...I wave...I feel free and unrestricted...I love the feeling of moving in the open air...How does the wind feel on my body?...Where do I feel the resistance of the wind? I glance at the pavement and see the sparkles of the stones in the cement as they reflect the sun...It's almost like a pattern of light that you can't catch up to...My rear end feels a little numb...I feel a little mesmerized by the sounds and the movement of the bike...What does that feel like? How does it manifest itself in my eyes?...What do I see ahead of me?... (Respond to one question at a time sensorially, but also involve all the other senses.) *I see the car in front of me...It's a Volvo...One of the taillights is cracked...We are both moving as if on a track together... What color is that car? How is the sun reflecting off the trunk?...I see the driver. Can't tell if it's a man or a woman...Who cares!...My arms hurt a little from this position...I smell hot dogs...Must be passing a restaurant...What does that smell like?...How many different odors do I smell?...Wait! I see the car in front. It's coming closer...Oh, my God! It's stopped...I feel...Hit the brakes...See it closer...Scratches on his trunk...See the license plate...Oh, God, I'm going to hit!...Feel myself squirreling to the side...Don't have time to lay it down...Going to hit... Oh God, my stomach!...I feel it dropped...Going over the top of the car ...I am in the air...I feel like I'm falling. No control...helpless...I am going to die...No, I don't want to die. I have no control. I feel like I'm going to hit hard...break my neck...Feel like my body is Jell-O...*(Even though all of those sensations are happening very fast, the actor must encourage all of his senses to work together to reexperience everything he felt at the time of the accident.)

I feel like everything has stopped, and in a few moments I'll be dead ...I'm coming down...I feel like I'm falling faster...I have no helmet... Please, God, protect my head!...I can't reach my head...My arms feel paralyzed...I'm coming down...trying to turn my body...I am turning... Hitting feet first...Feel the shock of the ground like electricity through my whole body...Falling forward...Feel like I'm flying again...Going to hit the ground with my body...Pushing my hands forward...Hitting... Feel the heat...burning my palms...My face is scraping the street...I feel the burn...the pain...I'm stopped...Don't know if I'm hurt...What do I feel?...I hear people running towards me...I'm looking at the sky...I don't feel hurt...but I must be in shock...I wonder if I'm going to die... Maybe my spine is broken and that's why I don't feel anything!...

The entire experience is filled with the re-creation of the images of the accident. By imaging with all five senses, the actor should be able to reexperience the fear, terror, and helplessness he originally felt. The imaging should be as detailed as necessary to accomplish the goal. If the actor needs to ask more questions or supply more details, he will know it by the degree of reality in the response. Since the obligation is to experience the terror of falling from the bridge, and since in every case the character either wakes up or snaps out of it before feeling himself hit the water, the actor can selectively emphasize specific elements of the event he is re-creating and end the process before the experience is over. Where he starts his imaging is dependent on how far back he must go to establish the reality so that he actually believes that it is happening. Just by the nature of this choice, it would seem that Imaging is a natural selection for creating the experience.

CREATING A PERSON

In this third example, I will suggest an imaginary person as the choice—a person from the actor's life who will hopefully stimulate the feelings, thoughts, and impulses of the character and thereby fulfill both the emotional and the relationship obligations.

The character is writing a Dear Jane letter to someone with whom he is truly in love. The reason he is thus stating his desire to end the relationship is that he has recently learned that he has a terminal disease and has only a few months to live. While he is still madly in love with this woman and knows that she would stay with him to the end, he doesn't want to subject her to the agony of witnessing his death. He also knows that unless this letter states that he no longer loves or wants her, she will not accept it. The emotional obligation here is complicated by a variety of feelings: He is very much in love with this woman but must tell her that he no longer loves her; he feels that this is a betrayal of truth, and yet he must spare her the pain of his disease. In addition, he is terribly sad about leaving her and the world but is resolved to "do the right thing." As we can see, there are a variety of very strong emotions here, mostly related to the woman he loves and his having to leave her. Accepting that the actor must first deal with the issue of the character's impending death and that this is the reason for writing the letter in the first place, we will explore this example by assuming that he has already addressed that responsibility.

The closest parallel in the actor's life was leaving his girlfriend to pursue his acting career. Knowing that a distance of two thousand miles would create too big a strain on the relationship, and having already had the experience of a long-distance relationship in the past, he chose not to "steal precious time from her life." He wrote her a letter telling her that he was engaged to be married to another woman—which was a lie. He did this knowing that it was the only way she would agree to end their relationship. The actor vividly remembers the pain and self-hatred he felt when he wrote that agonizing letter. This parallel seems close enough to the responsibilities of the material to warrant exploring it as a choice.

To re-create the intensity of the love he felt for that woman, the actor decides to approach the choice in two parts. He will first image all of the wonderful things about her, using Fragmented Imaging to supply the impetus he hopes will restimulate his intense attraction and love for her.

➤ First Part—Fragmented Imaging

The actor starts by clearing his brain of any background "noise" and starts his imaging journey by suggesting his first experiences with this woman—meeting her, dating her, sleeping with her, and so on.

Who is that stunning creature over there?...(He is imaging the very first time he saw her.) *Her hair...eyes...never saw eyes that color...Her lips...beautiful...What a gorgeous woman!...*(All of these suggestions are supported by all five senses responding in unison. He sees the place and the activity around him; he hears the sounds and experiences the odors simultaneously.) *Talking to her...love the sound of her voice... how she moves her mouth...the way she smells...Want to touch her...* (All of the suggestions—those that are voluntary and those that come involuntarily as a result of free-associating—are totally supported by what the other senses are filling in.)

Sitting across the table from her...see the outline of her perfect breasts through the sheer negligee she is wearing...She is truly the most beautiful woman I have ever been with...the way she smells and sounds ...the touch of her skin...Her naked body is lovely...(While all of these associations are happening, the actor is experiencing the full sensory impact in all of the suggested areas.) *Feel her mouth on mine...incredible...to actually taste another human being...I could devour her if only she would still exist after I digested every last incredible part of her...* (At any point of this sensorial exploration the actor might include fantasy as part of his imaging process.) *I feel her body shudder under me...It's like a wave of motion that starts in her stomach and moves rhythmically up and down her body at the same time...I hear the soft moaning sounds that seem like the satisfied purring of a cat being held and loved...If love is a feeling in the body that can be defined, I am sure that I feel it now...I feel myself vibrating and tingling all over...waves of excitement originating in my groin like the epicenter of an earthquake sending shock waves through my entire body...I feel like I might explode with an energy I have never experienced before.*

Having accomplished what he set out to do—to restimulate the love he had for this woman (his choice)—the actor moves on to the second part of his process. He has decided to use Fantasy Story Imaging as his technique in this part. Since he wasn't there when she received his letter, he never really knew how she responded or felt. So he launches into a fantasy that starts with her opening and reading his letter.

> ### Second Part—Fantasy Story Imaging

(This fantasy story is executed through Imaging Sensations.) *I see her excitement, as she almost relishes the anticipation of opening the envelope. She is smiling, and I can see that she is breathing deeply as she begins to insert the letter opener. She is beginning to read the letter...I see the immediate confusion creeping into her expression...It quickly molds itself into hurt and then pain...Her eyes fill with tears, and her mouth distorts in a downward turn...I feel such anguish seeing her like this...If only she were angry instead of hurt...I could deal with that!...I hear her sobs coming from the deepest places in her body...I feel like the lowest human on this planet...and yet I have no alternative...Better to hurt her now when she has the time and opportunity to create a new life than later when I have stolen precious time from her life...time that can never be replaced...I see her on the bed crying and sobbing...I hear her anguish...Even in pain she is so beautiful! Oh, how I wish I could change this!...I wish that I didn't have to lie to her!...I see her sitting on the edge of her bed...She looks completely destroyed by this...Her make-up has run all over her face...I see wrinkles that were never there before ...I can get a glimpse of what she might look like twenty years from now ...just because the impact of her pain has cut deeply into her face...I did that!...Oh, how angry and confused I feel now!*

After completing both parts of the exploration of this choice, the actor feels ready to address the obligations of the written scene.

The First Part

THE OBLIGATION: (Emotional/Relationship)	Incredible love for a woman, combined with the painful reality that he is dying

(This is not the complete obligation of the scene. The actor has opted to deal only with the depth of his love for her in the first part, thereby addressing only half of the original obligation.)

THE CHOICE:	A woman with whom he was deeply in love, but whom he rejected to pursue his acting career
THE IMAGING TECHNIQUE:	Fragmented and Free-Association Imaging, with selective emphasis of all the love elements
THE CHOICE APPROACH:	Imaging, using Imaging Sensations

The Second Part

THE OBLIGATION:	The ambivalence he feels about lying to her; his self-anger and his feelings of betraying her
THE CHOICE:	The same woman
THE IMAGING TECHNIQUE:	Fantasy Imaging, supported by Story Imaging
THE CHOICE APPROACH:	Imaging, using Imaging Sensations and selectively emphasizing fantasy elements of his choice's actions and behavior

The three examples given in this section included a piece of music, an event, and a person. As I explained earlier, a choice can be almost any kind of object—animate or inanimate—any kind of sound or experience. In fact, a choice can be almost anything in the realm of one's imagination. The *choice approach* is the method by which an actor creates the choice, and in these cases Imaging is that process. The basic trap of imaging is that most people will interpret it to mean strictly visualizing—that is, seeing the "picture"—and to compound this problem, they see that picture in their mind's eye rather than externally. All of this leads to an internal cerebral process of working and falls short of really *convincing* the actor that his choice exists in reality. For example, the first choice above was a piece of music, which is essentially an auditory experience. I suggested, however, that the actor create all of the other elements involved with the music—the sights, the sounds, and even the odors. This is because, if a person experiences an event, another person, or a place with all of his senses, he will have a better chance of creating the entire reality so that it really exists on an external level rather than in his head. Every choice an actor uses should involve a complete sensorial exploration. Imaging Sensations has already been defined as a way of imaging through all *five* senses.

I imagine by this time, having read all of my hypothetical examples, you are probably thinking, Where does he find all these actors who have such incredible convenient parallel choices?—right? Well, if you are not thinking that, I would be! Actually, since the examples are hypothetical, so are the actors I invent to address them. However, even if you, the reader, cannot find so many exact or literal parallels, not to worry: We all have tens of thousands of possible choices in our "life bags." Choices do not have to be either logical or literal. Anything that has some relevance or connection with the obligations of the piece can usually be adjusted and used. In my final example of the dying man who has to write the Dear Jane letter, the actor need not have such a perfect parallel choice in order to address the obligation. He can pick any number of choices that might produce similar emotional responses. Have you ever had to write a painful letter ending a relationship of any kind? Or have you ever had to hurt someone by lying to that person about anything? Have you ever had to make painful decisions or choices? Possibly you are presently in a relationship that has adjustable realities that would fit this circumstance. We have a tendency to make things very literal. Does death, for example, mean really dying? Does it mean a stone-cold body ready to go into the ground? No! There are many kinds of deaths: the death or ending of a relationship, the ending of a chapter or period in one's life, the death of trusting someone, and so on. Death is an ending; it is completion—or it can be. So, when looking for a choice, open your mind to the infinite possibilities available to you.

EMOTIONAL TRANSITIONS

In addition to addressing the emotional obligation, Imaging is a very good choice approach to use when, as happens in many plays and films, one must make a complete emotional transition from one moment to the next. This is difficult for most actors because the stimulus for the change must often come as a surprise. How does someone who knows what is coming and how he must change his emotional life still experience that moment as unpredictable? First of all, he must really be involved in the preceding reality and only on the eleventh level of consciousness know where and when to change stimuli. Then, he must use the correct choice and choice approach to make that transition. There are many approaches and techniques that can accommodate such an obligation: Sensory Suggestion, Evocative Words, various kinds of Inner Monologues, and so on; however, for the purpose of promoting an understanding of Imaging, I will use Fragmented Imaging, which is a particularly good technique in this case. If the responsibility is to go from one emotional state to another, the actor can begin to use fragmented images slightly before the transition is to take place. This is done with a kind of Creative Manipulation and not in a stream-of-consciousness fashion. Because the actor knows what the obligation is, he also has an idea of the kind of emotional change needed. Therefore, before starting the process, he must decide on the actual content of the fragmented images.

Making an Emotional Transition Using Fragmented Imaging

The scene: A friend enters the room. The main character is happy to see him and greets him with a great deal of enthusiasm. Almost immediately, however, he notices that his friend is somber and grave. The first obligation, therefore, is for the actor to be happy and excited to see his friend after a long time; however, as soon as he becomes aware of his friend's emotional state, the transition from excitement to concern must begin to happen. To fulfill the first obligation, the actor could use Available Stimulus, dealing directly with the other actor, or he might work for another person, using Endowments as his approach. Whatever the case may be, he must make the transition very quickly and organically. There is only a moment between the time when he first greets his friend and the time when he actually looks at his face and sees that he is somber. It is in that moment that he can begin his Fragmented Imaging. He might also suggest fragmented images related to the original choice he is using to greet his friend. Let us say that he is endowing the other actor with the features of a very close and dear friend, whom he has not seen for a long time. This endowment can begin before the other actor's entrance, in the form of imaginary expectations. Our actor can use fragmented images to create how his friend might look after all this time, how he might behave, what they will talk about, and so on. While waiting for his friend to arrive, he could create fragmented images about their life experiences growing up together, going to school, and sharing various events in their lives. As a result of this kind of imaging, he builds up an excitement and anticipation of his friend's arrival. All of the images are fragmented, skipping from one event and experience to another, not needing to be complete.

Freckles...See his pug Irish nose...smiling...separation in front teeth ...his laughter...sounds that come from him when he is excited...bright blue eyes...I see the sparkle...Tim...Timothy...How his mouth moves when he gets hurt...He smells like Ivory soap...Red hair all over his face ...falling in his eyes...See him on the football field...running fast...He's kissing Sharon...See how much he loves her...He's a little drunk... laughing...silly...

All of the images are sensorially experienced; all the senses are working in tandem with each other. These images can be stimulated or created in a number of ways: The actor can just say the name of his friend and see what images come up, or he can suggest a particular event involving his friend; he may creatively manipulate the entire exercise by using an evocative word to change the images, or he can use a stream of consciousness following the original suggestion. After all, he really knows in what direction he wants the images to go. Just the suggestion of his friend in the school auditorium could kick off an endless stream of fragmented images which would probably set him up to address the first obligation.

After the other actor makes his entrance and the initial excited response occurs, the main character sees that something is wrong. At that moment, the actor must begin the transitional Fragmented Imaging. He will naturally be able to use what the other actor has created. Relating to that, he starts his internal imaging:

See his eyes...sad...hurt...Something is wrong with Tim...His shoulders are stooped...Looks old and tired...Skin is gray and lifeless...Feel his fear and pain...His face has changed...

All of these images occur very rapidly, and there are no words involved—just Fragmented Imaging responses. They are all in contrast to what the actor had created in anticipation of his friend's arrival. If he was originally successful in eliciting a very positive group of fragmented images about his choice, the contrast in the other actor's behavior, followed by his own transitional images, should work very well. Sometimes there are only a few seconds to make an emotional transition, and the images must be created quickly.

CHARACTER

Our next obligation, CHARACTER, consists of four parts: the *physical,* the *emotional,* the *psychological* and the *intellectual.* Dividing it in this way helps us identify and understand the components that make up the character. In other words, we need to ask what the character is like in all of those areas: Who is he physically? emotionally? What is his psychological profile, and how does that affect his behavior throughout the play? What is his level of intelligence? How does his brain seem to function? Since none of these elements operate independently of each other, how does one influence the other? By determining all of this, an actor is better equipped to create parallel realities for himself.

The first step is to compare and contrast. Ask yourself: How am I like this person physically? emotionally? How am I different? It is not necessary, however, to try to equate what impels the character with what impels you. You may be very much like each other, but for different reasons. The stimuli that impel his behavior in the play will probably have very little impact on you.

The character obligation is very important to the play and to you, the actor playing the part. Many of the choices you will finally use to address the obligations of the play will have their origin in the character-background explorations. Once you have compared and contrasted your own traits with those of the character, you can start to create the differences and assimilate them into your own personality and behavior. There are numerous other techniques in this system that will help you affect and change your persona to fit the play, but Imaging lends itself particularly well to this area.

EXAMPLE USING FANTASY STORY IMAGING

For the first example, let us use Starbuck from *The Rainmaker*. He is a con man of the highest caliber! He is so good because he believes his own lies. There are many scenes in which he creates beautiful pictures and vistas for the people he is relating to; for example, the tack-room scene where he seduces Lizzie and the one in which he graphically describes his method for making rain and talks about the first time he realized that he was special and could actually make it rain. In a way, this is a perfect play in which to use Fantasy Imaging, because the character *is* actually creating a fantasy as he speaks. We do not know whether it is a rehearsed spiel or whether he makes it up as he goes along, but I'm inclined to believe the latter.

The part in which he describes how he creates the rain goes something like this:

"...I get out my big wheel and my rolling drum and my yella hat with the three little feathers in it! I look up at the sky and I say: 'Cumulus!' I say: 'Cumulo-nimbus! Nimbulo-cumulus' and pretty soon—way up there—there's a teeny little cloud the size of a mare's tail—and then over there—there's another cloud...and all of a sudden there's a herd of white buffalo stampedin' across the sky! And then, sister-of-all-good-people, down comes the rain! Rain in buckets, rain in barrels, fillin' the lowlands, flooding the gullies! And the land is as green as the valley of Adam!"

In this case, all the actor would have to do would be to parallel the material with his own magical fantasy. He could actually create one that would be totally related to making it rain, but only if it would stimulate impulses and feelings similar to Starbuck's. If not, he would have to come up with his own separate fantasy. For example, if we pretend that this hypothetical actor has always wanted to play Hamlet, his fantasy could consist of not only convincing Joe Papp (who unfortunately is no longer with us) that he can play the part but telling him how he would do it. He could start with the following preparation:

I see myself dressed as the brooding Dane in silks and with a ruff tightly fitting around my neck...I feel the tights embracing my thighs as I move to the front of the stage...I feel ripped apart with confusion...not knowing what to do with my life...to continue or to end it...I feel a mixture of pain and excitement...I can feel the audience anticipating the soliloquy...I stand motionless, deep in my contemplation...At last I hear the vibration of the first words bursting from my mouth almost like a striking snake lunging forward...I feel the brilliance of my emotions flowing out from a place of reality and conviction...I look at the audience studying their faces...I see their complete involvement, which impels me to go on...I feel powerful and complete. I pull the dagger out of its sheath and lift it high above my chest, threatening to plunge it into my heart. I hear the audience gasp...Aha! I have them! They are mine!

It is a hell of an actor's fantasy! We all have those, and sometimes—as in this example—they directly serve a specific obligation. If the actor did this as a preparation for the described scene it might put him in a place where he could start it. He could also do the Fantasy Story Imaging as an inner monologue while actually doing the lines from *The Rainmaker*.

BUILDING A CHARACTER THROUGH IMAGING

Another very important way in which one can use Imaging is in creating an entire imaginary background life for a character in a play or film. The first step to take when embarking on that journey is to read the script thoroughly! The actor should understand the character as written, absorb all of the information supplied by the author, and take note of what all the other characters say about this character, what the latter says about himself, and what his actions are throughout the play. Armed with this information, the actor can start out on the road to constructing the character's entire life prior to the first scene of the play, and he may even want to fill in the spaces between the different scenes. Besides its evident value in elevating his imagination, such an involvement would create a history for him. After all, a character's life does not begin with the first line he has in the play!

It helps, of course, if the actor has some perception and/or psychological knowledge about what goes into building a particular person's psychological profile—what has made the person the way he or she is. Having such knowledge is extremely helpful in creating the imaginary events, relationships, and experiences in the life of the character. Constructing a character background accomplishes many important things for an actor: It makes that character more dimensional and real for him, while at the same time supplying a greater understanding of who this person is and how he got that way. It also adds facets to the actor's behavior and establishes a much more specific "blueprint" for the nature and kinds of choices he will finally decide to use. In addition, if he uses some of his own experiences to create the character's background, he will solicit material from his unconscious—which will be enormously helpful in substantiating the realities of the material for him.

Any of the imaging techniques can be used to create a character background, but as I mentioned before, Story Imaging works extremely well in this area. As an example of how to use it, I am going to pick a play I directed in Germany in 1992, Agatha Christie's *Love from a Stranger*. A spin-off on the classic Bluebeard story, it is about a kind of serial killer—a man who seeks out women who have money or who have recently come into an inheritance, seduces them into marriage and then kills them. He usually buries each body beneath the cement floor of the basement of the house he shared with that victim. The character is attractive, incredibly charming and articulate, and he possesses an ability to romantically seduce most women. The play involves one of those relationships, and we gradually learn about the others in the dialogue.

In the first act and part of the second, the character seems normal and honest, although a number of things seem to contradict this—subtle things, which are designed to impact on the audience later, once they have found out who he really is. There is very little information about this man's life before the action of the play. We do learn about him through talk of newspaper accounts and of a book written about a man who has killed several women, but the book is only mentioned near the end of the play. It seems that the character has altered his appearance by changing the shape and color of his hair. There isn't much else, except an expurgatory outburst right near the end, before he attempts to kill the female character, in which he expresses his hatred for women and his frustration about the way people have treated him all his life. He talks about how his high-school principal used to punish him periodically and how others ordered him around—people who "were not as good as" he was! However, there aren't a lot of facts on which an actor could build the kind of background life that produces a Bluebeard—the incredibly impacting experiences that distort a person's ability to know right from wrong or, even if he does, cause him to have no conscience about his dastardly deeds. The actor can imagine what those experiences were, however, and re-create them through his process.

Before starting to build a character background through Story Imaging, the actor must decide whether to use total fantasy or to include some parallel realities from his own life. In other words, the imaging can come totally from his imagination, and he can build a complex scenario of the activities and experiences of his character as he imagines them to have been; or he can combine fantasy with elements from his own real experiences, either creatively manipulating them to fit the circumstances or selectively emphasizing only the usable parts. I think a good suggestion is to do the second, so that in effect this may turn into an acceptable Believability experience. This simply means that when one mixes reality with unreality, the two will merge into each other, so that down the line it becomes difficult to separate what is real from what isn't.

➢ *Story Imaging Example 1*

I am going to start the imaging at the age of five. I elect to use pure Sense Memory at first, as the springboard into Imaging:

What can I see from where I am lying?...(This is a visual sensory question, which is responded to by the visual sense. The actor "sees" what he is looking at.) *What does the window look like? What does the wood around the window look like?...Can I see anything through the window?...What?...What do I hear?...Where are those sounds coming from?...I hear my mother's voice coming from the other room...What does it sound like?...*(Asking more sensory questions about the specifics of her voice and responding with the auditory sense.) *What do I hear her saying?...How is the clarity of her voice affected as it comes through the wall?...I hear my name...Her voice sounds angry...and shrill...She is arguing with my father...I don't hear him say much...I look at the peeling wallpaper of my bedroom. I see the yellowed glue on the walls, and it looks like vomit...What do I smell? What are those odors like?...What do they remind me of?...I see the plaster peeling from the ceiling...*(All of the statements, visual or otherwise, are actually imaging responses and are not verbalized.) *I hear my mother say, "I never wanted him." I know she is talking about me...The sound in her voice is a mixture of rage, disgust and grief. "It was your idea to have him...Now I'm tied to this ugly place." I go to the window to escape the pain of what I have just heard...What do I see in the street below?...What do those people look like?...How are they dressed?...I see the garbage piled up across the street...The rats are all over it...I see them fighting over pieces of food...I hear the high pitch of their screams as they wound each other... Bang! My bedroom door flies open, and I look up into my mother's bloodshot, drunken, angry eyes...What does her face look like?...her hair?...What are the shape and position of her mouth?...Her clothes smell of urine mixed with alcohol...I suddenly feel the pain of her hand as it angrily connects with my face...I hear ringing in my ear...Everything is blurred for a moment...What is she saying?...What are those words?...It is hard to distinguish the words through the ringing in my ears!...Her face comes very close to mine...I feel her spitting up in my face...She is screaming at me...What is she saying?...What do her words sound like? "Why aren't you sleeping, you little no-good bastard?" I see the violence and pain distort her face...smell the stale alcohol and her bad breath from decayed and rotten teeth. "You're spying on us, listening to every word!" She stumbles back and hits the door...She hits me again...I feel the pain of her blow into my spine. "You little shit...you pushed me!" She leaves...I hear her stumbling in the kitchen, throwing pots at my father and against the wall...I hear myself begin to cry on the inside. I feel my tears, but only internally...The pain in my body is overwhelming...I want to strike out at something...I see an old stuffed bear on the floor of my bedroom...It's worn and ugly ...a hand-me-down from somewhere...I pick it up and begin to tear it apart...All my rage is in action...I don't make a sound...*

At the beginning of this Story Imaging, the actor starts with Sense Memory to establish the specificity of the images. As the episode continues, he moves into Imaging Sensations, where all of his senses

158

respond in unison to the creation of the experience. He creatively manipulates the continuity of the "story." It is important to note here that creating the background of a character is done through a series of episodes. The actor can arrange these in some sort of chronological order, but he should try to use meaningful events to promote the reality of the story. It would take the better part of the actor's life if he were to attempt to design his character's background day by day, so it is better to create some kind of continual collage of the latter's imaginary experiences, selectively emphasizing those that promote the underpinnings of the material. In the example above, the actor used only a little of his own reality mixed in with a lot of imaginary events. It is true that he was poor as a child and lived in a run-down apartment, that he felt unwanted by his mother and never received any affection from her. It is also true that his parents argued and eventually divorced. In other words, there were some real connections with the choice.

The purpose for constructing this particular character's early life is to create the episodes, events, experiences, and relationships that constitute the foundation of what turns a person into a selfish killer. The actor's intellect and his knowledge of what creates a specific character profile allow him to construct as complete a background as possible. The pain, rejection, and hurt that an individual suffers during his formative years create the underpinnings of all of his actions as an adult. Armed with this knowledge, the actor builds a series of episodes that support the hatred felt by the character in the play. The realities of a childhood of deprivation impel the killer to lash out at all the women who are symbolic of his mother. It is important that the actor find as many parallels from his own life as possible to combine with the imaginary elements he supplies. Of course, even the parallels will need to be selectively emphasized and enhanced.

After exploring this first episode to whatever conclusion he reaches, the actor might supplement it with other childhood experiences to establish a connection with poverty, deprival, and abuse from his mother. This kind of Story Imaging can take place over a period of time— certainly for the duration of the rehearsal period.

Having accomplished two or three other Story Imaging journeys into the character's early childhood, the actor could then explore other environments and relationships that collaborated in the construction of his personality.

➤ *Story Imaging Example 2*

This imaging exploration involves his school experiences:

I'm sitting in front of the class...on a stool higher than the desk... They are looking at me and quietly laughing because I am wearing a dunce cap...I see the teacher sitting at her desk...hear her asthmatic wheezing as she explains the assignment to the class...She is fat...I smell her body odor from here...Her glasses are so thick that they resemble the bottom of a Coke bottle...She glances at me sitting in the corner... Her eyes are so small they look like the eyes of an insect...She smiles at me with satisfied sarcasm...I feel humiliated...Jumping out of her chair, she waddles her mass of protoplasm towards me. "Are you chewing gum?" She spits those words out at me like the venom shooting from the fangs of a poisonous snake...I tell her that I am...She leans in to me, "Take it out of your mouth and fasten it to your nose! Sit there all day like that, you unruly boy!" Hear the silence...Smell the chalky blackboard...See all the others working on geography...I hate her...Mrs. Anderson...She's like all of them...

Of course, each of the imaging explorations must be infinitely more elaborate than indicated here. All of the senses must be specifically involved in the creation of every detail of the experience. The greater the sensorial involvement, the more the actor will succeed in creating the reality.

Other possibilities for this character include creating his relationships with girls as he deals with growing up—relationships filled with rejection and criticism—and his experiences with other children, who have parents who shower them with love and gifts, in contrast to his own. The entire Story Imaging creates a foundation for the actor that makes him ready to address the specific scene obligations of the material.

USING FANTASY IMAGING, WITH "I'M FIVE YEARS OLD"

In some cases, an actor might decide to use total fantasy in creating a character's background. He could then start in several ways: He might image the different environments where he supposes that the character grew up—filling in the actions and events in each of them—or begin with relationships and create imaginary circumstances involving the other characters prior to the time of the play, or even invent people who are not mentioned in the piece. He might also fantasize about all of the impacting events in the character's life—the kind of experiences that mold a personality. If he is confused about where to begin the fantasy, he might use another technique to impel himself to imagine, such as the "I'm Five Years Old and I..." exercise, which opens all the doors to childhood. He could start with his own memories first and then very quickly move into fantasy.

Knowing the written character well and having already developed some ideas of what his childhood might have been like, the actor would start the process with *I'm five years old and I...am playing in the back-yard...*(All of the responses are fragmented sensorial images. The actor "sees" the backyard and everything in it.) *I'm alone...playing with my blocks...building a house...I feel afraid...I don't hear anything and I'm cold...I begin to cry softly...Feel the sobs start in my belly, and my body is shaking...The yard is big and empty and nothing but dirt...I see the railroad tracks...It's cloudy, and I feel a sprinkle of rain...I feel alone... Where is Mommy?...Daddy?...I don't have a daddy...I try to remember his face...I can't...Mommy isn't home...She kissed me when she left...I hear that fat lady in the kitchen...She's mean to me...I hate her...I'll be quiet and she won't come out here...She pulls my hair...She hurts me...I want to go into my bedroom, but I'm afraid she will see me...I wish I could go to school...I would like a real friend...I know I have my bed-room friends...but they don't talk to me much!...I'm hungry...I don't like the fat lady's food...She is always watching television...What's her name?...I'm afraid of her...If I go to my room, I can hide and she won't know how to find me...*

For the sake of this example, let us say that the actor is playing a character who is very shy and painfully afraid of social involvement. He has isolated himself and lives a solitary life sequestered in a house with his sister, who cares for him. He is completely socially retarded, and his fear of people has reached the stage of phobia. By starting at the age of five and creatively manipulating his fantasies to create the underpinnings for the events that have shaped this isolated and reclusive personality, the actor could continue to create fantasies that will support and or-ganically justify his behavior in the play.

It is very important to note here that in every example I give, there may very well be a better choice or choice approach to use than the one given.

Of all the uses of imaging this is the most pragmatic: to help us create the choices that will stimulate the life of a character. If our goal is to become professional experiencers, then the process we work with must enable us to bring to life the realities that parallel the experiences of that character. In other words, the actor's job is to really go through all of the emotions of the character he is playing. To do so, he must introduce or create choices that affect him to the extent that he experiences the impulses and inner organic life of that character. Those choices are objects, people, places, and experiences from his own real life—from his past or present, from his fantasies if need be.

BUILDING THE CHARACTER BY IMAGING RELATIONSHIPS

As an example, let us imagine that the actor is playing the part of Biff in Arthur Miller's *Death of a Salesman*. In order to experience all of Biff's thoughts, feelings, and impulses, he must be able to create the numerous choices (stimuli) that will give rise to such feelings and responses. Let us confine our exploration to Biff's relationship to his father, Willy. This is indeed a very complex and involved relationship. The psychological ramifications of all of the ambivalent emotions these two harbor toward each other could fill a small book. To understand why Willy affects Biff the way he does, we would have to explore all of the elements that make up the character of Willy—truly a case history that would have challenged both Freud and Jung. I am convinced that an actor could spend his entire life working on Willy Loman and never completely fulfill the role! However, not to digress from the point here, which is Imaging as a choice approach, let us confine our attention just to Biff's feelings about Willy in certain scenes. For the sake of understanding the choice approach, let us say that the actor who is playing Biff is going to use his own father as a choice throughout the play. He has decided to create him in a variety of situations that parallel those in the text and has even thought of using events and experiences that do not specifically exist there.

There are many choice approaches that the actor could use to create his father in relation to the other actor. He could pick Endowments—done through either Sense Memory or Imaging—Imaginary Monologues, Evocative Words or Evocative Images, Sensory Suggestion, and a host of other choice approaches. Any or all of them could create the choice quite satisfactorily. Because this is a book about imaging as it relates to acting, however, I will give examples of several of the imaging techniques in relation to the various choices, in order to illustrate the use of Imaging as a choice approach.

To embark on his journey of creating the character of Biff, our actor decides to start with Available Stimulus realities. He begins by looking for any resemblance that might exist between the actor playing Willy and his own father, noting features, mannerisms, attitudes, physical rhythm, personality traits that are in any way similar. He does this so as to establish the relationship to his choice—his father. If at a later time he selects Endowments to create his father in relation to the other actor, he will already have accomplished the preliminary work. In addition, this Available Stimulus exploration helps him to get the essence of his father, which can serve as a foundation for any other choice he might use. Beginning this way may also allow him to hook into his unconscious. If he is successful in establishing enough similarities and in indeed getting an essence of his father in relation to the other actor, the entire rehearsal involvement will become a collaboration between his conscious process and unconscious responses. Remember that he is preparing to build the character of Biff, not just to deal with a scene-to-scene responsibility.

He might start the journey by doing an entire parallel imaging of his own relationship with his father from his childhood to the present time, selectively emphasizing circumstances, events, and experiences that service the relationship elements of the play.

Selecting Fragmented Imaging as the technique and Imaging Sensations as his process for creating the fragmented images, he begins around the age of six.

THE CHOICE:	All of the selectively emphasized experiences with his father from the age of six until the present
THE IMAGING TECHNIQUE:	Fragmented Imaging
THE CHOICE APPROACH:	Imaging, using Imaging Sensations

➤ *Example 1 (Fragmented Imaging)*

Baseball field...See grass...the dirt around bases...Smell the grass ...air...smell flowers blooming...Standing at home plate...feel real small ...wire mesh...screen behind...See my father, sleeves rolled up, red face ...His face in mine...Smell tobacco breath and sweat...He's angry... Hear him scolding me: "Can't you catch the ball once?...What's the matter with you?"...Feel hurt. "How you gonna be the best ballplayer if you can't catch?"...See the sky...want to run...clouds...hear music from somewhere. "'Cause you gonna be the best. All my children are winners or they must not be mine." Leather glove...smell glove oil...taste bubble gum...Throws ball...got it...His face red and happy...laughing...

163

Throughout the entire Fragmented Imaging process, the actor is responding with all five of his senses. If, for example, he is smelling the flowers, at the same time he is seeing his father and the field, feeling the ground beneath his feet, and hearing the sound of his father's voice and the other noises coming from the environment. Whatever the primary image may be, it is always supported by the other senses.

➢ *Example 2*

From the baseball diamond, the actor might go to another time in his life, perhaps about four years later. Take note that he is purposely emphasizing certain realities that mirror Biff and Willy's relationship in the play.

Table...food...it smells good...potatoes...tablecloth...Hear everyone talking...brother...sister...Dad is talking with his mouth full of food... boasting about his job...laughing...telling everyone how he outsmarted a customer...See his dentures moving...I hope I never need false teeth... Looking at me: "If you want to be popular with your classmates, you have to be nice...You have to be outstanding in some way." Heard it before...Looking at me...disapprovingly...Love him...want to be loved by him...Mom just sitting...not talking...looks sad...Hate that...Dad...still talking: "You're all gonna be special...You'll see...You're a Sullivan... and there ain't been a Sullivan in generations that wasn't special." Hear dishes in kitchen...Bedroom...pennants on the wall...colleges...pictures on dresser...Dad in football uniform...school team...smiling...happy... surrounded by teammates...Tired...want to sleep...looking at ceiling... want him to love me...What to do...confused...What would please him? ...Playing with baseball glove...kneading my fist hard in it...Feels good ...I am good...I'm shy, that's all...Be special in something...What?...

The actor decides on a circumstance and a direction and just allows and encourages all of the images to appear from his memory. The goal, of course, is to be successful enough in creating these images so that he gets a sense of really *being there!*

➢ *Example 3*

In this third example, the actor is attempting, through the use of Fragmented Imaging, to re-create his eighth-grade graduation ceremonies, an event that took place three years after the experience in the preceding section.

Sitting on stage...surrounded by other classmates...Smell the school smell...Polished wooden floors...lights in my eyes...Can't see anyone in the audience...Know my father and mother are there...Hope they are proud...Dressed up...hate the tightness of dress clothes...Feel the collar ...stiff...can't wait to get out of these clothes...I smell perfume...She sprayed it all over my face...I hate it...Hear the principal speaking... Don't care to listen...Can hear my father's cough in the audience... Made me nervous...I'm hearing names being called...Getting nervous... listening for mine...S is way down the alphabet...good...I feel sweat coming down from my temple...There's my name...hear it...Feel like everything just stopped...looking at me...nervous...See my dad—he's beaming...happy to make him proud...Outside now...great weather...My dad's arm around me...talking loud...Everyone turning to see who is talking...embarrassed: "Now off to high school...You'll go out for every-thing, make varsity, and get a college scholarship. I never made it to college. Had to go to work...but, my boy, you're gonna do it!"

Each of these Fragmented Imaging involvements could continue for any length of time, at the actor's discretion. When he should move on to the next experience would depend on how successful he felt with the one he was working on. During the rehearsal period he might cover as many as ten or fifteen specific events involving him and his father. He could repeat any of them as often as he wished. Even though he is using selectively emphasized realities, he might also include some Fantasy Imaging in his exploration.

The three examples given above are brief and serve only as an in-dication of how to use Imaging as a choice approach. The suggested process in all three is Imaging Sensations; however, if the actor had any difficulty in re-creating any of his life experiences, he could use Sense Memory to support the fragmented images that occur.

➢ *Using Sense Memory as the Approach Technique in Example 1*

Baseball field...What do I see directly in front of me?...(Responding with the visual sense.) *How long is this place?...What are the colors I see?...*(The actor encourages the other senses to respond, but the em-phasis is on the response to the specific sensorial question.) *The dirt around the bases...What is the difference between the grass and the dirt?...Color?...texture?...What is the distance between the bases?... Smell the grass...What is that odor like?...*(Olfactory response.) *The air ...what does that feel like on my face?...What is the temperature of the air?...Where do I feel the temperature?...*(Tactile responses.)

All of the senses employed up to this point are still responding to the original sensory questions and are now working together in the hopes of creating the whole reality. At any point, the actor can move into Imaging Sensations, or he may just continue the sensorial queries.

Any of the seven imaging techniques can be utilized to create the choice. If Story Imaging was selected, the actor would image the same experiences as a running story—a flow of events—instead of fragmented pieces.

> ### Using Story Imaging in Example 1

I'm on the baseball field...(The actor is using Imaging Sensations and supporting everything with sensory responses.) I'm looking at the whole field. I see the pitcher holding the ball in his glove...I can see all of the other players in the field...I imagine being in a real game... Suddenly, I see only my father standing on the mound...I feel really small...He is standing very still with a cigar in his mouth looking at me intensely...His sleeves are rolled up and his face is red...He suddenly throws the ball at me...It is coming very fast...I feel afraid and move out of its way...I see him walking towards me—angry...His face is very red ...He comes very close to me...He begins to scold me...I can smell the tobacco on his breath, see the sweat rolling down his face: "Can't you catch the ball once? What's the matter with you?" I look away...I see the sky and the clouds...I want to run away, "You are gonna be the best ...All my children are winners, or they must not be mine." I feel the tears welling up in my eyes...He walks back to the mound, winds up and fires a fast ball at me. I stand still, terrified but frozen in place. I put my glove in front of me, and I feel the thud of the ball as it connects with my glove. His face is red and happy. He shouts a flurry of words that I can't understand, but I know from his response that he is pleased. I smile, as a tear runs into my mouth. If I do well, he will love me!

As usual the imaging technique is selected because it best suits the circumstance. If Story Imaging creates a better connection with his realities, and the events of his life are clearer and have a greater impact on him when he uses that technique, the actor would choose it instead of Fragmented Imaging. The goal is always to create the choice so that one can really experience it—see it, hear it, feel it, smell it, and taste its components.

During the course of creating the background life of his character, the actor will probably use many of the imaging techniques. It is quite unlikely that his life experiences will parallel all of the responsibilities of the material, so he might elect to use Fantasy Imaging to forge elements of the relationship between the character and his father. In that case he would create situations and events that have not really occurred but that are based on his real life. He could use Believability in conjunction with the Fantasy Imaging, mixing truth and reality with fantasy. Whatever he ultimately decides to do, he must be able to create the elements of his choice with Imaging as the choice approach.

There are three other obligations that the actor might have to deal with in a play or film: the HISTORICAL, the THEMATIC, and the SUBTEXTUAL. (There is a complete description of all three in *Irreverent Acting,* starting on page 113.)

The historical obligation refers to when the play takes place, at what time in history. In dealing with this obligation, the actor must address many elements, such as the customs, the mores, the morality, religion, superstitions, and concerns of the people at that time. He must consider what their politics were, as well as their knowledge of medicine or science, and so on. He needs to address all of those realities and can use any of the imaging techniques to do it.

The thematic obligation has to do with what the author is saying in the piece—his statement or message. If the author chooses the character the actor is playing to carry that statement, then it is up to the actor to select choices that would create the elements or the emotions that would promote the behavior manifesting that thematic statement. The same is true for the subtextual obligation also. This obligation refers to the essence of the play, the emotional quality that runs through it. The style and behavior of the characters, expressed either in their words or their actions, promote this underlying quality. If, for example, there is a feeling of hopelessness throughout the play or, on the contrary, it is filled with a quality of hope and joy and a sense of life that makes the audience feel that anything is possible, the actor would have to accommodate those elements in every one of his choices. Here too, Imaging can be extremely productive in creating the quality and underlife of the piece.

Imaging is a fabulous choice approach for many reasons. It is a multifaceted tool embodying seven imaging techniques (with or without fantasy) and two approach techniques, which afford any actor a multitude of options. Whenever you identify an obligation or responsibility, there is a choice from your life that you can use to address it, and Imaging will create that choice very dimensionally. Imaging is also a powerful conduit to the unconscious, as I have said repeatedly. As is true for all the craft work, you must use this process daily in order to master it. Create a daily work schedule, and be sure to include imaging in it.

IMAGING AS A CRAFT TECHNIQUE

A CRAFT TECHNIQUE or approach technique is a choice approach that supplies the practical process for another choice approach that doesn't have one built into it. For example, the choice approach Objects That Come into Contact with the Body does not have an approach technique. In order to create an object that comes into contact with the body, you need a process or approach. If you are working to create a particular piece of clothing that you are wearing, because that piece of clothing affects you or stimulates the kind of impulses that you are after, you need a *craft technique* that will do that. Let us say that I am working to create a tuxedo. The character is not dressed that way in the scene, but in order to feel what I think the character feels, I have selected a tuxedo as my choice, because when I wear one, it makes me feel somewhat rigid and formal, as though I were not really myself. I act and behave differently. So, the *object that comes into contact with my body* is a tuxedo. However, I need a technique to create that tuxedo—in this case perhaps Sense Memory. That is called a *craft technique,* because it is a choice approach used in tandem with another. All of this may sound somewhat confusing, but it is really quite simple. In this example the original choice approach is Objects That Come into Contact with the Body, and the craft technique is Sense Memory, which is the process I use to create the tuxedo.

THE OBLIGATION:	To feel somewhat rigid and formal
THE CHOICE:	A tuxedo
THE CHOICE APPROACH:	Objects That Come into Contact with the Body
THE CRAFT TECHNIQUE:	Sense Memory

I could also use Sensory Suggestion or Imaging as a craft technique here. Once I decided that a tuxedo was a good choice, I would launch into creating a sense of it in relation to my body. In other words, I would create the reality of wearing a tuxedo. How I do that is called *the craft technique.* If I opted to use Imaging instead of Sense Memory, the craft technique would be Imaging. Using Imaging Sensations to create the tuxedo would be another way of making the choice approach work.

Choice Approaches that Need a Craft Technique: Endowments, Objects That Come into Contact with the Body, Externals, Affective Memory, Essences and Abstracts, Illnesses and Restrictions, Personal Realities, Believability, Prior Knowledge, Subpersonalities, and *Selective Enhancement*—all of those choice approaches need a craft technique to make them work, and Imaging can serve with all of them. There are a number of other choice approaches that can be used as craft techniques also. For example, with Prior Knowledge or Personal Realities, the actor can use a variety of Inner Monologues to feed in the information to himself. These can be personal Sharing Monologues or Imaginary Monologues. Believability could be approached by doing Imaginary Dialogues with another actor. It is interesting to note, however, that all of the choice approaches that do not have a built-in approach technique can be made effective through Sense Memory, Sensory Suggestion, or Imaging.

IMAGING AS A CRAFT TECHNIQUE WITH ENDOWMENTS

Endowments as a choice approach is the process of changing the properties of an object so that it either becomes another object or takes on features and elements which make it different from what it was originally. If the actor were working in a scene with another actor and his choice was a person from his life who would stimulate the impulses and relationship feelings demanded by the material, he would *endow* the other actor with the features, personality, behavior, attitudes, sounds, essence, and so on, of the person that he wanted to create. He can usually accomplish this by using Sense Memory to compare and contrast the two people. Starting with the available similarities and then moving into the contrasts, he would progressively sculpt his choice onto the actor with whom he is doing the scene. This can also be achieved by using Imaging as the *craft technique*.

Suppose the actor is working in a scene with an actress to whom he has to be intensely attracted, and in addition, the relationship responsibilities indicate a history of sexual intimacy. Obviously, he does not have such a history with the actress, since he just met her on the soundstage two hours ago, and furthermore, he does not find her particularly attractive. What does he do? Of course, he can explore the Available Stimulus possibilities, but it is unlikely that he would be able to supply a sense of long-lasting intimacy without using imaginary stimuli.

To endow his scene partner with another person through Imaging, the actor might start in the same way as he would if he were going to use a conventional Sense Memory approach—by looking for any similarities that exist between the actress and his personal choice. For the sake of this example, let us say that he is using his own live-in girlfriend. He starts the process by comparing hair and skin coloring, as well as eye shape and color. He may delve into qualities and essences that are similar to his girlfriend's or that remind him of her. This part of the exploration exists as available stimuli, and all he needs to do is look at, see, listen to, and smell the existing components. Once he has exhausted the available stimuli, he can begin to image his girlfriend's features and essence in relation to the actress, thereby *endowing* the latter with all of the properties of the former.

➢ *Example, Using Fragmented Imaging and Imaging Sensations*

Smell her odor...See that little yellow fleck in her right eye...Her nose...(The Fragmented Imaging suggestions are responded to immediately in the sense at which they are aimed, but all the other senses are working simultaneously, responding to the endowments in each sensory area. In other words, when the actor fragmentally suggests the fleck of yellow in her right eye, his olfactory sense is picking up her odors, searching for the smell of her perfume as it mixes with her body chemistry, reaching for unique odors that are only hers. At the same time, his auditory sense is creating the familiar sounds of her voice and of her breath as she exhales.) *Hear her breathing...sound of her clearing her throat...She's smiling...See her lip as it turns up...A peek at her front teeth...the texture of her skin...her cheeks...Can feel her skin next to my face...I feel how it moves against my cheek...The shape of her nostrils...*(All of the imaging responses are related to the actress he is working with. She is slowly and progressively taking on more and more of the features and qualities of his girlfriend.) *I see that look in her eyes when she is getting turned on to me...how the color of her skin changes. I hear her little laugh when she responds to my touch...see the laugh lines around her eyes...the crinkle in her nose...Smell her breath... Smells just like her...See the bulges of her breasts outlining her sweater ...Can see the shape of her body through her clothes...feel the skin texture around her waist...It's different from her cheeks...I can see her face—the way it is when we are making love...Hear the sounds she makes at that time...how she says my name...*(Every sense is supplying its own questions as the endowment process continues.) *The way her eyes look that tells me she loves me...the taste of her skin on my lips...*

tongue...the movement of her head...body...her unique rhythms as she moves different parts of her body...her eyes...how they look when she is hurt...how the tears form in the corners...that glint in her eyes when she gets excited...

The imaging can last as long as it is necessary for the actor to truly get a sense of his girlfriend in relation to the actress with whom he is doing the scene. As in any Endowments involvement, the two people become a "conglomerate"—which means that, while he is getting a very strong sense of his girlfriend, the actor must respond to what the *actress* is doing or saying and how she is behaving. It is as if everything that is really happening on the stage were coming from his girlfriend or her very strong essence. He actually begins to feel towards the actress the way he feels towards his girlfriend. The two women blend into one.

The actors could also opt to use other choice approaches in tandem with Endowments and Imaging. For example, they could decide to do an improvisation, using Imaginary Dialogues and Believability. The improvisation could start with a situation parallel to that of the written material.

➢ *Believability and Imaginary Dialogues Example*

He: I know things are bad, but why do you blame me for the condition of the economy?

(The dialogue almost literally parallels that of the scene and relates to a conversation the actor really had with his live-in girlfriend. It will have some truth mixed in with a lot of untruth, thereby becoming a Believability improvisation. The fact that both actors are talking to other people in relation to each other means that they are also using Imaginary Dialogues—another choice approach—as a craft technique. At all times, both actors are using Imaging with Endowments to see and hear the persons they are attempting to create.)

She: Well...you could do something...I mean, find another job maybe! (All the while she is using all four approach techniques: Imaginary Dialogues, Believability, Endowments, and Imaging.)

He: Oh yeah? And where else could I have this kind of earning potential? (He continues to image the features, behavior and attitude of his girlfriend, to create the sound of her voice and her vocal patterns.)

She: (Creatively manipulating the Imaginary Dialogue and the Believability into the parallel areas.) Potential? Does potential pay the rent?...The fact is that you aren't earning anything at the moment!

(The imaging process can include the place and the time of the real experiences as well as the various behaviors of the imaginary people involved.)

He: You know that times are bad now...It's going to pick up...and we have to get through this period, you know?

She: No, I don't know!...I see other people taking some kind of positive action instead of sitting around and waiting for things to change!

The above example actually employs four approach techniques all in tandem with each other. The dialogue is an improvisation using Believability, which is the process of combining a little truth or reality with a great deal of untruth or fantasy. The craft technique used is Imaginary Dialogues, which means that the two actors are talking to their choices (his girlfriend and her boyfriend respectively) in relation to each other. The second choice approach is Endowments, which means that the actors are *endowing* each other with their respective choices. The craft technique is Imaging, which they use to actually create the imaginary choices in relation to each other. This last approach not only encourages them to see, hear, feel, taste, and smell the persons they are creating, but it also supports the Believability and Imaginary Dialogues. It seems a bit complex, and a lot of work; however, it really is much simpler than it sounds. Each of the approaches meshes with the others, so it is like doing a single task. Of course, as shown above, this scene could be approached simply by creating the person in relation to the other actor.

IMAGING AS A CRAFT TECHNIQUE
WITH AFFECTIVE MEMORY

When using Imaging as a craft technique related to Affective Memory, the process must be somewhat more detailed and specific. Ordinarily, Sense Memory is used as the approach technique to trigger an Affective Memory experience. To effectively execute Affective Memory, an actor must have a substantial knowledge, and even mastery, of the Sense Memory process.

To begin with, Affective Memory is the technique of re-creating a complete experience, from before it actually occurred, up to and including the important or impacting part. The goal is to consciously supply enough of the specific elements of the experience to pique unconscious responses and actually relive the event as it originally happened. In order for the actor to reach these unconscious responses, every detail of the experience must be specific, accurate, and real for him. If he decides to use Imaging as the craft technique to create an Affective Memory experience, he must be very specific and chronological in his approach to the re-creation of the original event. I would suggest that he use Story Imaging and a combination of both imaging approach techniques—Sense Memory and Imaging Sensations. It would be advisable to start the imaging process using Sense Memory and later sneak into Imaging Sensations.

➤ *Example*

For this example, I am going to use an early acting experience I had. When I look back on it, I find it quite humorous, but at the time it was traumatic and devastating, and it took me years to get over it. I was hired to play a young criminal in the teaser for a television show called *The Court of Last Resort*. It went like this: The character goes into a grocery store and tries to hold it up; the owner reaches for a gun, whereupon our young criminal shoots both him and his wife. In the very next scene (still in the teaser), my character is seen being led into a prison cell; he turns to the guard and defiantly spits at him. Originally, my part had no lines, but the director later added one, as you will see. The director was a foreigner, who had some difficulty with the English language—not to mention a lack of talent and of sensitivity towards actors. To say the least, everything that could go wrong on that set did— and maybe a few other things besides! Since it was only my second film-acting job, I was understandably tense. This was compounded a hundred times by having a director who was impatient and lacked communication skills. To make a long story shorter, let me say that we did about eleven takes on the robbery part alone!

My instructions were to enter the store, look around, see the woman behind the counter, who asks if she can help me, then take the gun out of my pocket—making it obvious that I am holding up the store and not looking for a gunsmith, right? No, wrong! O.K., we are ready for the first take. I hear, "Action!" walk onto the set, and begin to look around the store—when I hear "Cut!" The director comes onto the set and in a very thick German accent says, "No, no, you don't make vit de eyess. You moofe di head," at which point he selects places on the set I should look at—a post and, about fifteen feet to the right, a coffee can. Very creative, wouldn't you say? At this point my heart is beating very rapidly, and I want to do it right. "Take two! Action!" I enter the store, mechanically look at the post, turn my head, look at the coffee can, and proceed toward the counter. The woman says her line, I reach into my pocket, draw the revolver, and—I hear a screaming, "Cut!" Again, the director walks onto the set with glaring accusation shooting at me from his beady eyes: "How she knows you make holt up if you don't say it?" I helplessly shrugged and said, "But I don't have any lines here!" He shook his head at me, behaving as if I were retarded, and exclaimed: "I giff you lines. You make vit de gun and you say, 'Up, up!'" I looked at him, terrified to say what I was thinking, which was, Up, Up? Why not, "This is a stickup!" or "This is a holdup! Don't move!" or something that sounds vaguely American?

"Take three!" While I was offstage waiting for take three, I noticed that the pocket of the suit jacket I was wearing—circa the 1930s, which is when this scene was supposedly taking place—had a very small opening and that I had been given a very large revolver, which I knew I would have trouble easily retrieving from that pocket. So to avoid any mishaps—such as the hammer snagging on the opening of the pocket—I held the gun completely out of sight but near that opening, with my thumb over the serration of the hammer. "Action!" loudly from the other side of the stage. I enter, look around—at this point seeing nothing, too tense to see anything—look from point to point, walk towards the counter, and hear a bloodcurdling scream: "Cut, cut, cut!" I freeze in place. He saunters onto the stage, spewing a stream of words that sound more like a German machine gun than like language: "Vit de hant in de pocket ve know you go to make schtickup! Take out de hant from de pocket!" At this point, I had to speak up and tell him what the problem was—so I did; I showed him the size of the gun and the opening of the pocket, and I even showed him what happened when I tried to take the gun out of the pocket. Surely enough, it caught and pulled the jacket up but didn't come out. Not satisfied with this, he tried it a couple of times himself, and the same thing happened. At this point, he was performing for the entire crew. With an impatient, long-suffering, indulgent moan, he screamed, "Costumes! Ver is de costume purson?" Very quickly a little munchkin woman, whom you would definitely cast in the part of a costume mistress, appeared in front of me. I showed her the problem, and she proceeded to rip out the lining of the pocket, leaving the opening exactly the way it had always been! Knowing that that would not solve the problem, but too scared to say anything, I readied myself for take four. The bell rang, I heard the assistant director yell, "Quiet on the set!" I heard the cameraman say "Speed!"—and there it was, a very loud "Action!" I entered, looked at my two points, walked toward the counter, reached in for the gun, and...it wasn't there! Without a pocket, it had slid into the lining of the jacket and found a resting place in the middle of my back! Not knowing where it was or what to do, I quickly felt around the lining looking for it, and because I had to stick my arm down into the lining, going towards my back, I must have looked like a deformed contortionist doing his thing! "Cut! Cut! Got in Himmel, vat is dis?" I heard all of that before I saw him, red faced and angry, enter the set. "Vat now? Vat is da matter? You can't take a gun frum out de pocket?" I did my best to explain what had happened and even showed him my plight, but he was unimpressed. All he could do was glare at me and share his burden with looks to the crew. "Take out frum de pocket de gun and put in de belt!" I did it. Unfortunately, the waistband was three or four sizes too big, which is why the trousers were being held up by suspenders; nonetheless, I took my position for take five. "Action!" I entered like a robot. With glazed eyes, I pointed my head in the direction of the first point, then the second, walked mechanically towards the counter, and, as if from the end of a long tunnel, heard some sound like that of a woman's voice—at which point I reached for the butt of the gun, which promptly slid down my right pants leg, hit my shoe, and slithered across the stage like a snake! I just looked at it for what seemed like two hours, when the director slowly walked over to it, picked it up, and brought it to me. Not a word was said, but his attitude was enough to humiliate a rock! I knew I had to think quickly. How was I going to keep that gun in my waistband? As I was walking offstage to my start position, it came to me: I would extend my stomach, pushing it hard against the gun, hopefully holding the weapon between my distended belly and the waistband. At this point, it didn't matter to me that I looked nine-months pregnant! All that was important was getting this nightmare over with! By God, I was ready for take six and resolved to do it this time. The bell, "Action!"—I was out there. It was all happening as if in some slow-motion dream. I found myself in front of the counter, heard my cue, reached past my bloated belly, grabbed the butt of the gun, and with one aggressive upward movement, jerked it out of the waistband, trapping the bottom of my necktie between the butt of the gun and the heel of my hand, at which point the tie flew into my face, causing me to respond as a punch-drunk sparring partner would to two sharp jabs to his nose! At this point, hearing him scream "Cut!" was anticlimactic! We did two more takes, and finally I heard the golden word: "Print!" I was exhausted—but it

175

wasn't over yet! On the close-up of me shooting the storeowner, the director told me he would give me the cue when to pull the trigger. There I am, standing in my tape marks, hear "Action," ready myself for his cue—and what do I hear? "No!" So standing offstage, I look at him, not knowing why he said no, when he screams:

"Why didn't you shoot?"

"You mean 'No' was the cue?"

"Ya, dat's right! No!"

We did it on the next take...The second part of the teaser—when I was being led to my cell—went off without a hitch, but as I was leaving the set, I heard the boom man mutter almost inaudibly, "Keep your day job, kid!" To say the least, I was devastated, humiliated. My confidence was shattered, and for years after that my tension level was at a peak at the beginning of every film I did.

I thought it necessary to describe the entire experience so that the reader would get a complete understanding of it—what had happened, how it had affected me, and how, if I re-created it as an Affective Memory experience, it could take me back to that time in my life and stimulate those feelings. For several years after it had happened, when I retold the story, people would laugh and even howl at it. I could never understand why they thought it was funny, when I had felt so violated and damaged by the incident.

To approach this as an Affective Memory experience, I choose to start with my arrival on the set, getting into costume and makeup and dealing with all the activity, sounds, and odors of a soundstage grinding up to go into action. Since I was forty years younger then, I will start with the way I looked and felt at that time. All exploration in an Affective Memory process is done in the here and now. All images and sensory questions are framed in the present.

➤ *Affective Memory Example*

I'm getting out of my car...I'm on the studio lot...I feel the anxiety beginning to creep into my stomach...What do I see ahead of me?... (Respond in sensory images.) *How far away is the door to the soundstage?...What is the temperature?...Where on my body...face...do I feel that?...Looking at my reflection in the window of my car, what do I see? ...*(I would have to see myself as I looked forty years ago!) *As my feet hit the pavement on my way to the soundstage, what do I feel in my feet? ...legs?...Can I identify the areas of my tension?...Where are they?... How do they move around?...Reaching for the door handle—what does it look like?...color?...material?...As I grasp it, what do I feel?...Where in my hand do I feel that?...What is its temperature?...As I enter the stage, what is the first thing I see?...How many people do I see?...Who are they?...What do they look like?...How are they dressed?...*(I must deal with each one of them, encouraging all my senses to work simultaneously.) *What do I hear?...How many sounds can I identify?...Where are they coming from?...What are the odors?...How many can I identify?...How do I feel?...Where do I feel my responses?...I'm standing on this stage and feel frozen in place...As I look around, what else do I see?...What do those flats look like?...What are their colors?...shapes? ...Someone is approaching me. What does she look like?...How tall is she?...How is she dressed?...What is the shape of her face?...Her eyes? ...color?...How old does she look?...*(etc.) *She begins to speak to me... What do I hear?...How is her mouth moving?...What is she saying?... What is the sound of her voice?...Do I hear it?...She says my name: "Are you...?" I hear that!..."Yes." I am responding...Feel the tension elevating in my body...What does that feel like, and where do I feel the changes?...*(Everything is taking place in imaging terms. I am experiencing a hundred times more sensory responses than I can list here on paper.) *She is the makeup lady, and she leads me to the makeup table... As I sit down, what does the stool feel like?...What do I see in front of me?...How many different objects are there on the table?...As I look into the mirror, what do I see?...How do I look?...What is the shape of my face?...color of my eyes?...shape of my nose?...Can I see how I feel?...Where do I see that?...What do I hear?...What are the sounds around me?...*

(At this point I might stop asking questions and begin the Imaging Sensations.) *Smell coffee...Feel the cold of the sponge on my cheek...I feel a shiver run up my body...I hear people yelling on the other side of the stage...I feel like I have to go to the toilet...I see my expressions change as I look in the mirror...smell her perfume...I feel the warmth of her breath as she applies the makeup to my face...see her hand flashing past my eyes...and hear the dulled sound of the insulated soundstage... Everything seems to have a muffled quality...Looking at the clock...feel anxious about working...feel scared...I see the director in the reflection of the makeup mirror...He doesn't know that I see him...He's looking at me...strange expression on his face...Maybe I'm imagining that...I feel frightened...I feel the texture of my sweater...That somehow feels reassuring...I taste the mouthwash I used this morning...I hear a bell from the other side of the soundstage...I am wondering if they're already shooting a scene...I feel a combination of fear and excitement...*

As you can see, this example could continue for thirty or forty pages if it were documented specifically. When doing Affective Memory, you must address almost everything in chronological order, everything that leads up to the experience you are attempting to relive. It is impossible to list all of the sensorial responses in the example, but I hope that you will get the idea. If I were to really do this Affective Memory, using Imaging, and to be specific in all of the sensory areas and address all of the component parts of the event, it might take me a couple of hours or more. However, as I repeatedly practiced it, I would ultimately be able to shorten the time down to just a couple of minutes. If I wanted to experience the frustration, the fear, and the devastating humiliation I felt at that time, I could use this experience, and if successful in re-creating its reality, I should be able to get the entire impact of being in that place at that time. Doing Affective Memory successfully depends on a variety of factors: being enough of a craftsman to use Sense Memory and Imaging Sensations with experience and facility, remembering enough of the components of the experience to be able to re-create it, being patient and specific and taking nothing for granted. If I were to leave out important elements or parts of the experience, I could very likely fail to re-experience it as if I were really there.

EXPLORING IMAGING WITH OTHER APPROACHES

Recently, two actors in my advanced class were working on a scene from Clifford Odets' play, *Waiting for Lefty*. For a number of weeks they attempted to address and fulfill the relationship elements. I worked very closely with both of them as they experimented with a number of choices and approaches. A large part of their exploration involved imaging. That is why I have decided to use it as an example in this section.

This is a depression play, which was written in the thirties and first performed by the Group Theater. It was well received at the time because it addressed many of the issues and concerns of the people. Unionism was relatively young then, and the unions were becoming the champions of the workers' rights. The conflict between them and "the establishment"—the corporations and companies that objected to and fought the rise and power of the unions—constitutes the underpinning of this and other plays of this type in that period. The play is laced with socialistic philosophy, which attacks the establishment and accuses "the big boys" of exploiting the working class (Clifford Odets was later investigated by the House Un-American Activities Committee for his Communist leanings). It comprises a number of scenes depicting the struggle of the people in the midst of a crippling depression. These scenes, which are somewhat separate from the main action of the play and are complete in themselves, are all brought together by the threads of each character's involvement in ultimately deciding to strike for better wages and working conditions.

The scene we will be exploring is the "Joe and Edna" section of the play. I chose it because it is extremely rich in relationship elements. Even though the play is dated and the dialogue antiquated, these relationship conflicts are timeless.

The action starts as Joe comes home to an empty apartment. He is a taxi driver, who works for a large company and is having a very difficult time earning enough even to pay his rent. He enters, sees that the room is virtually empty, and asks, "What happened to the furniture, honey?" Edna, his wife of five years, tells him that it has been repossessed because he has not been making the payments. Obviously angry, depressed, and feeling helpless, she then launches into a critical attack on him. She denigrates him for being in this place and not doing anything about it. The conflict continues with Joe's feeble attempt at defending himself by blaming the depression for all their woes. Edna informs him that their "two blondie kids" asleep in the next room are hungry and get colds one after another. The argument grows more passionate as her emasculation of him intensifies. She suggests that all the cab drivers go on strike for better wages, which he initially rejects as fruitless. She continues to humiliate and badger him and even threatens to leave him for her old boyfriend, "who makes a living," until he capitulates and is energetically catapulted into some kind of action to change the situation. He tells her that he is going uptown to talk to some guy in the union "that was just the other day saying..." They kiss and make up, and he leaves.

Essentially that is the action of the scene. There are quite a number of relationship responsibilities for the actors to address:

- A five-year relationship, which seemingly started out with a great deal of love and respect and has now disintegrated into blame, resentment, and disrespect; the history of five years of going to bed and waking up together, of eating and laughing and experiencing the conception and birth of two children, of knowing each other's likes and dislikes, and so on—all the life that is shared between two people in five years.

- The helplessness that they both feel in their inability to communicate or to change the situation; for Edna the frustration of not being able to motivate Joe into taking some kind of action.
- Joe's feelings of helplessness and the self-flagellation that results from his feeling unable to fulfill the "male provider" role.
- The mutual fear of losing each other and the children, and the guilt produced by feeling inadequate in providing for dependent and helpless youngsters for whom they are responsible.
- The desperate need to look for and find a shred of hope in each other, and the frustrations that come from the impasse in which they find themselves.
- The oppressive atmosphere of the times and the environment.
- The impact of the time and place on the relationship (having so little and having to struggle to survive are realities that have a strong impact on the erosion of the relationship).
- Edna's resolve to do something drastic to wake Joe up!

These component elements are what the actors must address as their responsibilities to this piece in the area of the relationship obligations. Once these are identified and defined, the actors can embark on their mutual journey of exploring the choices they will experiment with. As in any exploration leading to the fulfillment of the obligations of a piece of material, certain choices will take care of some of the responsibilities, while others will address different ones. Finding the right choice is usually a complex exploration of one's life experiences. In the case of these two actors, Shaun and Priscilla, I suggested that they start with an Available Stimulus exploration of each other. They began by attempting to find out how they really felt about each other and what they could use for the scene as a result of their discoveries. The obvious truth when deciding to use Available Stimulus is that it is almost impossible to reach the depth and complexity of the relationship in the material when, as here, the actors do not have much more than a classroom relationship with each other. However, by starting with what is available, they begin to include each other in the exploration of the relationship responsibilities; they become meaningfully involved with each other and avoid falling into the trap of using each other only as "armatures" on which to create their choices.

Proceeding with the Available Stimulus exploration, both actors might opt to add Selective Emphasis to their journey and creatively manipulate the available realities to include more of the issues found in the material. They thus have an opportunity to lead the relationship closer to the dynamics of the scene. Selective Emphasis is the process of looking for and emphasizing things about the other actor that might make you feel about him or her the way your character feels about the other one in the scene. For example, Shaun might look at Priscilla and selectively emphasize any critical things he sees in her eyes or hears in her voice—critical about him. He could selectively emphasize her lack of attention to him as blatant evidence of rejection. She, in turn, might interpret his smiles and levity as a lack of commitment to their work together. Other choice approaches that work in tandem with Available Stimulus might be added to further the relationship involvement. By starting this way, the actors are better prepared to look for a choice from their own personal life. First of all, they have created an involvement with each other, and secondly, they now have some of the same feelings as the characters do for each other.

In this scenario, both actors decided to use prior relationships as their choices for the scene. I am not sure how or where they started to create the parallel realities, but they did isolate particular experiences that matched the action of the material. Over a period of weeks, both of them tried a number of different choice approaches, such as Imaginary Dialogues, Sense Memory (to create time and place), Believability, Sensory Endowments, Inner Imaginary Monologues, and so on. Some of these choice approaches were supported by the use of Imaging. I suggested that each of them try Fantasy with either Story or Fragmented Imaging to attempt, at various times in their rehearsals, to image themselves in this situation together. The use of Fantasy Imaging is a strong addendum to Available Stimulus. I believe that it was then suggested by one of us that they approach the scene using Imaging as the craft technique for a complete Affective Memory exploration of the various events and experiences they had shared with their respective choices which could lead to parallels to the situation in *Waiting for Lefty*. They launched into working separately to create those experiences—not necessarily in any chronological order—through Affective Memory, using Imaging as their approach technique. Having already experimented with Fantasy Imaging, they could now use Imaging in relation to another MEGAPPROACH—Affective Memory! Since Shaun and Priscilla did their work silently and I was not privy to the specifics of their individual processes, I will create a hypothetical example.

➢ *Affective Memory, Using Imaging as the Approach*

(Keep in mind that this is an imaginary parallel to the circumstances of the play.) The actor starts with the conventional sensorial approach, asking sensory questions and responding directly with the sense involved. At this point, there is no difference between Imaging and the conventional Sense Memory approach. As the exercise continues, the actor begins to image on many levels at the same time, and the imaging process outdistances the conventional sensory question-and-answer approach. In effect, the actor's instrument is responding with all five of his senses at once. Usually, it is at this point that the conventional process of Sense Memory ceases and Imaging Sensations takes over.

Where am I standing?...(Visual response.) What does this place look like from here?...What does the room look like?...What's missing?... What does that space look like now?...The carpet—is it different from the rest of the floor?...(All of these responses are visual, but the actor must always allow for the possibility of other senses to respond simultaneously. Without asking an olfactory question, for example, he might experience the unique and specific odor of the place.) *What sounds do I hear?...Where are they coming from?...How many sounds are there? ...What is creating those sounds?...*(The actor could stay with this sense for a dozen or more questions before going on to the next sense.) *Who else is in the room?...Where is she?...How far away is she from where I'm standing?...How does she look?...What is the color of her hair?... Can I see the color of her eyes from here?...What is the expression on her face?...What is it that tells me that something is wrong?...What is the attitude of her body?...body language?...Where is the light in the room coming from?...Are there shadows?...Where are the shadows?... Are there any parts of the room that are too dark to see?...What do I feel in my body?...Where is that tension?...What does it feel like?... Does it move around?...Where do I feel it now?...Can I feel the ambience in here?...With which senses do I experience the feeling of this room?...As she gets up and begins to cross towards me, what changes do I see in her body?...her face?...movement?...How is she moving her arms?...hands?...*

For the sake of brevity I will stop here, but I encourage you, the reader, to supply other questions. Imagine that in each area the actor might ask ten or twenty more. At that very point when he begins to image with all of his senses, the questions can stop, and the rest of the technique will be done by the instrument. From here, he sees her approaching him and hears her clear her throat as she prepares to speak;

182

he notices the pictures hanging on the wall in front of him, and he feels like retreating...She begins her tirade of criticism, and he can smell her perfume at this distance. He feels the palms of his hands beginning to perspire...Her voice has a shrill accusatory sound that he is familiar with...He listens to the onslaught of her razorlike indictments and feels his own anger, as it rises from his abdomen into his chest. His body begins to shake as a gigantic bellow comes out of his mouth, the sound seeming to come from a distance down a long tunnel and exploding in this place. It is difficult to determine whether it was accompanied by any words. Everything in the room now seems blurred, except her vivid presence, which seems to have become brighter and more radiant...

All of those images occur automatically in most or all of his senses. The Affective Memory experience unfolds and goes to its conclusion. The actor might repeat this process a number of times during the rehearsals of this scene. Each time he does the scene, it should take less time for the experience to become real. Ultimately he should be able to start the written scene at the beginning of the imaging, and the Affective Memory will unfold as the scene progresses.

After the actors had done a fairly complete Available Stimulus exploration, we all thought that exploring the "choice" relationship would create and dimensionalize their feelings about each other. It had not been decided that Affective Memory would actually be one of the choice approaches they would end up using. What actually happened was that their explorations gave them more information about their choices. It brought into focus the physical and emotional components that they could later use in their imaging.

To this point in their rehearsal process they had used: Available Stimulus, Endowments with Sense Memory and Imaging, Imaginary Dialogues (talking to their respective choices in relation to each other), Inner and Outer Imaginary Monologues, Believability, and Fantasy Story Imaging, which was used to create imaginary parallels to the material—experiences and events that would mirror those of the characters in the scene. This type of exploration is usually confined to the rehearsal process, where the actors have the time and freedom to experiment and explore with the permission to be irreverent to the fulfillment of the material. When they arrive at their final choices and have decided which choice approaches are the most accurate and expedient for those choices, they will confine themselves to those selections.

In the case of Shaun and Priscilla, the final decision came out of what they had discovered during the many weeks of rehearsal. Having dimensionalized their own relationship by exploring each other in available areas, they had already reached many of the impulses and feelings that Joe and Edna experience toward each other. What they could not achieve in their repetitious exploration of each other was the five-year history and the intimacy that Joe and Edna share. For this responsibility they turned to Affective Memory, which they repeated a number of times using Imaging as the *craft technique*. They finally decided to use their own parallel relationships with their real-life partners as their choices and limited their choice approach to Endowments, with Imaging as the approach technique for creating their choices "on" each other. Where there weren't exact or usable parallels, they employed Believability, promoted by imaging their choices saying or doing things that they hadn't really said or done in reality—although those choices were amazingly close to the realities of the material for both of them.

Let us note that, throughout the rehearsal period, Priscilla and Shaun emphasized the use of Imaging and that they tried many of the techniques—*Fragmented Imaging* while exploring the Endowment process, *Story Imaging* at various times when using Affective Memory, and *Fantasy Story Imaging* when paralleling the circumstances of the piece. Whenever an actor is using an event as a choice to promote the emotional life of a scene, he will often experience a stream of images related to the experience that is being created. This *Involuntary Imaging* can also be used in a structured approach later in the rehearsal or performance. Both of these actors did experience many involuntary images during the rehearsal period, and they were able to convert some of them into structured choices. At times, one or both of them verbalized their images, thereby also including *Verbalized Imaging* in their rehearsal experience. It isn't often that an actor gets the opportunity to apply as many imaging techniques as these two did, but when that is possible, it is a rich and rewarding experience. The approach process was Imaging with Sense Memory, as well as Imaging Sensations.

For Joe (Shaun)

THE OBLIGATION: (Relationship)	His feelings for his wife of five years: he loves her, feels inadequate, experiences conflict, lack of communication, an inability to make her understand, frustration and anger with her. He also has the impelling desire to solve the problems.

THE CHOICE: A former girlfriend with whom he had lived for eight years—parallels in that relationship.

THE CHOICE APPROACH: Endowments, with some Believability created through the use of Imaging as the craft technique.

For Edna (Priscilla)

THE OBLIGATION: Her feelings for her husband of five years: intense frustration and a sense of helplessness. She feels at the end of the road, desperate, but resolved to change things.

THE CHOICE: A person and a former relationship with many similar parallels (Priscilla's relationship was shorter term).

THE CHOICE APPROACH: Endowments, also with the use of Believability, and Imaging as the craft technique.

Each of the actors also created a place from his or her own life experience, which stimulated feelings similar to those of the characters in their empty apartment. Both of the actors' places also came from a difficult period in their lives when times were hard. By creating this environment, they put themselves in a pre-preparatory state that lent itself to their choices. Both Shaun and Priscilla started every rehearsal by working for their respective places, using Imaging as their choice approach.

By now you must understand that imaging can serve for a large variety of purposes. There are many built-in options concerning its use as an acting tool: It can be employed as a choice approach to create any kind of object, place, event, relationship, or experience, as a preparation to get ready to act, or as an interim preparation to take you closer to the desired emotional state. You may use any of the seven imaging techniques to address any obligation, selecting the most expedient one to do the job. Imaging can also serve as a craft technique helping you to pragmatize another choice approach. In short, when you use imaging for acting purposes, you will find it to be a multifaceted tool in your acting toolbox!

CHAPTER 6

IMAGING AND SUBPERSONALITIES

A REPRISE ON SUBPERSONALITIES

Subpersonalities is yet another choice approach that can be used in conjunction with Imaging. I am devoting an entire chapter to it because it is such an important MEGAPPROACH, as well as the twenty-first choice approach in my system. There is a section in *Irreverent Acting* that explains what subpersonalities are, how they function in our lives, and how they are used as acting tools.

The originator of the concept was C.G. Jung, who put forth the theory of the *archetypes*, which we all have in common as facets of our collective unconscious. His identification of these archetypes, or energy patterns, explained many things in psychological and behavioral terms. He felt that a person under the control of any of these entities behaved and functioned with the energy of that particular archetype. Without awareness of this phenomenon an individual could spend his entire life being ruled by one or two of these entities and, in essence, would have no control over his own life beyond the desires of these "beings."

My first exposure to subpersonalities came quite by accident, over fifteen years ago, when I was recommended to a therapist, Dr. Hal Stone. He and his wife, Sidra, had put forth the concept of *subpersonalities,* based on Jung's archetypes, and were doing work using a technique they had innovated, called *voice dialogue.* This is a two-person process involving a facilitator and the person being facilitated. The facilitator starts by asking to speak with one of the various subpersonalities, and the subject attempts to get in touch with that part or energy by moving into an area which he feels it inhabits (later I will give a detailed example of how this is done). The facilitator then speaks to each of these various parts and in doing so, helps the subject to create an AWARE EGO. The theory is that, once the subject becomes aware of a particular "self," from then on the aware ego, who knows that it exists, can gather information on how it functions in his life. With repetition the subject becomes more and more knowledgeable about how his various selves relate to the world and how he may get stuck in a particular pattern of behavior, which deprives him of experiencing all of those selves. The goal is to attain balance and to be able to EMBRACE ALL OF ONE'S SELVES!

When I first met them, Hal and Sidra, who are both psychologists with Ph.D.'s, were using voice dialogue as a form of therapy. Two years ago, when I took a five-day workshop from them at their home in Mendecino, I realized, however, that their process had evolved and been modified a great deal! They now believe that working with subpersonalities serves to expand consciousness, elevate awareness, and understand the dynamics of how the various selves function in our lives; but they no longer seem to consider it psychotherapy and frequently say that if someone you are facilitating needs therapy, you should make a referral! Hal and Sidra have written a number of books on the subject—*Embracing Ourselves, Embracing Each Other, Embracing the World,* and *Embracing the Inner Critic,* to name a few. For further reference, and to go deeper into the exploration of subpersonality work, you can explore their books and tapes.

Of course, my focus is acting—how this approach is related to acting and how you can use it as a CHOICE APPROACH. However, before we can translate it into that area, we must first have an understanding of the theory and concept of the various selves and of how they function, of the evolution of awareness (meeting the selves and establishing an aware ego), and, most important, of the various techniques for accessing these subparts—bringing them to the forefront and using them to do our acting! Among the various techniques for accessing our selves is *Imaging*. I have created a four-part imaging approach for eliciting the various subpersonalities, which will be explored in great detail later in the chapter.

THE THEORY: WHO ARE THE SELVES, HOW WHERE THEY CREATED AND HOW DO THEY FUNCTION?

From the very moment we become conscious as newborn infants, the process begins! Our PRIMARY SELVES or subparts are created to protect the VULNERABLE CHILD from the consequences of life. They are the subpersonalities—or *selves*, as they are called—which in the very beginning appeal to our parents or caretakers and receive approval. As we grow older and our sphere of relationships expands, we become aware of what behavior is acceptable and which is not. Thus, the creation of the primary selves continues on into adolescence and often beyond. These consist of such energies as the PROTECTOR, the part of us that runs interference and protects us from harm and from doing the wrong thing, and the CONTROLLER, the part that calls the shots and comes into action to take control of our behavior when it feels there is danger or negative consequences. These two often work together, as we move into one and then the other. There is also the PLEASER, a subpart whose entire energy is devoted to doing the right thing and pleasing everyone. We have all known or experienced people who always seem to be concerned with pleasing and getting acceptance and approval. The PUSHER is another of the primary selves, one whose entire energy is devoted to *pushing* us to work, accomplish, achieve, and so on. This is the one that whispers in our ear to "get out of bed" in the morning and "get to work" and reminds us constantly of all the chores that need to be done!

Next comes the INNER CRITIC, a part of us that is always critiquing us, that tells us that our performance isn't good enough or that we need to do more to accomplish our goals. It often teams up with the pusher, who pushes us to achieve while the critic stands in the wings criticizing our efforts. The inner critic is a very powerful subpersonality and very necessary to our life, as all of our selves are! But if it seizes control, gets into "the driver's seat," and refuses to relinquish its hold, our life can become a living torment!

Another part, the MIND, or intellect, is the one who thinks and evaluates things. Its emphasis is on intelligence; it puts a premium on knowledge and the use of the brain to accomplish our goals. Then comes the ACHIEVER, who is totally involved with accomplishment. Its energy is active only in areas of achieving. If this one takes over, a person can become blind with ambition and allow no room for anything else. Finally, the WORKAHOLIC is the energy that dedicates its owner to working constantly, thrives on working, and sees little else in life except work!

As I said earlier, the primary selves are created to gain acceptance and approval, so some of them exist only in certain people, since which ones get formed depends on the environment a child grows up in and on the influence of the people in his life. If, for example, someone is part of a very religious or pious family, he will most likely develop a MORALIST subpart, better known as the MARTIN LUTHER subpersonality. There are other selves that can make up the primary-selves cluster, such as the perfectionist or the conciliator; however, those I have listed are the most common.

For every primary self you identify and become familiar with, there is an equal and opposite energy or subpart! So one of the opposites of the controlling parts listed above might be the easygoing, permissive part that goes the way the wind blows and is the opposite of protecting and controlling. You have experienced people in that energy. They are kind of kicked back and very allowing and accepting of everything that goes on around them. It is almost like the entire sixties generation was infected by that virus. They were all inhabited by that subpart! The pusher's opposite is the beach bum, the part that likes to do nothing but vegetate and loaf. The opposite energy to the responsible self, of course, is the irresponsible self! The opposite of the pleaser is the part that is self-involved and doesn't care what anyone thinks about him! It is a fairly antisocial energy. These opposite energies are pushed into the background by the primary selves, because they pose a threat to the security of the individual. In some cases they even threaten the vulnerable child and some of the other child archetypes. If an opposite self is too threatening and even considered dangerous by the primary selves, it becomes a DISOWNED SELF and is *pushed way back into the unconscious.* The more threatening it is to the primary selves, the deeper it goes into the unconscious. Disowned selves have a need to be heard and recognized, however, and if that isn't done, they can become malevolent and dangerous. The deeper a disowned self is consigned to the unconscious, the harder it is to access consciously. If it is left there for too long, it will retaliate through the unconscious by creating issues, problems, and self-sabotage.

The disowned subpersonalities come to us in our dreams. They reach out for recognition and speak to us while we sleep, asking to be heard—which is another very important reason for us to pay attention to our dreams! Some of the selves are less dangerous than others, so they are more accessible through voice dialogue and other techniques.

Examples of opposite and disowned selves are some of the child archetypes—such as the magical child, the mischievous child (its counterpart, the obedient child can exist as one of the primary selves), the vulnerable child, and the frightened child—as well as the warrior, the killer, Aphrodite (the female sexual energy) or Don Juan—its male counterpart—the satanic or demonic energies, the dictator, the beach bum, the needy ones, and a variety of others. Once you have identified the primary-self structure, you can pretty much expect that you will find its opposites in the disowned regions. Voice dialogue and some of the other techniques help you to communicate with the various selves and to liberate them, to create an aware ego, expand your consciousness and become cognizant of the forces that affect your life. Once you have established an awareness of these selves and their dynamics, they can no longer take control of your life. The aware ego sits between them and can hold them in balance, asking any one of them to relinquish its position and give way to another. It can raise or lower the energy of any of the selves and objectively relate to and include all of them.

The actor must become familiar with his instrument and with the mechanics of subpersonality work, and he should identify the primary-self and disowned-self structures. He must understand the dynamics of how they function as well as the "dances" they get into with other people. He can achieve this by doing voice dialogue or working with some of the other techniques involved, such as paying attention to his dreams or keeping a dream journal and identifying the voices of his disowned selves as they plead for attention and recognition. Quite often it is in our dreams that these disowned selves find their only means of expression. Immediately upon awakening, before you lose the dream, ask questions about who were the ones in it, what they were doing and what they said to you or to anyone else. You might even try some *active imagination* with the figures in the dream, as I will explain in the next chapter. This is an excellent way of identifying disowned selves and learning about them and what they want.

A number of years ago, while I was in a workshop with Hal Stone, I had a dream, which I shared with the group: I dreamt that I was in a place with this little boy, possibly five or six years old, who seemed

191

innocent, only I was aware that he was Adolf Hitler! Because of that, I hated him but knew I had the responsibility to take care of him and see that he came to no harm! I identified the ambivalence I felt, but I still had the need to protect this little child, no matter who he was. Hal interpreted the dream by saying that two of my disowned energies were trying to break through to my consciousness. The dictator energy was asking to be recognized in the guise of my innocent and vulnerable child. Both of those selves were calling for recognition of their existence and, in some way, asking to be included in my life. The fact that I had this overwhelming need to care for them and protect them was the responsible part of me telling me to pay attention and apprizing me of my obligation to take care of those energies. Shortly after that experience, I was able to access those selves in voice dialogue and, with a little work, to embrace them as part of my entire personality.

There are times after having had a specific dream when, as a result of re-creating it through imaging, I receive a clearer picture of the message in it. I am able to identify with greater clarity a disowned subpart, whereas in the dream it was unclear to me who that was and what it was trying to communicate.

SUBPERSONALITIES AS AN ACTING TOOL

Almost at the very beginning of my experience with Hal Stone, I recognized the potential of this work for actors. I knew that, as with the entire craft, there was an instrumental responsibility to subpersonality work that needed to be addressed first. Understanding the theory behind this phenomenon was a prerequisite to using it as a choice approach. In the beginning, before translating energies into vehicles for addressing scene obligations, I had my students do a lot of voice-dialogue work. As we tried to become aware of these subparts, and before employing them to work for us, we became very conscious that those selves were real and that when they took over, they completely controlled our behavior. We learned that every subpersonality exists only to be and do what it is there for. The pleaser only exists to please; the protector is only interested in protecting its charge; the inner critic's only obligation is to find things to criticize; when a female student accesses her Aphrodite subpart, she is only concerned with her sexuality and with addressing sexual impulses, and the same is true for a male student when he accesses his Don Juan subpersonality. And so it goes with every single subpart.

As time passed, I asked my students to try a monologue when under the influence of a particular subpersonality. The results were amazing! The monologue, even though it was being approached irreverently, took on incredible facets and dimension. Each subpart would bring new and different colors to the same piece of material. We went from there to identifying the obligations of the material and selecting the right subpersonality to fulfill the author's intent. Many characters in dramatic literature either live in a single subpersonality throughout the piece or go from one to another. If you can specifically select and access in you the subpersonality which happens to match the one that impels the character, you can depend on it to take you through the whole piece. What is so incredible about eliciting the help of a particular subpart is that it knows exactly how to relate and respond to the other people in each scene. It will behave just the way it has been programmed to, without commentary or redirections. Because the potential of this area is so vast and infinite, it has become a MEGAPPROACH in my process, which means that it could constitute an entire system of acting by itself: After the actor has identified the obligation he wants to address, he can select the specific subpersonality and then use one of the approach techniques to access it. In short, the subpersonality would be the *choice,* and the approach technique (voice dialogue, imaging, creating a choice to elicit the sub, and so on) would be the *choice approach.*

While there are times when the selection of a specific subpersonality is perfect for the character in terms of his behavior and actions, you may also access a subpart because that is the most complete way to approach the emotional responsibility of a character. This is appropriate when the character doesn't seem to be under the influence of a particular self but is expressing emotions that are very indigenous to one of your subpersonalities and is behaving accordingly. Let us say, for example, that you are addressing a character-element obligation of an angry and aggressive person but that, while this character is aggressive and freely expresses his anger, you are not convinced that any specific subpersonality is in the driver's seat of his life. There are a number of choices and choice approaches that you might consider using to fulfill the emotional obligation, but for the sake of this example, let us suppose that you chose to approach it by accessing your warrior subpersonality. You would do so because you know that, when you elicit that energy, you become aggressive and sometimes angry. Accessing any of your selves could fulfill a multitude of obligations with a single choice and a single choice approach, whereas you would ordinarily have to make two or three selections in order to address all of your responsibilities. If you choose the right subpersonality, it will accommodate all of the character obligations, the emotional obligations, the relationship obligations, and carry the character's sense of life all in one fell swoop! It can greatly simplify your process, while cutting down the number of choices and approaches you need to use in a piece.

Another important way to employ subpersonality work is to allow one of your subparts to select the choices you need in a scene or play. If, for example, you have identified the nature of the subpersonalities through which your character journeys, you can access your own parallel parts to deal with some of the other obligations of the piece. You can let those selves select choices for the time-and-place responsibilities, the thematic obligations, the various relationships the character has, and so on.

To clarify this, let us suppose that the character in this hypothetical piece has a variety of relationships with the other people in the play—his wife, his mistress, his father, his brother, and the major antagonist. His emotional point of view towards each of them is a result of which of his selves he is in when he relates to them. If you, the actor, are coming from a different energy, you might have difficulty selecting the proper parallel choices to address those relationship responsibilities. If, on the other hand, you identify from which energy the character is relating to his wife, for example, then you could elicit that subpersonality and make a much more accurate parallel-choice selection.

Subpersonalities can also be used as a preparation. You may elect to facilitate a specific self because it makes you feel the way you want to feel *before* you start to address the demands of the material. For example, before you tackle the obligations of the first scene, you find it necessary to elevate your ego state, as well as to confront the tension and fear you feel before starting the creative process. So you decide to access the hero subpersonality, because you know that that part of you is fearless and has a positive ego. The hero subpart usually exists in the primary-self structure and is fairly easy to access. Or let us imagine that you feel the need to be more powerful. There are a number of selves whose basic superstructure is built on power: the protector, the controller, the judge, the killer, the warrior, the evangelist, the messiah, and the perfectionist—to name a few.

There are many ways to use this megapproach in your work. It is multifaceted. Before you attempt to use subpersonalities as an acting tool, however, you must first become instrumentally familiar with who they are, where they are, and how they function within you. By doing a lot of work exploring your instrument and using the various techniques to facilitate and bring these various subparts to the forefront, you can establish an aware ego and become familiar with the various techniques for doing so. It is then that you can begin to use this choice approach in your acting.

BECOMING FAMILIAR
WITH ALL OF YOUR SELVES

As I mentioned earlier, the archetypes are the subpersonalities that all people have in common. In addition, we all create and have individual selves, which may resemble those of other people but do not exist universally. Their number is potentially infinite. We continue to discover new ones throughout our lives, some of which may be offshoots of others that we do know about!

Self-awareness is one of the first prerequisites to becoming familiar with all of your selves. Most people go through life in a semi-conscious state. In other words, they function and behave with a conditioned rote attitude. They go through life with a kind of tunnel vision, not seeing or observing the world around them or being aware of their own feelings and moods. If a person functions as the result of a particular primary subpersonality without being conscious of it, then that self is predominantly responsible for his behavior and personality. However, he will move from one primary self into another as the circumstances around him change. These changes are usually precipitated by some kind of new threat or responsibility and stimulate different moods and behavior. For example, he is sitting at his desk staring at the wall, when his boss enters the room. He immediately moves into his pleaser self and then shifts to his responsible self. These changes can take place with lightning speed, and while our subject is aware that something has occurred, he is completely at a loss to know what the specific dynamics of his emotional changes were! This lack of awareness is more the rule than the exception in our society. It may be caused by a conditioned need to protect oneself, or it may be a lack of emphasis in our educational curriculum. I don't remember having had any classes in sensitivity training or observation-and-awareness training. I do, however, remember my teachers' scolding me for looking at my classmates during class: "Keep your eyes on the desk in front of you! Why are you so interested in what Mary is doing?" All of you have heard these kinds of admonishments all of your lives, right? Well, if you hear them often enough, you begin to quell your curiosity and "shut down." There is a scene towards the end of the movie *Invasion of the Body Snatchers* (the newer one) in which everyone has been inhabited by the aliens and all these people are walking down the hallway of an office building, going to lunch or finishing their workday, seemingly unaware or unconcerned with anything or anyone around them. They walk in a kind of unison, almost robotlike in their demeanor. In a sense, we too have had our consciousness snatched by the disciplinarians who have successfully "robotized" us!

Fortunately, the human instrument is very malleable and adjusts easily to new impetus. If a stimulus is repeated consciously and often enough, we learn! We adjust! We change! So becoming aware of our behavior and of the changes in it is the first step in *meeting our selves.*

Ask yourself many questions continually: How do I feel? What is making me feel and behave this way? Be aware of sudden mood changes, and attempt to analyze what caused them. Begin to identify your primary selves and how they function. Look for the opposites and recognize them when they break through. Listen to the voice of your inner critic, and try to understand how that part of you influences your life. As you become more aware of the various selves, attempt to separate yourself objectively from particular energies. You will feel it when you detach yourself from a subpart. If you are successful in self-stimulating an aware-ego state, you can ask a self to relax its hold on you and invite another to step forward. Unfortunately, this is not easy to do. Most people need help in creating an aware ego. That is where voice dialogue comes in. With the help of a qualified facilitator, a person can be facilitated through the process of recognizing how the selves operate, and thereby begin to create an aware ego. There is, however, much you can do on your own. Just becoming aware of the way you function on a moment-to-moment basis will bring you to a level of consciousness that will create the momentum for change.

It is important to know that all of our primary selves are not benevolent. They are there to protect us and our vulnerable-child energy, but they are also there to keep us in line—to criticize us when we are not doing the right thing, to judge us when we are shirking our responsibilities, and if we have an active perfectionist as part of them, to constantly push us toward perfection! The danger in all of this is that there isn't any *balance!* If we do not allow our opposite selves to come forward, we are in danger of working ourselves to death and not having any relaxation or fun nor being able to indulge ourselves in any form of recreation. My father was a perfect example of someone taken over by the workaholic and achiever subparts. He worked seven days a week and never took a vacation in his entire life. His first heart attack occurred when he was sixty! It is easy to trace his subpersonality pattern. He was a Russian immigrant, who had to struggle to make a living. His entire existence was based on survival, on supporting his family and fulfilling his responsibilities. When he was a boy growing up in Russia, the circumstances were very similar. His primary selves were created at an early age, and the work ethic was solidly established. His survival and his being accepted were predicated upon working and achieving! So it is with many people. Their subpersonality chart can be identified and justified once they understand the components of their formative experiences and the forces that precipitated the creation of their primary selves.

It is important to remember that we need all of our selves, and we must be careful not to make judgments or create favorites! Every part of our subpersonality structure is vital to our lives, and we must embrace them all. The danger is when they take over and we are helpless to prevent it. If we create and establish a strong aware ego, that will not happen! With an aware ego we can hold all of our selves in balance and call forth the necessary energy to be there when we need it.

THE SUBPERSONALITY ARCHETYPES

The PROTECTOR, the PUSHER, the CRITIC, the GOOD FATHER and the BAD FATHER, the GOOD MOTHER and the BAD MOTHER, the PLEASER, the WISE PERSON or wisdom voice, APHRODITE—the female sexual energy— or DON JUAN—the male sexual energy—the child archetypes—the VULNERABLE CHILD, the FRIGHTENED CHILD, the MAGICAL CHILD, the MISCHIEVOUS CHILD, the LONELY CHILD, the REBELLIOUS CHILD—the OBEDIENT SON/DAUGHTER, the REBELLIOUS SON/DAUGHTER, the JUDGE, the MESSIAH or the GURU, the MASTER CONTROLLER, the HERO, the KILLER, the WARRIOR, the SATANIC or DEMONIC energies, the SPIRITUAL OR MYSTICAL energies—these are the most common subpersonality archetypes. Some of them comprise the primary-selves structure, while most of the others constitute the opposite or the disowned selves. You should know who and what these energies are so that you can communicate with them and include them in your life! Again, the first step is awareness, becoming conscious of your behavior patterns and being able to identify which subpersonality is speaking or what the energy is at any specific time. Once you become facile with identifying the different parts, you will achieve a greater understanding of how they function and how to control them. If you wish to delve deeper into this area, read the books I listed earlier.

CHARACTERS IN DRAMATIC LITERATURE WHO ARE IMPELLED BY SUBPERSONALITIES

As I mentioned before, some characters in dramatic literature are under the control of specific subpersonalities. The character Kane in the film *Citizen Kane,* for example, is obviously motivated by an OBSESSIVE ACHIEVER and DICTATOR. His entire energy is impelled by achievement and accomplishment. Because of his success, he becomes dictatorial with the people in his life. An actor approaching this role would profit greatly by exploring those subpersonalities.

Eddie and May in Sam Shepard's *Fool for Love* are obsessively tied to each other. Their sexual obsession controls their lives and is the major impetus in their relationship. The actors addressing these roles might investigate their DON JUAN and APHRODITE subpersonalities respectively and explore the obsessive part of these archetypal selves.

The character Jessie in *'night, Mother* decides to commit suicide and tells her mother, the only other character in the play, of her plan to kill herself in the next couple of hours. The motivating subpersonality in Jessie's life is the VICTIM; however, by the time she announces her intention, she is in another subpart, the rational part of her RESPONSIBLE SELF. She is rationally resolved and fairly relaxed with her decision. Whatever subpersonality the actress finally settles on, she must explore her victim subpersonality to create a structure that will lead her to the final decision to kill herself.

Othello, the WARRIOR, then the VICTIM and then the KILLER, can go from one of these subpersonalities to another as the material dictates.

Romeo fluctuates between his ROMANTIC CHILD energy and his DON JUAN subpart. The actor must decide how to access and balance these selves and possibly how to combine them so that they work in tandem with each other.

Hamlet, a complex character by anyone's definition, experiences the energies of a variety of selves. He starts with his HELPLESS VICTIM, moves from there into a cunning ACHIEVER, and then into a WARRIOR/KILLER energy. At times, his HERO subpart takes over. Not only is this character complex, so is the process of subpersonality facilitation in this case. This involvement demands experience with subpersonality work and exploration of this area.

Felix in *The Odd Couple* has a couple of subpersonalities that propel his behavior. As a matter of fact, several of his subpersonalities have teamed up and are working in tandem with each other: the PUSHER/ PERFECTIONIST, the RESPONSIBLE SELF, and the JUDGMENTAL SELF. The character seems to be controlled at one time or another by all four of these subpersonalities and is often going from one to another or expressing the impulses of two of them working together.

In the film *Wall Street* the character of Gordon Gecko is an insensitive, driven person, ruled by blind ambition and greed. There are a number of subpersonalities that you might explore in order to achieve his superstructure. The impetus of his behavior and possibly its origin or nucleus lie in his insecurity. So it might be an intelligent first step for you to explore one of the subpersonalities that live in that area. You could experiment with your FRIGHTENED CHILD energy. I know it seems like going in the opposite direction for this character, but from that place you might discover the subpersonalities that were accessed to compensate for the fear, which may be the MASTER CONTROLLER, the part that takes over control of everything, the ACHIEVER, and the PERFECTIONIST. Add a little of the WORKAHOLIC and you may have the recipe for Gecko's character.

Salieri in *Amadeus* is hurt, jealous, and envious. While there are several potentially good choices an actor can make, I would start by investigating the ABANDONED CHILD subpersonality. I think that it is the basis for Salieri's behavior. He feels overlooked, passed over, and abandoned. His vindictive behavior can come from another subpart, possibly the WARRIOR or a SATANIC energy.

The son in the play *I Never Sang for My Father* seems to go from an OBEDIENT SON to a REBELLIOUS SON, while the father fluctuates between the GOOD FATHER and the BAD FATHER. Two actors working together might possibly create a bonding pattern which would produce a relationship dance that would service the play. When the father is in the good-father subpart, the son is in his obedient-son subpart, and when the father moves into the bad-father energy, the son dances into his rebellious son. This is the way bonding-pattern dances go. The positive bonding pattern gives way to the negative one, and the dance can continue indefinitely until it is interrupted by the creation of an aware ego.

Those are just a fraction of the characters you will encounter that can be serviced well by using a subpersonality as a choice and choice approach.

THE APPROACH TECHNIQUES TO ACCESS THE VARIOUS SUBPERSONALITIES

At present we use ten separate techniques to access and elicit the various subpersonalities. In all of my system there are many tools available to the actor—not as a bigger collection of alternates, but so that he can have enough variety to be able to select the right tool for the job. I have always been an advocate of the *less is more* philosophy, so I am not looking for a way to multiply the exercises or techniques indigenous to this system. Having a variety of approach techniques in this area enables the actor to choose pragmatically what works best with certain material and the way that material is structured. If, for example, he is working alone, he cannot do voice dialogue, which needs another person to facilitate him. It will become very clear how each of these techniques work and how they can best be utilized.

VOICE DIALOGUE

Voice dialogue is a two-person process. The facilitator relates to the person being facilitated, talking to the various selves as they manifest or asking to speak to a particular one. The technique makes it possible for the person being facilitated to disengage these selves from his total personality or, in other words, to relate to them as separate parts. The facilitator addresses each subpersonality as a distinct entity, encouraging that specific part to talk and express itself. At certain intervals in the voice-dialogue process, he might ask the subject to move into his aware ego, at which times the person separates himself from the part that was responding and physically moves to another place in the room. When the subject feels detached from the self that was just there and experiences objectivity, the facilitator can relate to the aware-ego state and point out things about what the self said and where it was coming from. This process allows the subject being facilitated to become conscious of his subparts, while at the same time creating a facility to control them. Each of the subpersonalities has a distinct energy pattern that inhabits the subject's being—physically, emotionally, and in all behavioral ways. Being in one of the selves is often a transformational experience that seems to put the person into an altered state. In my own personal experience with voice dialogue I have witnessed incredible changes while the subject was "in" a particular subpersonality. Often, it altered his physical appearance. His facial structure seemed to change, as well as his physical posture and attitude. It is truly a remarkable phenomenon. Each of our subpersonalities looks at life and experiences it very differently, and each has its own responsibility to our life. Going from the warrior to the vulnerable child, for example, can visually transform the person being facilitated from a tall and aggressive physical being to a visually smaller, frailer person with a higher, halting voice. It happens right before your eyes and is an amazing experience.

THE VOICE DIALOGUE PROCESS

The facilitator must relax, stimulate objectivity, and in no way be threatening to the subject being facilitated. In fact, if he can acquire a benevolent demeanor, the various subpersonalities will be more disposed to coming to the forefront. He must *never* disagree or engage in conflict with the part that he is relating to. It is normal to want to succeed in a voice-dialogue facilitation, so the facilitator has to be aware of his own inner pushers, critics, or any other energies that might obligate him to encourage a successful session. He must be able to hear the vocal changes, see the physical cues, and notice the emergence of different energy patterns while conducting the voice dialogue. He starts the process by encouraging the subject to speak about anything, especially what is going on in his life or at this moment. By starting that way he will most likely be able to identify who is there, what subpart or self is speaking, and what the various voices are which interrupt or are standing in the wings ready to take control of the subject. He can thus get an overview of the person—or establish a "psychic map of the territory," which is what Hal and Sidra call it.

➢ *Example of a Voice Dialogue Facilitation*

The facilitator is usually seated facing the subject, who can either stand or sit. The facilitator may be silent for a few moments to allow the subject the time and space to get comfortable. Either one may start. Usually it is the facilitator:

Facilitator: Hi, how are you?

Subject: (After a short pause.) I'm all right...I guess.

Facilitator: What do you mean you guess? Are you unsure of how you are feeling?

201

Subject:	Well, no, I'm not unsure, but I'm a little nervous about talking about myself...I mean that I don't really know you, so I'm not sure about what you want to hear.
Facilitator:	(Being aware and making note that the subject is tentative and somewhat insecure and that she obviously wants to please him.) Well, why don't you just talk about anything you want to?
Subject:	(Looking slightly relieved.) Well, O.K., I mean...I'm not sure what to say...(At this point another voice breaks in. The subject's attitude changes drastically: She stands much straighter, her posture becomes rigid, and her voice drops several octaves.) What do you want? What are you asking for? Do you want her to bare her soul to you? (All of the subparts refer to the subject as separate from themselves. It is "her," not "me.")
Facilitator:	(Immediately noting the energy shift.) No, I don't want you to do anything that isn't comfortable! Who are you? I mean, I am interested in knowing you!
Subject:	(Still seeming somewhat guarded and suspicious.) Why do you want to know me?
Facilitator:	Well, I see that you are somewhat protective of Shirley, and I would like to put you at ease and find out how you function and what your job is.
Subject:	*Job?* Did you say *job?* I guess you did! Well, if you want to call it a job, I guess you can! What I do is take care of her, because she can't do that for herself! She's a wimp!... And I am here to see that she stays out of trouble and doesn't get into any situations.
Facilitator:	Oh, I see. Well, that's a pretty responsible job, isn't it?
Subject:	That's for damn sure! It's full-time employment!
Facilitator:	I'm curious about what you mean when you say, "get into situations"?
Subject:	Well, for God's sakes, she is so gullible and vulnerable that if I weren't here running interference, she would be constantly taken advantage of! She's not very strong, and sometimes I think that she isn't very bright either!

At this point it is quite clear that very soon after the voice-dialogue facilitation began, the protector/controller jumped in and took over. At first, it seemed that the subject, Shirley, was in one of her child energies, possibly her shy child. There was some pleaser energy evident also, so it is quite possible that there were more than one subpersonality operating. It also became clear to the facilitator that in addition to the protector/controller energy, there seemed to be a very active critic—which would indicate that these three are working together. At this point the facilitator could go in several directions: he might continue to talk to these subparts, he might ask to speak to the first subpersonality he started with, or he might attempt to talk to the aware ego, moving the subject into a place where that energy lives. He decides to opt for the first alternative.

Facilitator: I see...So in essence you take care of her?

Protector: Yeah, that's right! She has got into a lot of trouble before!

Facilitator: Trouble? What sort of trouble?

Protector: Well, when she was a little girl and before I came into the picture, her parents would verbally abuse her!

Facilitator: You mean that they would yell at her and criticize her?

Protector: That's putting it mildly! They yelled constantly and called her stupid and even began telling her that she was retarded!

Facilitator: That sounds very serious! Is that about the time you came into Shirley's life?

Protector: No, I was always there, but there were "others" that kept me from expressing myself! I tried—God knows that I tried!

Facilitator: You said there were others. Who were they?

Protector: Well, you see, Shirley always wanted to be loved by her parents, and so she would do anything to please them! She was very obedient, and those wimps were, for a time, impossible to break through.

(Making a mental note, the facilitator understands that Shirley had a very strong pleaser as a child and also a quite well-nourished obedient daughter. They were obviously strong enough to make it difficult for the protector to do her job adequately.)

Facilitator: So how were you finally able to succeed in being heard?

Protector: Well, I'm not sure! It seems like I got some help from somewhere, but I couldn't tell you where it came from. It was about the time Shirley went into the first grade that she started to be belligerent and disobedient. She became down-right rebellious towards everyone and everything! It was at that time that I could express myself, and I'm telling you that things really changed!

Facilitator: It seems that there must have been some kind of internal change for Shirley at that time! Well, it was very nice talking to you, and possibly we might continue this later, but I would like to speak with Shirley now. Would you mind? (When the facilitator asks to talk with Shirley, he really means Shirley's aware ego.)

Protector: Yeah, that's O.K.

(At this point the subject moves away from the protector/controller energy to another place in the room.)

Facilitator: Hi, Shirley. Are you in an aware-ego state?

Aware ego: Yes, I'm here. (Visually Shirley's entire behavioral state has changed. She seems much more relaxed and together.)

Facilitator: I assume you heard everything that went on and was said?

Aware ego: Yes, I did. It's very clear what's going on. I noticed that the protector was quite belligerent towards you in the beginning but seemed to mellow out as you talked to her.

Facilitator: Yes, I noticed that too. Were you aware that there are a few energies in operation there? I mean that there is quite a bit of critical energy as well as some responsible judgment taking place.

Aware ego: There are a number of them looking out for her. I'm aware of them, and it gets clearer all the time—I mean, about how they operate!

Facilitator: Have you been able to sit between these selves? Have you been able to talk to them?

Aware ego: Well, not a lot yet. I kind of just came into being.

Facilitator: What do you mean by that?

Aware ego: It's only recently that Shirley started to become conscious of all of these selves. With the help of voice dialogue and a few sessions *I* was created!

Facilitator: I see. Well now that you are here you can relate to the various parts of Shirley and ask them to back off or lower their energy!

Aware ego: Yes, I intend to become much more involved, and I feel stronger and more aware each time we do voice dialogue.

Facilitator: Thank you. It's a pleasure to know that you are here and ready to balance all of Shirley's energies. Could I speak to the first one who started in this session?

Aware ego: Sure!

(She moves from that place in the room and wanders for a few moments until she settles on a place further back. The facilitator, sensing that this self is reticent and tentative, waits a few moments before beginning to speak.)

Facilitator: Hi, how are you?

Shy child: (Moves a foot or two backward.) I'm all right! How are you?

Facilitator: Oh, thank you for asking...I'm fine...anxious to talk to you.

Shy child: Why? I mean, why do you want to talk to me?

Facilitator: Well, in the few moments that we had earlier I felt a very nice, warm quality from you, and I wanted to get to know you better!

Shy child: You like me, huh?

Facilitator: (Hearing a little pleaser energy.) Yes, I do like you. Is that important to you?

Shy child: Well, yes. I mean...I was never sure that her parents liked me. I would look into their eyes, and I never saw anything that said they liked me!

Facilitator: Did you do anything about that? Did you talk to them about whether or not they liked you?

Shy child: No. I was afraid to ask them that! I was afraid that they would say no.

Facilitator: So what did you do?

Shy child: I was quiet...I was very good...I did things that I thought they would like.

(At this point the facilitator makes note that there are a couple of voices coming through. The physical change in the subject is incredible. When she was in her aware ego, she seemed mature, self-confident, and relaxed. When she moved into the shy-child energy she seemed a foot shorter and slightly bent forward, and her voice became thin and a little inaudible.)

Facilitator: I hear someone else trying to break in here. Would you move over a little and let me talk to her? I promise I will come back and talk to you later.

(The shy child is a little reluctant to give up the space but with hesitation moves a couple of feet to her right.)

Pleaser: Hello! She's so shy—but really nice, don't you think so?

Facilitator: Yes, I do. She seems very nice.

Pleaser: I try to help her do the right thing. She's very fearful you know!

Facilitator: Yes, I can see that. Tell me about *you*. What do you do?

Pleaser: Oh, well, I make sure that everything goes right, that everyone is happy. I try to make sure that everybody likes her. It isn't always easy to do. *She* comes out and wrecks everything! I don't know what to do about her!

Facilitator: Who is *she*?

Pleaser: The one nobody can do anything with. She's so spoiled she's a brat!

Facilitator: I'm sure that's very difficult to handle, especially if she won't listen to anyone. I'm curious about her. May I speak with her for a moment or two?

Pleaser: Oh, I'm not sure that you want to. You see, once she gets out she never wants to leave! Well, all right, I'll help you.

(She moves out of that space and walks to within two feet of the facilitator, in an "in-your-face" position, so to speak. Again the subject's entire persona has transformed: she is standing with her weight shifted to one side, hands on hips, with an incredibly challenging attitude.)

Facilitator: Hi, it's nice to meet you.

Rebellious child: Don't give me that crap! You don't care anything about me, and I don't know who the hell you are and I don't care!

Facilitator: I see. Well, as a matter of fact I do care, and I would like to hear more about you.

Rebellious child: Like what do you want to hear? I'm not going to do any of that goody-goody crap for you! I'm sick of all the crap that goes on around her. If it weren't for me, they would have rolled over her a long time ago—you know, her parents, the kids in school, everybody!

Facilitator: I see that you are very concerned about her well-being. It seems that you have also protected her quite a bit.

Rebellious child: I don't know if you can call it protection. I just stood there and wouldn't do anything I didn't want to, and none of them could make me either!

Facilitator: Well, I think that you are very determined, and that's good! You seem very mature also.

Rebellious child: I had to grow up real fast around here! If I couldn't handle it, who would? I mean, those others wanted to protect and hide her, but I wasn't about to let them put her into some kind of box—know what I mean?

Facilitator: Yes, I think I do. I really enjoyed talking to you. I learned a lot about her life, thank you. May I speak with Shirley now?

Rebellious child: Yeah, I guess that's O.K.—as long as you didn't ask to talk to any of the others! (She moves back to where the aware ego was sitting.)

Facilitator: (Taking a moment to make sure that Shirley's aware ego is back.) Well, hello again. So you can get a clear idea of all of these selves, right?

Aware ego: Yes, I'm getting clearer about them. I still don't know who all of them are or how they function, but I'm learning very rapidly.

The facilitator does a brief recap of everything he observed. He might ask Shirley to come and stand at his side in the WITNESS STATE. The witness state or subpart is a nonverbal self who is not attached to the outcome of the session or the dynamics of the relationships between the selves. It *witnesses* what happens, takes it in, but is not involved in communicating with any of the subparts. It is different from the aware ego in that the latter is totally involved with the communication of the selves and can control their energy and participation. As he recaps the entire session, the facilitator makes some comments and shares his conclusions. At this point he will return the subject to one of the primary selves, because these are the parts that are most familiar to her, the ones she grew up with and is most identified with.

Facilitator: (Speaking to the aware ego.) Thank you, I'm sure that each time you experience a session you become more aware of everything.

(The aware ego gets up and moves to another place in the room.)

This example was a capsulized version of what a voice-dialogue session is and was designed to give the reader an idea of the process. An average session can last as long as an hour or more, as the facilitator spends more time with each of the selves. In this instance, the emphasis was *instrumental*. The purpose of the session was to help the subject develop an aware ego and become knowledgeable about the energies that exist in her. For an actor this is a very important prerequisite. He must first understand who his subparts are and how they function, before he can expect to use this process as a choice approach and acting tool. Once he is familiar with how to access the various subpersonalities, he can use voice dialogue to elicit the desired ones to do his acting, but he must initially understand who they are, where they are, and how to call them forth. Using this as an acting tool takes two experienced people, the facilitator and the subject. They must both know what they are doing and have experience with the process.

ROLE-PLAYING

This next technique, role-playing, is one I devised to help the actor. It is a one-person involvement but is similar in essence to voice dialogue. It might be called *voice monologue!* As an approach technique, it is initiated by the actor, who gets into his aware-ego state and asks for a specific part of himself to come forth and speak. This technique should only be implemented after one has had considerable experience with voice dialogue. If the actor attempts to access his various selves before knowing who they are and what degree of difficulty he will experience in getting them to cooperate, he will most likely fail in organic terms. What that means is that he will sometimes resort to imposing a concept or assuming the energy of a particular subpersonality, instead of really being inhabited by it.

The process is rather simple. After achieving an aware-ego state, the actor asks to speak with a specific self. The major difference between this and voice dialogue is that this is not a two-way conversation. Once the actor has elicited the energy of a subpart, he encourages it to express itself. If he attempts to communicate with it once it has inhabited him, the experience will become confusing and distracting. The initial approach is also different from voice dialogue. In role-playing the actor *asks* to speak to a certain part and encourages that part to come forth and express itself—to talk about anything it wants, almost in an uninterrupted monologue. If the subpart begins to meander or other voices interrupt it, at that point the actor can move back into an aware-ego state and become the conductor or facilitator again.

➤ *Example of Role-playing to Address a Subpersonality*

The actor relaxes, clears any mental background noise, and attempts to encourage an aware-ego state.

Actor: I would like the part of myself that is critical to come out. Talk about all the things going on in my life at present and anything else that you are critical about! (After a brief pause the actor moves around the room or stage until he finds where that critical energy is.)

Inner critic: (Looking around.) Wow! This is surely a seedy place! Why is it that most theaters look so natty? Give an actor a new piece of furniture, and in a few days he will destroy it! This whole place reeks with desperation! It hangs from the ceiling and sticks to the walls! Actors—the legions of the walking wounded! What a bunch of losers! Damaged goods, dripping with insecurity and looking for love in all the wrong places! "Look at me...look at me...look at me... do you think I'm pretty? Do you think I'm good-looking? Tell me I'm talented! Tell me I'm going to make it!"

Please! Get a job, you lazy piece of shit! Yeah, you're an actor, right! What restaurant? (Talking to another part of himself.) And you, how can you encourage him to pursue something he hasn't the aptitude for? You're full of shit too!

The monologue can continue for whatever length of time is necessary to establish a connection with the subpersonality. If the actor is using it as a choice, he can move into the scene or monologue as soon as he feels permeated with the critical energy, and he can then continue to promote and express that energy through the words of the piece.

USING A JOURNAL

Another way an actor can facilitate his own subpersonalities is through a journal. The main reason for using this approach technique is that it appeals to the subparts that are reluctant to respond to verbalization. Another reason for it is that there are times when an actor cannot speak out because of the environment or the circumstances in which he finds himself.

Using a pad of paper, the actor again promotes the aware-ego state before he begins. He starts by writing, "I would like to speak with...the vulnerable child" (for example), leaving space on the pad for that part to respond. Provided it does, he begins to write:

Vulnerable child: I'm not sure what to say...(Pause.) I'm afraid to be here.

I: Well, I promise you that you are safe with me in this place.

Vulnerable child: I always get hurt. No matter what anybody promises, I always get hurt. I don't like that they are all so cold and insensitive.

I: I understand how you feel. Please take your time and say anything that you would like.

Vulnerable child: Well, I wish I wasn't so afraid all the time. I would like to play and enjoy myself. There are so many things that I like and could do, but I'm so sad a lot of the time! I would like to be happy, but so many things make me sad!

210

Once the actor feels inhabited by the energy of this part, he can carry it into the material he is addressing. If he is using this particular subpart as a preparation for something else, he could move to the next subpersonality by asking to speak to it through the journal. Journalizing is very similar to voice dialogue because it is in fact a *written* dialogue.

USING A TAPE RECORDER

The actor can also use a tape recorder to "speak" to his subparts. This technique can be practiced in an environment or in circumstances that allow for it, and it is a very good tool for exploring the various selves. Often, it is done at home, as homework or preparation. The "facilitator" records his questions first and leaves blank space on the tape for the subpart to respond. The actor then moves into that subpersonality and records the responses. It ends up as a dialogue which goes back and forth between the facilitator and the self being facilitated. It is important that the subpersonality move into a physical space that its energy occupies, as is true for journalizing also. Each self is an energetic entity and occupies specific space. When moving from one subpart to another, the subject must physically shift positions.

USING MOVEMENT AND/OR DANCE

Some of our selves are not responsive to voice dialogue or any of the other verbal techniques. Their energy is more instinctual than rational. Their makeup is nonverbal, and they respond on a physical level rather than with words. Some of them exist in the sensual or sexual areas or at the primal levels of our being. Sometimes they are part of the child archetypes—the mute child subparts. You can access them by experimenting with a wide variety of movements and rhythmic dances, thus discovering who they are and what appeals to them and elicits their energy (it can go from aggressive Primitive Abandonment to very delicate and graceful gestures). Sometimes, just the act of gracefully making large circles with the arms will bring forth an energy response. If an actor wants to incorporate this technique into his system, he must explore and experiment with it for a while before being able to depend on it.

USING ART—DRAWING AND SCULPTING

As I said earlier, there are an infinite number of selves incubated by our instrument. Their makeup is often very complex, and it is entirely possible that we will never access or know them all! Have you ever wondered why some people end up doing what they do in life? What is it that creates a computer genius or a musician who, at an early age, is a virtuoso with more than one instrument? What makes a Van Gogh? We could ask these questions indefinitely without finding the answers. There are many theories: These talents are due to genetics—they are in the DNA and are inherited—or they are the result of environment, of exposure to certain endeavors, and so on. But maybe they are the manifestation of a subpersonality which has entrenched itself in the person's life and does what it does! Maybe that "artistic subpersonality" took hold of Vincent and never let go! Certainly, if you know anything about Van Gogh's life, you know that he was obsessed with painting—enough to forgo eating to buy oil paints!

There are a number of ways to approach this area. Get a sketch pad and, using pencils, crayons, charcoal, or any other medium, invite yourself to draw in a stream-of-consciousness manner, encouraging anything that is put on the pad to be there! Allow yourself to get into the feelings stimulated by the pictures, and become aware of the energy produced by the activity.

Another interesting exercise is to draw the previous night's dreams. Shortly after awakening, get your pad and draw your impressions of each dream, using your feelings to guide your hand. Encourage whatever ends up on the pad to be there, no matter how abstract it might look. Don't concern yourself at this point with interpreting the drawing or understanding its relationship to your dream. Just allow yourself to feel whatever it stimulates. Be aware of the specific energies that come to the surface, and if possible, identify those responses in subpersonality terms.

Sculpting is very much the same as drawing or painting, with one very important difference: the physical process! When we sculpt, we get into it directly, using our hands to make contact with the clay or whatever other material we might use. In some way this direct contact seems to appeal to other parts of our subpersonality structure. For some reason that I cannot explain, that contact and the molding process itself seem to stimulate other energies. In preschool and kindergarten children finger-paint and use clay and other molding substances. In other words, we all begin to create with our hands at a very early age; but in most cases we lose this connection as we grow up and matriculate into the higher grades. It is possible that these early childhood experiences are somehow linked to subpersonalities that did not continue to evolve and were consigned to the unconscious—only to be resurrected by the process of sculpting. Of course, it is just a theory!

The process is similar to drawing. The actor sits with a clump of clay and begins to sculpt in a stream-of-consciousness fashion. He works until he has created something. He should be aware of any impulses or feelings that come up while he is sculpting. It is quite possible that his involvement with the clay will pique some subpersonality with whom he is unfamiliar and open a door to others that can be accessed through this process. A couple of years ago at the same five-day workshop with Hal and Sidra Stone I mentioned earlier, our group sat at a table, sculpting with clay. Some of the people created human figures, while others made pottery. Some attempted to sculpt the figures in their recent dreams. What I found interesting about the experience was how it affected all of us. Everyone, including myself, seemed to move into a different energy. Afterwards, we sat in a circle and discussed it. We all noticed that there was an entirely different energy dynamic between us and that some of us seemed to behave quite differently.

I encourage you to spend time exploring this approach technique. The more tools you have as an actor, the richer you will be as an artist.

USING CHOICES

As I have said before, a choice can be almost anything in one's living experience. Quite often, in the normal process of creating a choice, the actor will inadvertently access a subpersonality!

This is one of my own personal favorites among the approach techniques for accessing subpersonalities. Even though I have used all of the techniques and encourage all my students to do the same, I favor this one because it has a built-in fail-safe device. With some of the others an actor can assume and impose—or represent—the behavior of a subpersonality. He can "indicate" that behavior rather than organically experiencing it. While it is still possible to do that when using a choice, it is less likely to happen if the actor is really involved with that choice. I guess, in a way, it is also like having a favorite pair of shoes! I have many kinds of shoes, but I seem to wear the same ones again and again. Perhaps I also like this technique because it is one I myself designed specifically for actors.

As you work with material, do scenes, monologues, plays and films, you should pay attention to the kinds of choices that appeal to specific subpersonalities. While you may not be attempting to elicit a subpart when creating a choice, become increasingly conscious of how various objects work to access the different energies. As you become more aware of which choices or categories of choices appeal to your subpersonalities, you will be able to use the right ones when you are trying to access a specific self.

Some selections are just a matter of common sense. Let us suppose, for example, that you wanted to access and liberate your sexual subpart. The choice would obviously be something or someone that stimulates attraction or lust or both. If you wanted to address the child archetypes, you would choose an object or experience that you know would appeal to the specific child energy. It could be a toy, a stuffed animal you slept with as a youngster, a place—a playground that was special, for example—friends who were in your life at that time, or even a favorite television program that was important in your childhood. Let us say that you wanted to access your warrior energy or even the killer. Again, you would select an object or person that piqued it. When I pick up one of my rifles—even when it isn't loaded—and I walk around with it, I feel aggressive and after a short while very much in touch with my warrior. With a minor adjustment, while still holding the rifle, I can elicit the killer part of me. All I have to do is relate to people in the world I would like to kill—people like the dictators who have been responsible for the death of thousands of people (Sadam Hussein for one) or serial killers—particularly the ones who hurt little children! I might use any of the choice approaches to create those choices. For my rifle example it was Available Stimulus; Sadam Hussein could be created through Sense Memory, and other people through Imaginary Monologues or Evocative Images. A very rich choice approach that is multifaceted in accessing subpersonalities is Objects That Come into Contact with the Body. The rifle example fits into that category. There are many objects, clothing, and jewelry that, when we are either wearing them or holding them, appeal to our various selves. In short, there is a bottomless well of choices that stagger the imagination. Explore them and use them to access your subpersonalities and to communicate with those selves!

USING MUSIC

Music definitely falls into the choice category, but the reason I am putting it separately is that it is so vast! It seems to be a continent all its own! Music appeals to many parts of us. It can stimulate patriotism, excitement, sexual and romantic feelings; it makes us vulnerable and nostalgic; it can create sadness or be inspirational. Its impact on human beings is phenomenal! It is used in films to promote the feeling of each scene as well as to support the emotions of the characters. A good composer of film scores can be extremely creative and manipulative with his background melodies. Music is used in television commercials to enhance the appeal of the product. Religion has depended on music to deliver its message almost from the beginning of time, and primitive people throughout the world have used music to worship and pay tribute to their gods.

Recently, I saw an interview with Diane Keaton in which she said that she had listened to a particular piece of music before doing a very emotional scene for the film *Marvin's Room*. She had walked around the set with earphones, listening to this piece right up to the moment when she had started shooting the scene.

Start experimenting with various types of music and see what appeals to your subpersonalities. I am sure that many of you who are reading this already have an idea, if not certain knowledge, of which pieces elicit which subparts. If not, start to catalogue music as a very important area for accessing subpersonalities.

EXTERNALS

Externals is one of the twenty-seven choice approaches in my system and a MEGAPPROACH, a very powerful tool for actors to use! There are four parts to it: ANIMALS, PEOPLE, INSECTS, and INANIMATE OBJECTS. By following the steps of the process, the actor, through his own body, can achieve the sense of the animal, person, insect, or inanimate object he is working for. Once he has achieved its essence, he translates it into human behavior. (For a complete description of the process, refer to *Irreverent Acting*. It is listed as the tenth choice approach.) This is used for a variety of purposes. The results it yields are very rich and dimensional. When an actor is successful in achieving the sense of a particular animal and is able to translate it or "humanize" it, the impact is totally transformational. It affects every part of his instrument. It changes him physically and stimulates a plethora of impulses and emotions.

The technique is used to address a wide variety of material obligations. It can create character behavior as no other choice can. It piques emotional life that is sometimes primordial, and it stimulates a thought process that very few other choice approaches can produce. In short, it is a dynamic megapproach!

Besides all the wonderful results it provides, it often accesses subpersonalities, catapulting them to the surface with surprising impact.

When I first began to study animals and at the time when I was creating the specifics of the approach, I experienced energies that seemed to take over my very being. That was long before I had been exposed to sub-personalities, and I didn't have the awareness or knowledge of what the phenomenon was. When you achieve a complete sense of one of these Externals, you know it! It is an undeniable feeling! It completely takes your body into another dimension. You feel the animal or other person inhabiting you; your rhythms change; mannerisms that are not you appear; you move, talk, relate, and behave differently. An actor uses this transformation to address the responsibilities of the text.

As impacting as this experience is, it is different from the feeling created when you elicit a subpart. While getting the sense of the "object" you are working for is extremely invasive and influential, it is not the same as being inhabited by a subpersonality. It is difficult to describe the difference—very much like trying to describe pain to someone who has never experienced it! While an external sense of an animal affects and totally changes your behavior, it falls short of constituting an *altered state of being!* When the actor is inhabited by the sense of the animal, he behaves differently, thinks differently, moves differently, feels different, but he still retains his consciousness and energy; whereas under the influence of a subpersonality he moves into a completely different energy. In essence he *becomes* that other part of himself, another being!

The Externals choice approach is yet another tool for appealing to and accessing the various selves; however, several things must precede its use. First, you must become facile with the entire process of studying, exploring, and experimenting with its four parts. Secondly, you need to experience the various animals, people, insects, and so on, so that you know how they affect you and which of them appeal to which subpersonality. There are a variety of circumstances that come into play and must be addressed and acknowledged. For example, it isn't always the particular animal you are working with that elicits a subpersonality; sometimes it is the way you approach getting the sense of that animal. It also depends on what specific self you are in when you start the process. Let us imagine that you are in a primary self, the inner-critic energy. Well, that part is very resistant to being permissive, and it could easily block the impact of achieving the sense of what you are working for. The variables and the way in which you deal with them are predicated on your experience in this area. As with every part of the craft, you must fail in order to succeed! If you learn something from each failure, you will ultimately reach your goal! At the beginning of your Externals exploration find out which of your selves is the most amenable to working with the process. Get into that self and begin to study the animal from that place. After a period of time, you will learn which of the Externals appeal to which of your subpersonalities, and, if working with a particular animal or person piques a certain part of you repeatedly, you will come to expect that result over and over again.

WORKING WITH ANIMALS

Certain animals by their very nature appeal to certain parts of our subpersonality structure.

The APE FAMILY—gorillas, chimps, gibbons, orangutans, and so on—seems to appeal to our more basic primitive subparts. Any of those animals can pique the earthy selves, as well as the aggressive energies. I have seen actors use apes to access the primal part of their Don Juan or sexual energy. Gorillas are very shy animals and most often run away from a confrontation; however, they are also very territorial, and when their space is invaded, they will become very aggressive. So getting a sense of the gorilla can appeal to a variety of subpersonalities. The gibbon seems like a shy and mellow ape, content to swing in the trees and look for food. The MANDRILL, on the other hand, is somewhat of a showman! It has a brightly colored face and most of the time seems very aggressive. Working with any of these creatures could open up a treasure chest of subpersonalities that you could use in your work.

The BIG CATS—lions, tigers, leopards, mountain lions, and so on—are essentially predators. They are meat eaters, and so they hunt and kill for their food. They have a totally different essence from that of the apes. They move with different rhythms; they stalk and are very quiet in their stealth. Using these animals as a choice approach will definitely appeal to a different kind of subpersonality. I have used big cats to address sly and deadly characters. In a film I did a number of years ago, I used a leopard as a choice for a character who was a Middle European hired assassin. It certainly piqued my killer subpart. These animals can be used for characters who stalk or are quietly dangerous. You must experiment with a large variety of these cats to get the results they achieve.

The ELEPHANT, another interesting animal, can be used to pique the more stoic parts of us. MONKEYS have an entirely different rhythm and energy. I have found that they pique the frenetic subparts, while SQUIRRELS, POSSUMS, and RACCOONS, totally different from monkeys in structure, rhythm, and activities, have the potential of appealing to our organizer, perfectionist, or responsible subparts.

BIRDS come in infinite varieties, all different from one another. Exploring the hawk or the eagle can potentially pique a variety of sub-personalities. Many years ago, I was playing Jocko De Paris in the play *End as a Man,* and I used the sense of an eagle with great success. I am sure that I was able to appeal to some of my unconscious and disowned subparts. The mind and killer energies were piqued and seemed to work together as a team!

REPTILES are another extremely interesting group of Externals. They are somewhat more difficult to do because of our limitations. If, for example, you work for the sense of a snake, your arms and legs have to be taken into account. It is nevertheless possible to successfully accomplish getting the sense of a reptile and to translate it into human behavior. Reptiles seem to appeal to the instinctual subpersonality energies. They speak to our disowned parts, which comprise the cold-principle energies—the satanic or demonic, the killer, the negative parts of the critic, as well as others.

PEOPLE

I have always adhered to the theory that whatever the external behavior of a person was—his rhythms, his mannerisms, the components of his persona—it reflected who and what he was internally. So I explored people in an attempt to find out what their inner life was like. At times, I achieved uncanny results, really getting a sense of the person's inner life, and stimulating thoughts, attitudes, and a specific sense of life, complete with the individual's personal points of view. I knew that I had succeeded because I was intimately familiar with the particular person, and when I wasn't sure of my results, I would ask that person for answers.

This area has very rich potential for accessing subpersonalities. If, for example, you experience a person in a specific subpart and you know him well enough to understand his subpersonality structure and to observe his particular patterns as he goes from one primary self to another based on external stimuli, you could work to get a sense of that person under specific circumstances and possibly access the corresponding part in yourself. It works better if that person is most often in a simple subpart, if that is his *modus operandi,* or if he lives almost exclusively in a narrow pattern of primary subpersonalities. At any rate, it all comes down to experimentation. The joy of this process is in the exploratory journey. Don't forget, for example, that, even though I described various animals and what subpersonalities they might appeal to, those are just suggestions based on my own personal experiences. The animals listed may not affect you that way at all! You must find your own answers!

INSECTS

Insects are approached in very much the same fashion as animals. The major difference is that they are much smaller and harder to study. Their rhythms and tempo are infinitely faster and extremely difficult to achieve in relation to our own bodies. They are, however, wonderful choices, and I have seen actors have great success with them. I would strongly recommend that you master animals before embarking on the journey to explore this category of Externals.

INANIMATE OBJECTS

The fourth area comprises nonliving things—a chair, a piano, a lamp, the fireplace, a bed, and so on. Success with it depends more on your imagination than on applying the specific parts of the Externals process. There aren't any active rhythms, tempo, or mannerisms to address, so you begin the exploration by assuming the physical position of the object you have chosen to work with; you then attempt to sensorially get a sense of its mass and weight and then try to imagine its static rhythm through your body. I realize that this sounds somewhat abstract, but I personally have experienced great success using inanimate objects, and I have seen scores of other actors do the same. It is yet another tool for exploring the process of accessing your subpersonalities.

IMAGING AS AN APPROACH TECHNIQUE

Imaging joined the other approach techniques at a much later date. It is a highly imaginative and creative approach for accessing subpersonalities. It is made up of four parts, which are designed to enable you to access and use specific subpersonalities when you are acting. Pragmatically, you can work with several of the imaging techniques in your pursuit of the selves. Always settle on the one that *works best for you!*

THE FOUR PARTS OF THE IMAGING APPROACH

Before you start the imaging process, it is important that you get into an AWARE-EGO state. You must not be attached to any of your subpersonalities or identified with it, since it can misinterpret or interfere with the creation of the selves that you are attempting to image. Relax, get comfortable, and decide which of your selves you are going to create with the imaging process. Once you have selected the specific subpart, choose a place in the environment you are in, and start the process. Do not arbitrarily pick a spot; take the time to *feel* where that energy might inhabit. The decision is largely dependent on your experience and your intuition. Once you have settled on a place, begin to imagine what that subpersonality might look like. Do not impose a concept, but image it intuitively. If, for example, you are attempting to create a satanic subpart, instinctively get an image of that energy without thinking too much about it! Once you have a sense of the general outline or appearance of the subpersonality, you can begin to create it through Imaging, using all five senses and either of the imaging approaches. You might want to start with sensory questions or just use Imaging Sensations throughout. The subpart can be any of your primary, opposite, or disowned selves. Whatever you decide to create, you must have a sense or feeling of it. If you start with a mental image or a visual concept, you can expect it to undergo some changes as you pursue the process. It is one thing to have a mental picture based on a concept, but what your senses produce is quite another image!

➢ *Example: Creating One of the Child Archetypes*

Having decided to work for the MAGICAL CHILD subpersonality, you begin to image that child in the space you have selected:

How far away is he from where I'm sitting? (All sensory questions are responded to with all five of your senses simultaneously. Remember that the senses do all of the work.) *How tall is he?...What is the color of his hair?...shape of his face...nose...mouth?...What is the color of his eyes?...Do I hear any sounds?...What are they like?...What is the expression on his face?...What is the attitude of his body?...What is he doing?...What does his voice sound like?...What is the pitch?...What emotions are in his voice?...Can I tell how he feels by the sound of his voice?...*(At this point in the imaging process you might want to switch to Imaging Sensations.) *I see him jumping up and down...*(All of your senses are responding at one time. You see him leap into the air, you hear the joyful scream as he lands, you hear the movement of his clothes, and you can smell the soap on his freshly washed face.) *His blond hair is moving rhythmically as he jumps into the air...His cheeks are shiny and red...I can almost feel the texture of his smooth babylike skin...His laughter is contagious...his eyes are wide with wonder and curiosity!...And I can almost feel his excitement...He looks so young and innocent...Happiness exudes from every pore in his body...I see him looking at everything in this place with such a sense of wonderment...If he weren't a human being, he might resemble a gorgeous little puppy filled with the love and magic of a young animal!...*

All of the imaging sensations take place in the senses, and the thoughts are a result of what you see, hear, feel, taste, and smell. All of the descriptions in this example are an expression of what the senses are supplying. There is *no verbal or intellectual involvement.*

Whatever the subpart selected may be, it is always approached in the same manner. Starting with a mental image of what it might look like and how it might behave, you begin to fill in that image with sensory responses. In a sense you are "sculpting" that subpersonality from your imagination. It leaves the realm of that imagination as it takes on the meat and bones supplied by the imaging process. At the point when you have a tangible figure in front of you, when it really exists, *move into that exact space,* and allow yourself to inhabit that energy. It is like putting on an overcoat. You encourage your entire being to STEP INTO THAT ENERGY FIELD AND BECOME THAT ENERGY! In this example, as you begin to feel that self merge into you, it will become apparent that you are experiencing the magical child!

The next part of this process is to find a mirror, look into it, and continue the imaging process. Observe any physical changes anywhere in your body; look at your face, and see if you can find that magical child's presence there. Observe the texture and color of the skin on your face, look deeply into your eyes, and see whether you can detect that childlike wonder and excitement! Allow the sounds that you feel deep in your body to be expressed; move around the room and feel the lightness of being in that state. Go back to the mirror, and image the features of that magical child until they totally fuse with your own. Once you have experienced that to the fullest, begin to look at the environment through that magical child's eyes. See everything through his energy. Then begin to image objects and people that are not in the room—whatever the magical child wants to image. It might be the circus, or sitting on the back of a pony, or going down a waterslide in an amusement park. The people may be parents and friends from your childhood, and the places those where you lived when you were young, always seen through the eyes of the magical-child subpersonality. None of the images need to be attached to the material into which you will ultimately take that energy.

Allowing this self free reign in a stream-of-consciousness imaging process really solidifies your being in that subpersonality.

The imaging process can continue for eight to ten minutes. You may use any of the imaging techniques you want. Try several and see which of them best supports the creation of the specific subpersonality. When you are deeply connected to the magical child, encourage it to begin relating to the text (at the eleventh level of consciousness). At this juncture the magical child might just relate to the available stimuli—the other actors in the scene—or he can begin to image things that are directly related to the material.

The first step of the imaging process, therefore, is to create the image of whatever subpersonality you wish to access and engage. Being familiar with many of your selves is necessary. Knowing in which part of your subpersonality structure they dwell makes it easier to access them. The PRIMARY SELVES are almost always in the forefront; their OPPOSITES are further back and somewhat less accessible, and the DISOWNED SELVES are even more difficult to coax forward, but with experience with some of the other approach techniques, you can develop the ability to access almost all of them.

We all have a feeling or an idea of what these selves look like. Take, for example, the child archetypes. They all look like different children! The magical child has features that are different from those of the vulnerable child. They all possess different energies and physical structures and may even be dressed differently. The rebellious child may even be bigger and more muscular than the others. Other subpersonalities might also have their distinctive look. The protector could be dressed in a military uniform and resemble General Patton! The controller could look like a bank president, and the master controller like his boss! The mind energy might resemble someone like Albert Einstein—and so on. Of course, these are just general suggestions to give you an idea about the way you may see the various selves. The capacity to create these subparts is highly dependent upon your ability to imagine them and your intuition about them. Develop trust in your feelings, and take chances. Be careful not to fall into clichés. Avoid a comic-book connection to these selves. They must come from an internal place.

Once you have successfully created the specific subpart, the second step in the process is to move into that energy. The best way to describe what we would like to happen is to say that it is like a morphing process! At first, you *feel* the energy flooding your body; then it feels as though you were being absorbed into the image, and finally, you are completely fused with it. You actually *are* that part of you!

The third step is to look into a mirror. It is a very important part of the imaging involvement! Actually seeing the manifestations of the subpersonality in your physical structure promotes the existence of that self. It helps to verify that you have embodied that energy and to see its transformational impact on you. A long time ago, when I was doing summer stock, I would get to the theater a couple of hours before curtain time, and I would leisurely apply my stage makeup, carefully creating the features of whatever character I was playing that week. The process would take about an hour, and with each brush stroke I would come a little closer to seeing myself transform into that character. That was thirty years before I knew anything about subpersonalities or imaging! I had, however, some intuitive understanding that the process of applying makeup had a transforming effect on me. I can't really say that I accessed a specific subpersonality, but it is certainly possible that some energy transfer would take place. Looking into that mirror as my features changed had a great impact on me! I had knowledge of the character in the play: I had drawn certain conclusions about who he was and what impelled him to behave in a certain way (I would even write a detailed character background on each part I played), and that knowledge must have affected me in a meaningful way and certainly influenced the manner in which I made myself up to play the part. I remember that I would stare at myself for fifteen or twenty minutes and would not leave the makeup table until I felt full of the feelings that my reflection created for me. In the same way, make sure that you take time with this part of the process. Stay with the mirror until you see and feel the impact of the subpersonality.

Once you are totally inhabited by the subpart, the fourth step is to encourage it to relate to the environment from its own energy field. The various parts of us see and relate to the world very differently. On my weekend workshops in the mountains, when we are working with subpersonalities, we go on a nature walk through the beautiful environments and wooded areas of a mountain paradise. I instruct my students to do half of the nature walk in one subpersonality and the other half in a polar opposite. Using whatever approach technique they elect, at the halfway point they move into the second subpersonality and continue the walk back to the house we work in. It is amazing and even mind-boggling to hear about the difference between the two subparts. The environment, of course, remains the same, but their impression of it is completely different in each of the subpersonalities—so different that you would imagine they were two totally separate environments. Not only do the subpersonalities see different things, but their emotional points of view are totally opposite also!

After relating to the environment from the subpart you have created, encourage the latter to image imaginary objects, people, and other places. These images should be impulsive and without goal or obligation. Encouraging the subpersonality to image whatever comes to it supplements its emotional impetus.

The final part in this involvement is to take the images into areas that fulfill the material and gently move towards the character obligations.

Subpersonalities in its own right is a powerful MEGAPPROACH, which can address almost all of the obligations in dramatic material. When used as an approach technique in relation to Imaging, it has an equally powerful ability to access and elicit the various selves. While only one of the ten subpersonality approach techniques directly involves it, Imaging can be incorporated into all ten. It is such a natural process and so easily promoted that we image intuitively and involuntarily. For example, when we use voice dialogue, our various subparts experience images as they are being facilitated. When we select a choice, an imaginary object that we create through Sense Memory, we are imaging. During the process of role-playing, images are formed while we relate to the various parts. When we listen to music, images are stimulated. When we use movement and dance, images come to us while we are engaged in the activity. What are drawing and sculpture if not images committed to paper or clay? When we use Externals, what images appear while we are under the influence of a particular animal, person, insect, or inanimate object? Imaging is a very large and important part of all of our lives! Use it to access your subpersonalities in conjunction with the various approach techniques contained in the Subpersonalities MEGAPPROACH.

CHAPTER 7

IMAGING AND THE UNCONSCIOUS

All through this book I have been saying that Imaging is a marvelous approach for accessing the unconscious. *"The trouble with the unconscious is that it is unconscious."* I believe C. G. Jung said that. What it means is that we understand very little about the unconscious. Countless numbers of books have been written on the subject, and no doubt countless more will be written, but for our purposes it is only necessary to understand how to use the unconscious in the creative process. We do not need to know the complete pathology of the brain or to unravel all of its complexities and mysteries—we just have to find ways of communicating with our unconscious. In my book *Acting from the Ultimate Consciousness,* there is a very good section on the importance of consciousness in communicating with the unconscious. If someone is not in touch with himself or the world around him, then he will surely not be connected to his unconscious impulses. How can anyone know what is going on internally when he is not even involved with his immediate environment?

The journey to the unconscious begins with elevating consciousness, becoming aware of external and internal stimuli, knowing how we feel, what makes us feel that way, and how the various stimuli that bombard us daily affect us. One of the most important goals of psychotherapy is to make us aware of how and why we function in the way we do. If we, as human beings, are not conscious of our behavior and do not understand why we respond to experiences in certain ways, then we are functioning much like the lower forms of animals—on instinct! It is a hell of a way to go through life! Fortunately, there is a process for elevating consciousness, and that is where we will begin this exploration of the unconscious.

BUILDING A CONSCIOUS STATE

As I have already stated in *Acting from the Ultimate Consciousness,* the component parts of consciousness are curiosity, imagination, awareness, sensitivity, perception, interest, knowledge, and a concern for all life—having an affinity for life and the entire world and being actively in touch with everything around.

Start with yourself! Ask questions! Do Personal Inventory. Find out how you feel about everything you see, hear, touch, taste, and smell! I know that might sound like giant self-involvement and indulgence, but it actually starts you on your journey to becoming aware of the things that affect you and cause you to feel and behave.

PERSONAL INVENTORY

I have described and defined Personal Inventory numerous times in my other books. It is one of the most important acting exercises you will use as an actor. Its purpose is to make you aware of what and how you feel on a moment-to-moment basis. It allows you to identify your thoughts and feelings and the obstacles to expressing your impulses. It also helps you to identify *unconscious* impulses and the images that float up from your unconscious into your conscious awareness.

Everything starts with the question, How do I feel? and continues from there.

➢ *Example*

"How do I feel?...I don't know!...How do I feel?...I'm thinking...I feel a little confused...How do I feel?...I feel O.K. I mean...I really don't know how I feel!...(It is all right not to know how you feel. Just keep asking the question. It will lead you to other impulses.) How do I feel?...I feel frustrated...I feel as though I can't seem to get any deeper into what I feel!...How do I feel?...I'm anxious about doing this right... I feel obligated to do this exercise!..."

As you do Personal Inventory, each impulse and its expression will lead to the next feeling or thought. Just keep asking yourself how you feel. While you are responding to the question, you might also encourage *images* and allow yourself to accommodate all those that occur. Some or even most of them may not be clear or understandable; however, they are definitely connected to something that you are experiencing as a result of the exercise, the environment, or some unconscious impulse that wants to be seen or heard. As you become more aware of your images, you will even be able to experience the subliminal ones. Doing Personal Inventory every day is very important in elevating your state of consciousness. You should also include Personal Point of View to your exercise schedule.

PERSONAL POINT OF VIEW

Personal Point of View is done in much the same way as Personal Inventory, except that you add the question, How do I feel about...? and explore your feeling responses to all the objects and people in the environment and your personal point of view toward anything else that comes up—people who are not present, as well as thoughts, impulses, or images that surface while you are doing the exercise.

➢ *Example*

(Start the process after a Personal Inventory workout, as a part of it, or totally separately from it.)

"How do I feel about this place?...I love it here!...How do I feel about the view?...It's inspiring!...How do I feel about that painting on the wall?...I'm not sure...My feelings change...Sometimes it makes me feel warm and cozy, and at other times it looks lonely...Right this minute I am unaffected by it...I just got an image of walking in that empty lot between those adobe houses in the painting...It makes me feel afraid ...alone and as if something might happen to me...How do I feel about that feeling?...I don't know where it came from...I hear the wind and see the trees surrendering to its force...How do I feel about that?...It excites me...I feel that I want to go out onto the deck and be blown by the wind...I can almost smell the pines and the lake..."

This exercise can go on for as long as you want to do it. Both of the inventories are designed to stimulate an awareness of what and how you feel—which is a necessary part of getting ready to communicate with the unconscious. As you establish a greater connection with your consciousness, you invite more unconscious impulses and images into it. Expanding your consciousness is a life involvement and must be done every day.

In addition to doing the various inventories, an actor must develop and elevate his curiosity, stimulate greater interest in many things, develop his imagination, and increase his perceptions. Having a rich fantasy life is also important. It encourages the imagination and gives birth to imaging. The various techniques for creating and elevating all of these areas of consciousness are specifically detailed in *Acting from the Ultimate Consciousness*. As I said earlier, before an actor can expect to communicate with his unconscious and use it as part of his creative process, he *must* be aware and conscious.

THE UNCONSCIOUS

When I think about the unconscious, it is like thinking about the universe. I have difficulty accepting that the universe is endless, that it is infinite! That concept boggles my mind. Doesn't everything have an end? The unconscious too seems bottomless, endless, infinite. Jung talks about *"the collective unconscious"*—that we are the receptacle of all the knowledge and experience of mankind from the beginning of time. If that is true, then we possess all the knowledge of all the ages locked up somewhere in our unconscious—all of the experiences, emotions, discoveries, thoughts, and inventions of mankind. Think for a moment about the potential of just a minute fraction of all that wealth to an actor's experience and expression! If we as actors could only find a way to access the power stored in the unconscious, what would be the results? We are influenced by the unconscious every moment of our lives, even though we do not have direct communication with it. We have thoughts, feelings, and impulses whose origins are not directly traceable. We do, say, image things that seem to come from mysterious and intangible places. How many times have you said or done something only to question why a moment or two afterwards? We all have images which do not seem connected to anything we are experiencing at that moment. The unconscious is constantly ventilating impulses and images into our conscious behavior. Most of them are vague and subliminal and go unnoticed. When we sleep, our unconscious is awake and active. It liberates its messages and desires in the often complex dream scenarios we experience. This is the time when, like a mythical vampire, the unconscious awakens and takes us over. Sometimes I muse about what early prehistoric man must have thought about dreams: Did he think they were supernatural messages from the gods? Did the superstitions of the time make him fear his dreams? Did dreaming of his own death really frighten him to death? In his waking state did he carry out the actions of the previous night's dreams? I wonder! When you think about how far mankind has come since then, how much more we know and how psychologically sophisticated we think we are, it is somehow shocking to realize how little we still understand about the unconscious! While we are no longer total victims of our ignorance, we still have come a very short distance in communicating with the unconscious or being able to harness its incredible power. A few of us interpret our dreams, try to understand what they mean, learn from them, and modify our conscious behavior as a result of the messages received, but what have we done to make the unconscious work for us? Virtually nothing! Because we don't completely understand it, we often have a healthy fear and respect for it. To me, it is like being in a foreign country where you don't understand the language, the customs, or the behavior of the people but you have to function nonetheless. What must you do in order to survive, fulfill your needs and desires? YOU MUST LEARN THE LANGUAGE! You must become familiar with the customs and workings of that particular society!

And so, you must begin to learn the language of the unconscious, to understand and interpret its messages, to question its images. Most of us have been led to believe that the unconscious functions in coded symbols and that our dreams are deliberately abstracted so that we do not understand them. That is like saying that our unconscious is in some kind of conspiracy to fool or confuse us and that it will not surrender its genius until we break the code. That is total nonsense! A long time ago, in the midst of teaching a class, I said that I thought the unconscious spoke a different language. A number of years later, I read somewhere that Jung had said that "images are the language of the unconscious." What an incredible concept that is! I totally believe it! Think for a moment about what that means. If indeed it is true, then the *universal* language of this planet is that of the unconscious. Everyone on the earth receives images from the unconscious—no matter how these are translated consciously. In other words, the language of the unconscious and its communication with consciousness are universally the same. Instead of fearing the unconscious or accepting that we can never be its master, what if we embarked on a journey to finding some way of forming a partnership with it and exercising it like a muscle in our body? Is it not possible that with work, exploration, and repetition, we could create a connection with it, so that we could dependably use it to our advantage? Yes! Yes! It is not only possible but can be and is being accomplished with this work! I am not saying that there is a direct way to talk to the unconscious the way you speak to someone on the telephone. What I am saying is that if it is true that images are the language of the unconscious, then by using those images we have a system of communicating with it. Imaging as a technique and as a choice approach is a tool for communication and interpretation.

In this section I will discuss many techniques for establishing that communication and bringing the unconscious closer to conscious awareness and behavior. Before I get into the exploration of these processes, however, I would like to discuss the importance of the unconscious to the actor's work—what it means to the creative process and how it affects performance.

ACTING AND THE UNCONSCIOUS

The greatest part of an actor's talent is housed in the unconscious. Lee Strasberg repeatedly said that "ninety-five percent of an actor's talent lives in the unconscious." If that is true, then it stands to reason that we must find a way of excavating that recess. When an actor stimulates unconscious support in a scene, it is as though something invisible and magical took over. Unconscious inspiration is awe inspiring; it dimensionalizes and deepens the life of the actor on stage or in front of the camera. If the connection to the unconscious is deep enough, it will lead to an ULTIMATE CONSCIOUSNESS experience. When that occurs, the actor and the audience are transported to another dimension of theatrical experience. The actor need not do anything except get out of its way! An ultimate-consciousness experience happens when the conscious stimuli pique an unconscious response, when whatever choice the actor is working for appeals to some unconscious wellspring, which then spews forth a flow of impulses, thoughts, and behaviors that are alive with excitement, dimension, and colorful emotions. More often than not, the actor doesn't even know what happened! He is catapulted by this seemingly unstoppable rush of emotional impulses. The ultimate-consciousness experience will run its course, and the actor will return to a state of consciousness. There are various levels of conscious-unconscious connection on the stage; however, that ultimate-consciousness experience is the pinnacle of unconscious achievement. Unfortunately, it is not consistently achievable, and it is also extremely unpredictable. When an actor experiences such a phenomenon, he will never forget it, and neither will his audience. (See page 42 of *Acting from the Ultimate Consciousness*, for a detailed description.)

Although such an experience is devoutly to be desired, it is not the main reason for attempting to establish a liaison with the unconscious. The closer consciousness and the unconscious are to each other, the deeper, fuller, and more dimensional is the actor's work. The richness of experiencing unconscious impulses is incomparable. It is nothing like the average work we have learned to accept in the plays and films we see.

If an actor wants to be able to experience communication with the unconscious every time he acts, if he wants to elicit its support and inspiration so that every acting experience is somehow connected with its wealth, he must have a craft, a process he can depend on, which always stimulates a high level of reality. He must develop techniques that are designed to build a bridge between consciousness and the unconscious. This entire process of work, all of the instrumental and craft techniques, dovetail into each other so that he can achieve the kind of freedom and trust that allow for the impulsive flow which is mandatory in contacting the unconscious.

Unfortunately, most actors encounter enormous obstacles that stand in the way of their trusting their impulses. Before we can embark on the exciting journey into the unconscious, I want to say a few words about those major obstacles that block an actor from tapping into any kind of underlife.

The most common trap is the actor's need to know where he is and what is coming next—what is the next cue and how he is going to say his next line. This is usually due to insecurity and a need to be sure that he is doing "the right thing." This entire syndrome stands like a thick wall directly in the path of any unconscious impulse, which it prevents from finding its way into conscious behavior. The basic contradiction is that the actor maintains a conscious state but stands outside that state and, like an orchestra conductor, conceptually directs his behavior in a premeditated fashion, thereby cutting off the flow of his moment-to-moment impulses and completely inhibiting any connection to unconscious sources. Most actors function that way. The very idea of discovering the next moment in the next moment and at the very same time as the audience is terrifying to them. It is like giving up all control, giving up the known for the unknown.

In order to connect with the unconscious, the actor must do a lot of preparation, eliminating fears and dependencies, addressing his insecurities, and building a foundation of trust. He must start by encouraging himself to be more impulsive and irreverent to the concepts of the material. There are many exercises and techniques that encourage impulsive expression or address irreverence, but before any actor decides to confront his obstacles, he must first understand and commit to becoming a PROFESSIONAL EXPERIENCER.

ESTABLISHING COMMUNICATION WITH THE UNCONSCIOUS

The very first step on the journey to the unconscious is to become more aware of what you feel. As I suggested earlier, Personal Inventory is an excellent technique for finding out what's going on internally. Encourage a verbal expression of your feelings, and be aware of impulses that seem to come from nowhere. Once you are well into taking Personal Inventory, encourage yourself to be impulsively expressive of the responses to your questions. After doing the exercise on a daily basis for a short time, you will begin to notice that some impulses are richer, deeper, a little abstract and mysterious in their content. Take note of those after the fact, and question them. If, for example, you suddenly feel a violent impulse—one that does not seem to be caused by any stimulus—express it, go on with the inventory, and later try to find out what may have caused that feeling.

Such intrusions can come from a variety of places: Something expressed in your Personal Inventory piqued a parallel memory, or an object in the place where you were doing the exercise triggered a vague image of something you experienced long ago. For example, while glancing around your living room, your eyes almost imperceptibly washed past the fireplace and the poker leaning against the brick façade, and suddenly that piqued a vague memory of your father in a rage, brandishing the poker and threatening to hit your mother with it. The image happened quickly, without conscious acknowledgment. It was an experience that took place so long ago that you would not have been able to consciously recall it. It had burrowed its way into your unconscious memory banks, and there it had stayed until you revived it by a fleeting glance at an innocent poker languishing against the fireplace.

There are literally hundreds, possibly thousands, of such experiences in the space of a single day. Start to take note of them; explore each of them. You won't be able to understand them all or to trace their origin, but you will surely be able to pinpoint some of them. It isn't even necessary to know where they come from, but it is incredibly valuable to become aware of them and to encourage a continued exploration of these varied unconscious impulses that surface each moment.

Some of the responses to your Personal Inventory will come in the form of *images*. Some will be very solid and three-dimensional, while others will look more like very overexposed negatives. Allow yourself to respond to all of them, and express whatever your response is. Your expression may not be verbal; it may find its way out in a sound or possibly a deep sigh. Essentially, what you are doing is taking the first step in building a bridge to your unconscious. With constant exploration and repetition you will become much more aware of the dynamics of the unconscious and of how it sneaks into your consciousness.

RE-CREATING UNCONSCIOUS IMPULSES THROUGH IMAGING

Let us use the example of the response to the poker and its stimulation of a flush of violent impulses and suppose that, shortly after it happened, you chose to re-create the experience it liberated. Where might you start the process, and why would you do it to begin with? The why first: each time you re-create or explore what seems to be an unconscious impulse, you are establishing a conscious relationship with the unconscious. In other words, you are bringing it up to the surface again; you are facilitating communication with the source! It is much like forcing your open hand into a small hole in the ground and by so doing making the hole a little larger each time.

You can start almost anywhere in the experience, directly with the fireplace or with another part of the room. You could approach it with a variety of imaging techniques: Story Imaging, Fragmented Imaging, Verbalized Imaging, or even Involuntary Imaging. As usual, the selection will depend on which will work best. Imagine that you have elected to do it through Fragmented Imaging. The very nature of this technique rules out using Affective Memory.

➢ *Imaging the Experience with Fragmented Imaging*

(None of the images are ever put into words of any kind. All responses are imaged with the five senses. However, words are the only way I can describe the process to the reader.)

Bricks...gray and coarse...different sizes and shapes...stained by the black ash of hundreds of fires...Wood burning...smell it...Smoke rising, taking odd shapes like pictures in the clouds...Feel warm...Poker in the air...father...face red...distorted...Hear his voice, rasping and strained ...words..."Kill you, bitch!" Poker circling in air...larger and larger circles...mother...moving back...face frightened...couch between them and me...I want to stop him...afraid, want to hide...Feel hot...then cold all over body...His eyes are bloodshot...Crying...see shape of poker...It looks like a question mark...Feel my brain running away...I hear a shrill scream...It's coming from me...They both turn...see me...stop...Hear crying...don't know where it comes from...seems like it's coming from the back of a long tunnel!...

All of those images are coming very fast. Some are not even connected to the ones that came before. The "imager" should allow the images to run themselves out. The exercise might last only a minute, or it might go on for a while. It is important to allow yourself to feel everything that the process brings up. Do not edit your impulses. When re-creating an experience, you may feel completely different from the way you did the first time you stumbled upon it. For example, when doing the Personal Inventory and seeing the poker, you felt angry and violent, but this time you experience more sadness than anger. Go with the sadness. Remember that you are not trying to create the experience to address an obligation related to a piece of material but attempting to explore your connection to the unconscious and to establish techniques for doing so.

It is not necessary to re-create every image or suspected unconscious response to your inventories. Select the more impacting ones and those that you sense have a complex root system in the unconscious. With increased experience you will begin to know which images or verbal responses seem "loaded." Not all impacting responses come from the deep unconscious. Some are just memories buried several layers down. You will, however, begin to know the difference as you continue to explore the unconscious.

NONVERBAL PERSONAL INVENTORY

Another technique for communicating with the unconscious is Personal Inventory in sounds. You start this process by asking yourself, *How do I feel?* and from that moment on, you just attempt to respond in sounds that express your internal feelings. You encourage a moment-to-moment involvement in your expression, allowing yourself to be affected by internal and external stimuli. As you peruse the environment, you will be affected by the inventory and also by the objects around you. Encourage yourself to be impulsively expressive.

Even though the conventional Personal Inventory is very effective, the words sometimes can impede your impulses and get in the way of the liberation of images from unconscious places. As you proceed with the nonverbal form, be aware of all the thoughts, feelings, impulses, and images that come to you. Doing it just now, I began to feel very vulnerable. Possibly this came from the sounds I was making or from looking at the sky through the windows—I don't know! At any rate, I allowed the feeling to run its course and be replaced by whatever followed.

With this exercise you are encouraging yourself to explore your feelings. By doing just that, you are elevating your awareness and beginning to dig down into places heretofore unexplored. At the same time, having made a conscious decision to address your unconscious, you have set up the expectation of receiving signals from it. At first, you may have minimal success, but don't be discouraged. This is new for you! Continue to do your various Personal Inventories many times each day.

THE PRIMAL MOAN

When an actor seems cut off or extremely blocked emotionally, I will ask him to do a Primal Moan. I have been using this exercise in my classes for more than twenty-five years, mostly to stimulate and pique deep emotional impulses. It almost always crashes through the protective walls and liberates some of the most exciting emotional life possible. The resulting emotional flow comes from a very deep and seemingly primordial place and almost always has a transformational impact on the actor's behavior. Even though I was at first using this exercise to plummet deep into the actor's emotional core, and not as a technique to deal with the unconscious, it became obvious that it was tapping into layers of unconscious life. The resulting expurgations seemed filled with expression that reflected the kinds of emotions and impulses which have typical unconscious earmarks. The actor looked and sounded very different; the work that followed seemed deeper and richer. It was obvious that, for whatever reason, this technique solicited unconscious impulses that liberally expressed themselves outwardly.

To start the exercise, you assume the "fetal" position on the floor—curling up into a ball with your hands, palms together, placed between your thighs, very much like a fetus in its mother's womb. Slowly and at first quietly, begin to moan. The sound must come from a very deep place in your body, such as your lower abdomen. As the exercise proceeds, the moan should become louder and deeper. It should be held for a fairly long period of time—about fifteen to twenty seconds. If you are doing the exercise correctly, you should feel the sound vibrating from the lower part of your body. Avoid getting trapped in your throat! As you continue, the sounds will begin to embody emotional impulses ranging from vulnerability to rage. Very often an actor is overcome with emotions and cries uncontrollably. The emotional flow should be encouraged to run its complete course, since one emotion will give way to the next, and so on. During this process, many images occur that are usually disregarded, since the original purpose of the exercise is to liberate congested emotions. When the Primal Moan is used to explore the unconscious, however, those images should be acknowledged as expressions of unconscious impulses stimulated or piqued directly by the exercise. They may be prenatal images or associations with another time in your life when you made those sounds, or they may in fact be the expression of some primitive animal energy that was excited by the moaning. Whatever the source, they are another way of communicating with the unconscious.

After starting the moan, allow whatever images occur to do so without any leadership or expectations. Remember: images are not exclusively visual! You might experience a strong odor of some kind, which may or may not be definable. No matter, just make note of it and continue the exercise. Any image that rises up into your consciousness will almost always have numerous sensory components. During a Primal Moan, one of my students experienced the softness and warmth of a baby blanket, while at the same time smelling talcum powder. Other experiences have included nightmare-like sensations of being in a dark cave, where the air was dense and hard to breathe. Many of the images may be abstract and just fragments of a whole picture or sensory response. It is important to allow all of them to run their course. Do not try to hold on to any one response. By doing so you would run the risk of short-circuiting the flow of images.

After practicing this technique for a period of time, you may begin suggesting things to yourself during the exercise. Once you have created a flow of images, you could suggest a particular time and place in your life, producing, for instance, an inner image of one of your bedrooms when you were young. Or you might image a string of people as they appeared in your life one by one. These kinds of suggested images often steer the unconscious into specific areas that are pregnant with memories of important events, which have been locked away for many years. When you strike a "glory hole" of conglomerated unconscious feelings, these can spew forth like a geyser filled with exciting impulses and emotions that will catapult you over that line into the ultimate consciousness.

Using the Primal Moan as a technique serves more than a single purpose. With repetition you become more facile with the exercise. It is a tool that helps you add material to build that bridge to the unconscious, as well as a dynamic preparation for getting ready to act. Besides its obvious involvement value, it is a direct way of priming the unconscious into participating in your work.

PRIMITIVE ABANDONMENTS AND OTHER PRIMAL EXPLORATIONS

There is a whole cluster of primitive types of exercises, which can be used for a variety of reasons. As instrumental workouts, they are extremely liberating and serve as important impetus for piquing powerful primitive or animal energy—which is very fruitful if the actor is out of touch with this area. They also act as emancipators of angry or hostile impulses in people who are conflict phobic or so socially obligated that they are unable to access those emotions. In addition, they free sexual impulses and stimulate the flow of sexual energy throughout the body, immediately transforming a person who may not be in touch with his sexuality into a visibly sensual actor. They have an incredible impact on everyone who does them.

When you use these techniques to stimulate the unconscious, only a slight adjustment is necessary. First, you must become aware of the goal—which is to reach the unconscious. Then you must add the imaging process to each exercise. Begin to take note of the upcoming images, and whatever they may be, allow each one to have its effect. Encourage their flow to affect and change the nature of all your expressions. For example, let us imagine that you are doing a Primitive Abandonment (described below) and that the first impulses, stimulated strictly by the physical commitment, make you feel aggressive and animal-like. Suppose that, while you are feeling these emotions, you get an image of being ten times larger in stature than you are in reality. All of a sudden you begin to feel different about everything and everyone around you. Your original aggressiveness then gives way to a benevolent attitude towards everything. The sense of size brings with it feelings of omnipotence and of responsibility for all things smaller. The images may change with lightning speed, giving way to a wide variety of thoughts and impulses. Quite frequently, this exercise will elicit various satanic subpersonalities, demonic energy patterns that will often be replete with their own images, which possibly come from deep wells of disowned unconscious energies. **It is not important to understand everything that happens or what each image means!** Just encourage yourself to express the impulses that come to the surface. After all, the point is to establish a connection with the unconscious, not to interpret its messages.

THE PRIMITIVE ABANDONMENT EXERCISE

The Primitive Abandonment exercise, unlike the conventional Abandonment exercise, is done standing. Starting with a very large physical and vocal commitment, you begin to move with large abandonment energy, making sounds that are very loud and animal-like. At first, it resembles an ordinary Abandonment exercise, but it slowly takes on a rhythmical quality in sound and movement, becoming more and more animal in its expression. You may howl, grunt, or utter guttural sounds like those of a hurt or angry animal. The body should be encouraged to have total freedom of movement and able to use a great deal of space. There should be no physical restrictions. The exercise can go on for as long as you can physically endure the expenditure of energy. Remember to encourage animal movements and sounds, since that is what stimulates the basic primitive impulses. Whatever images are brought on by this involvement will automatically run their course as you do the exercise.

Students in my classes have reported seeing a wide variety of brilliant colors flash by as they did the exercise, or feeling uncontrollable power and getting flashes of animal images. Many mentioned feeling violent and malevolent. Sexuality is a recurring theme—not romantic sexuality but aggressive, forceful impulses. Other actors have said that they felt prehistoric and nonverbal. The exercise has been known to give rise to a wide variety of images, including some of people who were not recognizable or familiar to the participant. When we dream, we "see" people whom we do not recognize, even though we may have seen their faces somewhere before. Therefore, when images of this kind begin to appear in a primitive exercise, it seems certain that they are coming from an unconscious source.

After completing the process, you should allow several moments of quiet assimilation and encourage a meditative state. This gives your instrument time to embody whatever connection you made with the unconscious. When this technique is used as a preparation to get ready to act, the next step is to start working for a choice that addresses the material. In that framework, piquing unconscious connection brings the flow of unconscious impulses and support into your work. When the exercise is used to communicate with the unconscious, the purpose is to progressively condition the instrument to do just that.

CREATING THE EXPERIENCE OF BIRTH

While the next exercise is not necessarily a "primitive" experience, it too is somewhat animal in nature and is a very good way of appealing to unconscious memories. Rebirthing is a fairly popular therapy—at least in California circles—which is used to help the "patient" overcome the trauma of birth. There is a fairly widespread belief that many people suffer the effects of birth trauma throughout their entire lives and that undergoing a series of "treatments" which simulate the birthing process (being "reborn") will alleviate the impact of the original experience. This is done in a shallow pool of water, with the "midwife" or "birthing therapist" helping the patient through the simulated birth canal with kindness and support in movement and sound. While I personally have never undergone this process, I have heard a number of people attest to its enormous value to their own lives. I am open to anything that works and has a positive impact.

As an exercise to help create a liaison with the unconscious, it is done on "dry land." Lie down and once again assume the fetal position. Clear your head of all thoughts. Try not to verbalize or conceptualize. Erase the blackboard of your mind and avoid all relationship to language. Begin to move very slowly as you imagine yourself passing through the confines of the birth canal. Keep your eyes closed, and attempt to maneuver through this long, dark, and damp tunnel. Create its resistance against all parts of your body. During this process, you should experience a plethora of images, hopefully related to unconscious memories of your birth. At the very least, it should activate some unconscious responses. Continue the exercise for however long it may take to manipulate yourself through that tunnel. Keep your eyes closed until you come out of the "canal." When you open your eyes, encourage yourself to look at everything as if you had never seen it before. Discover each new sensation as if for the very first time. Do not attach words to anything you see or feel. Discover your own body movements without any understanding of their mechanics. Accept whatever images surface during any part of this exercise. Do not molest those images! Allow them to evolve and give way to others. The exercise may stimulate fear, anxiety, feelings of being out of control, wonderment, and a sense of being disoriented. The emotional responses are evidence of success!

There are other kinds of primitive or primal exercises that you might find useful. You could, for example, sit in a chair and do the Primal Moan in that position, or you could create a helpless sound, much like the one you start with in the Primal Moan, and slowly build it into a violent scream for survival. Continue this helpless appeal until things begin to surface—images, thoughts, and feelings of many kinds.

On a daily basis, or at least several times a week, explore those exercises in order to start the journey into the unconscious.

EXTERNALS (ANIMALS)

Another good approach to use is *Externals*. The process was already outlined in relation to subpersonalities; therefore, in this context and for our present purposes, I will limit my discussion to its animal aspect and use it only to access unconscious life.

I have been working with this technique for many years. When I was a student at Northwestern University, my teacher, Alvina Krause, instructed us to go out and "watch animals." She not only did not tell us *why* we should watch them; she neglected to mention what to look for or what to do with what we saw! Many years later, I was again encouraged to observe animals by my other teacher, Martin Landau—only this time, I was given some tools and told the purpose of this involvement. Over the years, and with much exploration on my own, I was able to construct a fairly complete system, structuring various components that made it possible to achieve a very specific sense of any animal I worked with. Long before I became involved with imaging or the unconscious, I was aware that achieving the sense of an animal brought with it supplementary and residual responses. In the early years of practice, I accepted these bonuses as part of achieving success with the process. I didn't know or realize that many of the images and impulses that came through were the result of having piqued unconscious responses.

If you elect to use this process to communicate with your unconscious, the first thing you must do is learn how to work with it. Once you have done that, become increasingly aware of the images that surface while you are in the animal position, before attempting to translate that animal into human form. As you crawl around your living room, working to get a sense of your animal, take note of what images or thoughts rise to the surface. These will vary from animal to animal. Some animals stimulate more images than others—I don't know why! The primitive and primal elements involved often have an impact similar to that of the other primitive approaches; however, I have also experienced different kinds of impulses with different animals and often felt fragile or frightened. Most of the images that float to the surface are abstract and vague—more like subliminal flashes than well-defined pictures. The unconscious makes itself clear in image terms when we are asleep. It is far more difficult to communicate with it clearly when we are awake. However, since what we are after is to establish a connection with it so that our work is richer and filled with dimensions, it really doesn't matter whether or not we achieve clear or detailed images.

FEARS

Fears are another very rich area to explore. Since our greatest fears are often denied or pushed deep into unconscious recesses, exploring them can present us with a potential bonanza of unconscious material. Our nightmares are almost always expressions of those fears.

You might start by addressing your conscious fears first, doing an audible litany of them in the form of a sentence-completion exercise. Begin every sentence with "I am afraid of…"and fill in the blank with whatever completes it.

➤ Example

"I am afraid of…dying. I'm afraid of getting hurt…I'm afraid of being sick…I'm afraid of being laughed at…I'm afraid of dark places… I'm afraid of ghosts…I'm afraid of losing a limb…I'm afraid of failing …I am afraid of being poor…I am afraid of being aggressed on…I am afraid…that I won't achieve my goals…I am afraid…to be dependent on anyone…I'm afraid of violence…I'm afraid of losing my children…I'm afraid of any body of water where I can't see the bottom...I'm afraid of getting a terminal disease...I'm afraid of pain...I'm afraid of the unknown...I'm afraid of high places...I'm afraid of falling...I'm afraid of strange and unfamiliar places...I'm afraid of being stuck with a needle ...I'm sometimes afraid when I am alone...I'm afraid of loneliness..."

This exercise can be repeated quite often, yielding new fears each time you do it. All of the fears expressed in the example are conscious; however, they might very well have a root system in the unconscious and therefore be worthy of further exploration. How then might you proceed? First, while you are doing the exercise, you could stop and image the fear. For example, "I'm afraid of dying." Image yourself on the brink of expiring or in a hospital, connected to a respirator. As unpleasant an image as that might be, I promise you that it will bring up some very impacting responses. "I'm afraid of getting hurt." Image that event. Feel the pain in the injured areas. "I'm afraid of being laughed at." Create an entire room of people laughing at you in the way you fear. You can use the imaging process to create the manifestation of all your fears. Use all five of your senses and you will be surprised by the results!

Another way to use your conscious fears is to allow yourself to stay with each one exclusively for a longer period of time. Once you have acknowledged a fear, just incubate it. Sit with it for a while, and let it run its course. For example, in the case of being afraid of dying, don't image anything. Just allow the fear to exist. Encourage yourself to find out what dying means to you. If, for example, it means another kind of life on a different plane, one that is horrible, like being in Hell, then your fear will take on a specific reality. Or dying may mean the end of all sensory experience or nothingness or giving up the joys of living. Each of those responses ignites other fears, which may be directly tied to unconscious ones. In any case, this exploration should hook into deep-seated emotional issues. The deeper the origin of the fears, the more energy they probably carry.

After spending a couple of hours exploring your conscious fears, take a Personal Inventory. See how you feel. If you have made a connection with the unconscious, you will feel it. It is somewhat like awakening after a night full of dreams, feeling some kind of residual hangover but not knowing exactly what your feelings relate to or mean.

Fears are not always rooted in the unconscious. We have justifiable fears, fears that tell us to use caution in certain situations or that signal dangers of many kinds. We can refer to them as *conscious, intelligent fears*. One way to distinguish them from those that live in unconscious spaces is to identify the logic behind each particular fear. If, for example, you are driving down the highway at ninety miles an hour and all of a sudden you imagine having a blowout at that speed, that is a conscious, intelligent fear! It is *logical* that such an accident could happen. Fears that are connected to the unconscious are usually less explainable. They lack justifiable logic. For example, you are sitting in your living room reading, and suddenly you feel an icy-cold chill creeping up your spine. You sense the presence of someone or something in the room. In seconds, you are filled with an unexplainable terror, not knowing where it came from. The book you are reading is a romantic love story, far from anything that could cause such a response; your living room is well lit and warm in its décor; as far as you can determine, you didn't have any frightening thoughts prior to having those feelings, so where did they come from? They could have been created by a very subtle or subliminal stimulus—the howling of the wind outside the house, a creaking or settling sound, a faint odor related to a past experience, a dream or nightmare you had had at another time, and so on.

You are sitting in a restaurant enjoying a good meal. While casually glancing around the room, you see a little old man in the corner sipping tea, and for some unexplainable reason you feel an immediate sense of discomfort and even fear. The man is old and frail and could not possibly be a threat; however, your reaction is very powerful, and your impulse is to finish your dinner quickly and leave. What causes these experiences is very hard to pinpoint. In this case it could be an association with another person at another time in your life, or simply that this little man reminds you of someone you once feared, or it could be something else. The important thing to remember is that fears that may be rooted in the unconscious should be acknowledged and catalogued. Whenever you encounter such fears, take the time to explore them. It is not important to understand their origin or meaning; it is much more important to *experience* your response to the object that stimulated the fear in the first place. Record the experience. Keep a notebook of such occurrences, and be very specific about every detail.

As part of your daily work schedule, you might elect to re-create your most recent fear experience, using Imaging as your approach technique. For example, if you chose that little old man in the corner of the restaurant, you might start by imaging your own table, tasting your food, and creating the ambience of the room. You would begin to glance around the place until your eyes landed on the face of that man, and you would then create every detail of him, allowing yourself to reexperience the fear you felt originally—only this time encouraging it to play itself out. Go further with it; feel it envelop you. Quite possibly it may ignite other fears related to the original object. Stay with it as long as possible. Remember that the purpose of all of this is to create a relationship with your unconscious. Every time you involve yourself with anything that might be tied in to the unconscious, you are establishing a stronger connection with it, which will make you more dimensional and infinitely more faceted and unpredictable in all of your work.

WORKING WITH DREAMS

Addressing unconscious fears also means that you must become aware of them in your dreams (I will get much deeper into dreams and dreaming later in this chapter). At first, just make a decision to remember your dreams when you wake up. Keep a notepad or a tape recorder by your bedside, and immediately upon awakening, record everything you remember about the night's dreams. Dreams fade away very quickly, so jump on it immediately! Once you have committed the specifics to paper, you may not have the time or want to deal with the dream immediately, but whatever the case may be, you have it recorded and can return to it when the time is right. Sometimes, you should explore a particular dream immediately. There aren't any hard and fast rules in making that decision. It depends on the nature or impact of the dream and is more a question of having a gut feeling about it.

When using a dream as a way of connecting with the unconscious, don't analyze or try to interpret it. Go back over the experiences in it and try to respond to them emotionally. There are several ways to explore your dreams. You can just remember the experiences intellectually, or you may want to re-create the images literally. Sometimes, just remembering the events in a dream or nightmare can raise your blood pressure or quicken your heart rate. You could therefore start there and see where it leads. When you re-create the images in a dream, using all of your senses, you are actually speaking to your unconscious. It is almost like feeding the images of the dream back into the computer from which they came. Since the unconscious is so mysterious and mercurial, that may get a response or it may not! A third approach is to share the dream with someone verbally or just talk about it audibly to yourself. Quite often, hearing something can ignite a response if one happens to be "rise-able" through the auditory sense. I encourage you to explore all of those approaches in order to use your dreams as a technique for communicating with the unconscious.

I have had recurring dreams for some time. They are not frequent but nonetheless follow a similar pattern. In the previous chapter, I detailed a dream about going over a cliff on my motorcycle on Route 1. In a couple of recent dreams I went through similar near-death experiences.

In the first dream, I was driving a car on a two-lane road at about sixty-five miles an hour. The road curved gently to the left, and as I negotiated the turn, it abruptly ended in a large body of water, possibly a very large and deep lake. I jumped out of the car, just as it plunged into the water and began to sink. At that moment I saw another man reaching into the water with his right arm and bringing his car back to the surface. I followed his example and was able to easily lift my automobile out of the water and back onto the road. It seemed logical for me to be able to do that! The size and weight of the car did not seem to present a hardship, and I was able to lift it effortlessly. I remember thinking that it seemed very stupid to build a road that led into the water, while at the same moment I thought that I had possibly taken a wrong turn somewhere. I could feel my heart beating rapidly, and the perspiration was pouring down my face. I really felt frightened! The greatest component of my fear was the possibility of plunging into the water and sinking down into a bottomless abyss.

I experienced the second dream several months later. While similar in nature to the first one, this dream had slightly different components. Here again I was driving, this time in an open convertible and with someone at my side. I don't know who the other person was, and I didn't in the dream either. The road ahead was clear and comfortable to ride on. All of a sudden, I ran out of highway and plunged over a cliff. I was able to see the surface below, and again it was water, a large body of it—not the ocean, but large enough for me not to see the opposite shoreline. I distinctly remember feeling the weightless sensation of falling, that peculiar feeling in the stomach that one experiences on a roller coaster. All of those sensations felt quite real. I remember thinking, I am dead; I hope it is fast and without pain! I could see the water coming closer as the car tilted forward. I awoke before hitting the water, and I am sitting here quite alive reporting the dream—fortunately!

Both of those dreams deal with fear, fear that is obviously attached to some unconscious source. They both involve water and falling or plunging to certain death. I accept that I must have a very active fear of death, particularly violent death. Where this fear comes from, I don't know. I am, however, convinced that the core of these fears is buried in my unconscious and thereby very usable in contacting it from a conscious place. When I was about twelve years old, before I learned to swim, someone pushed me into the deep side of a large pool at Franklin Park in Chicago. I still hold this memory very vividly some fifty years later! I recall hitting the water with my eyes open and feeling the shock of the impact, which was totally unexpected. I began to sink. I saw the bubbles rush past my face. All the noise stopped. I could no longer hear the other children frolicking and screaming with excitement. Everything was quiet, except for the sound of the water rushing by me as I sank to the bottom. It is true that your life flashes by you—or at least it did for me! I saw my father as he looked when I was much younger, as well as other family members who were laughing and talking to me; I re-experienced my first day in school and many other fragments of my life, which seemed to flash by on this "screen" just behind my eyes. I knew I was drowning! I had swallowed mouthfuls of water on impact and felt as though I was suffocating. I was still conscious as I collided with the smooth bottom, and I thought of using my legs to catapult me to the surface—which is exactly what I did. My fear and/or energy were so great that I was propelled up like a rocket and landed on my stomach on the lip of the pool, fully out of the water! I had gone to the park with my cousin Irving, who had witnessed the whole event and thought it was a sensational feat of gymnastic prowess! Little did he know the reality of what had just happened. I never did tell him the truth.

My fears of falling and of drowning in water could have begun with that experience—I don't really know. However, wherever they came from, they are surely locked up in some labyrinth of unconscious fears. So the question is, How can I use the events above as tools to create communication with my unconscious?

In the first place, my memories of those dreams and experiences are so vivid that just recalling them has an effect on me! As I remember each of the dreams, I feel uneasy and get the same physical responses as I did then. Fear is a definable feeling! I feel a similar fear, even though I know that I am sitting safely in a chair on solid ground! I also experience some vague and abstract sensations that are hard to describe. There is a feeling of darkness that surrounds both of those dreams. I am very much in touch with my mortality at those times. Just the act of remembering stimulates a connection with the origin of the dreams. I feel an energy in my body and my emotional life that cannot be defined.

Something happens to me that fills me with a certain kind of underlife that enriches my behavior and expression.

As I collect these dreams and recount them, I add choices to my repertoire that will help build the road into the unconscious. At this point I would like to remind the reader that our concentration here is on unconscious fears and the dreams and nightmares that embody them. There are many other kinds of dreams that are also very valuable in piquing the unconscious. We will explore those later.

> ### Imaging the Dream

Re-creating a dream is very much like re-creating any other experience. With Imaging as a choice approach, you start at the beginning and use all five senses to create all of the sensorial elements of the experience.

I am going to work on the dream I had about driving into the lake. Once again I want to remind you that I am doing this to practice communicating with the unconscious. If, on the other hand, I was using this dream (choice) as a preparation to address a specific piece of material, a scene that contained the emotional components embodied in the dream, my goal would be to prime my unconscious sources to liberate into my consciousness the elements contained in the dream. I would, in a sense, be soliciting unconscious support to address the emotional obligations of the material. It is not necessary to re-create every dream you have—only the most impacting and vividly memorable ones.

Always start an imaging exercise with a relaxation preparation. When you are re-creating a dream, that is even more important, since when you are asleep, you are relaxed! After achieving a relaxed state, close your eyes and begin to image the dream from the beginning. Allow the images to come up spontaneously. You may do this lying down or in a sitting position:

I'm in a car...feel the seat...smell the leather upholstery...Hands on the wheel...see the road ahead of me...broken yellow lines passing rapidly past my front tires...If I look at them for a while, it becomes hypnotic...dashboard...gauges...sixty-five miles an hour...needle quivering...blank horizon ahead...Hear the sound of air rushing past the open window...feel the vibration of the tires on the pavement...on my seat... on my back...There is something surrealistic about this entire experience ...I don't know where I am going...(All of the above is actually taking place without words or comments. All of my senses are working simultaneously in Imaging Sensations to supply the elements of my dream.) *I see the road gently bearing to the left...On the right I see the road I was on...turns into a dirt road...I feel my body leaning to the left as the car eases in that direction...The road ahead of me begins to tilt downwards...and instead of blacktop, it turns into light-colored cement...no lines...just white pavement...I see the reflection of the sun as the pavement rushes beneath me...I'm curious but not alarmed...All of a sudden I see where the car is heading...The pavement ahead of me leads directly into the water...very large body of water...The pavement looks like a boat-launching ramp...I feel panic...fear in every part of my body...I know I'm going in...*(At this point in the re-creation I allow myself to experience whatever surfaces. I encourage the feelings—the panic, the fear, the helplessness, and so on. It is important to note here that the greater the emotional involvement, the closer I am to piquing an unconscious response.)

I see the water coming closer...In the very next moment, I am standing on the edge of the road looking at my car beginning to sink...I don't know how I got out of it...I must have jumped, but I have no memory of doing that!...I'm looking at my car slowly going down...It is a 1930s vintage automobile, which doesn't seem strange to me at all!...At that moment, on the other side of the road, I see a man reaching into the water and pulling his car out onto the pavement...He is short and stout and has thinning hair...I look at his action without surprise and begin doing the same with my car...It seems quite easy to lift it out of the water...only it has shrunk in size to a model car and has changed color...

At this point the dream ends. I might repeat the re-creation of the experience several times, each time remembering more details. Usually, imaging an experience is done with the eyes open; however, in the case of a dream, you are encouraged to do it with your eyes closed. Since when we are asleep, our eyes are closed, the dream process and whatever images we experience take place with the inner eye. Also, understand that you will have many more images in all five sensory areas (Imaging Sensations) than what I gave you in my attempt to describe the imaging process—subtleties that will liberate themselves into your awareness.

Find time to re-create your dreams; set aside specific moments to address your unconscious. The more you practice this process, the fuller the responses and the closer you will come to unconscious connection.

IMPULSIVITY WORKOUTS AND EXPLORATIONS

The next area to explore is *impulsivity*. I use a variety of impulsivity exercises in my classes, usually to antidote concept and leadership in an actor's work. Encouraging himself to express each impulse with great speed and as soon as it formulates itself keeps the actor from thinking and premeditating his next expression or the next line of material. The goal is to honor every impulse on a moment-to-moment basis, thereby avoiding any thought of what to say or how it should be said. In this framework an impulsivity exercise is an amazing tool for antidoting dependency on logic and concept. At a certain point, I will ask the actor to carry his moment-to-moment impulses into the lines of a written monologue, of course being irreverent to the author's intentions. What he experiences then is a complete connection with his here-and-now reality, and freedom from his usual conceptual ties to the material. The experience of suddenly being connected to those words from an organic place and not attached to their meaning liberates the actor, while at the same moment opening a new door of awareness.

After many years of success with this technique, it occurred to me that it could also be used to stimulate unconscious impulses. Our moment-to-moment impulses come from what we see, hear, feel, and think, so why not from "hooking into" some unconscious trough? I began to look for expressions that didn't seem to originate from an identifiable place, abstract responses that seemed unconnected to anything that had preceded them. Unsure of their source and not at all convinced that they were linked in any way to unconscious life, I listened to the actor and closely observed him. When a particular impulse or a flow of them seemed to modify his overall behavior pattern, I suspected that the change was due to some kind of unconscious energy. I knew that the exercise as structured was too unpredictable to serve as a tool to reach the unconscious. So I devised a more dependable way of using impulsivity to pique unconscious responses.

DISCONNECTED IMPULSIVITY

Conventionally, this exercise consists of expressing whatever moment-to-moment impulses may surface. It is called *Disconnected* Impulsivity because the actor is encouraged to honor and express every impulse, even if it interrupts a sentence or occurs in the middle of a word. In other words, he must *disconnect* from one impulse and express the next one that surfaces at that moment, and he must do so at lightning speed. Rapidity is very necessary to the success of the exercise, since it does not allow the actor to think or to insert any commentary between his impulses.

➤ *Example*

In order to give you an authentic example of this technique, I recorded one on tape while sitting at a table in my house in Lake Arrowhead. As with all Disconnected Impulsivity exercises, you start with what you see around you and from there go anywhere, hopefully including your inner impulses and feelings. Even though the process starts very arbitrarily, it usually piques an inner flow of impulses and images that are often connected to conscious and unconscious memory banks.

The following is a transcript of the tape I made:

"Looking around...see...the floor...orange...orange sky...see clouds ...trees...rain...snow...it's going to snow...hate snow...little boy rolling in snow...cold wet...looking outside...fireplace...see the lake through it ...couch...leather...love leather...picture...paintings...see it—Santa Fe ...I see that...beautiful...I'm looking at the reindeer...remember getting that Christmas...feeling smells of that...the table—it's antique...love antique...trees...trees over there...pines...love them...smell it...fresh...the woods...hiking...Boy Scouts...love it, best time in my life...building fires...going snipe hunting...pines...knotty pine...den...sitting there... she's looking at me...laughing...looking around...lights...lights are out ...Fillmore Street...where did that come from? Used to live on Fillmore Street...Trombino lived downstairs...and I don't know, and my father... where is he?...and I don't know...and there are things over there...it's snowing outside...it's not snowing—why did I say that?...It's going to snow...I hate...snow...chains...and weather...see the bench...there are slats in the bench...I'm thinking about Chicago...Chicago...it's always cold...walking along the lake...Northwestern...University...it's freezing ...windchill factor...forty below zero...what am I doing here?...I don't know...and here I am and...looking...Northwestern...acting...theater... school..."

At this point, I discontinued the exercise. All of the above impulses were expressed with lightning speed, which gave me no time to think or premeditate anything. Much of what came out was the result of what I saw inside and outside the room I was in. I started the exercise arbitrarily, expressing the first thing that came to me, and then encouraged the flow of anything that followed. Many of the verbal expressions were accompanied by images, which impacted all my senses. The technique works very well to promote impulsive flow and to antidote concept and premeditation. It also provides a staging area for the unconscious to come through. In the above example, there are a number of expressions that are intensely connected to my inner life—meaningful references to times, places, and people that were very impacting in my evolution. If I had done the exercise as a preparation or as a technique for liberating unconscious impulses, those references might have activated a flow of unconscious life that would have supported my subsequent acting. It is hard to say for sure! When I finished doing it, I felt different. My emotional life had not changed drastically, but I began thinking about my childhood on Fillmore Street and having some images of people from that time. My thoughts also took me back to my university days at Northwestern—which had a strange and disturbing effect on me. I am not sure why I had those feelings! What did the reference to my father mean—wondering where he is when I know very well that he died in July of 1969—and where did it come from? Trombino was the name of the landlord of the building where we lived on Fillmore Street. We had a lot of conflicts with him. One time I thought he was going to hit my father, and I remember being terrified! The reference to the Boy Scouts is very important. As I have said before, even though it happened over fifty years ago, I still have strong and pleasant feelings about that special time in my life! I still have dreams occasionally about being back there in that church basement, with all my friends and Mr. Nemec, the scoutmaster, with his broad and benevolent smile, his false teeth so perfect, reflecting the light as he opened his mouth! I loved that man for who and what he was and for everything he gave all of us, including me! And there were Morty and Hogan and John Graff, who never forgave me for winning the vote and becoming assistant patrol leader. Many of the impulses expressed in that impulsivity exercise are connected to important periods in my life.

Although Disconnected Impulsivity used in this way is a good tool for piquing unconscious responses, it is nevertheless unpredictable. At times, it is rich with impulses that are rooted deep beneath the surface, while at other times it is filled with just obvious and superficial responses to the environment. When approached with meaningful suggestions, however, it can turn into a very powerful tool for accessing unconscious responses.

ADDING MEANINGFUL SUGGESTIONS TO
DISCONNECTED IMPULSIVITY

Let us suppose I started another impulsivity workout but this time injected into it the meaningful things that came out of the first exercise, starting with Fillmore Street and encouraging all the impulses that resulted from that suggestion. I would allow whatever thoughts, feelings, impulses, and images to run their course, and then I might insert a suggestion related to my father and see where *that* went. Following that, I could relate something from my time with the Boy Scouts, and so on until I ran out of meaningful suggestions. It is something like stacking the deck with "jelly beans"! Knowing that all of these suggestions are charged with meaningful agenda, I can expect that there will be some kind of communication with the unconscious.

There are a couple of ways to do this. The first one is to just start an exercise, see what comes up, make note of what seem to be important expressions, and then repeat the process with those things added to it to see what happens. Following every one of your exercises, do Personal Inventory to see how you feel. After completing the impulsivity exercise described above, for example, I had a combination of feelings. I was definitely affected: I experienced an uncomfortable flash of energy related to my experiences at Northwestern University, while at the mention of the Boy Scouts and Mr. Nemec, I felt vulnerable and nostalgic. Those feelings persisted for quite a while and gave birth to many other thoughts, feelings, and images related to that period in my life. If, when I was experiencing that flush of emotions, I had started to address an obligation in a scene, I think that the process of creating a choice might have been filled with some inspirational support from the unconscious.

A second approach is to immediately start with suggestions that you know have a lot of "juice"—experiences from very important periods of your life, elements from dreams, images you have had all your life, fears, people who have unexplainable impact on you, and any event that is supercharged with conglomerated emotions. Since the unconscious *is* unconscious, we have no guarantees that any process we involve ourselves with will yield that kind of support. We must hope, however, that we will access impulses that *do* come from places just below our conscious awareness. Added to other techniques, and with repeated explorations, either of the above approaches can be very effective in building that bridge to the unconscious or as a preparation for doing a scene. If you are just using Disconnected Impulsivity as a device for establishing a relationship with your unconscious, it doesn't matter what suggestions you start with. If, on the other hand, you have a specific result in mind, you should carefully choose suggestions that hopefully will elicit a particular unconscious life related to your goal. If you "stack" your impulsivity exercise with *choices* that you know pique unconscious responses, you could expect to be affected in a certain way, which will encourage unconscious support for the emotional life that you are obligated to experience.

The value of impulsivity explorations is that they *are* impulsive and unpredictable and allow unknown feelings and impulses to surface. Of course, you must repeat them on a daily or weekly basis and make the journey to the unconscious part of your training schedule.

THE SWITCH-TRICK EXERCISE

Another in the cluster of impulsivity explorations is the Switch-Trick exercise. Somewhat different in structure from the others, it has very few words attached to it. In a classroom, I switch the actors from stimulus to stimulus. Often, I will even supply the suggested stimuli for them to respond to. The exercise can be done as a two-person workout or be self-regulated. Here again speed is a very important element. The actor must respond with his first impulse to each suggestion and may express that response verbally, vocally, or even silently. If the exercise is done by two persons, the one directing it will switch the other from stimulus to stimulus very quickly, at times so much so that it seems the actor hasn't the time to respond at all. The goal, again, is to pique, access, or stimulate unconscious responses. If the exercise is done properly, its potential is incredible. Over the years, I have seen its impact on the many actors who have done it in my classes. As an impulsivity workout, it pushes the actor to a razor's edge of impulsivity and, as a bonus, often brings up congested emotional life that had been relegated to the unconscious. The result depends, of course, on the nature of the suggestions and on where the actor is at the time he begins. If he has done other preparations before embarking on this journey, he can be very accessible to internal and external stimuli; so it is suggested that he do some preliminary preparations before using this technique to "converse" with the unconscious. He might start with Personal Inventory, followed by a Sharing Monologue filled with meaningful experiences. He could also elect to do a Primal Moan exercise to elevate his vulnerability, or even share a meaningful dream. All of those preparations could prime his emotional pumps in a way that might appeal to his unconscious.

Following the preparations, and supposing that he was more accessible, he would start the Switch-Trick exercise by suggesting objects, people, places, pieces of experiences, events, encounters, imaginary circumstances, fantasies, people he knows involved in outrageous activities, and so on. If he did this without the help of another person directing him, he would switch himself from one stimulus to another with great speed. His suggestions should be impulsive and in the form of *evocative images.* He would encourage a flow of those images, switching from one to another. Quite often, the images would be modified by his impulsive suggestions. For example, he might image his dog running around the yard and suddenly add a second evocative image of the same dog lying dead in a pool of blood! He may even supplement that with another suggestion of the animal abruptly returning to life. The surprise trick-and-shock value provided by many of these impulsive responses keeps him off balance and away from premeditation or leadership. The dog in his image may relate to one that he had as a little boy and that has long since departed. While a boy and his dog may be a great American cliché, there could be a wealth of memories and experiences associated with that dog, and by accessing them, the actor might open a Pandora's box of "goodies" that will catapult him into an unconscious never-never land!

He may continue the exercise for some time, switching his images from place to place and from one time to another. The key to succeeding with this technique is to remain impulsive and to encourage the discovery of the next image in the next moment without any expectation. Surprise is an important factor.

This is a difficult exercise to do for a number of reasons. It is not easy, in the first place, to allow oneself to be totally open to the next moment without having some thought or idea about what should happen, and secondly, to avoid any kind of expectations. Actors who are dependent on knowing what comes next have a harder time with the technique. Practice and repetition often antidote the obstacles.

The advantage of doing this as a two-person exercise is that the actor cannot predict or premeditate when the "director" is going to switch him or suggest an object. Therefore, he is available to a response without interference from his brain! His evocative image is encouraged immediately without a split second to premeditate anything. However, when it is impossible to enlist the help of a second person, he can do the exercise by himself. Both approaches are valid. The two-person version is a very good rehearsal tool. As two actors are getting ready to do a scene, one of them could facilitate the other through a Switch-Trick preparation before the second one starts to work for his choice. It has a twofold purpose: it stimulates impulsivity and at the same time may elicit unconscious responses.

➤ *Example of the Two-Person Approach*

The director might sit or stand several feet away from the actor and start the exercise with a single suggestion: "Grade-school classroom." The actor is encouraged to respond with any image related to the suggestion. All of the responses are in the form of IMAGES. His first image may not be of a classroom but of a pair of short pants he wore in grade school. After a very brief pause the director will "switch" him simply by saying "Switch!" At this point the actor is obligated to supply the next image immediately as it manifests itself. It may be one of the schoolyard at recess accompanied by a collage of activities and faces from his past…"Switch!" and he goes to a completely different time and place: he images his mother standing over the stove cooking. "Switch!" He sees his sister busily involved with dressing her doll—"Switch!" The sound of the director's voice cuts through the air, interrupting that image and producing another one—of his father reprimanding him for fooling with the lawnmower. "Switch!" He is on a football field with an army of huge players from the other team converging on him—"Switch!" He feels the ball cradled between his forearm and his chest, hears the crowd screaming, and feels the ground beneath his feet as he presses forward—"Switch!" And there is a flurry of new images totally unrelated to the previous ones.

At any point the director may interject a suggestion for the actor to respond to. He may suggest that there is someone standing in the doorway of the theater. This is responded to with an image that the actor evokes impulsively. It could be anyone from any place in his life. The director may follow this suggestion by saying, "It's the last person in the world that you want to see," at which point the actor might image such a person. "Switch!" And the actor is on his own once more: His evoked images may be of a crowd of people standing in that doorway, or he may go someplace else entirely. "Look out!" the director shouts. "You are surrounded by dangerous things!" He must respond by encouraging an image of spiders or poisonous snakes or any other objects that he considers dangerous. "No," the director shouts, "they are not dangerous at all. They are adorable puppies." He must modify the image immediately. "Switch!" And again he must supply a new image.

And so the exercise may continue for as long as ten minutes. At the conclusion of it, the actor should feel many different things: He could, for example, be highly stimulated, feel adrenaline coursing through his veins, be energized and filled with impulses exploding and bottlenecking to be released and, right below the surface, converging emotions that seem hard to separate or interpret. Depending on the nature of his images and the director's suggestions, he should be experiencing the aftermath of whatever memories and unconscious life were piqued during the exercise. Besides obviously achieving greater impulsivity, the technique will also hopefully bring the unconscious closer to consciousness. Even if the life stimulated has nothing to do with a material obligation, liberating the unconscious so that it may support the actor's conscious behavior will enrich everything that follows.

> ### Example of One-Person Approach

The one-person version can be done almost anywhere and at any time. The evocative images are suggested silently. Any sounds or words come out of the responses to those images.

This technique can be used for a variety of reasons—to stimulate and encourage an impulsive state, to activate the unconscious, or as a specific preparation to address an obligation in a scene. Having identified the desired emotional state, the actor could suggest a flow of images related to a particular time or issue, expecting that they will hook into the unconscious and encourage its support.

The actor can do the exercise standing or sitting; however, my feeling is that sitting somehow cuts off a physical dynamic that is important to the process. He starts by suggesting an image. The suggestion is not verbal, but comes in the form of an image:

A place...(The words I use are to describe the imaging process and do not exist for the actor. He sees a room, a bedroom, replete with odors, sounds, and tactile responses.) *Model airplanes hanging from the ceiling...voices in the other room...indistinguishable voices...*(Switch to another image.) *Backyard...Fillmore Street...Corky...the dog...jumping, playing...Hear the train from across the street...*(Switch!) *Cemetery... people are standing around a casket...quiet...crying...Feel the wind... bronze casket...reflections of people...images...black...*(Switch!) *Going down fast, roller coaster...Marie...screaming...Feel the wind blowing through my hair...tracks...coming fast...Chasing the reflection of the sun on the track...can't catch it...*(Switch!) *Snorkeling...beautiful water ...blue-green...incredible fish...caught in current...moving fast...scared*

...What to do?...(Switch!) Standing on the summit of a mountain...see forever...smell the air...hear the wind...otherwise a kind of silence never heard before...(Switch!) Dark place...don't recognize it...maybe a dream...maybe it happened...confused...

All of the experiences come from the images. There aren't any words attached to the stimulation of those images. **It is important that the actor use all five senses in the imaging process.** After completing the exercise, he can take a brief inventory of his emotional state and determine whether or not he accomplished his purpose. If he isn't satisfied with what the exercise yielded, he can reinvest in it, possibly structuring the first group of images so that they relate to a particular experience or event.

➤ *Example 2*

For the second example, I am going to use a personal experience that happened many years ago. I was on Christmas break from school visiting my older brother in New York City. It was quite cold. At that point in my life, I had decided to become a professional photographer and had sent out a number of applications to photography schools around the country. During my visit, we took the Staten Island ferry, which passes the Statue of Liberty at some distance. I had borrowed my niece's Brownie camera, which was a simple machine, much less evolved than the equipment I had back in Chicago. I exposed an entire roll of film on the journey and took it into a drugstore to be developed. In those days there weren't any laboratories that returned your pictures in an hour, so it took three days to get the prints back. (I am taking the time here to describe an experience that was traumatic and life changing, and I must fill in all of the details in order for the reader to understand why I selected it.) I remember standing on a busy New York street as my brother opened the envelope that contained the developed pictures. I watched him take them out and saw his expression contort into what seemed like a demonic mask of repulsion and disgust. This metamorphosis was followed by an avalanche of critical and denigrating shouts. He spared me nothing: "What is this? You call yourself a photographer? These pictures are the worst things I have ever seen! You have no talent or imagination. My ten-year-old daughter takes better pictures than these! You'd better give it up, son! These are pathetic, a waste of time and money!"—all the while shouting at the top of his voice. People stopped, turned as they passed, looking at this scene, which was a little much even for New York City! I cannot describe how I felt. I was embarrassed, humiliated; I wanted to find a hole and crawl into it! His tirade seemed endless! His attack hurts to this day. Needless to say, I gave up my pursuit of photography and didn't touch a camera for ten years—which turned out to be a blessing, since I am doing what I love!

This example might be used as a choice to begin the exercise with. I might suggest the first image:

Deck...ferryboat...water...reflections...camera...looking through the viewfinder...Statue of Liberty...(At this point all of my senses are operating simultaneously.) *Standing on the street...drugstore...his face ...angry, distorted...shouting...Can't make out all the words...People passing...looking...Feel terribly self-conscious and embarrassed...hurt ...taxicabs...horns...Want to escape from here...Everything is blurred...*

Even though I understand that this is a Switch-Trick exercise, which shouldn't have any planning or premeditating, I take the liberty of structuring the first part of it as a way of stimulating a deeper connection with my inner life. Having done this, I am now ready to return to the demands of the technique. At this point, the images may vary and go into other areas and experiences. What I had hoped to accomplish by this was to elicit impulses from the unconscious and set myself on a course of deeper connection with it. I continue to evoke images on an impulsive level, expecting that the emotional life that follows will have been piqued and influenced by that impacting experience.

The impulsivity cluster is yet another area of exploration on the journey to establishing a liaison with the unconscious. Add it to your repertoire of exercises that seduce the unconscious into cooperating.

LOGY

This next preparation is ostensibly a relaxation exercise. I have had amazing results with it in my classes. Actors who had monumental tension problems have been able to antidote them by doing *Logy* before working. In addition, many of them report having images and impulses which seem to come from an unconscious source. At a particular point during the exercise, they seem to achieve a HYPNAGOGIC STATE, where they are not asleep but not entirely awake either. During that period, they experience a flow of images and thoughts that are often fragmented and unrelated. At the point when they become aware of those strange images and impulses, they are once again in a conscious state. When doing Logy, it is possible to go in and out of the hypnagogic state many times. As a result of the combination of relaxation and the hypnagogic experience, actors seem very relaxed and in a transformed state of being, and the work that follows is usually very good.

The actor does the exercise lying down in a prone position. He encourages a slothlike attitude and exaggerates his body weight until he feels as if he weighed five thousand pounds. At all times, he is making a sound that comes from that behavior and using the word "logy"! It is very important that he continue the sound through most of the exercise and stop only when entering into the hypnagogic state. At a point when he has achieved feeling the weight, he might try to roll over on his side to experience the enormous effort it entails. The exercise might last for as much as a half hour. Usually, I send students out to the lobby of the theater to do it, so that they will not be interrupted by the activities of the class. When they return, most of them look as if they had just awakened from a deep sleep full of impacting dreams. In almost every instance they seem permissive and benevolent—and definitely ready to work! The hypnagogic phenomenon does not occur every time, but it does happen often. If the actor feels himself beginning to "drop off," it is at this point that he should encourage his images and, on some level, be aware of them. With repetition of the Logy exercise an actor can become quite facile at "working" his unconscious. The downside is that he may fall asleep—which also happens. The trick is to be able to keep coming out of the hypnagogic state and encouraging reentry into it.

When you do this exercise, allow the images to go wherever they will, and, with whatever percentage of awareness still exists, make a note of them and how they make you feel. There is a fine line between awareness and the hypnagogic, and you must learn to treat it delicately. If you become too aware of the images and thoughts, you will shock yourself out of a hypnagogic state, but on the other hand, if you surrender totally to that state, you will probably fall asleep! So it is important that you develop a facility to walk that tightrope between the two states. Remember why you are doing the Logy exercise. In this instance it is not only for the relaxation benefits but mostly as a preparation to establish a connection with the unconscious so as to elicit its support to catapult you into a scene.

THE HYPNAGOGIC STATE

We can enter into the hypnagogic state at times other than when doing Logy. It quite naturally occurs when we are about to fall asleep. It is the time when, while we are still conscious but are between wakefulness and sleep, the unconscious is beckoned to the surface and begins to liberate its images into our consciousness. Unlike dreaming, this is a state when we are still awake enough to have a conscious response to the images, which often startle us into a fully awake state. It is often quite unsettling, and we may wonder in our awake state "what that was all about." The images and thoughts don't seem to be attached to anything that we were thinking about just before they occurred. In fact, most of the time they seem quite unrelated to anything! In most instances the hypnagogic phenomenon lasts only a few seconds. We either become aware of it or not. Most often we just drift off to sleep.

Your first step in harnessing the hypnagogic is to become aware of it and to begin encouraging yourself to participate in the activity of the unconscious. With repetition you will be able to prolong each hypnagogic episode. Remember that the goal is to use this state to prepare to act. For example, just before approaching a rehearsal, you might do a Logy preparation, fully encouraging the cooperation of the unconscious. Create a habit of seducing the unconscious by promoting the hypnagogic state. As you repeat the process, you can expect to become quite capable of experiencing the events. Following each of these preparations, begin working for the choices that you are using to address the obligations of the scene. If you decide to encourage and experience the hypnagogic response every time you go to sleep, you will establish a greater facility with the technique.

DAYDREAMING

Another important involvement that encourages unconscious responses is daydreaming, which we all do naturally. However, instead of doing it less than consciously, you can practice it daily. Either put aside some time in your work schedule to daydream, or consciously do it at various times each day. In the beginning, the decision to daydream is very conscious and can be quite structured. You may, for example, decide to daydream about playing the lead in a film you saw the night before, imaging yourself on the set and in each of the scenes. In addition to stimulating the various images, you can encourage your emotional responses to them and to the events of the daydream. If you do it for the pleasure and fulfillment that we get from daydreaming, you are likely to encourage the process more frequently. You may even create an episodic structure, picking up tomorrow where you left off today! While the elements of a daydream come mostly from a conscious place, the involvement leads to unconscious responses and participation. Very often you will experience images and responses that come from an unconscious place and can divert the daydream into a completely different direction. These should be encouraged. Allow for anything that comes up. It is like taking an unpredictable journey, and it can be very rewarding if you make it an adventure. Besides deriving enjoyment from the experience of including daydreams into your daily work schedule, you might use them as general unconscious preparations just before beginning to approach a scene or a monologue.

➢ *Example of a Daydream*

I was watching the news last night and saw the older couple who won the lottery—thirty-four million dollars! I began to imagine what that would mean to my life. I started to daydream about having won all that money, and soon I was off into a full-blown fantasy filled with incredible images of places I would go to and things I would do and have. I allowed those images to emerge impulsively, and in the space of ten or fifteen minutes I had created an entire life filled with all of the activities and indulgences one might fantasize about. A daydream can start with a thought and then move into logical or less-than-logical images.

I can do anything I want to!...I don't have to do anything I don't want to do ever again!...What would be the first thing that I would do? ...I might not do anything!...I would help my children and friends...I would play Santa Claus for a while, making their dreams come true... "What do you want? O.K., here's the money; go and get it!..." I would buy a large garage...and fill it with all the cars I have ever wanted...I would tell my wife to go out and spend money foolishly...

At some point I would encourage myself to move from thoughts into imaging:

I begin to image myself in a variety of places, dressed in different outfits and dining in different restaurants in different parts of the world. As I negotiate hairpin turns in the mountains of Italy in my twelve-cylinder Ferrari, I feel myself being caressed by the butter-soft leather of the seat and moving gently with the car as it rounds the curves. I smell the leather and hear the sound that only a Ferrari can make!...I feel the warm wind on my face and my hair dancing with it. The colors are breathtaking; the sun is warm and comforting...I feel pampered! I'm heading for the studio for a script conference about a film I wrote, am producing, directing, and starring in!...I catch a glimpse of myself in the rearview mirror. I look terrific—tanned and healthy, wearing clothes designed for me...

At any point in the daydream, I might begin to have impulsive images that are not premeditated or structured. I must encourage them, as well as other impulses and thoughts. They are very likely coming from unconscious places piqued by my conscious fantasy. Without premeditation I might have the image of myself in an entirely different environment with people I don't know, unaware of how I got there or why I was there at all. I could find myself in the midst of an argument with a person in my life I never stood up to! I might be saying no to everyone whose image pops in! *I hear inner voices asking questions... asking me what's important...I can't answer those questions...Sometimes the inner voices make no sense at all!...*

Creating a habit of daydreaming can be very profitable, as it encourages your imagination and elevates your willingness to believe. It is a way of seducing the unconscious and can be used as a preparation to act. Once you have enlisted the inspiration of the unconscious, it continues to flow into your conscious behavior, enriching it with unpredictable dimension and depth! In the next chapter on programming the unconscious, I will further explore the use of daydreams.

INVOLUNTARY IMAGING

In chapter 3, I described in great detail all of the imaging techniques and the variety of purposes they serve. The wonderful thing about this work is that there are so many ways in which you can use a single technique! It is like that story of the elephant: If you blindfolded two men and took them to a different part of the same elephant, they would describe the animal quite differently. If the first man only felt the trunk, he would describe the elephant as being supple, mobile, and almost snakelike in its form; while the other man, who was only exposed to the hind leg, might say that this was a solid, unmoving, stoic animal without grace. And so it is with many parts of this system. If you decide to selectively emphasize the use of a technique to address a specific area, then that is how it will work for you.

Involuntary Imaging can serve as a way of opening the door to let the unconscious pass through. To start this exercise, lie down on your back on a comfortable surface. Clear your brain, do some relaxation or deep breathing, erase the blackboard of your mind, and begin to encourage any and all of the images that you experience.

➤ *Example*

Nothing...I see nothing...just blackness...I'm trying not to think...I feel thoughts collecting somewhere in me and wanting to be acknowledged...I won't give in to them...I'm remembering a dream I had last night...no images yet...

(Don't push yourself to image anything. Try not to expect anything, and avoid any kind of leadership. You may not make contact with the unconscious every time you do this, but at the very least, it is a wonderful way to relax and practice your imaging techniques.)

I smell roasting marshmallows...feel that charcoal texture of a burned marshmallow on the tip of my fingers...can taste its sugary creaminess in my mouth...Lying on the ground in a large vacant lot... Feel the hardness on my back...stickers...hurt...Smell smoke from a train...Hear it going by...Chalk...throw us some chalk...Bobby Snell... See his red hair and freckled face...upside down standing over me... looks funny upside down...Watching a movie...nightclub...forties look... Remember that time...everything...people, décor...post art deco...Feel warm and a little sad...vulnerable...See images of the war...Errol Flynn ...Objective Burma, The Sands of Iwo Jima...scenes flash by like images on a screen...Excited...feel proud...overwhelmed with sadness and nostalgia...My eyes filling with tears...Want to stop imaging...need to continue...Riding my bike...brown and cream...can feel the wind on my face...see the light on the front fender...Pacemaker...that's the name of my bike...A warm and good feeling is washing over my body...I feel like closing my eyes and really being back there...

At this point I decide to stop the imaging process. I sit up and begin to go back over the experience. I really don't know where those images came from. I remember all those places, people, and things, but I don't know what started that stream of involuntary images. They were all connected to a time in my life, but that time was over fifty years ago! Why would I begin to image that time, those places? I was very affected by the exercise, so much so that I wanted to stop doing it. Most of the images related to a particular time during the Second World War, when I was in grade school and lived across the street from a very large vacant lot. A railroad train ran parallel to the lot on an elevated bridge-like structure. A bunch of us used to play there every evening and on weekends. When I think about that time, I do not feel particularly nostalgic; however, when I was experiencing those images, I was overwhelmed with feelings. I felt sad and nostalgic, yet warm and protected! I wanted to be back there. I actually experienced all of the sensory responses to the objects that crashed into my images: I tasted the marsh-mallow, heard the train go by, felt the weeds as the sharp points of the "stickers" penetrated my pants, heard Bobby's voice as he laughed—all of that and more became real for me. Obviously, there is an awful lot of "stuff" packed into that time and place! When I decided to explore the imaging exercise, I had no idea what I might experience, and I haven't a clue as to what started that rush of images. I do know that it felt as though a giant door had opened up, and, as in Fibber McGee's closet, it all came tumbling out. I really don't know how much of that relates to the unconscious; however, I am sure that the well runs deep! There is a lot of emotional life involved in that period of time, and I feel that what I experienced was just the tip of the iceberg. I know that the images tapped into a very large memory bank, and my instinct tells me that those memories are rooted in the unconscious. As I sit here committing this to paper, I still feel the aftereffects of the experience. The best way to describe my feelings is to say that I feel very much the same as I did when I watched the last scene in *Citizen Kane,* when Orson Wells is dying and almost inaudibly mutters, "Rosebud"! I certainly intend to explore this area of my life. Besides its potential for eliciting un-conscious flow, it is rich with the buried gold of many powerful choices for my work.

There are a great number of exercises and techniques that can be used to create a connection with the unconscious. One of the advantages of Involuntary Imaging is that there is no direction or premeditation in-volved. You just start with an empty blackboard and allow images to appear. This approach therefore discourages leadership and expectation. While the example above related to a specific time and place, Involun-tary Imaging can jump around from time to time and place to place and contain a large variety of objects, as well as fragments of many expe-riences. Many of those images can be abstract and contain sounds and odors that are seemingly unrelated to them. You probably will not understand many of your responses or be able to trace their origin, but that is not the only reason for using the process. It is important to remember that every time you use an imaging technique you strengthen your connection with the unconscious. If indeed the language of the unconscious is images, then speaking that language with greater and greater frequency will build the bridge!

Rehearsing with these techniques elevates your knowledge about the unconscious and begins the process of conditioning a communication with it. When working with a piece of material, you might select a choice that you suspect contains impetus that would pique unconscious life, because you have explored it before and already have some knowledge or experience with it. It is important to note here that there is a distinct difference between working with techniques to learn about and explore the conscious-unconscious connection and using the process as an acting tool. What comes first is the understanding of how the unconscious manifests itself in our conscious behavior. Much like you need to practice Sense Memory every day in order to become sensorially accessible and proficient, you must make the journey into the unconscious a daily involvement.

SYMBOLIC IMAGING

Another process that directly solicits unconscious activity is the involvement with symbolic images. There is a very good section in chapter 3 of this book that already explores this technique. Please refer to it.

LISTENING TO YOUR INNER VOICES AND IMAGES

Many times throughout the day we experience thoughts and mental voices that seem to come from nowhere. Almost always we wonder what they were and what precipitated them. Mostly we dismiss the fleeting event and go on with our lives. Well, I'm here to tell you not to dismiss it, but to pay very close attention to those little voices that surface. The fragmented and fleeting images that cross the screen behind our eyes are very important. They are messages from the unconscious, and besides being incredibly instructive, they constitute a connection with it that can be harnessed and used. They bubble up into our conscious state and are telling us something that should be paid attention to, much like the lessons we learn from our dreams. We may never know or understand what precipitates these voices or images, but the important thing is to create a conscious awareness of their existence, to acknowledge them, and, if possible, to interpret their meaning.

Quite frequently, I will get an image or a feeling of being in a place that I have not seen for twenty or more years. The sense of it is so powerful that I can smell the odors attached to it and feel things related to that time in my life. When I try to figure out what piqued the image, I am almost always at a loss to find a connection with the life that immediately preceded it. It could be an unconscious association with a sound or odor, or even the temperature at a given moment; but no matter what the subliminal impetus was, it is at those times that I am connected to the unconscious in a very "delicious" way! If you encourage an awareness of these voices or images as they occur each day, you will begin to communicate with your unconscious while awake. The more you practice this awareness, the stronger your connections will become. Sometimes you will hear your inner voice speak someone's name, someone you haven't seen or thought of in a long time; or you might hear something that was said to you a while ago. The voice is loud and clear, so pay attention!

Our inner voices come from unpredictable places and are usually impulsively liberated into our consciousness. When working with the various choices we select to address the different obligations, we pique many images and inner voices, which of course in some way were stimulated by our exploration of those choices. In this manner we elicit unconscious impulses from a conscious source. This happens whether we are addressing the unconscious or not. It is quite important to encourage and include those unconscious impulses that filter into our consciousness. If an actor evolves into a PROFESSIONAL EXPERIENCER, he will naturally include all of the moment-to-moment life that occurs while he is expressing his impulses through the lines. All of that unconscious life will become part of his expression. So, in short, if the choice is impacting enough to elicit unconscious voices and images and the actor includes those in his behavior, the audience will be privy to discovering the next moment in the next moment, exactly at the same time as the actor does.

ENCOURAGING A MEDITATIVE STATE

Meditating is another activity you can engage in to connect with your unconscious. When I refer to meditation, I am not speaking of any of the structured forms of it, such as yoga or transcendental meditation or any of the others, and I am not saying that you shouldn't use those forms if you are qualified to; I am just using the word to indicate a simple process of clearing your brain of thoughts and background noise and allowing whatever comes up to do so. You can do this at any time and in any place. It is a very good relaxation exercise and can as well open a channel for unconscious impulses. If you are not preoccupied or tense, it is much easier for the unconscious to break through. You can do this preparation in a sitting or lying position, with your eyes closed or open, progressively clearing out your thoughts and creating an empty blackboard on which your unconscious can draw its pictures.

NIGHT GAMES

When I was very young, I hated going to bed. It seemed like a waste of living time, and living was exciting! So, in order to persuade myself to get into bed, I created stories and adventures that I could continue each night. Ultimately, my "night games" became so exciting that I looked forward to going to bed!

Without my knowing it, that is where my imaging journey started. I would create an adventure, almost always making myself the hero. In addition to imaging the places and people in my stories, I would speak, cry, yell, and *act* through each fantasy. Maybe that is where my love for acting began? I distinctly remember my senses being involved in those games. If, for example, I was wounded in one of those adventures, I really felt the pain, which sometimes lasted till morning. I would often wake up with an ache in some part of my body, wondering where it came from. While on these journeys, I tasted various kinds of foods, I smelled the campfire while exploring for gold, and I heard the roar of the lions when on safari in Africa. I know that those night games influenced my dreams, but I also believe that they hacked out a path for my unconscious to follow.

I call these *night games* because that is when I play them. You can use them as a preparation for eliciting unconscious life and see where they lead. I assure you that you will elevate your imagination as well as have a lot of fun. It is my belief that the fewer the obstacles that stand in the way of the unconscious, the greater the connection. Night games should be played with Imaging as the approach technique. Most of them will be fantasy, so you can use Story Imaging, Fragmented Imaging or start with Verbalized Imaging. You may have a simple theme to begin with and make it up as you go along, or you can invent a complete scenario, like a scene parallel.

UNCONSCIOUS SUGGESTIONS

There is also a large group of stimuli that exist in the area of unconscious suggestions. They all come from your own living experience. As you explore them, you will think of even more things that you can use.

I usually do this exercise at weekend workshops on Imaging: All the actors are instructed to lie down and, at first, close their eyes and begin to image the places and objects that I suggest to them. After a short time, they can open their eyes and include the visual area in their imaging process. When doing the exercise alone, you will have to make the suggestions yourself. You might write all of the categories down on a three-by-five card, which you can use to remind yourself of them. A tape recorder may also be of use. I call the exercise *Unconscious Suggestions* because many of the images do pique the unconscious.

We all have thousands of memories and experiences associated with the places we attempt to image, and very often these burrow their way deep into our unconscious. By re-creating those various places and experiences, we liberate unconscious impulses. Their flow into our conscious state creates a connection that enriches our work on stage.

When we explore this at a weekend workshop, immediately after the exercise I instruct the actors to do a monologue they are working on, either irreverently or with specific choices designed to address the obligations of the piece. In either case the results are amazing! After the actors have spent an hour imaging all of the suggested places and objects, the depth and dimension of their work are incredible. Most of them feel a deeper connection with their emotions and with many more facets of their life—which expresses itself through the lines of the piece. All of those feelings are accompanied by a sense of inspiration and purpose. Not all of our memories are attached to unconscious life, and neither is necessarily the re-creation of a specific environment, but by "shotgunning" the various areas of experience, you are sure to access something that lives in your unconscious. With repetition you will remember more about the places you image, as well as the events that occurred there. Repeat the technique as often as you like!

When imaging these "suggestions," it is better to use Imaging Sensations than to stop to ask sensory questions, which might interfere with the flow and the impulsivity of the images. Various imaging techniques can be employed throughout. You might start with Fragmented Imaging, then quite naturally fall into Story Imaging, go from there to free-association images, and so on. At various times you might even be impelled to verbalize some of your images. Allow the imaging process to flow in whatever direction it naturally takes.

THE BEDROOMS OF YOUR LIFE

Start by imaging the first bedroom that you remember. Allow the images to create the walls, the ceiling, the furniture, the toys and other personal things you had at that time in your life. Image the odors indigenous to that place, the feel of your blanket, the shadows on the walls, and the patterns and shapes you saw in the wood on the floor or the plaster on the walls. Image the sounds in that room, the creaking of the house as it settled, the objects you played with and your feelings about each one. Tactilely re-create the shape, texture, and feel of each toy. Remember the names of your stuffed animals or dolls and how you related to them. Image the feeling of the bed you slept in and the smell of your pillow, the designs on the sheets, and the stories you may have made up about the characters on the wallpaper. Image your parents entering the room. Create them as they might have looked at that time in your life, listen to their voices, and image what they said to you. Try to re-create tastes associated with that room. Even if you cannot remember eating anything, there will be tastes that go with that time and place. Use all five of your senses in the process. Remember that they all function simultaneously when you do Imaging Sensations. During the re-creation of this particular bedroom, you may remember some of your dreams, even if they are only vague and impossible to separate from what may have been real. Encourage yourself to re-create them through your imaging process.

When you have exhausted all of your remembered images, move on to another bedroom. Most of us lived in at least three or four different places while we were growing up, so re-create every bedroom in your life, including those lived in after you left your parents' house and moved away to school or to be on your own. More than one third of our lives is spent sleeping and even more than that in our bedrooms. There are a lot of life experiences tied to those rooms, and a lot of that life has been submerged into our unconscious.

Each time you involve yourself in this kind of imaging process, you will remember and image more things in each of those bedrooms. If it is possible for you to reexperience some of your thoughts and fears from that time in your life, it would help pique unconscious responses.

THE SCHOOLROOMS, SCHOOLYARDS, AND TEACHERS OF YOUR LIFE

School is a very rich area for most of us. I personally remember the times I spent there as being incredibly impacting and often traumatic. My years in grade school and even high school often seem like a nightmare time in my life. It wasn't until I entered college that school became a positive experience for me. I am sure that that isn't true for everyone; however, when I recall those years, I experience a plethora of images of dark halls, claustrophobic rooms with dirty wooden floors, that famous picture of George Washington bracketed by the American flag hanging over the teacher's desk, and windows adorned with simplistic and infantile art work created by my fellow first graders; I see the fat, distorted face of Miss Anderson shrieking at me for chewing gum in class and feel the discomfort of that gum attached to my nose for the rest of the day; I hear Miss Bloom's voice bellowing commands and criticizing everyone. It was a no-win situation in her class: Even if you responded to her requests, she would admonish you with, "Oh, don't be so agreeable!"

Added to those insensitive assaults were the taunting and jeering of the class bullies, who made recess a nightmarish experience. I remember having fantasies of killing those boys in unimaginable ways. The torture I devised for them would make even *Nightmare on Elm Street* pale in its gruesomeness! Mrs. Lane, my seventh- and eighth-grade teacher, would not graduate me unless I agreed to sign up for a technical course in high school! She told me that I was intellectually retarded and had to learn a trade so that I could ultimately support myself!

There were many more such excruciating episodes, which I will spare the reader. I was severely damaged by those experiences. I think that what saved me was my daydreaming. I was able to tolerate the long days by escaping into fantasies.

My purpose in this preamble is to make it clear that those formative years are rich with events and relationships that layer the unconscious with their complexities. As a result of my own experiences, I can identify when specific subpersonalities surfaced in my life. I remember my preschool years as being happy and carefree. I had a pleasant personality and was very well loved by my family and friends. As a result of my school experiences, however, I began to feel anger and hostility. It was then that my warrior subpersonality emerged.

To access the rich well of unconscious material that is connected to those impacting memories, start your imaging process with a specific room that jumps into focus or with the face of one of your teachers or classmates. Use Imaging Sensations as the approach technique and begin to image.

➤ *Example*

I see the blackboard (visual response)...*smell the chalk* (olfactory response)...*hear a cacophony of blurred voices...stale-milk odor...the top of my wooden desk...discolored and initialed by students long gone ...empty inkwell...pictures of Washington and Lincoln hanging high on the wall in front of me...windows...trees with naked branches...struggling against the snow and cold...I see the back of the head of a fellow student...don't remember him...I see my feet under the desk...funny shoes...Buster Brown shoes...The floor looks worn and discolored...I hear the teacher's voice...droning...uninterested...robotlike...Watching the clock on the wall...waiting for the minute hand to move...the brass pendulum swinging rhythmically back and forth...All school clocks are exactly the same...I'm thinking they all must have had the same mother and father!...I smell the disinfectant they use to clean the rooms...It stings my nose...Feel the winter clothes itching me...I hate winter—it's so depressing!...I hear the bell...unique sound...means freedom for a little while...echo of the bell reverberating on the objects in the room...*

At first, the imaging is specific and conscious, but as you become more involved in the environment, other images from other schoolrooms may arise. Allow them to run their course. What may have begun as a logical story-type of approach may become fragmented and out of sequence. At some point in the process you may begin to feel strong impulses or responses to what you are creating. Go with your feelings— allow them to be expressed. Some of them will feel disconnected from the event. That is a sign that your unconscious is beginning to respond to the stimuli of your images. DO NOT COMMENT! DO NOT ACKNOWLEDGE OR EVALUATE YOUR IMPULSES! JUST EXPRESS THEM!

> ➤ *Example, continued*

See Mrs. Shaunessy's face...smiles...Like her...brown hair...funny laugh...long table...We are drawing...art class...flag...reminds me of history class...Mr. Bowing...bald...glasses...combs his side hair over baldness...funny-looking...gentle man...feel safe with him...high ceilings ...hanging lights...institutional...ugly...cold...Whoever designs schools and schoolrooms must be a sadist who sits for hours thinking of how to torture the helpless children who sit in those sterile rooms! Paper airplane flying past...Hagameyer...threw it...joker...smiling...See his teeth ...nice smile...I like him...Poking me...pushing me...Chris...you dirty bastard...I'm thinking...afraid of him and his cousin Ralph...Hurts me ...picks on me...tells me that I killed Jesus!...I see that hatred in his eyes..."I didn't kill Jesus! I wasn't even alive then!" Hits me in the face ...Running home from school, fast...being chased...I want to turn and fight...I'm afraid...too many of them...Feel my feet hit the pavement... almost airborne...Hear their jeering and name-calling...feel the tears running down my cheeks..."I pledge allegiance to the flag of the United States of America." My hand over my heart...I remember when they told us to stop pointing at the flag because it looked too much like the Hitler

salute. We were to keep our hand over our heart for the entire pledge!
Smell the schoolyard...many different odors...feel the stone gravel under
my feet...hear it crunch as I move...see the light color of the bricks on
the front of the school...smell the glue used by that factory two blocks
away...I see all of the kids playing...laughing...touching the chain-link
fence...at the edge of the schoolyard...Cold...shivering...waiting for the
bell...want to go inside...the blast of warm air as I enter the building...
Can taste the air...heavy and sweet...sounds of kids sitting at their desks
...unique sound...only in school!...

The imaging can go on for as long as it is fruitful. If there is a
verbal response to any of the images, express it and go on with the
imaging. Quite frequently you will experience a big surge of images
coming all at the same moment. It will seem as if you were in sensory
overload. Don't panic! Allow your senses to select and respond to whatever they choose to deal with, and don't concern yourself with the rest.

It is important to note here that for every one suggested image given
in the example, you may have six or seven accompanying ones in a
variety of sensory areas. It is very difficult to supply suggested images
as rapidly as they happen. Use the example as a blueprint for your
imaging process.

As you explore this area and repeat the exercise, you will discover
many more components. Repetition in any of these areas opens up your
conscious memory banks as well as appealing to the unconscious. As
you practice imaging, you will remember more and more about each
event and object.

School and all of the elements connected with it occupy anywhere
from twelve to twenty years of our lives. Some of those times were very
impacting and formative. Exploring this area can therefore be a very
rich experience, one that creates a solid conduit to the unconscious.

THE CHURCHES AND RELIGIOUS EVENTS OF YOUR LIFE

Religion is also a highly emotionally charged area for most people.
Its impact on the human race is documented throughout history, and the
millions of graves filled with the victims of organized religion dot the
entire planet. The Romans and the lions, the Crusades, the Inquisition,
the burning of heretics and witches (even in our own country, the Salem
witch burnings), the Holocaust (six million Jews exterminated just because of their religion), ethnic cleansing in the former Yugoslavia, the
Catholics and the Protestants in Ireland (they have been killing each
other for years!)—I would definitely say that religion has played an

important role in shaping our history, as well as our psyches! Much of our religious education occurs at an early age, at a time when we are very impressionable. Thoughts, ideology, concepts, and belief structures are implanted in us by our clergymen and other religious teachers. We experience a kind of brainwashing, which is totally supported by our parents. If God is love, then why do we hate? Why do so many think, My God is the only God and yours is a false god? So much of our prejudice is built on what we were taught by our religious institutions. As we become more informed and conscious, we begin to question some of those beliefs and hopefully antidote the damage they have caused us. Nevertheless, there is a bottomless well of experiences that were pushed into the unconscious but that can be liberated and used creatively.

Over the years, I have heard shocking accounts of the beliefs taught to impressionable children in parochial schools, distortions that have a lifelong destructive impact on their lives. A number of years ago, a twenty-five-year-old woman in my class related that, while in a religious primary school, she had been scolded by one of the nuns, who had told her not to sit in a chair that a boy had just vacated but to wait till it "cooled off"! Other nuns in the same school had cautioned all the girls not to polish their shoes too well, because then the boys might be able to look up their dresses in the reflection on their shoes! As outrageous as these things sound, they were nevertheless said! These kinds of admonishments multiplied many times can have an incredible effect on a person's entire life! Just imagine how these paranoid distortions affect people's relationship to sex. How can someone subjected to this kind of brainwashing grow up and relate to her sexuality in a healthy way?

I apologize for what seems to be a tirade and brutal attack on organized religion. However, I do believe it is a necessary prelude to this section of the chapter. My purpose here is to make certain that the reader understands the depth, scope, and impact of this area on our lives.

Just a word here to make certain that religion is not confused with spirituality. I am a very spiritual person. I believe in a higher power and feel that there is a reason for our existence, that we have a purpose and destiny, and that we are all connected to God—hopefully without dogma or other crippling stigma!

When you approach this area, you might start by remembering the many parts of your religious experiences—the houses of worship you attended, the altar, the stained-glass windows and religious images or statues, the pews, the sound of the organ and choir, the floor, the ceilings with their ornate carvings, the prayer books, the voice of the minister, priest, or rabbi as he delivered the sermon, the Christmas, Easter, or other services, the parochial schools, the nuns and other religious teachers, the classes and catechism, the prayers you said, the uniforms you wore, the punishments for transgressions, confession, the odor of incense, candle tallow, the echoes reverberating off the walls, and so on.

After preparing to explore the area by listing all of the elements that come to mind, create an environment—possibly one of the first houses of worship you were taken to. Using Fragmented Imaging, attempt to get a sense of that place through Imaging Sensations. Allow yourself to explore everything that you can sensorially remember, and encourage all of the emotional responses that surface, whether you understand them or not. You may stay with that one environment for as long as you like and then move on to another. By exploring your conscious memories of those places and experiences, you might possibly generate unconscious support, since any of your images could ignite unconscious responses.

➤ *Fragmented Imaging Example*

I see the backs of the people sitting in front of me. Everyone is taller than I am...Feel the hard bench on my butt...hear the choir in front... feel my mother sitting next to me...feel her presence...I'm dressed up... collar uncomfortable...See the beams in the ceiling...huge...heavy wood ...Smell incense...see the priest in his box dressed in satins...gray... balding...smiling...waiting for the choir to finish...see red-cover prayer books...in the backs of the seats...worn...old...psalms...Reading, mumbling with the others...Want to go home and play...sermon...droning... Not listening...Hear him shout...I'm listening now...His eyes are big and red...he looks angry...What is he shouting about?...banging his fist ...the Devil?...Satan?...Who is that?...I'm frightened...hold my mom's hand...warm, comforting...See a statue of Jesus on the cross...He looks sad...makes me sad...Looking down at my shoes...polished...bright... Hear everyone singing...Don't know the words...move my mouth...the blood of Jesus...the body of Jesus...confused...See people standing at the altar...

Hopefully, you will experience a variety of feelings and impulses while you image that place. Encourage the expression of everything that comes up. Feel free to use any of the imaging techniques, and go from place to place and experience to experience. For example, you may start with Fragmented Imaging and move into Symbolic Imaging, or you could approach a particular experience with Story Imaging. Whatever you end up using, encourage yourself to honor all the impulses that are liberated by your involvement.

Another interesting technique is to encourage a potpourri of images that involve your religious experiences from a wide variety of places and times in your life. The exercise could span your entire life.

➤ *Free-Association Imaging Example*

Nun...her face...wrinkles...hard...high voice...blackboard...prayer ...saying Hail Mary's...punishment for talking...Sitting on stool in front of class...dunce cap...I feel humiliated...confession booth...father...see his shadow...afraid to confess touching myself...recess...churchyard... uniforms...Everyone looks the same...plaid skirts...or blue trousers... Kneeling by my bed: "If I die before I wake..." blanket...soft...shadows on the wall...looks like the Devil's horns...afraid to close my eyes...See Judy...like her...and want to kiss her...afraid to think that way...desk... prayer book...Memorize prayers...dirty pictures drawn on blank pages ...hide them...I didn't draw them...church picnic...food...sisters serving ...smiling...different from classroom...Hate Sister Emily...She hits us with a pointer if we miss an answer...smiling...hypocrite!...Wonder if she is a virgin...can't say that out loud!...Raffles...for the poor...baskets of food for those less fortunate...bring can goods...Spaghetti O's...I am glad to give those away...Hate those...Passion play...no one wants to play Judas!...funny fake beards...George doesn't look at all like Jesus! ...The disciples look raggedy!...I wonder if God would approve of this play...Glad I'm not in it...Father O'Brien...stern, scolding me...office... big desk...white collar...All his words are blurred...I'm looking at him through a long dark tunnel...hear words: "bad...shame...evil..." Is he talking about me?...terrified...

The images can go anywhere, as long as they stay within the framework of religion. If you start to stray into other areas, include those images and reinvest in a religious object or place. Even if you are initially unsuccessful in accessing unconscious impulses, you will definitely discover and liberate memories of those times and places—which may be used as future choices.

Repeat the exercise as often as you can fit it into your daily work schedule. A good time to do Unconscious Suggestions is before you go to sleep at night. More than likely, you will have dreams that are related to the area you are working in. If that occurs, remember to record those dreams. The very next time you do this process, you can suggest an image that presented itself in one of your dreams. That is a direct connection with the unconscious. All of the areas in this section are important to us and are designed to pique unconscious responses.

THE PLAYGROUNDS OF YOUR LIFE

All of us had special places that we looked forward to—places where we played, created fantasies and games, and had special and memorable relationships. They changed as we moved to new houses and grew older, but they were the places where we gave ourselves permission to play and to be who we really were.

In grade school I had a close friend named John, whose basement was one of the playgrounds of my life. We would meet almost every day after school and play "pretend games" there. We would take turns being the hero. Sometimes a particular scenario would go on for weeks, much like the episodes of a soap opera. We both indulged in the fantasies of the stories and acted with superb realism. I remember really feeling the emotions of the character I was playing and the relationship between us, as the two characters always seemed to feed off each other. We related to each other naturally and, just as naturally, would respond to the way we were affected by each other. It seemed effortless and, most important, very enjoyable! Both John and I were in the school play at graduation, and to this day I remember thinking how different we both were when we were "acting." We were stiff and self-conscious then, and it wasn't any fun! Even before I ever considered becoming an actor, I remember wondering why we were so different on that auditorium stage from the way we were in John's basement. Of course, I know why now!

That basement was a special playground, rich with memories and experiences that are important to me even to this day. In addition to our daily pretend games, we sometimes had Boy Scout patrol meetings there—another significant experience. I can remember the aura of the place, the objects, the odors, and the feelings of that room. It seemed alive in some strange way. I could feel an essence in the air, almost like a surrealistic Alice-in-Wonderland environment. We created the magic in that place. Both John and I had fantasized so many different places and stories that eventually some of them had to be absorbed into the walls, the floor, the furniture.

Using that place as a choice to access unconscious impulses seems very natural. Just thinking about it stimulates a plethora of emotional responses. Who was I then? What were the things that impelled my behavior? What were my dreams and desires? How much of that little boy still lives inside of me? How did my experiences influence my life from that point on? As I sit at the typewriter and commit this to paper, I am filled with a kind of sadness. I feel the tears welling up in my eyes and that feeling I get in my throat just before I begin to cry. Why? I really can't answer that! I don't know why just writing about that place has such a strong effect on me. Certainly, I can guess that there are a great deal of remembered and forgotten events that are bubbling up to the surface, but why sadness? Possibly because I am mourning for that lost time and that little boy who found his place in that room. Whatever the cause of my response, it seems quite certain that John's basement is a very important choice for exploring the unconscious. I could elect to re-create it with any of the imaging techniques, but in this instance, I intuitively feel that I should start at the entrance to the room and move into it as I would in reality. I therefore decide to use Story Imaging and a specific Sense Memory process to re-create the place. There are times when you just know which of the techniques to use in relation to a specific choice. At those times don't question the feeling—just honor it.

➢ *The Exercise*

The first thing I do is to get a really good mental picture of the room. I try to see everything that I can remember about it: the walls—their color and composition—the floor, the ceiling, the objects in the room, the table we sat at, the books piled in the corner, John's father's framed awards and trophies for outstanding performance on the football field, the windows, which were taller than we were, the grass we saw from the bottom up, and the naked light bulb hanging over the square table that had become the center of our activities. (That single, crude red table hurriedly put together by John's father had become so many things over the years!)

Once I have created a fairly complete mental picture of the place, I can start the sensory process. Remember that when you use Sense Memory for imaging purposes, you ask the questions in the same way as when doing a conventional Sense Memory process but you encourage all of your senses to respond simultaneously, even if the primary question is just visual. Actually, you are combining Sense Memory and Imaging Sensations. The value of the former approach is that it stimulates a greater degree of specificity in the creation of each object, which is sometimes necessary to the success of a particular choice.

What do I see? (This is responded to visually, and at the same time, the other senses follow with their own specific responses.) *How far away is the wall from where I am standing?...What color is it?...texture?...Can I see shapes in the texture of the wall? How wide is this place?...Where am I in relation to the place?...How far away is the left wall?...the right wall?...How are the colors different?...How high is the ceiling?...What is it made of?...The floor—what does it look like?...Can I feel it on the soles of my feet?...If so, what do I feel?...What is the material the floor is made of?...Any irregularities?...How long is that crack?...*(As I said earlier, you may be asking one question at a time, but in the framework of that single question, you might experience a dozen images related to all of your other senses. It is important that you allow these varied responses to occur. Your success may depend on experiencing the total environment.) *What do I smell? How many different odors do I detect? What part of this odor is familiar to me? As I move forward, does the odor change?...If so, how?...What do I smell now?... What does it remind me of?...Can I smell John?...What is his particular odor?...Where is he standing?...How tall is he in relation to me?...What color is his hair?...texture?...What is the shape of his hairline?...How does the light reflect on it?...What would it feel like if I touched it?...* (Each time you switch your emphasis to another sense, you must specifically respond in that sensory area. Remember that you are receiving many sensorial responses to each question. You may even get multiple visual responses to a single visual question. Your goal, of course, is to re-create the environment so that you really experience being there. It may not be necessary for our purposes to get a complete sense of the place in order to start the flow of unconscious impulses. For me these may have begun as I started to write about John's basement. Since the purpose of Unconscious Suggestions is to establish a connection with the unconscious, it is important that you allow these impulses to elevate themselves into your consciousness without molesting them. Let them flow through you. As you begin to experience this connection with the unconscious, your feelings will change. You will experience deeper emotional responses, and, in fact, all of your behavior will take on added dimensions.)

What is the shape of his face?...of his eyes?...color?...eyelashes?... What does his nose look like?...How long is it?...What does his mouth look like?...If I only saw his mouth, what would tell me that it belonged to him? Shape of his chin?...neck?...What is behind him?...How much of those shelves can I see?...What is on them?...What does his voice sound like?...What are the peculiarities of his voice?...What other sounds do I hear?...Where are they coming from?...What does the air in

this room feel like?...Can I feel it on my face?...Where else do I feel it?
...What does this place make me feel?...Where do I feel those feelings?

When you begin to experience a connection with the unconscious, you might stop the questioning and allow yourself to relate to the room with Imaging Sensations. While the above example involves a specific sensory approach, most of the time you should allow each of the Unconscious Suggestions to stimulate an impulsive flow of images. As you respond to the various ones, you may creatively manipulate them with questions and other suggestions. There are times during this involvement when you will feel the need to go deeper in the exploration of one of the areas. By steering some of the images in certain directions, you can accomplish a richer connection with the unconscious.

Working with your unconscious is very much like exercising the muscles in your body. The more you work it, the more it responds. You may repeat a choice many times, discovering new things every time you do it. There are many playgrounds in your life: the park with its swings and monkey bars, the vacant lots, the tree houses, the woods and campgrounds, the amusement parks you went to every year, the baseball diamonds of your little-league period, the back porches and secret hideaways, the hangouts where you met your friends, the pinball arcades, the bicycle rallies, the Boy or Girl Scout outings and jamborees, the after-school pizza place, and so on. They change with age and geography, and each one includes new and different faces and varied experiences. As you grow up and become more mature in your selections, they get somewhat more sophisticated, but they are nonetheless still the playgrounds of your life, and they hold a virtual treasure of memories—conscious and unconscious. How many of your playgrounds have you assigned to the unconscious?

THE TOYS OF YOUR LIFE

Very often we also attach great meaning to toys and other objects we owned at various stages in our development. Toys embody an incredible conglomeration of meaningful energies. They symbolize our dreams and fantasies and contain all of the properties that we endowed them with. They each represent a particular period of our life. We give them personalities; we carry on conversations with them and wait for their responses; we sleep with them, cuddling close when we are cold or frightened; they make us feel special, and we have secrets we only share with them.

What happens to those precious treasures of ours? Where do they go when we outgrow them? It is like the elephant graveyard: No one knows where elephants go to die, and so it is with our toys! Our parents give them away to the Salvation Army, Goodwill, or some other charitable institution. Sometimes they end up in thrift shops, sitting on shelves waiting for another child to give them life. I often wonder where *my* toys are. Do they still exist? Who has them? Have they been destroyed or turned into scrap? It seems that nothing can ever take the place of the first one—or mean as much as it did. Recently, while wandering around an antique shop, I spotted some old toy cars and airplanes, the kind that was made of heavy metal, before the advent of plastic! I picked one up and was surprised by how heavy it was. I stood there with that metal car in my hand and went on a "trip." It took me back many decades to an apartment in Chicago, where I lay on the floor and played with my car, making motor noises and running into the legs of the chairs in the living room. I don't know how long I stood there reminiscing about that time. I was filled with feelings. The recognizable one was nostalgia, but there were others, which seemed harder to identify. I know that I was experiencing a flush of unconscious recollections that kept coming up for most of the afternoon. That metal car pushed a button much like the key on a computer and accessed a cornucopia of memories and feelings related to that time in my life. You might ask, So what? What does that mean? Things like that happen to everyone! You're right, they do—all the time! And when they happen to you, you are experiencing a connection with your unconscious! If you are an actor, that experience is extremely important. It means that you have elicited the genius and support of the unconscious to help make your acting impacting, colorful, and unpredictable. That is exactly why I am taking the time to explain these techniques.

As you explore and experiment in this area, you will remember more and more of your toys and playthings. Start with what comes to you, and encourage the images prompted by those memories.

➢ *Example*

I remember sending for a "Tom Mix ring" by mail order. It glowed in the dark, and if you looked through a hole on the top, you could see inside a picture of Tom Mix on his horse. As I image that ring, I see the ceiling of my bedroom on Van Buren Street, the faded plaster and the water spots where the roof must have leaked in the rain.

Looking at the ring...greenish white in color...See Tom Mix on his horse...The horse is rearing and standing on its hind legs. Tom has his hat in one hand and is waving to me...black cowboy hat...boots with spurs made of silver...Comic books stacked in the corner of the room... Daredevil...in his suit...half red, half blue...Captain Marvel...Shazam! And he is Billy Batson...Taste chocolate-chip cookies...milk...and Mary Jane candy all at once...looking at my slippers...furry—and they have a head and eyes at the toes...They look like foxes. I call them Mutt and Jeff...The left one is Mutt. See my model airplane hanging from the ceiling...I built it from scratch...Smell the glue from here...It's yellow and has numbers on the fuselage...When I get tired of it, I will put a firecracker in the nose, light it, fly it off the back porch, and pretend that it is being shot down by the Nazis!...Smell the food being cooked in the kitchen...chicken soup...my mother's favorite appetizer!...Hear the radio on the shelf in the kitchen...Thinking of my red wagon...see it over there in the corner...scratches in its bed from the soles of my shoes...it's a "Red Flyer," but it doesn't fly...I really want a two-wheeler bike...but my mother and father are afraid that I will get run over by a car, so I get a scooter...which is also red with huge yellow wheels...I can feel the pavement on the sole of my left foot as I ride it...on the sidewalk...I'm not allowed in the street...I see Howard and Burton...playing on the curb...They make fun of me and my scooter...They both have bikes...I feel angry...My brother Phil bought me a Daisy BB gun that I can only shoot when he is there watching me...I love that gun...I practice all the time...I'm good!...On Saturdays I put on a show for the kids in the neighborhood...shooting bottle corks at fifteen feet...They all hoot and cheer every time I hit the cork...They call me "Buffalo Bill." It makes me proud, and I feel special!...Looking at the rifle...It's bluish...and the wood is deep brown...and I feel the coolness of the metal barrel...I love the sound it makes when I cock it...whoosh, it sucks in the air...I see Phil—his round, smiling face...curly blondish hair...I love him...He is good to me...Corky is barking in the yard...what a crazy dog!...See his face, smell his awful breath...growling...O.K., I back off...crazy dog... He ran away, gone for three days...sick about it...Phil was walking him ...took off...Phil felt terrible. We both cry about it...All of a sudden I am washed with sadness...Phil is gone, and I miss him...In this moment I am flooded with images of places where he and I went...downtown...to see Tarzan movies on the day they opened at the Palace Theatre...riding the L-train back home...listening to the classical music from the radio he bought me..."The Piper Fudge Hour..." I can see that radio with its

white metal handle curving at the top...Its name is General Television...
That's funny because there isn't any television yet!...So why is it called
that?...

As I worked in this area, I was overwhelmed by the number of
images floating through my senses—too many to be able to list them in
this example. When I finally stopped imaging, I felt a complete connection to that time in my life. The images covered about a four-year
period. The effect of the exercise was very meaningful to me. I was
filled with a variety of feelings and fairly strong emotions. I felt happy,
nostalgic, sad, and angry with Howard and Burton for making fun of
me. I resented my parents for not allowing me to have a bike, felt guilty
about my brother's death, and missed him. I experienced his odor, as
well as the various sounds and smells of the environment. I went
through unidentifiable emotions—the kind of feeling you get when you
are trying to remember a dream and can't.

If I was doing this imaging workout to stimulate a connection with
my unconscious, I certainly succeeded! As a result of the exercise, I felt
very connected to my unconscious. If I had elected to do this to prepare
for a specific scene that required the kind of life that the exercise
produced, I would also have been successful!

The toys of your life are very important stimuli for accessing memories, both conscious and unconscious. A seemingly simple and in-
expensive toy can become a symbol of one of the happiest times in your
life, a time when you felt an optimism that made your heart soar. For
me, it was my two-wheeler bike—when I finally got it—which came to
represent my being grown-up and mobile. It symbolized my first sense
of freedom! I can see it now—its color, its wheels and spokes, the light
that never worked on the front fender, the handlebars, the rubber hand-
grips and how they felt as the rubber deteriorated from the years of perspiration in the palms of my hands! I still see that bike sometimes in my
dreams—and it was well over fifty years ago!

At the end of the movie *Citizen Kane,* when Orson Wells is dying,
the last word he speaks is the famous "Rosebud," which refers to a
crude wooden snow sled he had as a young child. That sled symbolized
a freedom and happiness he probably never reexperienced after he was
taken from his mother and raised in the privileged circumstances that
followed. A simple toy or other object can be filled with the enormous
energy with which we endow it. By re-creating that object, we can directly access all of the locked-up emotions that live in the unconscious
and by so doing, sometimes liberate a bottomless well of unconscious

life that bursts to the surface of our consciousness and enriches our behavior enormously. When such an experience occurs, it is possible to stimulate an ultimate-consciousness event. Include this area of exploration in your Unconscious Suggestions! It is rich with untold treasures. As you repeat the exercise, you will remember and image many toys you had forgotten. If you still have any of your childhood toys, use them as available stimuli to start the imaging process.

THE JOYS OF YOUR LIFE

The next area includes all of the high times—graduations, awards, victories, celebrations, and so on—all of the memorable events that created excitement, joy, or a feeling of accomplishment, the kind of events that you will remember and consider important throughout your entire life. There is a lot of emotional life attached to those happenings. Some people feel that the greatest events of their lives occurred in their early years, and as a result, they constantly refer to that period. They even become trapped in a time capsule and constantly relive their victories and celebrations. For whatever reasons, most people get involved with the responsibilities of life: They get married, have a family, and get mired in jobs they hate in order to fulfill their obligations. As we all know, time is a very fleeting thing. Years are piled upon years, and, before they realize it, their dreams and hopes have faded away into memories. Fortunately, this isn't true for everybody. Some of us have followed the "yellow brick road" and visited the Wizard of Oz! If you pursue your dream, you are surely reaching for those joys of life. Even if a person does not succeed on the level he had wished to, as long as he is on that journey toward Oz, the joys continue.

This area of Unconscious Suggestions has a lot of "juice." Along with these joyful experiences, we store a lot of emotions, dreams, fears, insecurities, and hopes that are stockpiled in the unconscious. When imaging some of these meaningful events, we may liberate a Pandora's box of unconscious emotional ore. With the expurgation of those impulses can come some very surprising life, far different from what we had originally expected.

For example, a euphoric experience you had can stimulate great depression, which happens as a result of your perspective of where you were then as opposed to where you feel you are now; or it may release emotions and a sense of life that you no longer maintain. It may remind you of people who are gone and relationships that have long since been over. Using this area as a way to access or connect to the unconscious is extremely valuable. If you decide to use it in a preparation for a scene, however, you may be disappointed with the direction it takes.

As with any of the other areas of Unconscious Suggestions, you start imaging a particular event, encouraging all of the images related to that time and place in all the sensory areas, through Imaging Sensations. Allow images from other events to manifest themselves as well, while encouraging *joyful* experiences.

Any positive involvement is a usable choice. An encouraging smile from an important person can open a door to your unconscious. The larger and more impacting events are a good place to start, however. I remember, for instance, wanting to play the triangle in kindergarten. I was on sticks and hated the fact that they made such insignificant sounds. When I was finally promoted to the triangle, it seemed like an overwhelming victory to me! Whatever that instrument represented, its meaning and importance are filed away in my unconscious memory banks. By resurrecting the experience, I might be able to free that entire unconscious file!

Being a patrol boy—that was a big one—learning to drive a car, getting my driver's license, driving to high school with the other kids looking at me, earning merit badges in the Boy Scouts, being promoted from one rank to another, going on overnight hikes, being in my first play, knowing that I wanted to be an actor, getting my first curtain call and hearing the applause, getting my first film job, getting a series, reading a glowing review, falling in love, seeing my first child as a newborn in the hospital nursery, attending all of my graduations—from grade school, high school, and college—receiving my honorable discharge from the army—each of us has many such events and experiences in his life, most of which are pregnant with impacting emotional and unconscious components.

THE ATTRACTIONS, CRUSHES, AND ROMANCES OF YOUR LIFE

There is also a lot of power involved with sexuality, and when those hormones start to kick in, many things happen to the body and mind! Attractions occur long before puberty. I remember being attracted to girls and women at the age of three! I wondered what was under their dresses. I remember having feelings about them, wanting to touch and smell them. It is quite possible that I was precocious in this area, but I think it is quite normal for children to have such attractions.

My first sexual experience occurred when I was seven. The girl was nine. My friend Danny and I had a full-blown sexual relationship with the girl next door, and somehow, without ever having been instructed, we knew what to do. We did everything adults do, and we all enjoyed it! I knew that it was not acceptable, and so did the others, but we did it anyway! I can still see the girl's face and the way she smiled and responded. I had feelings for her. I'm sure that they couldn't be described as romantic love, but they were strong, and I knew that I missed her when we were not together. I can recall many crushes in my pre-adolescent years, mostly centered on classmates. In the sixth grade I sat four seats behind and one row over from a gorgeous girl named Doris. Her family called her Dolly, and she sure justified that name! She looked like a china doll, with perfect features and incredible skin and hair, and she always seemed as if she had just bathed and put on perfume. I can still recall how smitten I was by her. I would stare at her hungrily, experiencing a tangible feeling of painful yearning. It was an event to walk by her desk, and I did so at every opportunity. I would inhale deeply and attempt to ingest every last molecule of her scent. When I could muster up enough courage, I would even say hello to her, fearing every moment that my voice would crack or that the words would not come out! Even though that was fifty-four years ago, I can still see her big blue eyes and perfect teeth as she smiled, and I think I can still smell her scent.

There was a long line of attractions after Doris, faces without names, which were very exciting at the time. Even though my first sexual experience had happened at a very early age, I waited a long time until the next one, because of the taboo of my generation. I grew up at a time when most women waited to get married before having sex. There was a great premium in taking your virginity to the marriage bed; so there were a large number of "making out" interludes—and I must say that I steamed up a lot of car windows—but "going all the way" was out of the question. My first love was in high school. I fell madly in love with a girl named Joyce, by my standards a real beauty! We dated, made out, hung out for about three years. We had a song—you know, a relationship song that symbolized our feelings for each other. We wore matching clothes and spent every free moment together. Everyone's first love is a memorable event! It seems that all the feelings are magnified. All of the nerve endings are extra sensitive. The highs are higher and the lows are lower; pain seems to be a part of it all, and jealousy is an acceptable ingredient.

I married my second love after dating her all the way through college. We also had a song! I was involved with a small number of women between my first and second loves and have used many of these relationships as choices for my acting. All of them were meaningful and different from each other.

A big part of all of our lives is devoted to dating, romance, relationships, and sex. Some of the strongest emotions surround love and attraction, so it follows that many of our memories and feelings in this area are assigned to the unconscious. Many of our relationships are replays of the preceding ones. People spend years in therapy attempting to find out why they continue to repeat the same pattern over and over again. This is a very rich area to explore!

Start the process of imaging by suggesting a person from your past. It needn't be one of your earliest attractions or crushes—it can be more recent. Begin to image that person, using all of your senses, and include the environment that you shared together. Encourage the imaging process to go wherever it wants to, and allow yourself to express all of the ensuing emotions. If you are impelled to express your impulses verbally, do so. Stay with each person until the images run out or some other face pops into visual range. Beginnings and endings are very important! Quite often, we forget exactly why a particular relationship ended. We often protect ourselves from the pain of breaking up, so we push the components into the background, and eventually they end up in our unconscious.

> ### *Imaging Example*

Let us approach this area of Unconscious Suggestions with Free-Association Imaging. Start with a name and a face, and encourage the ensuing images to impulsively evolve.

Doris! Blue-and-white checkered dress...(That is my first image in response to that name.) *Freshly pressed and clean...hair...beautiful... brown with red highlights...thick, moving in slow motion as she turns her head...Can hear her laughter...pink blush in her cheeks...breast bumps just beginning to form...round and perfect...Looking at me...feel that to my toes...smell her scent...like every flower in a garden...She is moving in slow motion...Her mouth...perfect in shape...opening...white teeth...I feel as if I could be a part of the desk she sits in...flash of insecurity...Why would she be interested in me? She's so beautiful!...I'm transfixed by the back of her legs...See the muscles move as she adjusts in her seat...The room around her darkens and blurs...It is as if she were the only object in focus...I taste my attraction and desire for her in my mouth...It tastes like the taste you get just before biting into something delicious...I feel a familiar emotion coming to the surface...I recognize it as a kind of yearning feeling...It isn't pleasant—on the contrary, it has some pain attached to it.* (The images are quite fragmented, and I am beginning to see other faces, other bodies.) *I feel myself in an embrace with someone whom I recognize but whose name I can't remember ...feels warm and sensual...We are fully clothed, but I feel the curvature of her body next to mine...Her odors are stimulating...different from Doris's...I'm sitting in a booth with someone else...holding her hand... feel the softness of her skin...Carole...don't know the rest...smiling... attractive...warm face...cute voice...I hear her squeak...She squeaks when she laughs...feel her energy...up...happy...uncomplicated...*

Of course, the more serious the relationship, the greater the content. As you work, allow for each image to present itself. Sometimes, the people you are imaging blend together, and you begin to experience mixed sensory responses. You may have a visual image of one person and an auditory response to another. Allow that; do not derail your process by commenting. Accept all images and allow them to affect you. When you access an image of a person with whom you had a serious relationship for many years and whom you possibly married, your images will probably jump from one experience to another. You will go through a variety of environments and subsequently many emotional responses. Volatile relationships carry a lot of unexpressed feelings that were not dealt with. After my second divorce, my dreams went on for months. I would wake up angry, and that feeling might last the entire day. Obviously, my unconscious was very actively trying to communicate with me, perhaps in an attempt to resolve issues that had not been resolved in the relationship.

> ### ➤ *Example Continued*

Hear her voice...shrill and indicting...her face tense...full of stress ...eyes tearing...angry eyes...see her pain...feel angry and hurt at the same time...She is sitting in the chair looking out at the view...depressed...low energy...body language...limp...I can feel her depression ...On the beach, she is smiling...beautiful day...hair blowing in the wind...happy face...When she smiles, her whole body smiles...soft skin ...Hear her voice...it's soft, mellow...not angry...loving look...Smell the ocean...feel the breeze...hear seagulls overhead...wonder why it can't always be like this...She's crying...sobbing...doubled over with pain...

not physical...emotional pain...What is it?...What can I do?...Feel con-
fused...want to run...escape...don't know what to do...intimate conver-
sation...see her looking at me...mellow tones...talking about her child-
hood...Feel pain for what she went through...feel helpless...confused...

Since this area is so rich with stimuli, you may return to it as often as you wish to. After you have finished the imaging part, take an inventory of the entire exercise, and make note of your emotional responses. Acknowledge all of your unconscious impulses, and use them as a springboard.

In this next section of Unconscious Suggestions, the areas of exploration begin to be more abstract and vague. The following are designed to encourage a deeper sojourn into your unconscious. By the very nature of these suggestions you will have to challenge both your conscious and unconscious memory banks.

ABSTRACT PLACES FROM CHILDHOOD

Some people can recall things that happened when they were one year old and sometimes even earlier, but most of us have difficulty remembering anything before the age of three. In my classes we do exercises to liberate early childhood memories. I find that there are a lot of actors who have difficulty remembering things that happened before they were five years old. In order to access early life experiences, I ask them to do an exercise I call *Perspective Inventory.*

Perspective Inventory

The approach is simple: For one week, each night before going to bed, you go over the day. The following week you try to recall as many of the events of the previous week as you can. In the third week you go back over the entire month, attempting to remember and go through the events, experiences, and relationships that took place. By the fourth week you are ready to go back over the entire year. Of course, you cannot expect to remember every detail of every experience you had in that whole year, so you focus on the memorable ones. As you recall those experiences, they will bring with them surrounding ones, things that happened just before or after. By the fifth week of the exploration, you can begin the process of remembering events and experiences that occurred three to five years before. Again, you start by calling up the ones you can remember, those that have branded themselves into the core of your memory—usually early traumas, deaths, life-changing events that may have scarred you. As these memories rise to the surface, you ask yourself what happened around that time—just before or immediately after each event. These questions will pique other memories related to that period of time, and hopefully those will rise to the surface, progressively allowing you to remember more and more from those times in your life. You might stay with the recollections from those three to five years for a couple of weeks before going back further. When you feel ready, you may attempt to access experiences that go back ten years or more, again using the impacting ones as a key to opening that door. As you do Perspective Inventory, you will discover that you are bringing up memories that you had forgotten until now, and that doors that had seemed sealed forever are now beginning to open. Behind them you will BEGIN TO DISCOVER YOUR LIFE! Because this exercise is progressive and cumulative, it acts as a lever to pry open sealed boxes in which your experiences had been locked away. In a sense, it is like drilling for oil. You go through layers of rock, then shale, and then water, and when you have bored your way to that well of oil, it gushes with incredible force to the surface. Ultimately you try to liberate your memories from your very early years—one, two, three years old. They are there! The Perspective Inventory exercise acts as a primer. It progressively loosens the events stored in the crevasses of your mind, and, like that gushing oil, they spew up into your consciousness and your dreams.

Actors I have worked with have told me that they can remember their birth and even before that! I find that a little hard to believe, but it is possible. As I mentioned in chapter 2, I remember being diapered by my mother. I distinctly can see her standing at that table and even hear her whispering endearments to me as she works. I see the ceiling above me and can feel the table on my back. I must have been less than one year old. Everything leading up to that event and everything that followed is a blank, however. My next memory is of standing in a long hallway, looking towards a room with a lot of light pouring through the windows. I feel unsteady on my feet, so I assume that I am just learning to walk. I can vividly recall many things from about the age of five: I remember being in kindergarten and my sister Ida's taking me to school. I told everyone she was my mother, because all the other children's mothers were about her age. I am the baby of my family, and my mother was forty years old when I was born, so I guess I was ashamed of having such an old mother! Seems that peer pressure starts at a very early age!

The word *abstract,* as I use it in this section, should be taken to mean places that are strange or unidentifiable, fragments that are unclear, objects that may not relate to anything in your conscious memory. Before starting to explore this area, do a relaxation exercise. Logy is a good one. Clear your brain of all thoughts, and just suggest that you are in a place that you remember from when you were five. At first, just allow any images that come up to manifest themselves. They might come from a very different age, but that is all right! Let any of them run by you, much like movie credits scrolling up on a screen. If you have trouble pinpointing a specific age or are unsure where you lived at that time, just suggest the age or go to a place you remember being in. This exercise can also be approached with "I'm five years old and I..." which I use for "choice hunting." Sitting up or lying down, encourage an imaging response to complete the sentence. Stay with one age until you have exhausted it, and then move on through your life. It is a good framework to hang your images on.

> ### Imaging Example

I see shadows drawn across a high ceiling...frightening shapes...feel soft clothes on my body...see pictures on the clothes...animal pictures... dark walls with scary shadows from trees that look like skinny people... (These are all images. The only internal verbal expression should be impulsive responses to them.) *I hear a siren...far away...It's dark...everything looks so big...A big round thing going round and round...people on it...screams...I cry...afraid...arms embracing me...hard beard scratching my cheek...*

Smell funny odor...a long box...shiny wood...head of a person... doesn't look real...people all around...silence...crying...I am afraid... Someone holding my hand...look down...my hand is so small...the other hand is big...See people walking by...don't recognize them...old people ...faces...Moving inside a machine...rocking...sitting on a seat made of woven straw...a person on each side...feel afraid...see other people... sitting...going somewhere...streetcar...tracks...big hall...empty...wood floor with cracks in the floor...see dirt between the cracks...alone here ...high walls...funny lights on the walls...gold and silver...night time... see reflections in the windows...me...two little lamps...made of Scottie dogs with beady eyes...

So many of those images seemed not attached to anything. I know they were part of a place or places from my early life, but I don't really know what most of them meant or where I was. When giving examples,

I really do the exercises that I describe. I feel that it is the only way to create authentic experiences. While I was imaging, I had eerie feelings. It was unsettling. After completing the exploration, I was bombarded by waves of thoughts and subsequent images. I can't be sure that I made specific contact with the unconscious, but it surely affected me. Even at this moment my body feels "hyper," as though I had had six cups of coffee. The exercise stimulated an overall sense of fear and a feeling of being out of sorts.

When doing this workout, you will notice that there isn't any continuity to it. It jumps all over the place. Don't try to figure out what the images mean or what they are related to—just allow them to flow through you. At this point, I would like to indicate once again that the imaging examples I furnish are usually very brief and only intended to give you a sense of the process. You should encourage yourself to image for longer periods of time. You may spend ten or fifteen minutes on a single area, and in some exercises even longer!

FRAGMENTS OF MEMORIES

Jung and Freud had a lifelong ongoing difference of opinion about the unconscious. Jung felt that the unconscious was where most of man's knowledge and awareness—the genius of mankind—lived, while Freud was quoted as having said that it was a great big "garbage dump" of discarded memories and experiences. I am not sure that he really said that or even felt that way, but it is something I have heard or read somewhere. At any rate, I use this to make a point. Even if indeed the unconscious is some kind of dump where all of our memories—significant and otherwise—are stored or discarded, we can dig through this refuse and salvage usable components when they are needed for a particular involvement. Good questions to pose at that juncture are: What do these individual memories or experiences contain? What are they attached to? How complex might a single memory be? Could a seemingly abstract and unattached memory be the catalyst to an entire anomaly? Possibly, it is the only remaining part of an entire complex emotional phenomenon. This is something like walking along a vacant lot and noticing a shiny piece of metal protruding from the ground; it may be only two-inches high, so you decide to dig it out, mostly to see what it is, and after hours of digging realize that it is buried hundreds of feet below the surface! In the same way, a single innocent memory may be deeply rooted in some dark region of the unconscious and, when liberated, bring up the strings attached to a plethora of unconscious life.

Unlike the previous Unconscious Suggestions exercise, this one does not follow any chronology. There is no beginning place where you start imaging fragments of memories. You just clear your brain, relax, and begin. You might suggest to yourself that you would like to receive images from any place in your life, any time, and any event. From the outset, discourage getting trapped in some story line. If necessary, in the beginning suggest images that are unrelated to each other. You will probably notice that they come from every period in your life and, if you are successful with this approach, become increasingly fragmented; that is to say that they will not be complete images, only fragments.

➢ *Imaging Example*

To give you an example of this exercise, I did it and recorded it on tape. The following is an exact transcript:

"I am lying down, and I am getting ready to do the suggested...unconscious suggestion...(Expelling a little sigh.) I am trying to relax... (sigh) and clear my brain...trying not to think about anything...This morning I tried to remember a dream...and I couldn't...and I worked really hard to pull a thread of it...anything...anything that would remind me of the dream, and that's the way I feel right now...I feel like I'm doing something which hopefully will become impulsive and automatic ...and I'm not sure how to do it...I mean I'm not sure how to start it... (Deep breathing, sigh.) I feel my mind going to places in my life... people...things jumping in...It is as though I wanted to grab a handle... Trying to avoid that...don't want to do that!...Phew!...I have memories, and they are clear...and I see things, and I'm beginning to image... but...they're not fragments of memories...(Long pause expelling air.) Nothing seems to be going on...I see a movie theater...long and dark, and I see the aisle...and the seats...(pause) and the aisle looks like a deep incline...(Sigh.) I don't know what that is...(Another long pause here and sigh.) It's dark...Sometimes I think there are things in the dark that don't exist when the lights are on. Ugh! (Another pause.) Nothing seems to be happening for me...(Short pause.) I see my sister's friend, Sadie...smiling...see her face...I don't know...I don't know what that means...I don't care what that means!...She is gone...She is dead... There's a green 1936 Pontiac...with a straight back...Bernie...Bernie's car...It has an Indian head on the front...(Sigh.) My cousin Leon...in his navy uniform...picture on the wall...smiling...all teeth...looking up ...(A lengthy pause.) I see little cards...cards from chewing gum...bubble gum—flat...the war...war scenes...cigar box...cards in the cigar box

...(Another sigh.) I'm feeling sad for some reason...I'm thinking about time travel...I don't know where that came from...(Sighing again.) This is difficult...this is hard...I feel like I can't pull on those threads...I see the threads...I can't pull on them...I can't get them up...(Ugh! Sigh. Feel the frustration in the sounds.) A lot of memories...and a lot of my images relate to Fillmore Street...Chicago...I seem to always go back there, and I don't know what that means...Phew! What period of life?... What was that like?...I mean, why do I go back there?...Flashes of images...I just saw Walgreens drugstore...Paul...the fountain manager ...skeletal face...Two guys put his hand in burning-hot water...Forget the guy's name I worked with...he was fast...Wooden floors...wooden ...wooden things they put on the floor...Mr. Solomon...pharmacist... Austin Boulevard...(Ugh! Almost sounds painful.) Oh...I see that man on the floor...epileptic fit...seizure—not fit—seizure...Oh...Oh...foaming at the mouth...first time I ever saw that...Oh, for a split second I thought it was my father...then I was relieved...I am relieved...I was relieved...(Sigh.) I feel like I'm trying too hard...feel like I'm leading myself...I feel like I want to grab on to something...instead of letting it come...Nothing is coming though...(Long pause.) I'm back on Fillmore Street...coal yard...walk by on the way to school...truck scale...coal dust...cold...bricks...dark...depressing...Even then, without knowing any better, I thought it was depressing...(Short pause.) No wonder I'm having these thoughts about life...(Big sigh.) I feel like I'm wondering what life is all about...At this moment, it means...I mean...I feel like I don't know if life has any meaning...I don't know why I'm thinking this way...(ugh)...I mean, what's the purpose?...It has a beginning, a middle, and an end...Boy, that's depressing! Where did that come from?... Phew! I feel like I'm suffering through this...It certainly isn't any fun! (Pause.) Streetcar...see my brother getting off...He's in the army...I get off...I'm going the other way...I feel...I feel like I'm there! Nasitir's Delicatessen...Flies getting killed on that electric grid on the door...ugh ...terrible sound...Oh God, oh...I don't know...I think I am going to stop this...I think I would have to spend more time with it...It seems like a lot of my memories are complete, and once I get them...once I get a thought—memory...an image...it seems to want to play itself out...but I know there are things there that I'm trying to remember and image, and it seems like they're under two feet of dirt, and then I can't reach down and get them...I know they're there—I feel them...Phew!...Wow! ...(Pause.) Interesting...I'm going to stop here."

When I listened to the tape, it was very evident that the imaging exercise had an enormous impact on me. I had to wait for half an hour before committing it to paper! I felt depressed, philosophically resigned, anxious, and in a strange place. I'm usually very up and optimistic, and even in moments of depression, I rarely question the purpose of life— why I am here and where I am going! I'm not sure that I have fully digested the exercise yet, but I do know that it had an impact on me. It took me a long time to get into it, but I think I piqued a connection with something buried down there. I think that the fragmented images started with that of the movie theater. Some of the people whose faces jumped in are people I haven't thought about in decades! The bubble-gum "war cards" came out of the blue, and I think that what followed were fragmented memories in the form of images. My entire relationship to Fillmore Street confuses me! My conscious recollections of that period of time do not seem to indicate that it was either stressful or particularly exciting. Nonetheless, there is something important about that time and place. I am somehow tied into it! There are a number of things I can conjecture about. I think that it was a time of "passages," a time when I passed through that tunnel between being a child and being a young man, a time of puberty and discovery. My whole family was together in that place, and I felt secure in that knowledge. I became mobile at that time. I traveled on buses and streetcars by myself, I learned to ride a two-wheeler bike, and I finally got one! My interest in girls came to the forefront, and I discovered independence! I imagine that those are enough ingredients to make that time and place important!

Using Unconscious Suggestions in this area should help you too to make contact with the unconscious. Don't get discouraged if it takes a little time to stimulate the fragmented memories. This is just another tool for accessing unconscious impulses to carry into your work. As a bonus, you get to know and understand yourself better!

PEOPLE YOU HARDLY REMEMBER AND SHADOW FIGURES

Quite often when we dream, and even in our nightmares, we see people we think we have never seen before. I could swear that many of the people in my dream world never appeared in my waking life; but if that is true, then where did they come from? Did I make up a face? Did I take features from a lot of people I know or once knew and create a composite, much like the police do from witnesses' descriptions? Where do these unfamiliar faces in our dreams come from? Perhaps we see those people passing in the street—so quickly that we take no notice of them. Our unconscious does though. I believe that, as if by an incredibly quick camera, their images are imprinted on our unconscious. Much like subliminal advertising, the images go so fast that we do not register them consciously. All through our lives, people come and go—people we know, friends of our parents or of our siblings, people who have worked for us, scores of faces who stared down at us as we lay in our crib, clicking their tongues and making cooing sounds at us. Sometimes those people stay in our lives for a period of time before they disappear. Some of them die when we are very young and leave behind a vague and shadowy image. Sometimes we can remember a name but can't attach a face to it. Most of those people didn't make any important impression on our lives, but some had an impact and, either negatively or positively, left their mark on our unconscious. It is a fact that children who are sexually abused block out the memory and, if that abuse was perpetrated by someone outside the family, even erase the person from their memory. The same can happen with other types of experiences.

Let us suppose that, while working in this area, you successfully access the face of a person who had a strong impact on you. It would follow that the events surrounding him or her would also be belched up at the same time. Fortunately, all images are not attached to traumatic events! Some of us lost our grandparents at such an early age that their faces seem impossible to retrieve; yet their love and affection at the beginning of our lives had an indelible impact. Going back and working to retrieve those images can bring a wealth of unconscious memories and emotions. Even the people who seem unimportant can be attached to events that *were* important. For example, your sister, who took care of you, showered you with love, and was always there when you needed something, became romantically involved with a young man for a very brief period of time. Her attention was diverted from you to him, and you experienced the first impacting feeling of abandonment. Therapists' couches are filled with people dealing with abandonment issues! Some of those individuals have an incredible fear of intimacy because of early experiences of abandonment. A single experience like the one above can create a lifelong psychological trauma. Because you were psychologically undeveloped and had not yet learned to objectify reality, your sister's taking her attention away from you and awarding it to someone else was a devastating rejection! You felt devalued, worthless, and cast off. It could have been the beginning of a total change in your personality. It could have created a pattern of behavior that compounded itself over a period of years and became an integral part of your personality.

So even though her relationship with that young man was short-lived, resurrecting his image could bring with it a bonanza of unconscious material!

Where do you begin to look for such "hardly remembered people and shadowy figures"? There are a number of ways in which you may start to explore this area of Unconscious Suggestions. First, you could go back to "I'm five years old and I..."—hoping that some of those images will present themselves—or you might do some Perspective Inventory of your very early years. You might re-create people you remember well and work to elicit the faces of their friends and acquaintances. Another possibility is to encourage an impulsive imaging workout, which is done in much the same way as Disconnected Impulsivity, with the emphasis on impulsively suggesting faces of people from your life. This approach can yield success by virtue of its speed and the trick element. The unconscious is quite often reluctant to give up its treasures, so tricking it into cooperating sometimes works.

➢ *Imaging Example*

All of the techniques mentioned above can be explored. For this example, however, I am going to work with the hypothetical incident I described earlier. Consciously starting with the image of your sister as she was at that time, encourage the creation of images of her relating to you, taking care of you, and showering you with her love. Use all five senses and Imaging Sensations as the approach technique.

I see her bending over me...her curly brown hair...big blue eyes...I smell talcum powder and baby oil...I hear music...feel her hands on my face...soft...loving hands...She is singing...flowered dress...apron...See the sides of my crib...light wooden slats...Furry pillow behind my head tickles my nose...Hear her laughing...see her white teeth...clicking her tongue...making faces at me...Feel myself laughing...feel happy...moving my arms and legs...want to sit up...She takes my arms...I feel myself being lifted...see the wall...pictures of little children, balloons...Being lifted out of the bed...being held in her arms...close to her...feel the warmth of her body...smell her...love to smell her...feel her hands on my back...moving in circles...warm and comforting...She is still singing to me...I feel her rocking me...and moving across the room...see toys... on the dresser...a panda bear...bigger than me...scary...See windows... snow...white everywhere...I hear the hissing of the radiator...see the steam...I don't know what that is...Hear voices in the other room...I recognize the voice...can't see the person...I feel her lips on my cheek... warm...

The imaging process can continue until you have a very clear experience of the person and place at that time. At some point, you begin to introduce the young man your sister became involved with. Since you do not remember him or how he looked, you might start with the image of his back.

I see her holding him...close to her...She is smiling...looks happy... See the back of his head...dark hair...shiny, oily...combed close to his head...big shoulders...taller than my sister...Can't see her...blocked by him...See her head on his shoulder...She isn't looking at me...Want to attract her attention...making sounds...She isn't responding...They are turning...Can see the side of his face...big nose...small chin...dark skin ...see him hold her tight...feel angry...They are dancing...Hear music... laughter...see his forehead...lines...black eyes...hear his voice...deep... strange sounds...He doesn't look at me...I feel like I'm not here...I see him...not clearly...but I see him...It's dark in here...Alone, looking at the ceiling...feeling things...afraid...voices in the other room...feeling myself crying...My voice seems as though it were coming from someone else...Hear the clock ticking...smell food...loud sounds...Where is she? ...I hear his voice in the other room...The darkness scares me...I feel funny feelings...feel alone...helpless...

At this point, if I were the reader, I would be wondering how a very small child could possibly have the awareness and the vocabulary to describe such complex images, responses, and feelings. Well, of course he couldn't! In order to explain the imaging process and the child's responses and commit the experience to paper, I have to use words that reflect the images and feelings engendered. It would be difficult for you to understand if I wrote "ga ga goo goo ma ma pa pa"—right? If you are successful in getting any visual response to that person, it should bring with it associations to the time and place. Any emotional response should be encouraged.

On the news recently, there was a report of a case where an adult woman reexperienced witnessing the murder of her mother by her father thirty years ago. Her mother's body was buried under a cement slab in the backyard. She led the police to the site, and indeed they found the skeletal remains of her mother! Obviously, she had blocked the memory of the event from her consciousness. I believe that it was retrieved in a therapy session. What was it that triggered the release of such a horrifying experience? It could have been a word, a sentence, an image that unlocked the entire episode. Whatever it was, it is certain that the whole event had been stuffed into her unconscious at a time when her conscious mind could not deal with it! I am not suggesting that we are all walking around with such horror stories buried in the recesses of our unconscious—I am merely trying to emphasize the power and complexity of what we all have locked in there!

PIECES OF DREAMS AND NIGHTMARES

In the next part of this chapter, I will be exploring dreams and dreaming as a way of communicating with the unconscious. In this section, however, I want to explore and experiment with imaging pieces or fragments of dreams. Again let me say that the language of the unconscious is IMAGES! We dream in images and may have as many as ten or fifteen dreams in a single night, most of which we don't remember. It is possible to grab an image or two from the dreams we had either recently or years ago. Sometimes a nightmare will startle us awake. We may not recall it, except for a fleeting image, which might, for example, consist of stepping into an elevator that isn't there, feeling that we are tumbling downward, and waking up at that moment. It is possible that stepping through that door into an empty elevator shaft was the entire dream, or maybe that was the tail end of it and we cannot remember what led us to that door. For our purposes it doesn't matter, since we are only trying to make a connection with the unconscious.

➤ *Imaging Example: Nightmare of Falling down an Elevator Shaft*

Start the imaging process by sensorially suggesting all of the elements that you remember about the dream—the shapes, colors, and size of things. Sizes, distances, and objects themselves are often distorted in dreams, so don't let your conscious logic keep you from re-creating the images as they were.

I feel myself moving very fast...I'm in a very long corridor...very narrow...I'm walking on gravel...the stones are hurting my feet...even through the soles of my shoes...(All of the images are responded to sensorially. Do not make any comments while re-creating the dream.) *I feel the need to get to the end of this corridor quickly...I don't know why... The faster I walk, the further away it seems...The walls on each side are very close to me...I can feel my elbows brushing the wall as my arms move...I know I am in some kind of building...I see a double door ahead of me...It is light green, and there is a slight separation between the two parts of the door...I'm increasing my speed...It is getting closer...but not fast enough...As I approach the door, it begins to open very slowly ...I'm thinking that it's funny, since I didn't push any buttons to call the elevator...No matter...it's important for me to get on it...I'm not sure why...I just know that it is urgent that I do...As I reach the fully open door and begin to take that step into the elevator, I realize that it isn't there...Too late...my right leg has taken that big step. I feel my body lurching forward, and I am falling...tumbling...I see the elevator shaft, the cables, and the steel grid...The cables look like braided hair...I feel myself tumbling, and I'm thinking that this isn't happening...I know I'm going to die...I remember thinking that I hope it doesn't hurt too much!*

At this point I wake up. I feel myself shaking and for a moment feel very disoriented. When I realize that it was just a nightmare, I feel a warm rush of relief go through my entire body. For a few moments I sit there trying to make some sense of the dream.

Re-creating a dream or nightmare is done to make contact with the unconscious. If you are successful, it should free some of the impulses related to that dream. If you explore the area of Unconscious Suggestions primarily to establish closer contact with your unconscious energies, then you should frequently repeat the exercises. You can also re-create an Unconscious Suggestion because you see a connection between the experience and the obligation of a scene you are addressing and are therefore using the dream as a choice to hopefully fulfill that obligation.

We often wonder where our dreams come from, what stimulates a particular nightmare. Is it fear? insecurity? our unconscious trying to tell us something? Is it wish fulfillment? Our dreams are all of those things and more! I really had the nightmare detailed above. It wasn't recently—about two years ago, I think. However, it wasn't until recently that I made a connection to its possible origin: When I was about ten years old, a good friend of my sister's fell seventeen flights down an open elevator shaft and was killed. I distinctly recall when we first heard about it. We were sitting at the kitchen table finishing dinner. My sister was reading the newspaper, when all of a sudden she screamed in shock and horror and turned white as a sheet. For a long while we couldn't get her to speak. When she finally was able to talk, she read the article to us. It seems that her friend had been walking along a corridor reading a magazine. He had pushed the button to call the elevator, but when the doors opened, he hadn't noticed that there was no elevator there, just an empty shaft. Still reading the magazine, he stepped off to his death. His name was Marty Brilliant. I didn't know him personally. I might have met him once or twice—I seem to have a picture of his face in my mind—but I'm not totally sure of that. The whole thing happened over five decades ago, and through those years I have thought about the incident several times, but I don't think I was ever preoccupied with it. It must, however, have had an incredible impact on me and burrowed deeply into my unconscious to be released fifty years later in a nightmare! You see, that is the point of sharing the event with you—to make it clear that experiences, events, encounters of all kinds have impact and meaning beyond our original awareness of their importance. Sitting in that "garbage dump" of the unconscious is enough material to fill the public library, and unless we are committed and dedicated to the emancipation of so much of what is available to us consciously, we will go to our graves without experiencing or sharing the untold wealth housed there!

The first step in using this area of Unconscious Suggestions is to try to remember these snippets of your dreams. They could consist of a single image; for example, you might remember looking up and seeing thousands of multicolored balloons rising high into the atmosphere. You could just re-create that image through the imaging process and see what it yields!

EXPERIENCES WHERE YOU CAN'T DISTINGUISH DREAMS FROM REALITY

The last area is an interesting one with which to challenge the unconscious. To this day, there are a couple of experiences that I am not sure about: Did they really happen, or was it a dream? I think I dreamt one of them, and yet it seems so real that I am not sure! It took place when I was still living in my parents' house. As I remember it, I had kept one of my handguns in a "gun muffin"—which is a suede case, with a fleece lining, that has a zipper running around its entire circumference—but when I went to look for it one day, it was gone! I emptied the entire drawer where it was supposed to be, frantically attempting to find it, but I didn't. I asked my mother about it, but she didn't know what had happened to it. Nothing else was missing, so I assumed that we hadn't been burglarized. Now, here is the strange part of this entire thing: I have no recollection of which one of my guns it was, and I surely would know if one of them were missing, right? Secondly, I don't recall owning a handgun when I was living with my mother and father! However, at this very moment, while I am sitting here typing this story, I am still convinced that someone took that gun. It is an incredibly strong feeling! Yet all of the evidence points to the fact that I dreamt the whole thing! How can a dream be so real? It has been a number of years since the event took place—or since I dreamt it.

There are other experiences that I'm not sure about. I am convinced that I attended an event with other people I know, in a place where I know I have been. I can describe what we did, what we talked about, and so on, and yet, when I mention it to those people, none of them recall such an event in such a place! It can be quite "crazy making" to know that you had an experience and yet not to be sure that it wasn't a dream! I am certain that as you read this, you will be able to think of one or two such feelings of your own. It doesn't matter how long ago the experience took place—what is important here is that you are not sure about its having happened! Was it a dream or wasn't it?

I have a theory about this phenomenon. I don't think that it occurs very often, but when it does, it creates this kind of confusion. Our dreams have an unconscious origin. They ventilate themselves when we are asleep. When we awaken, we know that what happened was a dream. We can attempt to remember it, analyze it, try to understand it, but we consciously know that it was a dream! We separate it, and we consciously can tell the difference. We have conscious memories and unconscious memories—they are separate. One of the reasons we record our dreams is that they fade back into the unconscious very quickly. In order to retain the memory of any given dream, we must remind our consciousness of its components. Then we remember it, but not on the same level as when we were experiencing it. It is quite different. My theory as to why we sometimes cannot distinguish reality from a dream is that, for some unknown reason, a particular dream may get trapped between the two memory banks. Our consciousness treats the dream, not as a dream, but as a real memory! Because there are evident contradictions and possibly some distortions of the experience, we are not sure whether it indeed happened or it was a dream. Now, assuming that my theory has any validity, my question is, What causes this phenomenon? Is it related to the nature of our sleep state at the time? Are we closer to a lucid-dream state when this happens? Do the components of such a dream somehow burrow their way into our conscious memory bank? Is the dream close enough to a parallel real experience? Why is it that whatever separates the two spheres disappears at certain times? Whatever the reason for such a phenomenon, we must learn to use it and take advantage of it.

How is that done? Well, first you must identify those types of experiences. After finding one, approach it with the imaging process that we have been describing throughout this entire book. Start to stimulate images based on your strongest memories of the experience. Approach it without making the distinction between reality and dream. Create each part of it in some chronological order, almost as if you were remembering it rather than pulling it up from your unconscious. Encourage the images to unfold, and allow them to affect you in any way they might. Remember that the goal here is not to determine whether or not this was a dream, but to make a connection with your unconscious. You may never know the truth!

The area of Unconscious Suggestions is a very rich one. If you work with it frequently and include it in your daily schedule, you will be surprised by its impact. After a short period of imaging Unconscious Suggestions, you will begin to notice thoughts, impulses, and memories that seem to come from a different place. The process will begin to inhabit your dream life, and you will experience a greater awareness of unconscious impulses that bubble to the surface each day. In addition to the suggestions already described and explored, here are some others that you might investigate:

- Funerals of relatives, friends, schoolmates
- Events that you have blocked from memory
- Early childhood traumas
- Early sexual images

Working with these areas will at the very least stimulate memories that you have long since forgotten and that are very rich with choices for your work. The goal, however, is to create a connection with your unconscious and to be able to elicit inspiration and support from it. As I said earlier in this section, you can use Unconscious Suggestions to make this connection in general terms, or you can specifically identify an obligation related to a piece of material and investigate an area that addresses it. If, for example, you are dealing with an obligation related to a religious experience or are playing a member of the clergy, you could explore all of your religious experiences through Unconscious Suggestions, creatively manipulating the exploration to address the particular demands of the material. In any event, you have a very rich area available to you. Remember to use imaging as the technique to access the stimuli in each area.

AFFECTIVE MEMORY

I discussed Affective Memory in chapter 5, but not as an unconscious preparation. The impact of Affective Memory on the unconscious is enormous. The theory is that by creating all of the components of a meaningful experience from a conscious place, you will hopefully trap the unconscious into responding as you had originally. It is a very precise and demanding involvement, and you must be very specific with your process. It can be approached through the use of Sense Memory or Imaging, but even in the second case Sense Memory is an indigenous part of the process.

Start by selecting a very meaningful experience or event, one that is loaded with unconscious potential—meaning that it contains issues that have a history in your life and that are deeply rooted in important relationships. The experience should be very full emotionally. Remember that in this instance you are not using it as a choice to address a piece of material but rather as a *general preparation* to pique unconscious life. If you are doing it to get ready to act, give yourself plenty of time to explore it, particularly the first time you approach it. If you are practicing for the purpose of exploring the unconscious, the time factor is less critical. Just start the process and continue until you have completed the entire experience. It will either access the unconscious, or it won't! Be prepared to fail! If you do indeed fall short of your goal, go over the process and try to determine how you can make it more specific and involving. Always approach Affective Memory in the here and now. All of your sensory questions must be phrased as if the experience and its components were taking place in the present. Start the process before the actual impact of the experience, and progressively create *everything* leading to the "moment"! If you create the place, the objects, the people, and the sounds, and pay meticulous attention to every sensory detail, you might really get a sense of being there. If that occurs, the possibility of success is very high. Once you step across that line into the reexperience and are supported by your unconscious, you are on the precipice of an ULTIMATE CONSCIOUSNESS experience. At the very least you will be in direct communication with your unconscious. Once you have achieved that, it will bleed into anything you do following the workout, on a very exciting level. For a very specific example of how to approach Affective Memory, look at the section dealing with "Imaging as a craft technique" in chapter 5.

The unconscious is a bottomless well of inspirational and mercurial emotional life, which liberates its product into the conscious expression of the actor, even in simple scenes. We have all seen actors who seem to have an inner life that is extremely compelling, even when they are doing nothing but listening to others. It is almost like some kind of internal radioactive generator spewing excitement through every pore in their body. Some people are naturally more connected to their unconscious than others, but whatever the case may be, if you want to establish this relationship, you must work at it. I have said this before, and I guess I will say it many more times: I would rather see an actor with less talent, who has developed that talent and become a master craftsman, than one who is endowed with a great deal of natural talent but refuses to learn how to access it consistently. If you are familiar with my other books, you know that there are a great many exercises and techniques that I encourage you to work with every day. Certainly a day is never long enough to do all of them; therefore you must design your work schedule so that you can concentrate on various areas at different times. Working with the unconscious is a monumentally important involvement. It takes time, energy, and motivation, but the reward is humongous!

DREAMS, DREAMING, AND THE UNCONSCIOUS

DREAMS AND DREAMING ARE A GIGANTIC PLANET IN THE SOLAR SYSTEM OF ACTING!

The discussion, telling, and analysis of dreams are an ancient involvement. Man has been addressing his dreams since the dawn of time. His religions, superstitions, and daily activities have been influenced and guided by his responses to them and his interpretation of their meaning. Only very recently, however, has there been a *scientific* exploration of what, how, and why we dream and what our dreams mean. C.G. Jung spearheaded it and wrote a great deal on the subject. He and Freud pioneered this incredible area, but hundreds of others have taken up the banner and made discoveries and contributions to it. Hundreds, possibly thousands, of books and papers have been written about dreams, as well as infinite techniques and suggestions given for understanding, exploring, interpreting, and learning from them. There are so many ways to relate to and use our dreams and so much to be gotten from becoming sophisticated about the dreaming process! If used properly, our dreams can help us antidote lifelong obstacles and inhibitions. They can teach us the lessons that the unconscious wishes to communicate and bring us a greater understanding of ourselves and the knowledge that will help us solve psychological and other problems. Unfortunately, they quite frequently lack continuity and can jump from one environment to another without any logical transition. They are also often rather abstract and filled with symbolism. Therefore, it takes some training or research to understand them and be able to use them creatively.

As acting tools, dreams can serve us in a variety of important ways. In the last chapter, I explained how we can use them to identify the existence of DISOWNED SUBPERSONALITIES. In this section, I am going to explore and emphasize dreams and dreaming as a way to create a connection to the unconscious and to seduce it into servicing our creative needs. In the next part the dreaming process will be investigated as a tool for preparing to act, and in the last chapter we will explore dreams as a device to PROGRAM THE UNCONSCIOUS to address character elements that we are obligated to fulfill. I will spend very little time interpreting dreams or trying to understand their meaning. That is for another book! The only analysis will be related to how we can use dreams and dreaming as tools for acting!

STARTING THE PROCESS

Where do you begin this incredible journey? That, of course, depends on where you are in the world of dreaming. If you are at the very beginning, you must start with DREAM AWARENESS. If you have been working and exploring your dreams for a period of time, then you can jump to the second or third step. In either case, I am going to explain a systematic process for becoming aware of dreams and using them to build a bridge from consciousness to the unconscious.

DREAM AWARENESS

You would be surprised at the number of people who think that they never dream, or at least that they do so very infrequently. We all dream every night or whenever we sleep. We may have ten or fifteen dreams in a single night. A number of them are quite subliminal, and we don't remember having had them at all. There are some which we are aware of while we are sleeping, but they evaporate even before we experience the first glimmer of consciousness. Some of us remember our dreams for a very few brief moments after awakening, but they vanish so quickly that we only have a vague sense of having dreamt at all! Others remember in great detail many of their dreams. There are many reasons for these personal differences. Certain people are just more closely connected with the conscious-unconscious process, and they also often have "lucid" dreams (I will explain lucid dreaming in the next chapter). Whatever the case may be for you, there is a process for remembering and using your dreams. It starts with AWARENESS!

The first step is to accept that you dream almost every time you sleep and that you *can* remember those dreams long enough to record them. Planting that knowledge in your consciousness will start the process of expecting yourself to dream. Once you have done that, you must ask yourself to remember what you dream. Upon awakening, stay in bed, preferably in the prone position, and go over the events and elements of a dream, allowing yourself to "feel the dream." Encourage a state of relaxation and, if possible, keep your eyes closed to avoid collision with the waking world and its distractions. Continue encouraging the state of not being quite fully awake and invite sensorial connection to the dream. In addition to feeling the dream, try to experience the sounds and smells you encountered there, and allow for the temperature of the place to affect you. Employ all of your senses! After doing that, quickly write the dream down. Keep a pad and pencil or a tape recorder by your bedside so that you can record the dream in detail and work with it later. The conscious habit of remembering and exploring your dreams in this manner will open that world up to you! This connection is a life-changing involvement, and there is no limit to how far you can travel on this journey. Many people who started on it became so involved in that universe that they spent their entire life pursuing and interpreting their dreams and becoming professionals in the field.

Once you are awake, and possibly at a later time, you may go back to your notes and begin to work with the dream (we will explore that process a little later in this section). After you encourage an awareness of dreaming, the next step is to prepare to dream.

INVITING THE DREAM

Inviting yourself to dream and encouraging yourself to remember the dream are conscious processes. There are many facets to this involvement. It starts with a very deliberate decision to have a dream or a number of dreams. As you get into bed, do any of the relaxation exercises that are indigenous to this system. Encourage a complete state of physical and mental relaxation. You might meditate, if that is a technique which you are familiar with. At a point when you are completely relaxed, tell yourself that you are going to dream tonight and that you will remember your dreams. Make the suggestion quite specific and firm: "Tonight, I am going to dream! I will remember all of my dreams. I know that I dream every time I sleep, so I am inviting those dreams into my life." As you wake up, whether it is in the middle of the night or in the morning, stay with the dream and do everything noted above to remember and record it. If you awake in the middle of a dream and there is still some sleep time remaining, try to reinvest in the dream. Tell yourself that you are going back to sleep and will pick up the dream where it left off. That doesn't always work, but sometimes it does! By doing that, you can possibly have a resolution to the dream—which may be very important to your sense of well-being for the rest of the day. In addition, each time you succeed in continuing the dream, you may be strengthening your connection to conscious-unconscious communication. Encourage yourself to dream every time you go to sleep. At first, you may only have a little success with your request, but do it consistently. The rewards will be forthcoming. Try to remember that this is very new to you and that the unconscious is not accustomed to taking orders! However, with repetition and encouragement, it will soon begin to cooperate.

DREAM CATCHING

The next step in the process is "DREAM CATCHING"—an expression Elizabeth Strahan uses. She is a Jungian analyst associated with the C.G. Jung Institute of Los Angeles, who has devoted much of her life to the study and interpretation of dreams. Besides writing many articles and papers on the subject, she has a videotape series called *The Language of Dreams*. Dream catching refers to the process of being aware of the dream—its parts and elements, the place, time, people, animals, and objects in it. Dream catching can occur while you are still asleep—if you become aware that you are dreaming—or when you wake up. If in those very few moments when you still remember the dream you note all of its elements, you can use them for later reconstruction.

Besides feeling the dream, which not only means identifying the way it made you feel but feeling into its fabric (dreams have a fabric, a quality, an essence that frequently cannot be described but can be felt), ask questions about it while you are still in the sleep state, such as Where is this place? Am I familiar with it? Does it feel like my environment? Who are these people? Do I recognize them? Whom do they remind me of? What are they trying to tell me? What is the plot of this dream? You might even talk to the characters in the dream and ask them what they are trying to communicate, why they are there, what they want, why they are doing what they are doing, and so on. Wait for them to respond! This is a very special time, when you are close enough to your unconscious to actually get answers that may even be startling! Most often, the characters in your dream are subjective, which means that they represent parts of yourself—things you need to address, to acknowledge and include in your life. Sometimes they are more objective—which means that they also represent other people in your life—and the dream may be telling you something about them or your relationship to them that needs to be clarified or paid attention to. Catching the dream is extremely important for a variety of reasons: first, so that you might be able to understand the message, and secondly, so that you have enough components to re-create and work with the dream from a conscious place.

IDENTIFYING THE SYMBOLS IN YOUR DREAMS

Almost every dream contains symbols—or actions that are symbolic. Usually, we don't understand or know what they mean. A symbol might be the key to a dream—its message. It might indicate what part of your life the dream pertains to. There are subjective symbols, which represent or relate to you, and objective symbols, which refer to others. A symbol can represent almost anything in your life. For example, on *The Language of Dreams* video a man talked about a dream he had, in which he was holding his dog on a leash. The dog changed into a cat and then into a much larger, seemingly dangerous animal. The dreamer was frightened by it but invited it to eat fruit on a tree in his backyard. It began to devour the fruit, which looked like figs with seeds inside. In the beginning the animal could have represented the man's puppy, but later, as it became larger and the man began to sense some danger, it might have meant something else. It was suggested on the tape that the figs could represent the dreamer's masculinity, his sperm, his "seed," which was being eaten by this strange animal. While the interpretation of this dream is not our concern at this point, it should be noted that by re-creating the animals and their actions, the dreamer would certainly reexperience his emotional response to the dream, while at the same time communicating with his unconscious.

When committing your dreams to paper, make sure that you list or underline the symbols in each of them. Make a note of anything that is abstract or that you don't understand logically.

I have noticed that in my dreams I will often be somewhere with a particular person, doing something or other, and a short time later that person will turn into someone else, only I don't note the change; I just accept the understudy. When I remember the dream, it seems strange that the switch took place and even stranger that I took no note of it. Sometimes, I will dream about an experience or an adventure with a person with whom I used to be romantically involved. In the dream, I know it is that person because of the way I feel and also because we are doing things we really did in life; however, the person is physically someone else—sometimes no one I remember knowing. I have also had dreams where the people were fighting each other with live fish! Recently, I had a strange dream about my father, who died in 1969. He looked just as he did then. He was dressed exactly as I picture him to be when I think about him, wearing a gray felt hat and a dark sweater. We were walking arm in arm over a large metal grate. He was happy and smiling, and he asked me if I wanted to have breakfast. I don't remember my response, but I do recall thinking in the dream that he would have been eighty-three on his next birthday if he had lived. So part of my unconscious knew that he was dead, and yet I accepted him as alive. The dream had a number of symbols in it: the place where we were, which seemed gray and long, the metal grating we walked over, and so on. I expect that if I worked to re-create that dream, I would be strongly affected by it. I haven't tried it yet, but somewhere down the line I will. Many of my dreams involve one kind of transportation or another, and I frequently end up in another conveyance than the one I started out in. Once I had one of those warrior-type dreams—you know, the ones where you are in a great battle somewhere—only my weapon was a large turkey leg! I am not even going to attempt to interpret that one!

I had a short but very interesting dream last night: I was driving a red Corvette without lights. Next to me was an old girlfriend. I knew it was she, but she looked like someone else. We were in an alley or narrow street with trees on the left side and a cement wall on the right. We were talking about health and taking care of oneself, when all of a sudden three hoodlums came from behind the corner of the cement wall. I knew they were out for trouble by the way they behaved and were dressed! They were in their twenties and were not part of any minority group. One of them was carrying a kerosene lantern that was not lit. He abruptly flung it against the cement wall, and it just smashed—no flames or fire. I remember at this point thinking that I hoped it had not damaged my car. Then they all converged on the car, making threatening gestures and sounds. I realized that my doors were unlocked but could not seem to move to lock them. I jammed the accelerator pedal to the floor, but the car would not move forward. I don't know whether the wheels were spinning or not. I knew I had a pistol in my right pocket and hoped that I had enough time to get it out before the hoodlums reached the car doors. As I was groping for the gun, I woke up! It was still dark outside, so it must have been the middle of the night. My heart was beating rapidly, and besides feeling fear, I was very angry!

I had a red Corvette twenty-five years ago, at approximately the same time as I was involved with the woman in the dream. As for the rest of it, I didn't recognize the place or the three hoodlums. Besides the car and the woman, I think that the unlit lantern and the fact that I could not get the car to move all symbolize important elements. The fact that I knew who the woman was but that she looked like someone else I didn't recognize also seems significant!

I believe that it was a very important dream. Before going to bed, I was watching a Charles Bronson movie, *Death Wish 3,* which was filled with episodes like the one in my dream. Even though that might have sparked the dream, I believe that the latter is much more deeply rooted in my psyche. There are a number of identifiable elements: I was aggressed on during my grade-school and high-school years. The abuse was formidable and left scars. I have incredible fears of being attacked and becoming the victim of a violent crime. I have taken various precautions and have armed myself. The nondescript hoodlums in my dream looked like a composite of the bullies in my life! I have also always been interested in high-performance automobiles, which have somehow become attached to my ego. At the time when I owned the Corvette, I was concerned with having a good image in front of that girlfriend.

All of the symbols in the dream might be usable as catalysts in its re-creation. Because I feel that it is very deeply rooted and that the issues in it are responsible for the construction of strong elements of my personality, I believe it would be a very good dream for me to use to access unconscious life and inspiration and open capillaries that would support any choice I might work for to create a dynamic unconscious life, which could inspire and dimensionalize my experiential behavior. I could also use this dream as a choice to address the complex emotional life it is attached to.

THE LANGUAGE, SYMBOLS, AND MEANING OF DREAMS

Although our dreams are indigenous to each of us, they often contain similar objects and characters. We have a common connection to many of their symbols. For instance, many individuals dream about snakes, engaged in a variety of activities. Most people are both frightened and fascinated by snakes, which often represent wisdom and instinctive energy. So, if a snake appears in your dream, you might want to talk to it and ask it what it is attempting to communicate. Large and deep bodies of water relate to the unconscious, so a dream of sinking down or drowning might not be what it obviously suggests but instead may indicate that the unconscious is telling you to pay attention to the messages it keeps sending you! If you disregard them, it will keep sending them to you until it gets angry enough to create some kind of emergency that you will not be able to overlook. Flying in a dream can mean a number of different things: It can suggest that you need to escape from what or where you are in life, or it can mean that you have the potential to soar to the heights. To understand the meaning of such a symbol, you must examine the content of your life—what is going on at present. Do you feel trapped? Are you underachieving? You must look deeply into yourself to understand the meaning of those symbols.

Another common dream is one in which you are standing in a public place completely naked. You feel embarrassed and ashamed and can't understand how you got there. This can mean many things. It can relate to a feeling of helplessness in your life, to feeling exposed to something out of your control, or it can indicate that you need to strip yourself of all of your protections and insulation. Again, you must look at what is happening in your life. If you ask enough questions about the context of your life, you may begin to understand your dreams.

Someone recently told me that he had a recurring dream of taking various people to his home (it doesn't always look like his home, but he knows it is). In this place there is a lot of disarray; junk is piled in corners, and his overall feeling is, Why did I bring these people to a place that needs to be cleaned up? That dream seems obvious: The unconscious is simply saying that the dreamer has to "put his house in order," to deal with his own life, before he invites other "energies" into it. Here again, there are probably other elements—and possibly other interpretations too!

If you have a violent dream with hostile aggressors, it may just be the unconscious telling you that you are not honoring a part or parts of yourself. The violent characters might be aspects of you that you have pushed into the background and that are now trying to tell you to recognize them and include them in your life.

Many dreams are about animals or have animals in them. Each type of animal symbolizes something specific. Dogs usually relate to relationship, warmth, or personal touch; domestic animals represent our civilized selves, while wild ones are closest to the instincts and the unconscious; fish, dolphins, and other such creatures relate to contents from deep inside our unconscious that want to come to the surface. When you dream of biting or being bitten, it often indicates that your unconscious wants to get in, that your ego needs to recognize it.

If you have a dream about an automobile (which I do all the time!), it can relate to your ego, to how you behave in your outer life. If, for example, you dream about speeding down the highway at critical speeds, the dream may be telling you that you need to slow down! Your life is moving too fast for your safety or health. If you dream of having an auto accident, it could mean that your ego attitude is leading you in the wrong direction and needs to be modified. Such dreams mean that you need to examine your outer life.

Dreaming about the opposite sex can objectively point to another person in your life and/or be subjective and relate to your feminine side if you are a man, and conversely, to your masculine side if you are a woman. You might have a dream where a woman appears—someone you feel you know but do not recognize. She is crying and wants your love and attention, but you refuse to pay any attention to her. This could mean that you are overidentified with your macho or masculine self and need to honor and accept your feminine energy, which contains your sensitivity, creativity, and warmth. If that dream recurs, it usually means that you *must* pay attention.

Those are but a few examples of the specific language and symbolic interpretation of dreams. I took the time to inform you of their existence because I feel that the more you know about the subject, the better you will be able to use it in your personal life as well as in your artistic pursuits. It would be wise for you to explore further and accumulate more information about what dreams mean. Even though our emphasis here is on using them as conduits to the unconscious, understanding their components will allow you to access elements that will plummet you deeper into the recesses of your unconscious. It is true that working to re-create a dream on face value information only will usually access unconscious impulses, but without understanding the symbols you might only be able to go just so deep! On the other hand, if the interpretation of an object in your dream or what it relates to can lead you to pushing other buttons, you may find the "open Sesame" to your unconscious. It may be somewhat of a cliché, but having more knowledge about anything gives you the control and the power to succeed.

ACTIVE IMAGINATION

Before I get into imaging the dream, I would like to introduce a technique created by Jung, called *active imagination*. This technique, with which I am somewhat familiar in the area of subpersonality work, is totally compatible with imaging. In fact, they complement each other. It is important to note here, however, that they are also different processes.

Jung felt that active imagination was an important way to consciously relate to the unconscious. You can proceed in several manners. First, you can "talk" to the people in your dreams by putting any of them in a chair facing you and starting a conversation. Ask questions such as Who are you? What do you want here? Why are you behaving this way? What were you doing in my living room? Where did you come from? and allow the figure to answer. This is a highly imaginative process, and since it originates in the dream world, the answers you get may surprise you! You can use the process in relation to all of the characters in your dreams. You may even ask questions about the place or the action of the dream. To combine active imagination with imaging, add sensorial elements and imaging responses as you relate to that person sitting across from you. Create him or her by imaging his or her features through Imaging Sensations. By combining the two techniques, you create a much richer and more tangible reality. The greater that is, the better chance you have at accessing the unconscious.

Another way of using active imagination is to write down your impulses and responses to the dream in a stream-of-consciousness fashion. Of course, you must first reinvest in the dream. You can use imaging to re-create its various elements and then begin writing your responses to the images. Working in a stream-of-consciousness mode will more than likely stimulate disconnected, sometimes abstract writing. Remember, however, that the stream of words you scribble onto the paper may be directly connected to your unconscious.

The third approach involves drawing or sculpting your dream. Again you should invest in the re-creation of the dream; then, as you become involved in it, start to draw the objects, animals, or people in it, as well as whatever images present themselves. You can also use clay or some other similar material to sculpt them. You need not be a great artist and must not let your drawing or sculpting abilities stand in the way of your using this technique. Whatever the results are, you stand to learn something about yourself, as well as to connect with unconscious impulses.

The last approach uses movement. Again, reinvest in the dream, and this time encourage yourself to move, using as much of your body as possible. (These techniques are very similar to those we used in the previous chapter to access subpersonalities.)

RE-CREATING THE DREAM THROUGH IMAGING

Using the dream about the Corvette I recounted earlier, I might start with the identification of its symbols. Before I begin, I might write the dream down, study what I have written, and allow myself to be attracted to the parts or words that seem to be symbolic. Assuming that I want to re-create this dream to increase my ability to communicate with my unconscious and strengthen my relationship to it, I might at first approach it through Symbolic Imaging. I might start by re-creating the Corvette. Looking over the hood, relating to the shape and colors, I would simultaneously create the smell of the leather interior, the sound of the engine, the way the seat feels on my back, and so on, using Imaging Sensations. From the car, I might go to the unlit lantern in the hand of one of the hoodlums and create it as it is being smashed against the wall, hearing the sounds. At this point, I might add some active imagination and ask the hoodlum why he is doing this to us or what he wants. Using Symbolic Imaging lets me jump from object to object in random fashion.

Another approach would be to verbalize the entire dream so that I could listen to the emotional emphasis on words and phrases, which could give me insight into what part or parts have the most impact on me. I would then encourage myself to feel the dream, allowing all of my emotional responses to run their course. At the point where I was the most connected to the dream, I would start to re-create it, using Symbolic Imaging and Imaging Sensations.

➢ *Symbolic Imaging Example*

It's dark...no headlights...(Even though my initial response is visual, all of the other senses are responding to the particular stimulus they come in contact with. I am feeling the seat on my back, I smell the odors, I feel the presence of the person next to me, I hear the engine, I am aware of the clump of trees on my left, I see the dimly lit cement wall to my right, and so on.) *I see the reflections of the streetlights on the hood of the car. The color is somewhat distorted...I hear shouting...*

314

ugly, high-pitched sounds...Don't know where they're coming from...
Can feel a sense of danger...See someone in a black leather motorcycle
jacket with a chain looped through the epaulet...face distorted into a
mask of anger...hatred...lantern dangling from right hand...swinging it
back and forth while shouting at us...Can't make out what he is saying
...Two others to his left...dressed in a similar fashion...moving towards
the car...See the lantern being thrown against the cement wall...hear the
crashing of metal and glass...feel the rush of fear...can't seem to move
fast enough...My movements seem labored and take so much effort to
execute!...I feel my foot pressing down on the accelerator...I feel the
firewall behind the pedal...and nothing is happening...I'm standing still
...I feel the fear of death...It has a taste to it...The gun in my pocket—I
must get it...I can't seem to move fast enough...Will there be time?...
(This is the point at which I woke up.)

Using Imaging Sensations encourages all of my senses to fill in the
blanks between the symbolic images in the exploration. By imaging
many of the surrounding elements of the dream that may not be crucial,
I am able to re-create the main symbols by building a frame around
them. Let us suppose that the important symbols are the car, the person
I am with—who doesn't look like who she is—the hoodlum with the
leather jacket, the cement wall, the lantern, and the gun in my pocket. If
those are the meaningful parts of the dream, they are somehow rooted
more deeply in my unconscious than some of the other elements. By
creating them, I can expect a response from my unconscious, which may
present itself in a number of ways. By pushing those symbolic buttons, I
might reexperience the entire impact of the dream—feel, in a conscious
state, the same things I felt while dreaming. On the other hand, I might
connect to many other feelings associated with that kind of experience.
In that case, my emotional response could be quite different: By re-
creating the dream in symbolic terms, I might be opening a Pandora's
box filled with a myriad of experiences and feelings that date back to my
early childhood. It would seem that the second response would be more
deeply rooted in the unconscious. In either scenario, however, I am
working with ingredients that speak to my unconscious. As I repeat this
process on a daily basis, recording the previous night's dreams and
working with them, I am creating a habit of communicating with my
unconscious. If I do this for a period of time, I can expect greater
cooperation and involvement from it.

As Sigmund Freud said, "Dreams are the royal road to the unconscious." If you travel that road consistently, you will reach your

destination. The key to success is repetition. As you become more facile with the process, you may be able to order up dreams in specific areas. For example, you may want to address some confusion that you are experiencing about how to deal with a particular problem or person, so you might ask for a dream in that area: "I would like to have a dream concerning my confusion about what to do about such and such a relationship." If you think about it several times during the day and before you retire at night, you just might get a dream that addresses the issue.

The residual bonus is that working with your dreams on a daily basis will ultimately promote a greater proximity to your unconscious in a waking, conscious state. By communicating with your unconscious on a regular basis, you receive impulses that come directly from it, so that even when you are not involved with some process that is designed to elicit its response, it continues to liberate thoughts and impulses into your conscious expression and behavior.

When re-creating a dream, you should explore the various imaging techniques outlined in chapter 3. The dream above might have been explored through Fragmented Imaging, Story Imaging or Verbalized Imaging. A particular dream may respond to one technique better than to another, but the only way you could know that is to experiment with all of them. Using some of the modalities of active imagination can yield wonderful results also. Drawing the people or animals you dreamt about can act as a catapult into the entire dream. If, for example, you draw or sculpt the image of a character in one of your dreams and you get repeated physical and emotional responses to the drawing or sculpture, you can use the product again and again to ignite your unconscious responses. For an actor this is like carrying a powerful choice in his pocket! Imagine collecting a number of drawings that relate to various dreams you have had! All you would have to do to stimulate emotional life or a connection to your unconscious would be to look at the appropriate drawing! You might even place it somewhere on the stage in an unobtrusive place, and when you needed to address a particular emotional obligation, you could saunter over to where it was, and bingo, you would be there! Of course, that might not always work! But whether you use the results as choices or just to remind you of particular dreams, drawing and sculpting are viable techniques.

THE PURPOSES FOR WORKING WITH YOUR DREAMS

Working with your dreams enables you to do the following:

1. Establish connection with your unconscious. Since dreams come directly from there, developing a relationship to them and using them create a direct line to your unconscious.
2. Learn from the dreams, understand more about yourself, and affect your conscious life as a result of your discoveries.
3. Bring your unconscious into closer proximity with your consciousness.
4. Use dreams as choices for your acting obligations.
5. Accumulate choices for future use.
6. Learn the language of dreams. As you gain more knowledge and do more research on dreams, you will begin to understand what they are telling you. A greater understanding of their language and symbols will make it easier for you to translate their content into impetus for your work.

If you become interested and involved in the study of dreams and dreaming, there is a great deal of literature on the subject. I will recommend a number of good books in the bibliography.

This seems like a good place to fill in a little background about this field. As far as I know, there has not been a lot of time or energy put into the use of dreams in acting. None of the people I studied with or the acting books I have read deal with dreams to any important extent. As I mentioned earlier, Lee Strasberg quite frequently said that "ninety-five percent of our talent lives in the unconscious," but I never heard him say anything about using dreams as a way of accessing it! When I have heard acting teachers refer to dreams, it was a cursory statement that dreams were important, and that is all. Well, I believe dreams constitute an entire universe, filled with known and unknown things, bottomless, endless, and infinite, possibly containing all the knowledge from the beginning of time! We have not even begun to fathom what the unconscious holds. Possibly, as Jung believed, our collective unconscious could possess all of the knowledge of man since his appearance on this planet, passed on from one generation to the next through genetic inheritance. It is possible that the coding of our DNA contains all of the history and stories since the "big bang"! But even if none of that is true, we do know that the genius of the unconscious truly exists and that to harness even a small part of it would put us in a category unique in human behavior. Dreams and the telling of dreams exist in recorded documents and literature that date back to 3000 B.C. (1600 B.C. in Egyptian writings)! There are numerous references to dreams in the Bible, and many ancient civilizations had a religious attachment to them and their meaning. Some believed that dreams were messages and instructions from God, telling them how to worship and live their lives. The messages needed to be carefully interpreted, though, because they might also come from the Devil, who was always looking for ways to seduce people and lead them astray! In modern times the individual study of dreams has been somewhat abandoned, except by primitive people like the Senoi of Malaysia and the Native Americans, who have kept their spiritual connection to the meaning and purpose of dreams.

In the early 1900s, Freud began his scientific research into dreams. Jung, who had read Freud, took up the banner, and both of those brilliant men built a road into understanding dreams and their meaning and impact on our lives. Their paths later separated, and each of them created his own relationship to dreaming and the unconscious. On many issues they agreed, but on many more they did not, as each became interested in other aspects of the psyche as well.

USING DREAMS AS CHOICES

Dreams make particularly good choices. However, working to re-create a dream with any choice approach is more complex than using a simpler choice. So why and when would you select a dream to address a piece of material? The first answer that comes to mind is, Anytime you want to enlist the support of your unconscious. Well, suppose that you wanted your unconscious to inspire you every time you acted, wouldn't it be wise then to always use your dreams as choices? The answer is no! In some cases that would be like attempting to kill a fly with a shotgun! You do want unconscious support every time you act; however, not every obligation demands the complexity of life that comes from using dreams. In many cases, it would suffice to do a preparation that would elicit unconscious impulses. Every choice you work for, depending on its impact, will affect your unconscious in some way, so in a manner of speaking, you are almost always somewhat supported by responses from the unconscious. I know that may sound a little like double talk, but it truly isn't! In some way the unconscious is involved in everything we do, but like the evening star, it can only be seen when the "sun" goes down! Just because we can't see it, it doesn't mean it isn't there! Quite often in my classes, I will tell an actor to "raise the stakes," make the choice more meaningful and impacting. In other words, I am encouraging him to use something that affects him more powerfully on a conscious emotional level. What appeals to our conscious state may also impact on our unconscious. If the actor is already connected to his unconscious as a result of his daily exercises and has done preparations in this area, his work will contain the components of unconscious life. Why are some actors so compelling, even when they are just sitting there doing nothing? Yeah, right, that's talent! But then I ask you to define talent! Is it not possible that what makes an actor's inner life so interesting is a connection with the unconscious? It could be!

There are times when a dream is a perfect choice! Many obligations call for intricate and dimensional emotional life. Many characters in dramatic literature who are very complex psychologically could be approached through dreams that come from deeply rooted areas within us. We have all heard the statement, "That character might be out of your emotional range." On a conscious level, and based on what you have or have not accessed in your acting career, that might be true! However, is it beyond your *unconscious* emotional range?

The decision whether to use a dream as a choice should depend on your sense of where the life of a particular character comes from. If you feel that the obligations can be addressed from a conscious place and with a conscious process, you needn't go into the unconscious, except for preparation. On the other hand, if you lack conscious affinity for the character and can't find justification for his inner life and his behavior, you might begin to explore your unconscious to find connections.

CHARACTERS WHO CAN BE CREATED THROUGH DREAMS

There are many roles in theater and film that could be well serviced through the use of dreams as choices. In chapter 3, I described a dream I had about vampires and the helplessness I felt in relation to them and the power they seemed to have over me. I interpreted that dream and, if you remember, came to the conclusion that I could use it as a choice to address a character who felt helpless and victimized by a woman, or women in general, as did the character played by Henry Fonda in *The Big Street*.

There is a long list of other characters who require inspiration and support from the unconscious. Hamlet, for one, is a complex character, tortured by his father's death and his own inability to do anything about it. He is visited by his father's ghost and haunted by his mother's relationship to his uncle. He has an ambivalent and complex relationship with Ophelia and her brother, his friend Laertes, whom he ends up killing in a duel. He contemplates suicide, kills his uncle, and generally creates mayhem for a couple of hours on stage! That is quite a feat for a nineteen-year-old boy! No wonder most of the famous actors who played him were a least twenty years older than he! Nonetheless, Shakespeare obviously thought it was possible. Dreams might certainly be used to create the dimensional character profile of Hamlet.

In the film *A Double Life* Ronald Colman played an actor who is doing *Othello* on Broadway and who gets so deeply into the character that he begins to imagine that his wife is doing to him what Othello thinks Desdemona did. In a jealous rage, he kills a woman and ends up killing himself on stage! I have no idea how Ronald Colman approached the role. He was a fine actor and was very good in this film. But if you were going to play this character and you wanted to access the kind of insecurity, jealousy, and outrage at being betrayed that are needed, you might have to go into your unconscious to liberate the conglomerated facets involved. If you had been cataloguing your dreams and committing them to a dream journal or diary, you could begin the search for the right one or at least for the area that might access that hidden well in your unconscious. In the event you could not find such a dream or cluster of dreams, you might order one up!

Willy Loman, in *Death of a Salesman*, is another character who walks a tenuous line between reality and illusion. He is also tortured and filled with delusional priorities—the need to be rich and respected, to have many friends, to have hopes for his sons, to accomplish what he has dreamt for himself, and especially "to be well liked"! When almost everything he holds paramount in his life is shattered, he begins to hallucinate and has many conversations with his dead brother, who had gone to Alaska and struck it rich. He is yet another character whose behavior seems to come from very deep sources. Since an actor playing the role would necessarily have to be in his late fifties or early sixties, he would have a lifetime of dreaming to draw from.

Amanda in *The Glass Menagerie* is another desperate character, who lives on hopes and dreams and survives by re-creating the successes of her past. Her daughter, Laura, also lives in illusion for most of the play, creating a fantasy world inhabited by glass animals. Laura's brother, Tom, a poet and dreamer, lives his life in the darkness of movie theaters, where "all of those actors in Hollywood have all of the adventures for the rest of the world." He finally deserts his mother and sister to pursue his own adventure, only to find that he cannot enjoy it because the guilt of abandoning Laura constantly haunts him. He is also the narrator of the play and relives the events for the audience. All three of those characters are rich and dimensional and could very easily be approached with dreams as choices.

The character in the film *The Three Faces of Eve* can be fulfilled by the use of subpersonalities, which may be accessed through dreams. The film is about a woman with three separate personalities, who are unknown to each other. Multiple-personality disorder is a real psychological abnormality, which has been researched quite intensely since that film was made. Since there are three distinct parts to this character, the actor playing her would have to identify and separate three specific parts of her own personality. She could access and liberate those selves by facilitating the proper subpersonalities or by using dreams to ignite those energies.

Macbeth and Lady Macbeth are also very complex characters, whose needs, drives, and actions are motivated from very deep and convoluted places. Here again, identifying the right dream could go a long way toward the creation of their characters.

Let us add to the list the antithetical figures of Dr. Jekyll and Mr. Hyde—another example of multiple personalities, which illustrates the good-versus-evil theme—and the preacher in Somerset Maugham's *Rain,* a moralist who totally denies his sexual energies, judges Sadie Thompson, condemns her life, and finally succumbs to his overwhelming sexual desire. Those are just a few of the thousands of characters whose psychological structure calls out for support from the unconscious. I am certain that as you read this, many more will come to mind from films or plays you have seen or even parts you have played.

When you read a play or film script, ask yourself some questions about the character you are interested in: What kind of person is he? What seems to impel his behavior? What is his psychological state? Does his behavior seem to come from identifiable places? How does he relate to the world around him and to the other characters? Are his actions rational or irrational? Is he always coherent? Does he allude to inner pressures or forces that motivate his actions? Does the author indicate instability or neurosis? Does the character seem driven by inner voices? Is he obviously in denial of specific personality elements? Is his personality the result of abuse or trauma in his childhood? Does he overreact to certain people or behaviors? Is he expressive, or does he suppress his emotions? How does he relate to himself physically? The answers to those questions will help you construct a blueprint of the character, which will be very instrumental in the identification of the various obligations and choices.

A clue you might look for when deciding to use a dream as a choice is whether the character's personality is the obvious result of inner and unconscious forces. The character Kane in *Citizen Kane*, for example, spends his entire adult life compelled and driven by inner demons created in his childhood. When you approach that kind of character, you might construct a profile by following the events of his early experiences and the way he responded to them, exploring the people in his life and the way they treated him, tracing the visible evolution of his personality and the development of his defense system—the compensatory behaviors and suppression of emotions that would come out later in his life, more often than not in destructive ways. Once you have created this blueprint, you could start looking into your own life for parallels and choices. Let us suppose that you have identified a strong theme that existed in his evolution from childhood into maturity and that had to do with suppression. He was never allowed to play with other children, he was isolated from the outside world and surrounded only by adults, and he wasn't allowed to attend public or private schools but was educated by tutors. His guardians were very judgmental and critical of anything they did not approve of. He was left to his lonely world, which was filled only with the comfort of daydreams and fantasy, and he suppressed his resentment and hostilities. His thoughts were constantly directed towards growing up and finally being free. Filled with resentment and the desire to retaliate and prove himself to his "warden" and "guards," he grew up with enormous suppressed frustrations, which later manifested themselves in ruthlessness and insensitivity. His entire thrust was towards succeeding at any cost. You might begin by identifying experiences in your own life that stimulated similar feelings. In order to create the many elements of this character structure, you could look into dreams that related to similar childhood circumstances. You would then attempt to re-create those dreams in the hopes of reexperiencing an unconscious relationship to those times, places, and events. Building on any success you might have with this process, you could then "layer" it by selecting more dreams that addressed the same or similar feelings and experiences.

For example, let us imagine that an actor playing this role can remember that, at an early age, he had many dreams related to abandonment. His mother worked nights and had to leave him quite often in the care of an older lady, who drank too much and would fall into a deep stupor, completely unaware of him or his needs. Many nights, while his mother was at work, he would have no dinner and would cry himself to sleep. If he ever needed a drink of water, he had to fend for himself and had a very difficult time reaching the faucet. His first feelings of abandonment had come when his father left, which was why his mother had to work. During this period of time, our actor remembers having had numerous dreams, which he later came to understand were the result of his feelings of being abandoned. One of those dreams put him naked and alone in a dark forest. The trees were huge, and his neck hurt just to look up to their top. He would continually step on sharp stones, which cut into his bare feet. He would walk endlessly, not knowing where he was going or which direction to take. He would try to cry out, but when he opened his mouth, nothing would come out—he had no voice. As the dream continued, he would roam the forest until it was too dark to see, at which time he would sit naked on the ground and wait for morning so that he could continue walking. He remembers that he had this dream or a similar one over and over. It gave way to other more sophisticated ones as he grew older, but the theme and meaning were the same. Our actor grew up with the scars of his abandonment deeply etched in his unconscious. As a result, many of the events and relationships of his life were influenced by those unconscious memories and dreams. In every relationship with the opposite sex, he became possessive to the point of destroying it. He was constantly uncomfortable when alone and therefore sought company even if he didn't particularly like the people involved. He had an enormous drive to prove his worth, and he became a workaholic. This and his tunnel vision alienated people, and he would often feel abandoned by his friends.

If our hypothetical actor were to approach a role like Kane, he might begin his journey by following his character blueprint and re-creating those dreams that he remembered from childhood. He might work on the same one many times, emphasizing different elements and symbols each time. Then he might move to the next dream or cluster of dreams relating to the same feelings, at all times encouraging his unconscious to give up its treasure. As he layered the elements of character, using the stimuli yielded, he could work for dreams he had as he grew up, which he would add to the ones he had already been working with, and hopefully he would begin to experience the layers of the unconscious fabric of the character. In a sense, this actor would be creating the experiential life of another person from his own unconscious raw materials, embodying the thoughts, feelings, and impetus that would make him think, feel, and act like the character, *from a real place.*

This example was designed to give you an idea of how you might use your dreams as choices to address the responsibilities of material. It is too much to expect that every character holds some kind of parallel to your life. However, whenever you can identify a theme that you can relate to, you might be able through the use of dreaming to access and liberate your unconscious to *play the part for you!*

Another example not quite so hypothetical has to do with a film I saw recently, *A Time to Kill.* The character Samuel L. Jackson plays is a black man in the rural South, whose daughter was raped and killed by two white rednecks. The men were caught, but as they are on their way to the courtroom to stand trial, the Jackson character bursts in and kills them both with a semi-automatic assault rifle. He is arrested and goes to trial—and so on and so forth. The outcome is not important for our purposes. Obviously, the character, who grew up in the rural South, had already experienced bigotry, insults, abuse, and all kinds of indignities. The death of his daughter at the hands of those men was the "straw" that made him take violent action.

Let us imagine that I am going to play a part like Samuel L. Jackson's. The character has been aggressed on, ridiculed, abused in untold ways, and at a point in the film decides that he has had enough and becomes his own judge, jury, and executioner. These types of situations are common place in movies, but how often do we see in an actor the dimensional behavior that would allow us to believe that the character's feelings have been subliminally present from the moment he appeared? It isn't hard to *indicate* the emotion necessary to grab a gun filled with blanks and pretend to kill someone. The real art is to *create* all of the conscious and unconscious realities that fester from a lifetime of experience, to work with dreams to access the component parts of deep hurt and anger which might finally erupt in violence. Let us return to my Corvette dream, which I feel was very significant. It is not the only one of that sort I have ever had. There have been many other similar ones. In some I stand and fight, and in others I run, but they always leave me hurt and angry. Sometimes it is hard to contain my violent feelings, and I wish for a chance to go back and confront those bullies! I have often thought, God help the person who aggresses on me now, because he will get it for all the others!

Returning to the dream and imaging it, encouraging all of my unconscious impulses to surface, I am on the journey to addressing the character responsibilities. I might supplement the dream with a number of others that reflect the same type of emotions, use some Creative Manipulation of the impulses liberated, and possibly add other relationship choices to my work.

Dreams can also help to address other obligations than character, such as very dimensional relationship or emotional obligations, as well as historical or thematic obligations. They can be used to create time and place, moods, ambience, and emotional states that are inherent to the character. They can lend a surrealistic quality to place and behavior or elicit disowned subpersonalities that can only speak from the unconscious. They can open up a world of emotions that an actor may not be able to access in any other way.

THE DREAM JOURNAL

Keeping a record of your dreams is mandatory! You cannot remember all of them over long periods of times. Even if you train yourself to hold on to a dream for a while, in a short time it will become vague, and you will lose important elements in it. You will forget key symbols and events—which might be like cutting the heart out of it. Therefore take the time every morning to record all the dreams that you can remember from the previous night. Even if they are not complete, collect the fragments, since they might contain significant symbols that you will understand later in another dream. Some people dream in episodes; that is to say that they dream about a theme, which is then repeated the following night. Write down all of the parts, even if you think some of them might be irrelevant. After doing so, leave a section underneath to record your responses to the dream and/or feelings about it. This is very important, particularly if you do it immediately. Since you may still be somewhat connected to your unconscious upon awakening, your feelings and comments may prove to be very valuable, as the following example will show.

➤ *Example of a Dream Journal Entry*
"April 6, 1997

"I had a number of dreams. Most of them seem very far back there—like looking at figures through twenty-seven layers of gauze! I was arguing with someone at a table—real muscular guy, who was being very belligerent and threatening. I told him to back off. I was very firm and not afraid at all! He did nothing except stare at me. I told him that if he tried to get physical with me, I would kill him. I can't remember what his response was. I do remember that I made an internal comment after saying that. I said to myself that I was serious and that it was not an idle threat. He just sat there, glaring back at me. I remember saying to myself that I had seen him somewhere before but could not remember where. I turned to someone and told him to call the Highway Patrol, not to protect me but to keep me from killing him. That's where the dream ended.

"Since that was only one dream out of many, I can't recall any feeling I had about it. In writing it down, I identified that it was another in a long line of dreams where I was being aggressed on or threatened in some way. I don't believe that this character in my dream was a subjective part of me—although he might be! I think he represented an archetypal person one associates with aggression and violence. The important thing that I am noticing lately in these kinds of dreams is that I am standing up to the threat and responding in kind! I am not sure what that means except that it feels very satisfying to me. Possibly I am continuing to receive messages from my unconscious telling me that I have the power to do that. Even a few hours after the dream, I can close my eyes and see his face.

"Dream Number 2: This one is more vivid and also more understandable. I'm driving along a road or street (another car dream) somewhere in an older, small white Chrysler convertible (totally out of character for me! The fact that I am in that kind of a car elevates this dream to nightmare status!). I'm driving, and I feel that I can't control the car, which keeps bumping into things. I feel very distressed and as if I had lost one of my physical faculties. I sideswipe parked cars and damage mine a little, which concerns me somewhat (I remember looking at a small crease in the right fender and not liking it much), but my major concern is that I can't seem to handle the car or get it to go where I want. I feel very upset by the situation. I think that when people get old they lose their reflexes and judgment of distances. I think that might be happening to me, and I feel frightened. At one point someone—I think it was a woman, but I don't remember seeing her—says that there are two parts that fit under the car that would stabilize it, and if I got the parts, control of the car would return. I have a visual image of what those parts look like. They resemble two average-size pink rubber donuts. I am still all over the place, and I collide with a parked car—only it is the side of my body that hits the car. I feel pain in my left hip and thigh, but I am relieved that it was my body that hit the other car and not my car. That is the end of the dream.

"Since I am aware that automobiles in dreams represent the ego—and in my case even more so—I think that my dream is telling me to look at the context of my life—what I'm doing, how I feel about it, and whether there are any areas where I feel I am not in control. In the dream my car kept crashing into objects and other cars, which may indicate that I am repeatedly doing the same things over and over again. Maybe my unconscious is telling me to look at all of my activities and determine what I need to change. A woman I did not see (I only heard her voice) was telling me that my car was missing parts that would stabilize it. This indicates that I need to change something or add something to my life. The fact that the voice was a woman's might mean that I should heed the advice of a woman or that the feminine part of myself needs to be listened to. I consider myself a superb driver, so feeling out of control behind that steering wheel really upset me! I had a feeling that I was losing my abilities or physical faculties, which really concerned me. That feeling of loss might indicate that I need to pay close attention to the messages in this dream, or I might really lose something important."

Your dream journal can be a specific report of your dreams, without any commentary. You do not have to be totally accurate in the interpretation of a dream. Instead, try to trust your feelings and instincts about it. Ask yourself how it made you feel, how you felt later when you read your journal, and how you think the dream relates to your outer life. If you have an emotional point of view about it, you could add it at a later time. In any event, give yourself permission to comment or to interpret the dream at those times when you feel confident about your responses. For acting purposes you might also add your thoughts about how this dream might be used as a choice at a later time.

There are several reasons for keeping a dream journal: to record your dreams so that you remember them, to identify patterns and messages, to create an understanding of the unconscious and what it is attempting to communicate, to identify the unconscious forces that operate within, to become facile in communicating with the unconscious, and to discover choices and choice areas that can be used in your work. If you are in psychotherapy, a dream journal can also be a valuable tool for your therapist. Since a third of our entire lives is spent sleeping, and a good part of that time dreaming, using and enjoying those years of experience can be quite fulfilling.

At a weekend workshop in Lake Arrowhead in March of 1997, we shared the previous night's dream experiences and attempted to identify the meaning of the dreams and to see whether there were any disowned subpersonalities that needed to be heard. In addition, we wanted to determine if the dreams or their component parts were good material for choices. The following is a transcription of the audiotape I made:

Marty: I had a dream that was related to something that happened at work last week. There's a guy I work with who's a friend of mine. I got very mad at him over the phone...He had gone over my head to talk to my boss about something, and what he was talking to her about was relatively innocuous, but I really got angry about it, and uh...I called him up on the phone and yelled at him about it, and he got very offended...My dream was about a fight behind the barn, like if somebody said, O.K., we're going to take this out behind. The dream was that I was a witness to this fight, and this guy I got angry with, the one at work, was in a fight with two other guys, and I was in the hayloft watching the fight. So I was not a participant, but I was watching this fantastic fight. These three guys—it was sort of... like...they were mauling each other, and then they would just be beating each other, and sometimes it would seem like it was the two guys against my friend, and sometimes it was like it was all three just beating on each other with their fists and mauling each other and trying to push each other onto the ground. Then there was, out behind the barn, like a stack of wood, two-by-four boards, and as part of the fight they would pick up these boards (it was a brutal fight), and they would just beat each other with the boards and hit each other over the head. At a few points it seemed like the fight was over, and one of them would start to walk away...and another one would pick up a board and slam him over the head, and one would fall down, and then they would get back up and go at it. That was the whole dream...and I was in the hayloft watching the whole thing and thinking that this was amazing—like I'm witnessing this amazing fight—and I didn't relate it back in any specific way to my friend...there was no overt connection—I didn't make an overt connection—but it was an amazing looking fight, a really brutal, bloody fight.

Eric: And then you woke up?

328

Marty: And then I woke up.

Eric: O.K., that's interesting too. It's almost like a lucid–non-lucid
dream. Let me explain what I mean. Obviously, you were in
the hayloft. You were the witness. You were in a witness state.
It's almost like when we're in a witness state watching our subpersonalities. It's not a lucid dream because you don't know
you're dreaming, but you know something is happening there,
and you're not a part of it, but you're watching the action...
Well, in subpersonality terms all three of those people are you,
and all...of that energy, that violent, bloody energy is part of
your subpersonality structure—elements, specific parts of you
in that area of killer energy. Your dream is particularly interesting to me because it really manifests how I see you as a
person. You have a certain kind of...civility. You're up above
it all in some "hayloft," looking at all those other energies, and
you do not take part in it; but yet, you were almost—can I say
that you were transfixed watching this, and very interested in
it? You didn't turn away from it, you didn't blanch, you didn't
run, but you were way above it... You were in a hayloft up
above witnessing this carnage, this violence, this blood and
gore and maybe even enjoying it a little bit, who knows? But it
really speaks very loudly of the energy I get from you. You
have a kind of detachment from getting your hands dirty, so to
speak. You manifest a kind of intellectual above-it-all kind of
thing, and you're very civil, you have a lot of civility, you're
very evolved as a person, you're very articulate, you're very
cerebral, and that experience you shared about your friend over
the phone probably accessed those violent energies that you
have not recognized and have separated yourself from. You're
way up in this hayloft, and you're kind of enjoying it, but
you're not getting your hands dirty, you see? So does it mean
that you're going to pick up a two-by-four or hit anybody or
kill anybody or shoot anybody or whatever? No! But it means
that there is some part of you that is telling you that you had
better get out of the hayloft and recognize that energy in your
life and make it more a part of who you are, because your
ethereal energy keeps you from being *earthy*. It keeps you from
being planted in the earth. It keeps you from the darker energies, *which must be recognized!* You see? So that's a fairly
clear dream really. If I didn't know you as well as I do, I might

have a little more difficulty understanding or interpreting it, but as I have experienced you now for months, I see how this totally fits into what your persona is. Good! Are you understanding this? All of you? How you can look into your dreams?

If Marty was keeping a dream journal, he might divide his entries into four sections: First, he would record the dream specifically, leaving nothing out. Then, he would make some attempt at interpreting it; that is to say, he would record his feelings about it, note any symbols that he recognized, and translate them into some kind of understandable meaning. He could ask himself how the dream related to his conscious life, whom the people represented, whom they resembled, whether they were objective or subjective figures or both, whether he identified with their energies, was repulsed by any of them or disliked their actions, and whether he recognized any of them from his life. He could ask them what they were trying to communicate, or he might use some *active imagination,* putting each of them in an empty chair and confronting them with queries about their actions. The third step would be to identify the components and the people in the dream and translate their impact into choices that he could catalogue for future acting obligations. Based on my interpretation of it, Marty's dream would be a valuable tool for accessing his warrior or killer energies. If, for example, he were obligated to play a violent person in a play or film, he would be able—in the fourth step—to re-create some part of this dream and possibly access some of the feelings he had when he experienced it originally. Since his role was that of an observer, that would probably be his response when he re-created the dream. However, he would most likely stimulate a very different response if he were to IMAGE HIMSELF AS ONE OF THE PARTICIPANTS IN THE BRAWL! He could use almost any of the imaging techniques to re-create the dream. If, while imaging himself involved in the violence, he felt the energy inhabit his being, he could use part of that dream as a choice to access those violent impulses for the scene.

As I've said before, remembering and recording your dreams constitute a valuable experience, which helps you to know and understand more about who you are and the forces that impel your life. It helps you identify behavioral patterns and repetitious, circular behavior that may be trapping you in the same maze. It helps you become more perceptive and increasingly conscious about what your dreams mean or are attempting to tell you! For an actor it is an incomparable tool! Your dreams can become a cornucopia of impelling choices that fit a great variety of dramatic responsibilities! Just a single dream could supply five or six choices.

THE STRUCTURE OF A DREAM JOURNAL

Using Marty's dream as a framework, we can list the four sections of a dream journal as follows:

1. **Describing the dream and all of its parts.** Record the dream immediately upon awakening, just the way Marty related his at the weekend workshop. Remember to list all of your comments and feelings as well.

2. **Interpreting the dream.** Look for the dream's meaning and message. Identify all of the symbols or symbolic behavior, listing all of your feelings and reactions. Recognize any of the people—who they are and what they are communicating—and ascertain whether any of them symbolizes you, is part of you. Create a dialogue with them, and ask them what they are trying to tell you. Some research into dreams and dreaming will help you understand archetypes and specific dream symbols that are common to everyone.

3. **Translating the dream into components, choices that can be used to access parts of you or impel specific emotional life.** As an example, Marty could approach his dream in a variety of ways. He might re-create the entire thing, using Imaging as his choice approach (this would probably stimulate his original feeling of being a very interested witness to the violence that was taking place below him), or he might image himself as any of the three men who are beating each other.

4. **Re-creating the dream.**
   A. *Re-creating it from the original perspective, as you dreamt it.* Using any of the imaging techniques, Marty could begin to reconstruct his dream from the beginning. With Story Imaging he would follow a continuity, beginning at the beginning and re-creating all of it, or he might elect to explore it by using Fragmented Imaging to see what that technique might yield. After going through the process, he would be able to identify his responses to the dream and ascertain how it could be used as a choice to address a piece of material. At this point, he should make a note in his dream journal, recording his emotional responses to re-creating the dream.

➤ *Example of Dream Journal Entry A*

"I used Fragmented Imaging to re-create the dream described above. I remained loyal to its structure, and I followed the continuity as I remembered it. During and after the imaging involvement, I felt a similar excitement from watching the fight, while at the same time I felt personally uninvolved in the brutality. Again, I experienced the feeling of being a witness to something that I was glad not to be personally involved in."

Having made this entry in his dream journal, Marty could return to it at any time and possibly use it as a choice to address a parallel obligation. As I said earlier, there are many ways to use a dream. You can explore it from a variety of perspectives.

B. **Re-creating the dream from an entirely different perspective, assuming the identity of one of the characters in it.** The second way Marty could approach the dream would be by assuming the identity of one of the men in the fight, possibly the one being beaten, and imaging himself in the center of that melee, feeling the blows and hearing the sounds of the combat, smelling the sweat and fear emanating from the bodies twisting and turning with violent impact. Even though this is not the structure of the original dream, approaching it from this perspective might allow Marty to embrace one of his subparts which he has disowned, the warrior energy. Besides being a liberating experience, it very likely might put him in touch with parts of himself that he has denied all his life. Having felt the emotional impact of re-creating the dream from this perspective, Marty might easily identify the result as another potential choice to be used in a different framework.

➤ *Example of Dream Journal Entry B*

"I approached the dream using Story Imaging, starting somewhere in the middle of the fight. At times, I used Verbalized Imaging in an attempt to make it more real for myself. I re-created the physical energy, the sensory feelings of hitting and receiving blows from the other two, who seemed not to have features—just blocks for faces. I felt the pain of being hit, combined with a violent excitement of striking the others. At times I felt like a killer, while at other times I felt victimized and ganged up on. I found myself yelling and screaming as I re-created this part of the dream. I could use this as a choice if the obligation demanded some kind of physical violence or even the potential of violence."

Having made two separate entries about the same dream, Marty can return to his journal at any time and peruse it to find a choice that addresses the various obligations of the material he is working on. Having accumulated many dreams in his dream journal, he would have a multitude of choice possibilities covering a large variety of material obligations.

> ***C. Re-creating the dream objectively, as if you were watching it, but not actually involved in it.*** This third approach would remove you from any participation in the dream and could help you to objectify and identify the elements and components you might have missed when you were directly involved.

There are a number of ways in which you can approach re-creating a dream. Exploring and experimenting can only open up a multitude of possibilities. Feel free to make adjustments and changes in your approach, always listing what the exploration yields and how you might use it in your work.

USING SPECIFIC UNCONSCIOUS PREPARATIONS TO FULFILL MATERIAL

As I described the exercises and techniques in this chapter, I repeatedly explained how they could be used both as *general preparations* to elicit or access unconscious support, and as *specific preparations* related to the content of material. In other words, if you were addressing an obligation in a scene that called for an emotional state or involved a particular subpersonality or character element, you might use one of the techniques discussed above or maybe a dream that would pique an appropriate response. Of course, before you start your journey of exploring possible unconscious choices, you must identify very specifically the fabric of the character and his emotional state. Once you have mapped out the components of the character and the obligations of the particular scenes, you essentially know what you must create experientially. It is at this point that you can select specific unconscious preparations.

The first step is to understand the character, as I have explained before, and, if possible, to try to identify the unconscious forces that influence him. Ask many questions about his behavior, and then create a behavioral graph charting all of the elements. Once you have done that, ask some questions about the experiences he may have had growing up that could have structured his personality. If this information is not supplied in the material, read between the lines and use your knowledge and imagination to supply the history. After you have established a concept or theory about the character and what his childhood may have been like, start looking for any parallels in your life. Again, this doesn't mean that you are specifically *like* the character, only that we are all driven by the same impetus and subject to similar influences in our lives. What you are looking for are threads that connect you with the unconscious impact that is at the root of the character's fabric.

For example, let us imagine that the character is motivated and influenced by enormous fear, that the impelling force behind most of his actions is fear. You, the actor, arrive at the speculation that he must have been exposed to many experiences that produced that underlying feeling. Maybe as a child he was left alone at night because his parents had to work, and, in addition to feeling abandoned, he had to deal with the fearful shadows on the walls of his bedroom—the "things that go bump in the night." Compounding these fears were tired and impatient parents, who were insensitive to him. So our character grew up finding ways to protect himself and to compensate for his fears, and he became aggressive and impatient with the sensitivities and fears of others. Because of his need to survive, he created a strong protector sub-personality, which totally disowned his frightened-child energy, and because the latter was a disowned part of himself, he hated it in anyone else. The protector energy became the force which motivated his actions and behavior. He ruled his domain with an iron fist, in complete denial of his own sensitivity. His children feared him, and his wife, whipped into obedience through fear, became all of his disowned parts. (I have already explained how we can be taken over by a primary subpart and be totally unconscious about its control of our lives.)

Having determined all of this, you wonder where you should begin to look for connections with *your* unconscious. Deciding that this character is unconsciously motivated by fear might be a good starting point. It is important to remember that in this instance you are not addressing the scene obligations—you are searching for a *specific unconscious preparation*, one related to your own life experience, which will hopefully create an unconscious foundation for the evolution of the character.

I loosely structured the description of the character above on the father in the play *Papa Is All*, which is about a Mennonite (Pennsylvania Dutch) family ruled by a harsh, unbending disciplinarian. It is a well-known fact that most spouse and child abusers were indeed abused children themselves. Using Selective Emphasis as a craft technique, you should begin to explore your own fear areas. Having speculated that the character suffered a great deal of fear in his childhood, that is where you would start your own unconscious exploration. Since delving into the unconscious isn't an exact science and is not exactly like looking through an alphabetized card file, instinct and feelings will play a large part in the selection process. There is a bottomless well of possibilities, so you might begin with the most obvious area of exploration, *your own fears!* You could start by imaging the things you fear, trying to parallel what you believe the character's fears are based on. Starting with conscious fears, you could use a sentence-completion exercise, such as "I'm afraid of..." If you had identified the area of fears the character experienced, you could steer yours into similar areas.

➢ *Example*

"I'm afraid of...being alone...I'm afraid of...the dark...I'm afraid of...the sounds I hear...I'm afraid...that someone is standing outside my bedroom door...about to come in and get me...I'm afraid of...being afraid...I'm afraid of the things that I can't see..." and so on.

At any point in the sentence-completion workout, you might stop and IMAGE the things you fear. Or at this juncture you could explore one of the areas of Unconscious Suggestions, such as the bedrooms of your life, selecting one of the bedrooms in which you experienced fear. Using any of the imaging techniques, you would start by creating the room and the objects in it, emphasizing the elements that produce fears. Work for the room in partial darkness with ominous shadows spread across the walls and ceiling; create the sounds of the wind and the creaking beams of the house; encourage the fear, and allow yourself to imagine all of the things that are stimulated by your images.

In the area of Unconscious Suggestions, you might also look into "abstract places from childhood," "fragments of memories," "people you hardly remember and shadow figures," or "experiences where you cannot distinguish dreams from reality." They are all rich with stimuli that pique the unconscious! After you have explored all of them, you will probably experience an unconscious connection to your childhood fears. Re-creating nightmares is also useful for this exploration, since they are the direct result of fears. Emphasize those that address the origin of the character's fears. If you were working on this character, you could repeat your exploration as often as necessary to establish an unconscious foundation. Remember that you haven't begun to address the character in relation to his scene responsibilities; you are only laying a foundation in the unconscious on which to build his reality. If you have approached it properly, your natural adjustment or compensation will be similar to how the character has redirected his fears.

Every character in dramatic literature has structure—which relates to who he or she is, what he or she is like physically, emotionally, psychologically, and intellectually. It isn't always so simple to identify the unconscious underpinnings of each character; however, there are clues in his or her behavior that can direct you to a proper unconscious preparation.

THE CHARACTER OF WILLY LOMAN

Let us look at a specific character in dramatic literature and explore the numerous possibilities for using specific unconscious preparations. I have already mentioned Willy Loman, from *Death of a Salesman,* as a man haunted by his lack of success in the world and the discrepancies between his dreams and the realities of his life. To escape his harsh disappointment not only with his personal life but also with his two sons, who never even came close to his image of their futures, he indulges in fantasy and illusion. Finally, however, the impact of the disintegration of his hopes leads him to suicide.

This is a very rich character in a very dimensional play. Where do you start to address the unconscious components that go into its makeup? The only information supplied by the author about Willy's family is in reference to his dead brother Ben, who went to Alaska, where he struck it rich, and with whom Willy has imaginary conversations in his backyard throughout the play. That's not much to go on in relation to his childhood and adolescence! You might, however, make some educated guesses about Willy's father, a man who was driven by obsessive energies to succeed and who, like Willy, failed to reach his goals, always demanding that his son achieve the position and respect that he himself had not. "To be well liked" is a phrase often repeated in the play. As an actor looking for a specific unconscious preparation for this character, you might start by re-creating experiences where great demands were placed on you to accomplish, to be successful, to compete, to achieve. Start by taking an inventory of all such events and experiences, and then re-create each of them, using any of the imaging techniques. By selectively emphasizing only those kinds of experiences, you might ignite the unconscious in those areas, which will supply a connection to Willy and the unconscious forces that drive him.

Using my own life as an example for potential choices, I can select experiences I had growing up in a home with two older brothers and two older sisters. The sibling closest to me in age is a sister eleven years older. My brother, the oldest, was twenty years older than I. So there you have the picture of an environment that was inherently demanding just by virtue of the variance in age. As far back as I can remember, there always seemed to be expectations placed on me. Whether they were real or imagined, I'm not sure. I do know that I always felt that I needed to run fast to catch up with the rest of them. When I found out that I couldn't compete, I made myself unable to! My oldest brother was very abusive psychologically, always making fun of me and humiliating me at every opportunity. Seeing that I couldn't live up to the real or imagined expectations, I unconsciously created an intellectual inability to understand and measure up. If I couldn't, I wouldn't be expected to! Consequently, I did very poorly in grade school. It seemed that I couldn't comprehend things as well as the other children; my reading ability was extremely poor, and I couldn't spell well. Mathematics was a nightmare I thought I would never wake up from. As I mentioned before, my eighth-grade teacher almost refused to graduate me and insisted, as she put it, that I "learn a trade in the woodshops or machine shops at school," so that ultimately I could earn a living and take care of myself. I did graduate from grade school and went on to high school, where I took a technical course, soon to find out that I didn't like woodshop or machine shop. I very quickly changed my major to general science, where I was more comfortable. Unfortunately, due to the psychological damage I had undergone, I had to take remedial reading instead of regular English courses (I suffer to this day from that lack of opportunity). I graduated after four years, but not with my class, since I had to complete summer school first. (I had failed a number of classes and had to go to summer school twice to get my diploma.) The damage was so deep and so faceted that I still believed I was stupid! After high school, I started junior college but dropped out because of what was a continuation of the school pressure, which only made me aware of my inadequacies. I had failed to inform the college administration of my decision to drop out, so I was awarded an "F absence." I then took a job working on a punch press in a children's phonograph factory. I had a car that my father had bought me, so I worked eight hours a day and after work ran around with girls and drank beer with my buddies. It seemed like an O.K. life.

After I had spent about a year in this blue-collar existence, my brothers got together, and, because of my actions and school record and because, I think, they were humiliated at having a brother who was content with that kind of life, they decided to send me to a psychologist for therapy. He was an old school chum of my oldest brother by the name of Ruby Segal. I mention his name here because, as it turned out, he was a significant person in my life. In my first weeks of therapy with him, I was sent to take a battery of tests on eight or nine successive Saturdays at various universities in the Chicago area. They lasted all day long and were combinations of multiple choice, essay, and mechanical tests. I continued to work in the phonograph factory while going to therapy two or three times a week. This went on for about a year. One day, at one of my regular sessions, when Ruby asked me to come into his office, I sensed that something was wrong, since he seemed troubled and a little distraught. He sat down behind his desk, which was piled high with folders and papers of all kinds. On the left side was a pile of folders and manila envelopes, and directly across on the right was a smaller group of folders. Several minutes passed, and finally, with a very troubled and confused expression, Ruby said, "You know, Fred" (that's my real first name, Fredric. I later adopted the second half of it and became Eric), "I have a problem!" My immediate response was one of panic: If he had a problem, no matter what it might be, where was I, since *I* was supposed to be the one with the problems? He continued: "My problem is this: Do you see all these papers on the desk?" I nodded affirmatively. "Well, on the left side of the desk is what we might call your 201 file. It is a complete record of you in all of the schools you attended, your grades and all of your teachers' comments—and let me tell you, I had a hell of a time getting it all. Now, on the other side of the desk, are the results of the tests you took about a year ago." I had forgotten all about those tests and expressed that to him. He went on: "Well, Fred, this is the problem I have: Your school record from kindergarten to the time you dropped out of junior college indicates the profile of a high-grade *moron,* while the tests you took indicate an I.Q.

in excess of ten points above mine! How do you explain this?" We looked at each other for a very long time without speaking, when I finally broke the silence by saying, "The tests must be wrong, Ruby!" He lowered his head and released a long, painful sigh. Finally, he looked up with an intensity I will never forget and said, "No, Fred, that's impossible. These tests—and that is exactly why you took so many of them—are graded on an intelligence curve. It would be impossible for the margin of error to be more than a point or two." From that moment on, the therapy went into high gear! For the next year, we confronted the demons that had been created and had almost crippled me for life. It became clear that as a result of the age difference with my siblings and the constant abuse and ridicule I had suffered at the hands of my oldest brother, I had convinced myself that all of the things he had told me were true: "You're stupid!...You can't do anything right!...Why don't you read anything but comic books?...You're an apple head!..." (That was the name he gave me.) Those are but a fraction of the criticisms he leveled at me.

I returned to junior college on trial because of my "F absence" status and graduated two years later with a 3.8 grade-point average! I continued my studies at Northwestern University, where I graduated in the upper five percent of my class! I shudder to think, but for the grace of God and Ruby Segal, where I might be now.

I took the time and space to fill in this background because it makes it very clear that there is a wealth of unconscious life involved in those experiences, a background I could definitely use to explore unconscious preparations for the character of Willy Loman. The pressures of expectation, the need to be successful in the eyes of my family, the competitive elements, the priorities of others, the need for acceptance, the psychological pressures and demands, and so on—all of those realities were played out in separate experiences and events in my life, all of which can be re-created to elicit all of that energy locked in the unconscious. If I had not been fortunate enough to have therapy, there could be a direct parallel between Willy Loman and me! Thanks to therapy, I was able to overcome the damage of my childhood experiences and allow myself to become successful, while Willy was never able to deal with the damage caused by what may have been similar experiences in *his* childhood!

If I were going to prepare to play this part and wanted to involve my unconscious in the preparatory stage, I would begin by using specific unconscious preparations. I might start with early memories of my experiences with my family, progressively adding the elements which made me feel that I needed to compete or to fulfill their expectations. I would continue to add successive events that would hopefully pique unconscious memories and impulses that existed at that time in my life. Using Fragmented Imaging, I would create the environments and the people, as well as the experiences at that time and in those places. I would structure a specific chronology of events, like a storyboard, and would image them and possibly encourage dreams related to them. Once I had created the underpinnings of an emotional fabric that impelled me towards success, I would address the specific obligations of the material, in character terms and scene by scene.

The unconscious is infinite. It is like its own universe within the universe. Working with it on a daily basis and using the techniques described in this chapter and the next will help you build a conduit into it, which will enrich your life beyond what words can describe!

Imaging is truly an incredible technique for reaching into the unconscious. Once again, "IMAGES ARE THE LANGUAGE OF THE UNCONSCIOUS," so it logically follows that the unconscious is predisposed to images and that they are therefore an incredible way of communicating with it. Nothing worthwhile is possible without work and commitment. When I think of what Jack Nicholson wrote in the "Foreword" to *No Acting Please,* "This work is not for everyone," it reminds me that to be an artist and PROFESSIONAL EXPERIENCER is the work of a lifetime and that you must explore, experiment, investigate, and practice every day of your life. The work is a twenty-four-hour-a-day involvement. You even work when you sleep; dream work is an important component of this system! So, if you think that all you have to do is to memorize and say your lines, THIS WORK IS INDEED NOT FOR YOU!

CHAPTER 8

PROGRAMMING THE UNCONSCIOUS

As I said earlier, direct communication with the unconscious is not possible—except under hypnosis, and at that time consciousness is not involved. So we need to find more ways of eliciting the support of the unconscious, and that is what *programming* it is all about. The word should not be taken literally. In this age of the computer, it conjures up an image of introducing or feeding information into a machine, which will then process this information and structure it in such a way as to make it useful for a variety of purposes. For the actor the goal is to introduce events, experiences, and relationships that will hopefully involve the unconscious even further in the creative process. There are a number of techniques involved in this approach—which is what this chapter is all about.

I am sure that the processes contained herein will raise many eyebrows and will be the subject for much controversy. I am accustomed to that kind of response to my work, so I will not tiptoe lightly in any attempt to avoid it! There are, however, some words of warning related to this area, and they should be heeded.

First, let me say that the actor should only use these techniques for major roles—characters that are dimensional and multifaceted. He should not program the unconscious for small parts that are not well defined or integral to the story. Secondly, as is true with almost all of this work, he should be psychologically stable and have a strong hold on reality. If he is prone to getting lost between reality and fantasy and cannot at times distinguish between them, he should not be involved with this process! As in all organic acting, the actor must have a well-developed *eleventh level of consciousness* (I will get much more specific about the eleventh level of consciousness later in this chapter).

The goal of these techniques is to encourage, pique, and seduce the unconscious so that it will participate in the creative process, so that it will inspire and dimensionalize the life of the character to a level that goes way beyond what we have become accustomed to seeing in films and plays. This is done through the use of IMAGING. Using his own relationships and experiences as the raw material, the actor parallels the relationships and experiences of the character in the text, thereby in a sense merging with him in a way that makes them one with each other. In other words, the actor is organically going through the emotions and all the other realities of the character FROM HIS OWN LIFE EXPERIENCES.

AN OUTLINE OF THE PROCESS

The process of programming the unconscious consists of six important steps:

1. The first one is to read the play. Note the character's background, his physical structure, his emotional points of view towards everything, and his personality traits. Record everything that describes him and everything that is said to or about him. Become totally familiar with his actions and with what he says about himself and about others in the piece.
2. Once you are completely familiar with the play and the character you are going to approach, you can begin the *imaging* process. At first, using your own personal experiences, image events that do not exist in the text but could have happened in the character's life prior to the beginning of the play. You could begin to image these experiences as an observer, seeing yourself being involved with people the character might have known and events that might have taken place in his life. This would be like watching yourself in a movie. The other approach would be to

create the experience around you so that you are actually there having it. Which technique you opt for depends on which one creates the reality more dimensionally for you.

3. The third step is to deal with all of the relationships of the piece. Image every one of them, using people and relationships of your own in parallel to the character's. Identify the specific dynamics of each relationship in the material, and look for similar ones in your own life.

4. You are now ready to address the text scene by scene. Up to this point in your process of programming the unconscious, you have created parallels from your own personal experiences that mostly address the events outside of the written material—those that take place before the play begins and in between the scenes and map out the evolution of the character in terms of your own history. You have chosen a parallel person in your life for every one of the other characters in the play and have created numerous imaging experiences with each. At times you dealt with sections of the material as written, but not with any continuity. Now it is time for you to take the next step. Carrying all of your previous work into it, start to create a parallel to each scene in the play, imaging the events in it in terms of your own real experiences.

5. You can also image yourself successfully playing the part. Create a series of images of yourself being with the other people in the play and moving through all of the experiences of the character with great involvement and success.

6. At the very beginning of the process start a programming journal, and record everything in it. Doing so is extremely important for a variety of reasons, which will be explored later in the chapter.

THE VARIOUS TECHNIQUES TO USE

As you go through the steps of the programming process, keep in mind the following:

1. All of the imaging techniques should be used. There are times when INVOLUNTARY IMAGING may open doors into the unconscious, while at other times STORY IMAGING will be the most expedient technique. To cover a large variety of experiences in a short interval, FRAGMENTED IMAGING might be the best approach. SYMBOLIC IMAGING should also be employed at the

proper moments, since it seems so closely tied to the unconscious. Of course, fantasy is extremely valuable as well.

2. At any point you can also use the *Walter Mitty* option. In a sense, this is a *fail-safe* alternative, but it isn't limited to being only an option; it can also be a total approach to programming the unconscious. As I explained earlier in the book, Walter Mitty is a Thurber character who lives almost entirely in his fantasies and as a result of his vivid imagination, creates wonderful and adventurous exploits, which his own real life doesn't afford him. In the same way, this option consists of creating experiences that you haven't had in reality. If, for example, you cannot find a parallel for a scene in a play, you can create a totally imaginary one (imaging is particularly conducive to the imagination) by imaging all of the actions and emotional life that occur in the scene as if they had really happened to *you*. You may repeat this process a number of times, putting yourself in the center of the action repeatedly, until you actually feel that it *did* happen to you. With the help of the unconscious and the programming process you will hopefully confuse reality and fantasy. Using this option, you can "mix and match," so to speak, using real parallels whenever possible and fantasy when a real experience is not available; or you may elect to approach the entire programming process with the Walter Mitty option. As usual, that depends on which one of these approaches works best in a particular circumstance.

3. Both the pre-hypnagogic and the hypnagogic states should be used as well. During those few fleeting moments when the conscious mind is very connected to the unconscious, you can plant the seed that might produce an important dream which will connect the unconscious to the play. In the pre-hypnagogic state, with a plan in mind, you can create a series of images that relate to your character or to the events in the scenes. If at that time, when you are still quite conscious but in bed preparing to sleep, you can produce vivid sensory images, these may very well be carried into the hypnagogic and subsequently produce a series of dreams connecting the unconscious to your conscious relationship to the character.

4. Encouraging and using dreams to program the unconscious are also very helpful. Besides what you can learn and what choices can be culled from them, dreams are excellent programming

devices to establish direct communication with the unconscious. If the goal is to get the unconscious to inspire and dimensionalize the reality of a performance, then you should definitely use dreams as a major component of programming the unconscious to do your acting for you.

STEP 1: READING THE PLAY

You may first want to read the play several times to objectively relate to it in its entirety and get an overall feeling for it. We will call this *the objective reading!* The next reading can be to understand the dynamics of the piece—the relationships between the characters, the author's statement, the theme, and so on. By the last reading, you might address *your* character specifically. Concentrate on his actions and relationships and make note of the environments and their effect on him. Start a mini-journal related to him, and write down all of the significant elements that you personally identify with. Make specific notations related to the similarities between you and him, and record the dissimilarities and contradictions. Be very specific with these details. They will be very important later as you begin the imaging process. Detail all of the character's relationships, and begin to list people in your own life who have a similar impact on you. You might end up with three or four people for every character. That is O.K. You can determine later which of your choices is the best for the play. Identify the variety of places where the action takes place and find parallels for them too. At some point, you will probably make a determination of the character-element obligations—what the character's psychological structure is, how he behaves emotionally, where his intellect is, and how he relates to his body and to the world physically. You will identify the specifics of his thought process. If you specifically note his speech patterns, the way he expresses things, the unique individuality of his sentence structure and the content of his words, you will probably be able to determine much of his thinking patterns. Also identify the forces that impel his behavior—what drives him, motivates his actions, his needs and desires, and so on. Understand how his important relationships affect him. Trace their influence and their impact on forming his character. Record your observations in your programming journal, and draw the similarities as well as the differences. Using your own psychological knowledge, you may conjecture about how his personality was formed through his childhood experiences. Whether you identify with all the elements of his character or not, you can imagine what events and experiences might have occurred earlier in his life and find specific parallels in your own to re-create later in your imaging workouts. Write everything down in your journal with alternate options. You may end up with several experiences to explore. Write down all of your discoveries and comments.

For example, let us imagine that the character is extremely insecure and that his insecurity was created by a punitive and demanding father, who was very critical and abusive and constantly negated every one of his accomplishments. As a result, this character developed an overwhelming need to prove himself and to achieve success and acceptance. As the actor approaching these realities, you might identify a group of experiences from your own life, then string them together and re-create each so as to fashion a similar underpinning reality for yourself. It is an amazing phenomenon how, when you successfully create a parallel reality that is at the basis of a character's behavior, everything seems to fall into place! All of a sudden the relationships seem to gel, and the impetus for the character's behavior also impels your behavior on and off the stage.

In this first phase of programming the unconscious, you should concentrate on gathering information and committing all of your discoveries to paper. You will also identify the parallel choices in each area and make notes about what specific experiences, events, and relationships you will want to explore when you start the imaging process. Include characters who don't actually exist in the play but did exist in the character's life before. They too must be addressed and created so that they are real to you as you play the part.

STEP 2: STARTING TO IMAGE

I already detailed the various imaging techniques earlier in the book. When re-creating a personal experience, you may use any of them. Selecting the right one is a matter of trial and discovery. Of course, after spending considerable time with the various techniques, you will become aware of which one works best in which situation. So as you go into a choice, you will already have the knowledge from prior experience as to which technique you will try first.

Another decision you must make as an actor is where to begin. Should you start with the environments, re-creating personal places from your life, or should you launch right into addressing the various relationships the character has in the play? This too is a decision that depends on the nature of the piece and the priorities of the material. Remember that at this point you have not started to address the written scenes of the play. You are only *laying the foundation* for the background of the character and his relationships. Which of your personal experiences you choose is up to you and dependent on the character and your understanding of him. Using selectively emphasized experiences and **imaging them repeatedly** create the life of the character outside of the material and apart from it. This brings a dimension to the play that would not otherwise exist.

After spending some time creating the events that take place before, after, and in between the written scenes of the play, you can begin dealing with those scenes by finding your own life parallels and imaging those events. By selecting experiences similar to the character's and imaging them, you begin to create a life that is parallel to his. Since the events of your life are real and have actually happened, stringing them together as they occur in the life of the character begins to make the entire experience real for you. At first, this imaging process is quite conscious, but later you can create these images in a hypnagogic state, hoping to pique the unconscious and have the images inhabit your dreams (I will say more about that later in the chapter).

STEP 3: IMAGING RELATIONSHIPS

The next step is to follow the blueprint of the character and the way he relates to the various people in the play and to find parallels in your own experience that you can create using the imaging process. They do not have to be literal parallels; they can contain different types of activities, but they must be similar in character-relationship content. Image experiences that you had with your choices that may not be in the play but might have happened to the character. By imaging events that the author didn't write about, you create a history with each person, which carries into the play. As you act in it, depending on how successful you were in "downloading" these imaging events into the unconscious, you will really feel as though you had experienced all of these realities with the other characters. Whenever there is no exact parallel, use the closest one you have. Create an unconscious connection and history with every person your character relates to, no matter how casual the relationship may be. By doing this you create a real relationship with everyone, a history of experiences with each person that actually happened to you, the actor, in your real life.

347

EXAMPLES OF PROGRAMMING THE UNCONSCIOUS

For the sake of an example, let us approach a relationship responsibility.

This hypothetical example is about a man's relationship to the most significant woman in his life. The play opens in the Sloan-Kettering Hospital in New York. The woman is dying of cancer, and our character is at her bedside. They have had many years together and a very loving relationship. He met her in college, and they have been together ever since. He is trying very hard to keep it together, not wanting to upset her, but it is very difficult for him to hide the devastation that is racking him internally. Given this role, an actor might just find some parallel and work for that specific experience, but if it did not embody the history of a long, loving relationship, it would lack the depth it needs and would not involve his unconscious to support the reality. The actor therefore decides to re-create through Fragmented Imaging the history of his relationship with this woman, starting with their first encounter. He picks that particular technique because he is going to do a *montage* of experiences, from their first meeting to their present relationship. Fragmented Imaging usually takes less time than Story Imaging.

The actor in this hypothetical scenario elects to use the relationship he had with his college sweetheart, whom he later married. Fortunately, there is a strong parallel to the material. Both he and the character fell in love with a woman in college and had a long-lasting relationship. The major difference is that the actor's wife did not die! Instead, they got divorced. The separation and subsequent divorce, however, were almost as devastating to him as the impending loss of his wife is to the character. Essentially this is a good parallel. The reason for creating a series of experiences related to his life with his wife is twofold: First, by so doing he will stimulate the memories and the history of a long and meaningful relationship, which will be present in his inner life when he approaches the written scenes; and secondly, he will most likely liberate many memories, feelings, and impulses which had been consigned to the unconscious. As he images these experiences and works with them, he releases many unconscious memories related to the years they spent together—the feelings they shared, the dreams he had about her during their courtship and their marriage and after their divorce, and so on. These dreams and nightmares were produced by the unconscious. By re-creating many of the realities of the relationship, the actor is stirring up the "silt" at the bottom of his unconscious "pond"! As this occurs, many thoughts and impulses float to the surface. Some of them break into his conscious awareness, while others are subliminal but still have an emotional impact on him. By doing this, he brings into the scene the history and emotional dimension that make the character's reality more believable to the audience, while at the same time allowing him to organically experience what the character is going through.

Another option the actor might choose to exercise is to re-create some of his dreams about the relationship. He may use the imaging process to specifically re-create some of the ones he had when he and his wife were still together, in order to stimulate an unconscious connection to his Fragmented Imaging montage of their relationship; or he can encourage himself to invite new dreams which deal with the loss of his wife, the separation, the divorce, and so on. By encouraging both the re-creation of dreams he had in the past and the occurrence of new ones that address his present state in the relationship, he may be able to connect the past with the present in unconscious terms.

➢ *Imaging Example*

He starts with the first time he saw his wife at the student-union cafeteria:

I smell the hamburgers on the grill...burnt oil odor...greasy...meat smell...don't like it...I feel the back of the booth on my back...Formica tabletop...stained...gray...ugly...carved initials...gathering grime and dirt...(All five senses are working at the same time. He is using Imaging Sensations as his approach technique.) *Hear the cacophony of voices in an unintelligible din...Looking around...see people eating, reading textbooks...colors...clashing...see her...she's beautiful...almost as if surrounded by a white light...sitting alone...hair...brown...skin...white... pink...She moves in slow motion...I feel overwhelmed by the sight of her ...feel my heart beating faster...aware of the fluorescent lights above... They cast an eerie glow on this room...She stands out...changing the colors around her...She is speaking to someone passing her table...I'm trying to read her lips...her teeth...white...beautiful...*

(Since this exercise is approached as a montage of many experiences in the course of their relationship, the actor will jump from one to another without any transitions.)

Walking with her arm in arm...See the leaves of the trees turning red...brown...feel the chill in the air...hear her voice...I'm putting my arm around her...feel warm...in love...See the campus as I never have before...smell her odor...incredible...feel the texture of her sweater and the warmth of her body coming through it...I'm kissing her...feel the softness and moistness of her lips on mine...unbelievable feelings in my stomach...feel the excitement coursing through my entire body...In bed together...feel the warmth of her entire body next to me...so excited... feel out of control...lying there...heart beating so fast...kissing...touching her all over...Can't believe this is happening to me...looking into each other's eyes...wanting to be so close—almost as if merging through each other...feel the satin sheets...sliding down...laughing...listening to the silence...tasting her on my lips...feel her hair touching my shoulder ...Standing in front of him...gray hair...nice, kind face...wrinkles... smiling, talking...saying something...can't hear the words...Collar tight on my neck...feel nervous...See her...tears in her eyes...looking at me with love..."Do you take this woman?"...My heart jumps...Yes!...Yes!... I'll take her...anywhere...I love her...We're making love...in this over-done honeymoon suite...can't get enough of her...See her face...flushed red...happy...feel the sand crunching under my toes...Holding her close ...feel the ocean breeze...smell the kelp...blue sky...white puffs of clouds ...I feel happy...Kissing her on the hot sand...tasting her lips...sand in my mouth gritty...laughing in a symphony of sounds together...love her laugh...See her standing on the chair...Looking at her body...wanting her...hanging picture...Looking around the apartment...feel like it is home...warm all over...eating at this new table...tasting the food...looking into her eyes...never felt so happy...Picture on the wall...hers... child with a teddy bear...looks like she must have looked as a child... That picture means something to her...It means something to me...I look at it when she is not here, and I feel closer to her...Hear the shrill sound of her voice, see the anger in her eyes...face distorted...screaming at me ...words run together...I feel angry...hurt...She doesn't understand... face red, heart beating fast...walking away...slamming door, thunderous sound...Where to go?...Feel alone...empty...She's crying...Holding her close...feeling sad..."I love you!" She responds...crying...hurt...Coming home...face looks strained...She looks older...stressed...don't see the light in her eyes...miss it...Holding her, trying to kiss her...feel her coldness...don't know what to do, what to say...Alone...sitting on the couch looking at that picture of the little girl with the teddy bear... lonely...feel lost...

The fragmented images spanned a period of years in their relationship, from their first meeting until their separation. The sensorial journey brought back all of the feelings related to those days and that person, while at the same time it hopefully accessed unconscious impulses and responses. Relating to our hypothetical scenario, the actor may repeat this process many times, adding other elements of his experience to the images. All of this is done before he addresses the scene as written. He may urge himself to image before going to sleep, suggesting images to himself and encouraging them to filter into the hypnagogic state. He may ask for a dream relating to his ex-wife and their life together. He could re-create a memorable dream he had about her recently or even one from a long time ago. Re-creating a dream just before going to sleep is very conducive to encouraging oneself to dream in that area. Quite often you may involve yourself in Symbolic Imaging, as you re-create the symbols contained in a dream. In some instances those symbols act as triggers which liberate the entire dream and a plethora of feelings related to the person involved in them. This phenomenon is extremely important because it may be used later in performance to trigger unconscious responses.

For example, let us imagine that the actor discovers something symbolic in one of his dreams, which he may or may not understand. The person in his dream is holding a bag filled with living fish jumping and wriggling around in the bag. Neither he nor the other person acknowledges or responds to the bag of fish. They just continue their conversation. The actor can't understand what those fish represent or mean. However, he may re-create the image in a waking state and see what it may yield, or in a rehearsal or even a performance, he may flash the image of those wriggling fish to see if it piques anything related to his dream or the relationship he is using as a choice.

As a result of the time he has spent working on the history of his parallel relationship, the actor will bring a lot of life into the scene that would not have existed if he hadn't done this work. Programming the unconscious encourages an inner life that liberates itself throughout in very subtle and powerful ways. In a sense, it is like letting the genius of the unconscious do your acting for you.

So our actor has done much work on the relationship parallel and has repeated the imaging process many times. He has asked for dreams related to the issue and has even taken the parallel into his daydreams. He may also have done some work creating the environment related to that period in his life and dealing with other relationships involved—his in-laws, his friends, neighbors, and so on. Let us also accept that he has done all of his preparatory work on his own character parallels, the personal issues that motivate his actions in the play, and so forth. He is now ready to address the written scene: sitting at his dying wife's bedside. Since his real wife is still alive, there isn't an existing parallel to the scene obligation, so what does he do to accommodate it? Well, he has several options. Using an imaging process, he could re-create the events surrounding his divorce, or he might creatively manipulate a series of experiences that might stimulate a very similar state of life. If he was still in love with his wife, divorcing her was a kind of death, a loss of a person in his life. Using Imaging in the same way as he did earlier, he might fragment images that embodied the events leading to the separation.

His second option could be to endow the actress playing his wife with the features of his own real ex-wife and elect to use the Walter Mitty option: He could image her in this hospital dying of cancer and create the ravages of this terrible disease all over her body. This is very much like using Believability as a craft technique related to the imaging process. He could also try both techniques and decide on the one that worked best for him. A third possibility, and a somewhat more abstract and challenging approach, would be to create the entire scenario, complete with a prior relationship and all, with the actress playing his wife. He could image himself and her together and start from the same place as he did his parallel earlier. He might use Fragmented Imaging or Story Imaging to create the entire relationship prior to and including the action of the play. With dedicated repetition of his imaging process, he very well might succeed in consigning it all to the unconscious, thereby eliciting its support to verify the reality. If in the images he created he progressively endowed his wife with the features of the actress playing the part and he repeated that endowment from the beginning of the programming process and every time he imaged the events, it is quite possible that, much as it happens in dreams, his wife and the actress would gradually become one in his unconscious images of the experiences he was creating. If this occurs as a result of the endowment process, the actress and his wife will become a conglomerate reality, which would antidote any possibility of confusion for the actor.

THE EXAMPLE OF 'NIGHT MOTHER

In the play 'night, Mother, which I used as an example earlier in the book, Jessie, one of the two characters, talks about her father, her husband, and her son, none of whom appear in the play. Each of those characters is important in her life and has some influence on her decision to commit suicide. The main relationship takes place between her and her mother, who throughout the entire two hours of the play pleads with her not to kill herself. The actress playing Jessie would have to create a relationship with all four characters. She would have to make those who do not appear in the play real to her, while at the same time creating parallel realities to the material. In order to appeal to her un-conscious, she would image experiences and events with each of the people whom she chose to represent those characters. She could use her real father, creating an entire life parallel with him, using experiences that the character talks about in the play, as well as events that are not discussed there. She could creatively manipulate her experiences, so that they would impact on her in much the same way as the character's father affected *her*. She would essentially do the same thing with each character, creating a dimensional parallel to each of the people in the material.

An interesting practice is to commit all of the elements of a rela-tionship to paper. The actress could write down all of her thoughts and experiences with each of the characters throughout her life and later use those "character journals" as a blueprint for imaging the experiences and events related to each of them. For Jessie's mother, who does ap-pear in the play and is the only other character there, she could structure various experiences with her own mother that somehow relate to the play. As in the example described earlier, she might use Fragmented Imaging to create all of the events that lead to the opening curtain. By doing this, she would build a foundation and an unconscious connection to the other characters, which would exist before she says her first line.

In addition, this character has been battling a multitude of inner demons for the greater part of her life. She is an epileptic; she has a son with a criminal mentality, who has stolen from her and others; she had an unsuccessful marriage with a nice man, but one who nevertheless didn't love her enough; she takes care of her mother, and her life is without pleasure or any kind of fulfillment. All of those realities must be addressed by the actress who plays the part. She can find parallels from her own life to deal with all of them and can begin the imaging process to create experiences in each of the areas, one at a time. Even if an event is not an exact parallel and does not totally fit the circumstances of the play, she can selectively emphasize and creatively manipulate the similarities to edit the experience and make it work. Selective Emphasis, Selective Memory, and Creative Manipulation are an additional set of tools an actor can use to turn an experience into a usable parallel.

For example, let us imagine that the actress has been fighting a weight problem or some other addiction. She could catalogue all of her experiences and encounters with this issue in a series of imaging involvements. If she can recall any of her dreams related to any one of the areas, she can also re-create it using Imaging.

This is a good time to remind you how valuable it is to record your dreams. Keeping a dream journal to which you can refer is like having a buried treasure in your backyard! Recalling dreams that you had, particularly if they apply to the circumstances of an obligation, is often a direct conduit to the unconscious. Frequently, people with specific liabilities or concerns that plague them have a series of dreams over the course of their lives which deal with the particular issue. Those dreams are filled with the angst the person lives with and often contain the knowledge of the origin of the problem.

If the actress playing Jessie had a physical problem that had plagued her throughout her entire life—such as being overweight—she could use that as an Available Stimulus choice. It exists and is real, and it has influenced her life. However, she has come to terms with it and is not affected by it in the same way as the character is by her epilepsy, so she decides to go back into her life to select some traumatic experiences dealing with being overweight. Using Fragmented Imaging, she creates a collection of experiences and encounters that are unrelated to each other but that all surround the horror of growing up as a fat girl.

➢ *Fragmented Imaging Example*

The actress starts the process by cataloguing the most memorable of those experiences, and then she begins the imaging process: *Standing in the doorway...excited to meet him...feel the perspiration running down the inside of my dress...thinking that when he comes he won't see me sweating...Smell my perfume...Is it too strong?...Looking at the texture of the wood on the front door...can hear my heart beating...feel it in my throat...Seeing outside through the little glass window in the door... porch light...listening for sounds...hear footsteps...See face through the window...blond...handsome...Heart beating faster...hope I don't stutter ...opening the door...standing there seeing him look at me...from head to toe...Can see shock, surprise, disappointment in his face...He tries to hide it...It's too late...it's unmistakable!...Hurt...laughing...trying to be nice...*

This was the Fragmented Imaging re-creation of a blind date the actress had many years earlier. She continues with a variety of other such experiences, re-creating each of them through the imaging process. With repetition and the addition of other events that she remembers later, she is activating a strong connection with her unconscious, which will support all of the other issues which she adds to this one. For the character's relationship with her son, our actress substitutes similar issues with a younger brother. For the character's husband, she has a perfect parallel with her own former husband.

Most of the work in programming the unconscious takes place before one addresses the actual material. By the time the actor deals with the play scene by scene, he has already paralleled much of the responsibilities of the character in relation to all of the people the character relates to and even those he encounters before the play begins. He has dealt with the variety of environments and with how they affect the character, by supplying his own places and creating a parallel relationship to each one. He has assigned to his unconscious the components that have sculpted his character, by selectively emphasizing similar events, experiences, and relationships from his own life. From a conscious place he has imaged each event with sensorial specificity, creating those images again and again until they are fed back into his consciousness by the flow of unconscious thoughts and impulses. He has encouraged dreams related to his character, carefully noting the components of each dream and underlining the symbols that appear in it. In fact, our actor has recorded all of his dreams while working with a particular character. Even if many of them do not obviously relate to what he may be working on, they still may contain subliminal messages that he can use in creating an unconscious relationship to the material. Once he is ready to address the play in a systematic way, he is already predisposed to the character's emotional points of view.

Here is a taped excerpt on programming the unconscious that I recorded at a weekend workshop:

"All of our subparts, all of our subpersonalities, the collection of everything we are and everything we have become, are the result of all the experiences we have had and of how we were affected by the people in our lives. Let's take a character named John Jones, who is angry and resentful and feels rejected by society because he had an overbearing father and mother, bad teacher-student experiences, or possibly a couple of bad love affairs. It turns out that he hates the world, and he ends up killing his wife. The screenplay opens with his being on trial for murder. The entire film takes place in the courtroom; however, pieces of his life emerge in flashbacks and in what people say about him. He has killed his wife in a rage as a result of a series of events that relate to the way he was brought up and the abuse he suffered at the hands of his parents, teachers, and other disappointing relationships. Essentially, that is a thumbnail description of the character I'm using to illustrate some important points about how we program the unconscious. All right, for the sake of the example let's say that I'm going to play John Jones. O.K., I had an abusive brother—not physically abusive, but psychologically so. But my parents were good. I do not identify with John Jones. You might ask, Eric Morris, is he like John Jones? No, not really! Not in terms of my personality—how I have turned out, by the grace of God! I'm not John Jones, but I *am!* Everybody is! That's the point, and that's how you program the unconscious. Suppose I only selectively emphasize, isolate, and enhance those experiences that totally parallel John Jones' life and I do not allow the infusion of any of the other *balancing* experiences that were responsible for my becoming a decent human being—I only use the events and the people that parallel those that actually built the character's structure, the fabric of John Jones, and I selectively create all of them in my life and relate to them, enhancing, isolating, and selectively emphasizing them, including the discrimination I experienced from other students when I was growing up. Every day I was chased home from school; I was beaten up, humiliated in front of my female classmates, all because I was Jewish and lived in a neighborhood devoid of other Jewish people. My life was a living nightmare, filled with fear, anxiety, and resentment. One day, as I was being chased home, I ran into the house, grabbed my BB gun, and shot one of my pursuers in the head. I could have blinded him! I'm eternally grateful that I didn't, but I was in a place where I didn't care whether or not I did permanent damage to him. I had been pushed as far to the wall as I was willing to be, and if that had been a real gun, who knows what would have happened! You see, that is the point I am making. Wait a minute, I think John Jones is surfacing here, isn't he? But you see, as time went on and other experiences and balancing factors in my life took over, I didn't turn out like him, thank God! But suppose we only take those experiences, those relationships, and those feelings and influences in our lives that totally parallel the fabric and the "red thread" of the character—we selectively emphasize and *image* our lives in that way, repeatedly and exclusively—are we not programming those components into our unconscious? **Always using the eleventh level of consciousness in this process** so that we don't end up like John Jones, we have the basic fabric that created this man (or this woman or this person). The basic collection of experiences exists in all of us. If we do not include the others but selectively isolate the ones that happen to affect us the way we want to be affected, every one of us has the potential and the ability to be almost anything, because we all possess all of the universal subparts. Your personality, like a DNA code, a genetic code, is specific to each of you; but suppose, as an analogy, that you altered the genetic code and only used portions of it hypothetically, wouldn't you then be a carbon copy of Electra, Hedda Gabler, Willy Loman, Hamlet, or whoever else exists in dramatic literature? If you altered that code, would you not mirror the personality of those characters? Therefore, if you really became familiar with the character and created all of the experiences that the author describes—what the character says about himself, what the other characters say about him, and his actions—you would get a blueprint and all of the instructions on how to create this character in unconscious terms. When I say *in unconscious terms*, what I mean is that you do it consciously, but you elicit support from the unconscious as an additional multifaceted system. You don't turn it totally over to the unconscious; there are a lot of conscious elements involved: the memorization of lines, the knowledge of your cues, an awareness of transitions, the implementation of other choices—much of the work is conscious. You do, however, relegate a lot of the responsibility for inspiration and support to the unconscious, and in essence you do that by living in that restructured behavioral code. Again, suppose you haven't had that experience. If you cannot find a parallel or even something that slightly resembles it, then you turn it over to the *imagination of the unconscious* (the Walter Mitty option). You begin by structuring a Fantasy Imaging process. Using your own real people, you create the experiences of the character that you cannot parallel, as if they had happened to you. You mix and match the imaginative elements with the real parallels until the real and the imaginary become so interrelated that you cannot tell the difference between them. So there is the Walter Mitty option if you can't find a choice or a parallel or you can't find a relationship. When you program the unconscious, you don't have to start with the material. You can start with your knowledge of the character, find the parallels that create his fabric and mirror image, and you live with it, you encourage it, you nourish it, you nurture it, until you begin to take on the personality elements of that character. Remember that you have to have a healthy eleventh level of consciousness. I would not recommend this to anyone who has a tenuous hold on reality or who is not well adjusted or who is a little psychotic. I WOULD DEFINITELY NOT RECOMMEND THIS WORK TO THOSE PEOPLE!

Furthermore, I would certainly discourage them from dealing with this area completely!"

STEP 4: ADDRESSING THE WRITTEN SCENES

Assuming that you have done all of the other programming work and are now ready to deal with the scenes in the play or film, the first thing you must do is chart the character's evolution throughout the piece. Scene by scene, you might outline the play, in the same way as you would create a continuity chart for a film (see the chapter on charts and journals in *Acting from the Ultimate Consciousness*). In the description of each scene, you can detail the obligations and the actions of the character, filling in the emotional life, the relationship realities, the effects of the environment, and so on. Having done all of this, you essentially have a map or blueprint of the play and of your character's involvement in it. The play is an entity. It has a beginning, a middle, and an end, and themes and subtextual elements that run through it. You, the actor, must be careful not to fall into the trap of separating or segmenting your scenes in such a way that one does not carry over into the next. You must follow the essence of the piece. What may seem like a wonderful parallel for a particular scene may have no relation to the rest of the play. If you have done your homework, have selected the proper people from your life to parallel the relationships between the characters, and have otherwise honored the components of the piece, you will make choices with the fabric of the play and your character in mind. The choices must specifically relate to the action of the text. In other words, each experience you select must have an emotional content similar to that in the material, the relationship dynamics must be very much the same, and the impact of your choices should mirror what the character feels in the respective parallel scenes. **As a result of selecting events and experiences that relate to the character, you are in a sense editing your life to match his.** At first, the work is done on a conscious level. You explore the imaging process in the same way as you would for any choice, using any of the various approaches. When you feel satisfied with your parallel choices and have explored them in great detail and depth, you should begin to image just before going to sleep, involving the hypnagogic state in your images. We only experience this state for ten or fifteen seconds before falling asleep; however, with constant repetition you can expand the time you spend there. Carrying your imaging process into the hypnagogic area puts you directly in touch with your unconscious. The images you are beginning to feed into it will hopefully influence your dreams. This is one of the ways in which we program the unconscious. Since everything we do and experience consciously is also fed into our unconscious and often liberates itself into our dreams, IF YOU CONTINUE TO IMAGE AN EVENT AND YOU EXPERIENCE IT OVER AND OVER, THE UNCONSCIOUS WILL ACCEPT IT AS IF IT HAD ACTUALLY HAPPENED. As a result, when as an actor you create a choice that is connected to one of these imaged events, the unconscious will begin to ventilate impulses into your conscious behavior, thereby dimensionalizing your impulses and actions.

THE GLASS MENAGERIE

As an example I have chosen *The Glass Menagerie* by Tennessee Williams, using Tom as the character that the actor will address to program his unconscious. I chose it because it is a classic American play, one with which most actors are very familiar.

There are four characters in the play: Tom, his mother Amanda, his sister Laura, and a "gentleman caller" named Jim. Tom has a relationship with all of the other characters, so the actor must define who they are to him in his life. There is a fifth character—who only appears as a photograph hanging on the wall—Tom's father, who "worked for the telephone company and fell in love with long distance." He deserted the entire family and has only been heard from once or twice in postcards he sent long ago.

Tom is the narrator of the play as well as a character in it. All of the narrative takes place many years after the events of the play. It describes and comments on the past—the period of history, the time, the characters, and the action that took place then. It is a "memory play" and is usually staged with a dreamlike ambience in set, lighting, and music.

Let us assume that our actor has charted the entire play and is ready to attack each scene armed with his parallels.

The First Narration: As narrator, the character first talks about what was happening in the world historically at the time the events of the play took place. He describes the characters—who they are and their relationship to each other. He talks about his father and generally sets up the play. Tom is a poet, so much of his narrative is very poetic in nature and style.

The Actor: Since he has done a lot of work in relationship parallels with whomever he has chosen from his own life to parallel the characters in the play, and since he has hopefully repeated these imaging parallels and committed them to his unconscious, all the actor needs to do as narrator is talk to the audience about those people and their relationship to each other. As for the period and history of that time, he would be far too young to relate to the Great Depression or the revolution in Spain, so he could create choices from his own life experience with which to parallel the realities of the material. For example, he might image the Gulf War or other recent events, re-creating the pictures broadcast every night on television. He could make those events very vivid to himself through the imaging process. As for the depression, he might choose Nixon and Watergate, the images of the hungry and homeless in this country or the rest of the world, or anything else. There are many choices that would make what the narrator talks about real for our actor. He might use Imaging as a choice approach as he is narrating.

Scene 1: In the first scene Amanda, Laura, and Tom are in the Wingfield apartment, at the dinner table. It is evident right from the start that there are conflict and tension between Tom and his mother. In the scene she incessantly carps about his not chewing his food properly or long enough and about his smoking too much. Her criticism and disapproval are quite obvious. Laura is obviously very uncomfortable about their conflict and the way they relate. Tom is very sensitive to Laura. He loves her and feels responsible for her. As a matter of fact, she is the only reason he hasn't left already! Amanda brings up the "gentleman caller" issue, which makes Laura even more uncomfortable. Amanda begins to reminisce about the days in her youth when she had a multitude of gentlemen callers. This is something Tom and Laura have sat through hundreds of times, and they have to brace themselves to listen to it again.

The Actor: Our actor has chosen to use his own mother as a parallel choice for Amanda. He has a little brother with learning disabilities, so he selects him as a substitute for Laura. His home life does not entirely parallel the play, but with Selective Emphasis he can manipulate the similarities to work for him. He chooses a time when he was simultaneously attending school and working almost full time. He was tired and overworked and had to listen to his mother's demands and criticism at every meal. His mother, an unhappy divorced woman, who blamed the failure of her own life on everybody and everything else, reveled in criticizing the actor, his brother, the neighbors, the government, and anything else she could think of. The actor decides to use a direct parallel from his own life. Since there were numerous experiences at the dinner table that directly mirror the first scene in the play, he chooses one that is very close and begins the imaging process. The technique he selects is Story Imaging.

➤ *Story Imaging Example*

Sitting at the table...feel the stiff-back chair against my spine...uncomfortable...wondering why someone would buy such an uncomfortable chair...My mother buys for looks and not serviceability!...(These are thoughts that come directly from the actor's images.) *I see the tablecloth ...white...spotless...smell the food on my plate...macaroni and cheese... My mother is a great cook...anything that comes in a can or box that can be heated up and served!...Hear her chewing...Avoiding looking at her but feel her presence...wallpaper...flowered...bunches of red roses ...on a beige background...old sideboard...family pictures on a lace doily...See my little brother, his face buried in his plate...in his own world somewhere...Thinking what it would have been like for him to have been born into a different family...feel tired...would like to leave the table and go to bed...Hear her voice...only she can make sounds like that... not listening...hear her say my name..."What?" I respond...with irritation...See her face...eyes big...blue surrounded by red veins cutting patterns like a road map in the whites of her eyes..."I said, Why aren't you eating your food?" I hear accusation in almost everything she says ...I respond: "I guess I'm more tired than hungry." Silence...I can feel her disapproval without even looking at her...The air in the room feels heavy...I can feel the tirade coming...She explodes into a nonstop verbal diarrheic onslaught on me and my actions...I hear her voice elevate in pitch..."Tired, tired, you are always tired. You are fortunate to be able to go to college. I didn't...My parents couldn't afford it...You have food on the table, clothes on your back, and a comfortable bed to sleep in... You do nothing around the house. I launder your clothes, clean up after you, and take care of your poor handicapped brother." I can feel my stomach doing flips...I feel the acid rising into my throat...My knuckles are white from my clenched fists...Music coming from the other room...I want to escape into that sound...distract myself...She continues to rail at me...I am now only hearing every third word...The sentences make no sense. I begin to laugh at the ridiculous nonsensical things she is saying ...I see my brother sink deeper into his chair as if trying to disappear into the bottom of it...I feel my blood rushing to my head...I want to explode but think better of it...I quietly say, "I work almost full time to be able to go to school. I contribute money to this household." I hold on to rationality...and try very hard to maintain control...I see her sitting there glaring at me...She is bright red and flushed with anger...I hear my brother begin to cry...see him...helpless and unable to do anything to stop this...Feel bad for him...I get up and go to my room...*

Of course, when the actor creates the Story Imaging parallel, it should be infinitely more detailed. There should be a much fuller sensory involvement, and it could go on for a half hour or more. The examples that I provide are indications of the structure of the imaging process, but the actor must fill in the specificity of the experience created. At those times in the example when there was dialogue, the actor is encouraged to express his impulses audibly if the environment so permits. He is creating his mother's words through Imaging. He can, however, speak to her and to the other characters aloud.

Each time he images the same experience he will discover that he has to do less and less to make it real for himself. With each repetition, he will also remember and find new things that he had not included the time before. I know that it is redundant for me to say it again, but I must remind you that the imaging process is sensorial. There are no words or descriptions of stimuli, only their sensorial creation with all five senses simultaneously (Imaging Sensations).

With repetition the actor continues to commit his imaging experiences to the unconscious, and if he starts the creative process before going to bed, there is the likelihood that it will carry into his dream life. He can ask to have dreams related to the issues. Very few people, particularly after a certain age, sleep straight through the night. I know that *I* wake up three or four times each night. It is at those times that we can remind ourselves of the parallels, and for the time it takes us to go back to sleep, we might begin to image a specific experience. I believe that it is then that we are most closely in touch with our unconscious. In the morning we also experience that *sleep-wake state* just before we are fully awake. This is also a hypnagogic state that can be used in our effort to communicate with our unconscious. The actor playing Tom should repeat each of his parallels many times, using his dreams as allies for unconscious support.

Scene 2: Tom does not appear in the second scene. It is between Amanda and Laura. This is where Amanda finds out that Laura has not been attending business school. Amanda is devastated since she had hoped that Laura would someday be able to take care of herself. She therefore decides on an alternate plan to help secure Laura's future.

Second Narration: Tom's narration is a discussion of the previous scene and of how important getting a gentleman caller has become. It has turned into Amanda's obsession. He talks about its presence even when

362

there isn't any discussion of it: "It became an obsession. Like some archetype of the universal unconscious, the image of the gentleman caller haunted our small apartment."

The Actor: The actor knows that his own mother, in spite of her ambivalence towards his younger brother (she often asked, "Why me?" in relation to him), also had some guilt and concern about the boy and on various occasions expressed her worry about his life and his future. He too was very shy and socially retarded, so much had to be done for him. On numerous occasions the mother had tried to enlist the help of our actor in some way, as she looked for solutions to this problem. This reality in the actor's life is a very close parallel, and his process is quite simple. Before addressing the material, he might have created, through Imaging, the various conversations he had with his mother about his little brother. By the time he is ready to deal with the play as written, he should have a backlog of imaging experiences that would totally support the content of this second narration. If necessary, he could supplement his process by using Fragmented Imaging as he says the lines.

Scene 3: Scene 3 begins with a heated argument between Tom and Amanda, which seems to have started before the lights come up, indicating that it has been ongoing. Unlike the previous scene with his mother, this conflict is very active and volatile. The argument escalates, with both of them railing at each other. She accuses him of jeopardizing his job and reminds him of his responsibilities. He defends himself, expressing how hard it is for him to go to work at that warehouse every day. She accuses him of doing things that he is ashamed of, and he finally explodes into an intimidating fantasy monologue about all of the terrible things he is doing (the famous "El Diablo" monologue that every male acting student, including myself, has done at one time or another). In their first encounter, the character exercised much more control, but in this scene he "loses it."

The Actor: Our actor, who has re-created many such events from his own life, decides to pick the one that most closely relates to the scene, an experience that was very explosive. He might approach that parallel by using a combination of Fragmented and Verbalized Imaging.

> ➤ **_Imaging Example_**

He starts with the verbalization of his images:

"I see her standing in the doorway of my bedroom...Her lip is curled upward, and I know what that means...She's ready to attack!... 'What do you want, Mother?' She stands there for a moment with her arms folded across her chest...She's wearing an apron...It's wet, so I assume she's been washing dishes...She speaks...Instead of saying the words, she spits them at me: 'What do you mean, what do I want? I want a little respect from you. You come and go as if this was a flophouse that you just crashed in—no acknowledgement, no hello, nothing!'" (During all of this the actor is sensorially imaging all of the events taking place. He is creating the room, his mother, the sound of her voice, and so on. He is seeing her clothing and listening to her words as they are expressed. Usually there are at least a dozen sensory images for each verbal expression.)

"'I leave very early...for school...I come home very late from work ...What the hell do you want me to do?...Wake you up at one in the morning and say, Hi, Mom, how are things?' She comes closer in one large aggressive movement...I can feel her breath on my face...smell her...combination of stale perfume, dishwashing liquid, and perspiration ...'Don't you dare speak to me like that! Do you hear?...I have sacrificed for you...You are no help around here...Your life—that's all that's important...Your brother and me don't exist in your selfish world.' See the spittle on her chin, feel disgusted, angry...Want to lash out to hurt her in some way...feel the muscles in my body tighten. I am beginning to tremble all over...losing control...'STOP IT! STOP IT!...Stop putting me down...You are always dumping on me...I'm sorry that your life isn't what you want it to be...and maybe if you were different, Dad would still be here.' I see that the last statement really hurt her...and I want to back away from my feelings...but I can't, I'm too angry! 'I'm trying to make something of myself! I'm working so that I can be somebody someday!...Do you hear that?' See her surprise at the power and energy that I am expressing my feelings with...I can see how hard she is trying to recover and reclaim her position...We both stand there silently for a moment or two. 'You mean to tell me all you do is go to school and work?...no fun, no recreation?...Tell me that you don't smoke grass anymore...Go ahead. I'll laugh right in your face...I smell it...Don't try to kid me!' I feel my heart beating so hard it feels like it's going to explode right out of my chest...'No, Mom, I don't smoke grass anymore. I'm using heroin...I'm also dealing crack...That's how I support myself...What you smell is not grass...I'm free-basing cocaine.' I can see she doesn't know if she should believe any of this or not...There is a long silence...I feel my energy draining out of every pore in my body... I see tears welling up in the corner of her eyes. She turns and walks away...I close the door of my bedroom...hoping for some moments of quiet and peace."

The actor chose an experience that was the closest parallel to the written scene and selectively emphasized the similarities. In the actual experience, he and his mother ended the argument in an embrace, both crying and holding each other very tightly. The Creative Manipulation process involves adding things that didn't actually happen and editing out things that did. By re-creating this experience over and over, the actor becomes very familiar with the sensory elements which make it more vivid. He should carry all of his imaging into his daydreams and night dreams.

Scene 4: The fourth scene takes place later that evening. Tom returns home quite drunk after having stormed out of the house announcing that he is going to the movies. The scene is between him and Laura. She helps him into the house, and he tells her about the wonderful movie and stage show. He talks about the magician and his wonderful tricks—how he poured water from one pitcher into another, and at first it turned into wine, then whiskey, and Tom knew it was real whiskey because he was called up from the audience to taste it, "both shows." Throughout his sharing of the experience, his dissatisfactions and frustrations come through his commentary. He tells Laura of the greatest trick of all that the magician performed: getting out of a nailed-up coffin without removing one nail! "Now there's a trick that would come in handy for me, get me out of this two-by-four situation!"

The Actor: Having had very few experiences with intoxication, the actor has only a couple of possibilities: He remembers that he and some of his friends went to a bar to celebrate the ending of final exams at school and that he got quite drunk on only a few beers. From there he went to his girlfriend's house, because he didn't want to return to his own in the condition he was in. They sat on her sofa, and he rambled for several hours about the world, the future, their relationship, and some of his troubles. It is the closest parallel he can find, and he decides to re-create it. At first, he attempts to create the physical state of being drunk, which he could approach sensorially—a wise decision, since he had that experience with his girlfriend while he was under the influence and the process of re-creating the whole event through Imaging would depend heavily on that fact. Having achieved the state of intoxication, he begins to use Fragmented Imaging in an attempt to re-create the experience at his girlfriend's apartment. Since it wasn't as close to the material as some of his other parallels, he might have to make some adjustments.

His personal experience didn't contain as much angst about his life situation as Tom, the character, feels, so he might introduce a "litany of his personal woes" as an addendum to the imaging process. This could supply a closer parallel to what the character is going through.

Scene 5: The fifth scene is longer and more complex than any of the earlier ones. It follows the drunk scene and Tom's explosion with his mother. In the beginning all three characters are present. Amanda won't speak to Tom until he apologizes for the previous night, so Laura pleads with him to do that. She leaves to go get butter at the market, which is the way Amanda gets her out of the house so that she can speak with Tom. Tom hesitantly apologizes to his mother. They talk, and Amanda makes an attempt at communicating with him. He too tries to be civil to her. It's obvious that she knows of his dissatisfactions, but she attempts to persuade him to be patient and accept his responsibilities in life. The thrust of the scene is that she wants him to help find a gentleman caller for Laura. She confides in him that she knows that he has received his Merchant Marine card and that he intends to leave. She beseeches him to wait until Laura is taken care of, married with a home of her own. He's late for work and anxious to get out of there, so he reluctantly agrees to help with the search for a gentleman caller.

The Actor: Those are the circumstances of the scene that our actor must address. Having done many parallel imaging workouts involving his mother, he is already consciously and unconsciously involved deeply in that relationship. What is necessary here is to find an experience that contains many of the emotional and relationship elements of the scene.

The actor has had very few heart-to-heart talks with his mother. He can remember many instances when she wanted him to do things for her or his brother, but she always expressed her desires in a demanding and guilt-inflicting way. In the scene from *The Glass Menagerie,* Amanda softens towards Tom, and some of the love that she feels is apparent in the way she relates to him. She communicates her understanding of his dissatisfactions and of the fact that he wants more than he can get from working at the warehouse. She expresses her fears that he may become a "drunkard" and that Laura may never be able to care for herself. He reassures her that he won't become a drunkard. In spite of her attempts to be loving and understanding, there is still an edge of criticism and conflict in the way she relates to him.

In selecting a parallel, the actor can choose from a variety of experiences he has had with his mother, instances where she wanted something from him. Since there is a variety of such events, he elects to approach the programming of this scene by doing a Fragmented Imaging collage of these events with fantasy images added (the Walter Mitty option). In order to create behavior that is quite rare in his mother, he will endow her with emotions and expressions that mirror the benevolence Amanda displays in the written scene.

> ### *Imaging Example*

In this instance the actor might use a combination of Fragmented, Story, and Verbalized Imaging.

Reading the paper, stretched out on the living-room rug...Feel her enter the room...I feel her presence...She isn't saying anything, but I know that she is waiting for me to acknowledge her...Continue reading ...I hear her clear her throat...and I reluctantly look up at her...She is dressed up...made up...and obviously getting ready to go out..."Yes, Mother, did you want to say something?" *She hesitates...then begins to talk about how little pleasure she experiences in her life. She has been invited to lunch by one of her friends—and would I look after my brother ...take him someplace, behave like a brother who cares?...*

All of the above is approached through Fragmented Imaging of an actual event. The actor's comments and verbalizations are a direct result of the images that he has created. In spite of the fact that his mother's request is subtly indicting and definitely guilt inflicting, he sees her pain and hears the need expressed in her voice. The pain in her eyes and the need in her voice are something that he creates in fantasy terms. He *endows* her with these emotional qualities in his images.

He may image several such experiences that he had with his mother, combining reality and fantasy. Using fantasy exclusively, he can also create a series of parallel experiences that never really happened. By repeating this process in relation to every scene in the play, he establishes a personal connection to the material that will hopefully inhabit his unconscious and be liberated into his work. At the very least, he will create a history of relationships and events that will support and dimensionalize his character and his performance. He may spend several hours creating this collage of experiences with his own mother, imaging numerous ones over a long period of time. He can creatively manipulate his process to accommodate fantasy images so that they become a part of the entire reality. Much as in a Believability framework, with repetition the fantasy images are accepted as reality.

> *Example, continued*

See her kneeling down and combing his hair...Looking into his eyes, I see a combination of love and sadness...He is smiling at her, and she kisses him on the forehead..."Now you look like a grownup young man!" He laughs...enjoying her attention...I see the concern in her eyes and in the way she touches him...I am moved by the scene and feel a closeness to her that I rarely experience...It isn't easy being a single parent and having to fulfill both mother and father roles...For a few moments I feel an empathy that is rare in this relationship.

To promote his parallel programming, the actor can endow the actress playing his mother with the features of his real mother, with Sense Memory or Imaging as a craft technique. By using Endowments, the actor will support his programming process without running the risk of short-circuiting his reality by dealing with another person. In other words, there will not be any contradictions or dichotomies in the relationships.

Scene 6: Scene 6 is the scene where Tom brings Jim, the "gentleman caller," home to dinner. He and Jim work at the warehouse together. They knew each other in high school, where Jim was very popular and successful. He was the captain of the football team and excelled in everything he did. Tom had always admired him and had expected him to be very successful in the world. Unfortunately, now, six years after graduation, Jim holds a job in the warehouse that is not much better than Tom's. He knows of Tom's habit of retiring to the men's room to write poetry and he regards him with humor and warmth. He calls him "Shakespeare."

At the beginning of the scene Tom and Jim spend a little time on the fire escape smoking and talking. Tom opens up to Jim and shares his dissatisfactions with working at the warehouse and his desire to be in the Merchant Marine. He shows Jim his union card and explains that he paid his dues instead of the light bill. Jim jokingly warns him that he will be sorry when the lights are turned off! The two men are not really close friends, never having spent enough time together to develop such a friendship. However, Jim shares the environment of the warehouse and understands Tom's dissatisfactions, since he too has other ambitions.

The Actor: For a parallel, our actor begins to explore a number of work-related relationships that he has had over the years. Needing to support himself and still pursue an acting career, he has worked at various times as a waiter in a number of restaurants around town. He has made friends with the other waiters and shared similar needs and

ambitions with them. Since there were a variety of people and environments, our actor needs to find the closest parallel to the play. After
some deductive exploration, he comes up with a fairly recent choice.
While working in a trendy restaurant on the Sunset Strip in Los
Angeles, he spent time with one of his co-workers, who had an ambition
of becoming a lawyer and was in the process of saving money to attend
law school. This young man, whom we will call "Harry," regarded our
actor with a friendly confusion, always making comments about acting
and actors and failing to understand why anyone would choose such a
profession. He was, however, supportive of the whole thing and made
jokes about it, such as: "Oh, so you're an actor! What restaurant?" He
thought that this joke was hysterical, and he frequently repeated it to
new waiters. There were many opportunities for our actor and Harry to
have in-depth personal conversations when business was slow. However, since Tom and Jim have not had many talks like the one they have
in the scene, it is not necessary for our actor to re-create a large number
of such experiences. Instead, he might select the closest parallel and
image that event.

> ➢ *Example*

To establish the place, he may begin with fragmented images of the
environment. These don't necessarily have an order or chronology but
should be supported, as always, by all five senses (Imaging Sensations).

*Leaning against the door jamb...feel its edge sculpting a groove in
my back...smoking...looking out at the alley behind the restaurant...It's
dark...see reflections of the street lights on the wet cement...distorted...
creating images...like seeing pictures in the clouds...Taste the smoke in
my mouth...smell the combination of food odors wafting through the
kitchen and being sucked out into the night...Feel the restriction of the
bow tie I have to wear as part of this disgusting uniform...hear the pots
...dishes clanking on the counters and in the sink...hear the voices of the
Spanish-speaking cooks...laughing at some ununderstandable joke that
they just passed to each other...Looking outside into the street past the
alley...it looks like the gateway to freedom...I feel imprisoned for eight
hours every day...feel the greasy floor beneath my shoes...Suddenly, I
feel the presence of someone behind me. I feel his breath on my neck...I
turn and see Harry smiling mischievously, "Thought it was the manager,
huh? It's O.K. to take a break. Lighten up!" He asks me what I was
thinking. I seemed a million miles away!...I look at him...who always
seems to have a smile somewhere on his body...He likes to joke and*

seems able to make the best of any situation...I look into his deep blue eyes...which always seem filled with a kind of optimism. I see some of the leftover acne from adolescence...He uses pancake makeup to cover the few small blemishes on his face..."I was thinking about how different I would feel if I were playing a waiter instead of being one!" *He laughs...really enjoying it...and begins to talk about what great training this is...studying people...behaviors...and so forth...*"When I become a lawyer, who knows? I might have to defend a customer who has had an accident in a restaurant." *I wonder why he always seems to be able to turn everything into a positive...I feel a little depressed...He sees it and asks me what's going on...I hear cars starting outside on the street...feel the wind blowing the night drizzle in my face...It's hard to tell him what I feel...I look at him. He is waiting for a response...*"I don't know, Harry...I sometimes wonder if I'm going to have to do this for the rest of my life! It depresses me. I haven't had an audition or interview in over a month, and sometimes I think that I'm wasting my life...I love acting, and that's what I want to spend my life doing, but sometimes it gets to me." *For a moment I see a look of understanding cross his face ...but it quickly disappears with a quip:* "Well, look on the bright side... You may own this restaurant some day! So what is it about acting that you like so much?" *I look deeply into his eyes before attempting to answer his question, wanting to be sure that it is sincere.* "It's hard to explain, unless you have experienced it for yourself. It's an incredible adventure...to be able to explore the inner life of a character and find ways to access those emotions and impulses in yourself...It's like taking a journey and not knowing the destination until you arrive there!" *I listen to what I have just said and am momentarily impressed with my articulateness.* "Yeah, and it's even more than that!" *I see Harry looking at me...not quite understanding my fascination with it...With a nod of his head and a gesture of his hand acknowledging me, he saunters off through the kitchen and into the dining room. I take a few deep breaths, pulling the outside air deep into my lungs as if to retain the air of a free environment for a few minutes, as I too return to my station in the dining room.*

There were enough parallels in the experience to mirror the scene between Tom and Jim. The actor's relationship to Harry was close to that between Tom and Jim, except for the fact that in school Jim had been Tom's hero. For this parallel, the actor can use his admiration for Harry's positive personality and his ability to make any situation work. He can respect that Harry's future is surely more stable than his own.

Our actor can also use the restaurant environment to parallel the warehouse, and his frustrations to address what Tom feels. By repeating his imaging of this experience he will certainly influence his unconscious, and hopefully it will bleed over into the scene. Each time the actor repeats the process he will discover other elements in the experience that make it richer. He may even add fantasy items that more closely address the written material. If he has worked with this experience many times over the rehearsal period, by the time he reaches performance all he might have to do is to start to image the restaurant environment, and everything else might fall into place. The ultimate goal of programming the unconscious is to encourage it to do our acting for us. Once that happens, the need for conventional choices and choice approaches is significantly minimized.

The imaging approaches used in the above example were:

1. *Fragmented Imaging* to establish the place
2. *Story Imaging* with a specific chronology following the original experience
3. *Verbalized Imaging* possibly when the actor spoke

The Walter Mitty option could be added to any part of the experience where the reality doesn't reflect the circumstances of the material.

STEP 5: IMAGING YOURSELF PLAYING THE PART

At any time during the programming process, you can also image yourself playing the part. You do this by standing outside yourself and seeing all of the environments that the character inhabits and yourself as the character moving from experience to experience with total organic reality, as well as real involvement and success. In a sense you are doing what a basketball player does when he images himself making perfect baskets from the other side of the court. You can start with this part in order to psych yourself up or wait until you have laid the foundation by creating parallel events from your life. Here again your success is dependent on exploration and experimentation, but Story Imaging seems to work best as a technique in this case.

STEP 6: THE PROGRAMMING JOURNAL

As you go through the programming process, make sure you record everything in your programming journal. The first reason for doing so is that it will help you to remember where you left off in your previous imaging journey and what techniques you employed. By detailing everything you do very specifically and noting all of the components of each experience or relationship, you can pick up the next exploration exactly where you left off the previous one, with a knowledge of all the imaging techniques you used up to that point. The second reason, and possibly the most important, for starting a programming journal is **so that you can deprogram the unconscious. If every step in the programming process is noted, detailed, and replete with your comments, you are equipped to reverse the process and clear all the images from the unconscious.** Keeping a journal of any kind is a very individual thing. The structure, notations and comments may take on personal meaning and be recorded in codes that only the writer may understand.

➢ *Example of an Actor's Journal*

(I will continue to use *The Glass Menagerie* as the material so that it is less confusing.)

"I am starting with identifying people in my life who somehow resemble those in the play. For Amanda, I am going to use my own mother, and for Laura, I think my little brother is pretty close. I'm going to have to make many adjustments and do a lot of selective emphasizing and Creative Manipulation because the parallels are not exactly perfect.

"To start with, I'm going to work for a number of experiences that relate to being at home with both of them. These may span a long period of time and will consist of our activities in the evening after dinner: mother washing dishes in the kitchen and listening to the radio, my little brother playing with his plastic building toys, me studying or doing homework or watching television, listening to my mother talk to a friend on the telephone, writing a paper for school, etc., etc. I am going to take those parallel events out of continuity, as I re-create them through Fragmented Imaging.

"Worked for several parallel experiences. Used Fragmented Imaging and jumped around quite a bit, but it seems to give me a sense of being home with my mother and brother. Tom spends a lot of time listening to his mother's reminiscences of the good old days, when she had as many as seventeen gentlemen callers, and watching Laura play with her glass menagerie. I had to do some Fantasy Imaging since my own mother hardly ever spoke to us of her former life, so I imaged her talking about when she met our father and about their courtship, the places they went to and the things they did together. I must make a note about adding other experiences to this fantasy as I pursue these parallels."

(The actor should continue to detail everything he does in the area of programming the unconscious, down to the last detail, listing the imaging approaches as well as his comments on what worked and what didn't. He might even include the preparations he did before each programming involvement. For example, he might need to do some relaxation exercises or to elevate his sensory availability by Sensitizing or doing an arbitrary imaging workout.)

Second Entry

"I want to create a background and relationship to Tom's experiences at the warehouse. I'm going to create a series of images of the restaurant where I work. At the warehouse Tom is surrounded by other workers, as well as by the warehouse manager and Jim. He has a personal point of view toward each of them. The other employees at the warehouse regard him as somewhat of an oddity and view him with suspicion. The manager is always on his case for being late and for disappearing into the bathroom. Jim is the only one down there that he can relate to. Having catalogued all of the information from the play, I can image the restaurant and use all of the available stimuli, since it parallels pretty closely.

"After the imaging workout: Did some Fragmented Imaging related to the place, the odors, the colors of the walls and tablecloths, the people, the cooks in the kitchen. Worked to create my uniform and the overall ambience of the place. I selectively emphasized all of the negative things there: I sensorially exaggerated the noise, the din of many people talking at the same time; I magnified the odors and made them distasteful; I created dust and dirt on the walls, faded the paint, looked for and selectively emphasized everything I find distasteful about the people, etc.

"Worked for a conversation I had with Harry (Jim's substitute). Used Story Imaging and did some Verbalized Imaging related to our conversation. Worked to create an experience with the manager and used a conglomeration of encounters I have had with him in the year I have been working there. Endowed him with behaviors and things he said to me that never really occurred (a little Fantasy Imaging there!).

Emphasized all of the things about that environment that make me feel claustrophobic."

All of the examples given above for *The Glass Menagerie,* as well as the ones used for every other scene in the play, would be included in the programming journal. The actor's comments on the results should be recorded also. Each journal entry should be scrupulously detailed and every imaging technique listed, described, and commented upon. How specific the actor wants to make it is up to him and his need for detail.

THE VARIOUS APPROACHES AND OPTIONS FOR PROGRAMMING THE UNCONSCIOUS

All of the examples for *The Glass Menagerie* deal mostly with parallel experiences, which the actor re-creates repeatedly, with Imaging as the choice approach. To be able to pragmatically apply this process to the written scenes, the actor can make various adjustments. First, he can endow the other actor with the features of the person in each of his parallel experiences and continue the imaging process into the written scene; or he may begin the parallel imaging and allow his responses to be the impetus for his behavior in the scene. Once he believes the reality of the material, he doesn't need to do much of anything except trust his impulses and allow the lines to come from his moment-to-moment reality. As is true in every other part of this work, if he dries up and loses his involvement in the scene, he can "reinvest" in the experience by returning to his imaging of it.

There are other techniques that you as an actor may have to employ as you re-create specific events from your life. If an experience is not exactly a parallel but embodies many of the elements indigenous to the material, you may have to use Selective Emphasis or Creative Manipulation, for example, to make it work. In other words, you may have to emphasize certain aspects while minimizing others, edit in things that help the parallel or edit out those that do not. You may creatively manipulate what the other person says or does, so that it serves your purpose. Remember that the unconscious accepts things on face value. It is not an analytical or evaluative function, so if you repeatedly create an experience and add elements to it that had not originally existed, the unconscious will ultimately accept your additions and adjustments as real.

It is helpful to address the material with some continuity; however, you can take scenes out of context and work with them individually. Using the material in sequence helps create a thread of behavior that puts the play into perspective. There is a natural evolution of events that takes the actor to the conclusion.

THE WALTER MITTY OPTION

When it is necessary to apply the Walter Mitty option, you may also image parts of the experience totally in fantasy terms, mixing reality with unreality until they merge into a single real experience.

This is not an alien technique. Most of us do it quite frequently. We daydream, have fantasy responses to other people's behavior, image and imagine all sorts of things in the space of a single day. As I have said before, imaging is a natural process, which we do from early childhood. Unfortunately, most people lose their ability to image by making a decision to stop. They "grow up" and become practical and mature! But creating imaginary circumstances and events can be quite pleasurable and fulfilling. People in dire circumstances, people in prison or in poverty often survive because they are able to image and imagine their lives as being different from what they really are. We have all heard the bromides and clichés: *Think and grow rich. See yourself as you want to be and become that!* and so on. Well, they may be worn-out tools of the positivity movement, but they work! Anyone who spends a great deal of time imaging a result may consciously create the behaviors which promote that result.

The Walter Mitty option not only fills the gap when you can't find a real-life parallel, it also connects directly to the imagination. It piques the child energy and seduces the actor into a pleasurable fantasy, which has the potential of creating a conduit to the unconscious. As with Believability, fantasy and truth become intermingled and ultimately indistinguishable from each other. Besides, since the process is very pleasurable, we look forward to doing it—which is a powerful plus in its favor. If a great part of acting is believing, then Walter Mitty can supply that belief structure. An actor can do an entire play imaging himself having all of the experiences of the character, thinking, feeling, and behaving just as the character does. With repetition it becomes more and more real, so that ultimately in the rehearsal process he may actually believe much of what is happening to him on the stage. The goal, of course, is to ignite and excite the unconscious and solicit its support. How many times have we fantasized about things that happened in our lives, events that we wish we could have changed or been different in? I cannot begin to list the number of detailed fantasies I had in which I beat up and destroyed all the bullies who abused and humiliated me in grade school and forced me to make a hasty retreat to avoid injury and taunting. I dealt with them in heroic fashion, at times using martial arts and at other times, like the hero in *High Noon,* having victorious shoot-outs against unbelievable odds! I relished my Walter Mitty exploits and looked forward to doing them. Perhaps they did impact on my unconscious in some way, because I no longer live in fear of being aggressed on, and I feel capable of defending myself in such situations.

To program the unconscious so that it becomes supportive of your work, you must repeatedly create images that you can feed into unconscious areas. Taking the example of *The Glass Menagerie* as detailed in this chapter, you could approach each of the scenes with the Walter Mitty option. Instead of finding real experiences from your own life to parallel the material, you could just create images that are directly related to the circumstances of the play. In other words, you could image yourself in the middle of the action and create all of the other people and events as they unfold. You may substitute your own real people, people who really exist in your life, for those in the play; or, if you know the other actors, you can use them as part of your fantasy. They can become the characters in the play. As a third possibility, you can create other people, imaginary or fictitious ones who only exist in your imagination. We dream about people every night whom we swear we don't know or have never seen. So whatever faces appear in our imaging fantasies, we can use them as part of the total reality. Here again, let me reiterate that you can use elements of reality mixed in with fantasy and re-create either a real place from your own background or the environment described by the author. Whatever works best is what you will end up using.

USING THE WALTER MITTY OPTION
FOR THE FIRST SCENE IN *THE GLASS MENAGERIE*

Taking, for example, the first scene in *The Glass Menagerie* between Tom and his mother, instead of finding a parallel, you can launch into creating the entire circumstance as being part of your own life. If you have already done some work to create the subtextual events of the play, it will be much easier to believe in the imaginary images that you create. Here again, you may or may not use the actress with whom you are working. That decision is based on what you feel more comfortable with.

We are all accustomed to imaging positive events and circumstances which elevate or aggrandize us. It is really very rare to find someone purposely having negative daydreams. So it will take some practice to approach material that is negative or depressing. The process of imaging is the same, however. The more often you use your images to create imaginary circumstances, the sooner you will become facile in believing them.

In this instance, you may follow the written scene verbatim. Your images would relate to the author's description of the set, to any pictures contained in the edition of the script, and so on. You would image yourself in that place. You would create it and fantasize about being a total part of that reality. Using Story Imaging, you would create the dinner table as well as Amanda (your mother) and Laura (your sister) eating their dinner. You could use the actresses in the play, creating the fantasy that they are really your relatives, or you could inject other substitutes for them. As your Story Imaging continued, you would supply in fantasy terms the dialogue of the play or a reasonable facsimile thereof. Your fantasy would promote your emotional responses to the carping, nagging Southern drawl that is Amanda's. Your images would include the discomfort and pain that Laura feels as a result of this conflict between Tom and his mother. The Fantasy Imaging would directly parallel the play, but instead of using your own personal experiences as you did earlier, you would create an entire fantasy and encourage yourself to become part of it.

➤ *Fantasy Story Imaging Example*

I'm sitting here looking at the cardboard lampshade...It's discolored ...like the walls of this room...That wallpaper must be a thousand years old...Hearing mother ramble on...(using the actress in this example) *can't stand the sound of her voice...You would think by now that she would have lost that irritating Southern drawl...I think she hangs on to it like a precious antique from her past...I smell the food on my plate... spaghetti...What a surprise!...See Laura trying not to listen to the shrill sounds shooting out of mother's mouth..."Chew, chew. You must eat more slowly, Tom." I try to disregard it, but it is difficult...She repeats everything she says...Hear music coming from across the alley...sweet... want to get up and have a smoke...get away from her...Laura seems helpless...I love her...She's so shy...and frightened of almost everything ...There she goes with her "gentleman caller" diatribe...Must I listen to this one more time?...I know where it is leading...How many times have we listened to her about how popular she was and how many gentlemen callers she entertained in one day...*

The imaging process may continue for quite some time, depending on how far the actor needs to go to make it a complete reality. The Walter Mitty option can be used at any time and in relation to any material. It can be total fantasy, or it can contain elements of the actor's reality. In either case, it will hopefully create a canvas of total reality for the actor.

Some characters in plays and films seem very close to us, while others appear quite alien to our life experiences. When we feel that we cannot find specific parallel realities in our own lives, we may find that this option is the only way to create a connection to the character. For the most part there is a common denominator in all human beings. The similarities, even if they are not exact, can be used to find parallels.

Approaching a piece of material using "Walter Mitty" throughout has some advantages: Since it is a highly imaginative process, it piques the creative impulses in an actor. If used properly and with disciplined repetition, it acts very much like Believability, in so far as reality and fantasy soon become so intertwined that it is difficult to distinguish which is which. At least, that is the goal. From my own personal exposure, I can share experiences created through Believability that became so real to me that for years I thought that what had been part of a Believability improvisation in my class had really happened.

THE HYPNAGOGIC STATE

There are two times each day when we may experience the hypnagogic phenomenon: at night, before falling asleep, and in the morning before becoming fully awake; or it may happen even more often if we wake up during the night and reexperience it as we fall asleep again. As I said earlier, the hypnagogic state consists of those very few moments that occur as our conscious mind begins to lapse into sleep and the unconscious begins to surface. The conscious part of us is not totally in a sleep state and is receiving images from the unconscious. Quite often, those images startle us awake, and we wonder what that was we saw or thought. Those thoughts and images seem to come from nowhere and to be totally disconnected from our last conscious musings. It is at those fleeting moments that we are most closely connected to our unconscious from a conscious place and that we can communicate with it.

Let us suppose that you are working on a character for a play or film and that you have been attempting to seduce your unconscious by creating experiences and events that you hope will elicit its support. It is specifically at those hypnagogic moments that you can plant an image in your unconscious—an image of your character talking to one of the others in the piece, an image of the place you have been creating—or even more specifically, a request for a dream dealing with the material. You must be quick! It is over in a few seconds! You are either totally awake, or you have fallen off to sleep. If you discipline yourself to use those moments, you may very likely succeed in eliciting help from that state. If you work at it, you can elongate the period of time when you are connected to your unconscious.

Make the decision that you are going to experience the hypnagogic phenomenon and that you already have a plan about what you are going to suggest to your unconscious. Be prepared to take advantage of that precious time. The images that you use can be as simple as seeing your-self dressed as the character or feeling his sense of life, particularly if it differs from yours.

With practice you will be able to take advantage of the hypnagogic state. If you have an image to suggest at that time, be ready to plant it at the very moment when you experience that connection. To me the hyp-nagogic phenomenon much resembles being on a tightrope, walking along that slim wire for just a few moments before falling into the abyss. As you become more aware of that state and make disciplined decisions to stay in it a few seconds longer each time, you can create the image you want to implant.

For example, let us return to Tom in *The Glass Menagerie:* He feels trapped—trapped in the warehouse, trapped in the apartment, trapped by his mother's carping demands and by his loyalty to Laura and his love for her. So this feeling of being trapped and helpless is the key here. If the actor understands that it constitutes the character's major frustration, he can create a wide variety of images to suggest to himself while in the hypnagogic state. These might be very literal, or abstract and symbolic. He might create a very short image of being bound, gagged, and tied to a chair in a very small and claustrophobic place or of being in a thick glass cylinder with water rising rapidly to the top, making sure that this cylinder affords no escape. There are endless images that would stimu-late the feelings of being trapped and helpless; for example, lying help-lessly under a ton of bricks and cement with just enough room to breathe and not be crushed, or being paralyzed and unable to move, almost as in that dream where we are being chased and cannot move away. Images like these will hopefully activate unconscious responses and promote dreams that will support the character's state of life. More conventional images are also appropriate. Any part of the parallel experiences that the actor has already created—such as sitting at the table and hearing the harsh voice of his mother criticizing him, or seeing the crying face of his little brother and the wallpaper in his dining room and smelling the odors of that place—can easily be used. Remember that there isn't time to create a complete image, only fragments of a place or parallel which you have spent time on. Repeat these images many times, and hopefully they will impact the unconscious.

USING YOUR DREAMS

I have already discussed dreams and dreaming in great detail and explained how they are used to communicate with the unconscious and access impulses from it. Many of the techniques explored in chapter 7 can also serve as programming tools. Some of them may need slight adjustments or modifications, but for the most part they can be used in the same way, as prerequisites to the programming process. Inviting the dream, recognizing the symbols in dreams, interpreting the dream, re-creating the dream, using active imagination, keeping a dream journal, using unconscious suggestions to stimulate a particular area, imaging a dream, re-creating a dream with the use of different imaging techniques, understanding yourself and the character from the dream you have, using dreams as choices, and so on—all are relevant undertakings in this context.

Our dreams are influenced by our daily activities. We dream on a variety of levels. For instance, I have noticed that my dreams contain information about things that are happening in my life at the present time. These dreams may be conveying a much more abstract and symbolic message, but they also contain elements from my reality that are neither distorted nor in any other way changed but that have become embedded in a complex dream. For example, a few months ago I dreamt that my car battery was dead and that I couldn't go where I had to. In reality, it turned out that my battery was indeed dead, and I had to replace it the following day. We have all had hundreds of such dreams—which makes a very important point: that our daily life, our activities and relationships influence our dreams directly!

While we are working to program the unconscious by creating parallel experiences that mirror the scenes in a play, we are therefore influencing our dreams. Whether we use real parallels or fantasy images, with repetition we impact the unconscious. As we do this, it begins to liberate those images into our dreams. The genius of the unconscious feeds those dreams back to us in terms of its own interpretation and perspective and, with these added elements, may give us a wealth of information that we can consciously use in creating the character. Besides the literal knowledge that we can glean from these dreams, we are providing raw material for the unconscious to support our involvement in the play. Even if we cannot point directly to an unconscious response, that support system dimensionalizes our work. When you see an actor with real depth and dimension, who seems to do so very little, you can assume that the inspiration for his behavior is coming from a very deep place, most likely from his unconscious.

It is necessary to have some experience with the dream process before embarking on a programming journey. All the work that the actor does before, during, and after the rehearsals will inevitably inhabit his dream life. All of his dreams should be recorded and studied. All of the information culled there can be transformed into imaging choices to elicit additional life pertinent to the character and the play. Whether the actor orders up a dream by imaging the events of the play or the behavior of his character, or the dreams simply come as a result of his concentration and involvement in the project, they can all be recalled and revisited if they are in any way related to the play or the character. The actor can consciously image components of the dream or possibly re-create one of the symbols.

This is why it is very important to keep a *dream journal*. There are a number of other reasons for doing so, but in this case it serves as a record of all the dreams one has while working on a specific role. These can be filled with enormously important information related to the character one is building.

For example, you are working with a character whose every action is impelled by deep-seated insecurities, which were created in his childhood and have severely damaged his ego and self-esteem. He covers and compensates for them by being arrogant and overbearing. During the period when you are looking for choices and parallels from your own life experience, you have a series of dreams related to your own childhood. These dreams are invaluable in your approach to this character. By keeping a record of their specific components, you can return to their various parts and gain knowledge that will help you to select choices as well as to re-create portions of the dreams in your journey to programming the unconscious. You may also use the information that you retrieve to create images that can be used to encourage additional dreams. While a single dream may contain many things, isolating a small part of it and creating a variety of images related to that element could indeed beget a series of focused dreams related to the spine of the character.

> ### *Example of Dream Journal Entries*

If we go back once again to *The Glass Menagerie* as an example, we might find the following entries in the actor's journal:

First Entry

"This dream was a result of my parallel imaging workout related to an experience with my mother, in which we were arguing about my lack of involvement with the family—her and my little brother. I completed the workout, had a glass of milk, and went to bed.

"I dreamt that I was who I am and as old as I am but that I had the body of a little boy. I was so small that I couldn't reach the tabletop from the floor. I felt frustrated because I knew that I was an adult, but I had the body of this four-year-old child. My mother didn't seem to care that I couldn't reach the top of the table. She seemed unconcerned. My food was sitting there waiting for me to eat it, and I was very hungry. I asked her to help me, and it seemed that she didn't hear me. I repeated my request for help several times until she finally looked at me, seemingly very irritated with me for asking her to help. She said that I would have to be patient and to wait until I grew up before I could eat...I remember feeling very abandoned at that moment, and I began to cry. That's where the dream ended.

"After reading what I wrote in my dream journal, I began to think about what all of this meant. I am a little confused by some of it, but I'm sure that it relates to Tom and my imaging parallels. Being too little to reach the tabletop is a manifestation of being helpless. Being a fully grown adult in a child's body means that I feel trapped in a small ego with the potential to do and be much more than my situation allows me. My mother in the dream seems to mirror my real mother's lack of understanding or concern for me. She seems to be saying, Accept your reality and be patient. Those are all of the elements in Tom's and Amanda's relationship in the play.

"How can I use that dream to promote my programming process? I think I am going to image myself as that little boy. I am going to create that image and see where it leads."

Second Entry

"Worked on imaging that part of my dream. I created a small body and related to my real environment, my own home. I walked around my bedroom and made all of the objects in the room large and over-whelming. I used Story Imaging to create a continuity of my actions.

"The result: I found myself enjoying the experience—which seemed curious. I caught myself laughing a few times at the size of my bed and dresser. I thought of Gulliver and of being one of the Lilliputians. I found it amusing—to my disappointment!"

Third Entry

"Imaged the dream again, with the same approach as before, creating a little body, but this time I imaged the environment in the play, combining it with our dining room. Wow! The results were startlingly different. I felt alone, abandoned, and as though no one could see or hear me. I introduced my mother in the image, and she ignored me! I kept trying to get her attention, to no avail. The results were very en-couraging: The fact that my own mother ignored me in my imaging process seems to indicate that it is beginning to work."

Re-creating a dream repeatedly can be very useful as a technique for programming the unconscious. Provided the dream is significant to the reality of the character and adds dimension to his personality, you may ultimately just create a single image related to that dream, and that will be enough to stimulate an unending flow of emotions and impulses that come from the unconscious and fulfill the behavioral reality of the character. Quite often, as I've said before, our dreams contain the pres-ence of *disowned subpersonalities,* which can only manifest themselves there! These selves frequently appear as threatening people or as entities that are dangerous to us. A good example might be a person in your dreams who wants to kill you. This person may take many forms or look like a variety of different people, but he is repeatedly there trying to kill you. Of course, you wake up before the act can be completed. This dream may be the manifestation of a disowned part of you. It may, in fact, be your killer subpersonality, which you pushed into the back-ground many years earlier. When we dream of such things, it is only the manifestation of one of our disowned selves asking to be recognized! It is saying, Hey, pay attention to me; I exist and I want to be included in your life as part of your total personality.

For our purposes in this section about programming the un-conscious, it is extremely important that we be aware of these disowned selves (listed in chapter 6). Most people disown the selves who are most threatening to their survival in society or who in some way threaten their vulnerable-child part. If functioning in the world and being accepted by family and friends are predicated upon how a person behaves, then it stands to reason that we would learn at a very early age to construct a group of primary selves which will promote our success in society and that we would banish the others into a disowned environment, which usually turns out to be a compartment in the unconscious. Unfortunately for many actors who have relegated their various disowned selves to the obscurity of the unconscious, the same energies often appear as characters in dramatic literature. So while working with your dreams, you must become aware of the presence of those selves and invite them into your life and that of the character. Because you are dealing with specific elements related to the play and the character, you are necessarily stirring up things that may be buried very deeply in your unconscious. If by Selective Emphasis you choose parallels in your life to mirror the character's experiences, you will most likely access many of his subpersonalities, whose equivalents for you may only exist in *your* unconscious. It is vitally important that you recognize those selves as they inhabit your dreams and that you find ways of bringing them to the surface. If the work that you are doing is responsible for their presence in your dreams, then you can encourage them to inhabit your conscious behavior and to become part of your character's personality. If this happens, it is possible that one of your disowned selves can become the superstructure of the entire character. A good way to repeatedly access a particular disowned self is to re-create a dream where that self originally appeared.

ORDERING UP A DREAM

As a result of cataloguing the dreams you have while working on a specific character, you will get an idea of the nature and kinds of dreams that are being activated in your unconscious. Each night before going to sleep, you might take an imaging journey related to the experiences and events that take place in your character's life. It may be an exact parallel experience from your own life that you would image your way through or a fantasy exploration of an experience that you have never had. In either case, be very specific with your images—using all five senses—and somewhere towards the end of the imaging process *order up* a dream related to what you have just imaged. Be very specific and demanding in asking the unconscious to cooperate with your request. Presuming that the unconscious does comply, record the dream and be very diligent in recognizing all of its components. In your next rehearsal or whenever you continue the programming process, attempt to call up the dream by working to re-create some of its images. If you continue this process for the duration of the rehearsal period, you may be successful in linking the unconscious to your conscious behavior as the character. In other words, you will hopefully stimulate a complete connection with the flow of unconscious impulses that inhabit you, the character, and the entire play.

LUCID DREAMING

There are a large number of books and articles dealing with *lucid dreaming*. Many of them define the phenomenon and instruct you on how to encourage it. First, let us define it for our purposes: You are having a lucid dream when you are aware that you are dreaming in the midst of it. This awareness does not interrupt the dream. In most cases you continue to dream, and your lucidity makes you an observer in your own dream. We will not get into an explanation of what causes or promotes lucid dreaming. There are many theories, some of them even related to what we ate before retiring! We have all had such dreams at one time, and we know that they do not occur frequently. I have personally experimented with lucid dreaming, consciously deciding to have a lucid dream, and in some instances it worked! Unfortunately, it is not very dependable!

Over the years, I have experimented with manipulating certain lucid dreams and even redirecting or changing their outcome. I have been moderately successful in this undertaking, but it is not a frequent experience for me. As for the possibility of using lucid dreaming as a technique to program the unconscious, there is some positive potential in it. Let us suppose that you have a lucid dream while you are working on a character and attempting to program the unconscious through the various techniques. The dream does not seem relevant to you or your character and does not appear to relate in any way to the play at all. What can you do with this wonderful opportunity? You can direct and manipulate the dream into the environment of the play and a specific encounter between your character and one of the others. By so doing, you are orchestrating the unconscious scenario. If this opportunity presents itself more than once during the programming process, it might be an indication that you are establishing a very strong connection with your unconscious! When re-creating such a dream, you should have a greater conscious understanding of its continuity and content, since you were consciously involved in its process.

A word of caution here: If you become too aggressive in your conscious participation, you will probably wake up and lose the dream. There is a very tenuous thread between the two states of consciousness, and if you are heavy-handed, you will interrupt the dream.

Lucid dreaming is probably the closest we ever come to communicating with the unconscious from a conscious place. It is a wonderful tool for programming purposes, so if it occurs or if you can encourage it to, use it wisely!

UNCONSCIOUS SUGGESTIONS
TO PROMOTE SPECIFIC DREAMS

In chapter 7, I listed a large number of suggestions that I feel appeal to the unconscious. Many of them dealt with childhood memories, while others were connected to fears and suppressed images. Once you become completely familiar with your character, his background, and the forces in his life that shaped his personality, you may be able to identify areas in your own life that resemble his experiences. By creatively manipulating the use of specific unconscious suggestions, you may be able to stimulate unconscious connections that will produce a series of dreams that you can use in the programming process.

Suppose you were approaching the character Jamie in Eugene O'Neill's *Long Day's Journey into Night*. This is a very dark play. Jamie has tuberculosis, his father is a penny-pinching tyrant, his mother is upstairs sick and hooked on drugs, and so on. Jamie is desperate to cure himself, but he doesn't have the money for medical care, and his miserly father won't give it to him. With this kind of scenario, it is obvious that you must seek out the dark sides of your past. The areas of unconscious suggestions could relate to people in your life who have died, funerals, shadow figures that you hardly remember, experiences with sick people and hospitals, and so on. These kinds of unconscious suggestions done at the right time and repeatedly might stimulate dreams that could be used to program the unconscious.

A BLUEPRINT FOR USING DREAMS
TO PROGRAM THE UNCONSCIOUS

To use dreams to program the unconscious:

1. Record all your dreams in a dream journal. If you would like to keep a separate one while working on a specific character, you may call it a *character dream journal.*

2. Be aware of all the information each dream contains. You will be stimulating specific dreams while working with other programming techniques.

3. Use all the information you glean from your dreams as choices or impetus to stimulate character parallels or other dreams. For example, let us suppose that a symbol repeats itself in a number of successive dreams. Even if you don't understand its significance, use it in an imaging workout and see where it leads.

4. Repeatedly re-create all significant dreams, and use them as addenda to your imaging character parallels.

5. Use the hypnagogic state to plant seeds that dreams can grow from.

6. Be aware of disowned subpersonalities that inhabit your dreams. If they seem significant to the character, find ways of accessing them, and include them in your conscious behavior.

7. Encourage and use lucid dreaming as a tool for programming the unconscious. If you have a lucid dream while working on a character, try to steer it into the environment and emotional content of the play and the character's experiences.

Most of the programming process is conscious. The actor consciously images the events that relate to the play; he consciously creates the parallel relationships and relates to the character's life before, during, and even after the play. Through the imaging process, he creates all of the conscious elements related to the play, continually encouraging unconscious involvement. If and when he initiates the dream process, he knows then that the unconscious is involved and ready to collaborate. Since we don't really know when the unconscious is liberating itself into our conscious behavior, we must assume that when an actor catches fire on the stage, that flame comes from the furnace of the unconscious.

THE ELEVENTH LEVEL OF CONSCIOUSNESS

The eleventh level of consciousness is a phrase I coined many years ago. It is the part of you that knows that you are acting—or a better term would be *experiencing*. It is the level of awareness that remembers your lines and cues and knows how you should hit your marks. It understands that you are experiencing emotional life from deep and often unconscious wellsprings, and it does not interfere with your experience. It is something like having a lucid dream: You know you are dreaming but do not participate in the dream.

Every actor *must* have this level of consciousness. Without it he has no control and can be dangerous to himself as well as to others with whom he acts. It is a developable facility, which grows simultaneously with one's craft and experience. I picked the number eleven because I felt that the actor should be totally involved with the reality of his character on the first ten levels of consciousness. When he begins to train, his level of consciousness in his early work is much lower. Most actors are self-conscious and aware of their presence on the stage. So we might say that their level of consciousness is a two or a three, which means that they are not very deeply involved in the reality of the character or the play. As their craft and their confidence grow, their level of consciousness is pushed further back, which allows them to create reality on a much deeper and fuller level.

It is an absolute necessity to encourage and nourish the construction of the eleventh level of consciousness, particularly in relation to this work! Even when an actor is in the grips of an overwhelming flow of emotions, he must have an awareness of his acting reality. He can check his eleventh level of consciousness at any time and must be sure that it is active and healthy before he embarks on working with any choice. It must be functioning at all times! When an actor works to create a choice, in the midst of an emotional breakdown on stage, he must have an awareness of where he is and what he is doing. This *must not interfere with his involvement* in the emotional life taking place, but he must have the knowledge of all the dynamics and the realities involved in his process and its results.

When the actor embarks on the journey into the unconscious and more specifically begins the programming process, he must have a strong and well-developed eleventh level of consciousness. The line between involvement and the eleventh level is a very fine one. If the actor is not really involved on the first ten levels of consciousness, he may begin to interrupt his involvement with commentary. When that occurs, his running comments on what he is doing and feeling short-circuit his reality, and we see an actor *acting!* It is as though he were standing outside of himself and commenting on everything he is doing. In a manner of speaking, creating and maintaining the eleventh level of consciousness is like holding on to a state of sanity. One is able to identify the difference between reality and fantasy, right and wrong, and to hold on to all of the civilized behavior of a psychologically stable person. If an actor is unable to meet these requirements at any time and for any reason, he should not be an actor—certainly not an *organic* actor involved specifically in this process!

I have spoken of the *ultimate-consciousness* experience in my previous book and in this one. It is a much desired state of being that an actor attains only occasionally when he crosses the line into the unconscious on stage and its power and creative genius provide inspiration that is unequalled at all other times. This inspired flow of life takes over, and the actor only needs to surrender to it. If he is working properly and knows how to access his own real emotional life, he can expect an ultimate-consciousness experience to happen five or six times in his acting life! I mention this phenomenon to make the point that even in such a state the eleventh level of consciousness must exist. It may move to a twelfth or thirteenth level temporarily, but it must be present or the ultimate-consciousness experience would become a psychotic episode. The end never justifies the means in creative terms if the end is irresponsible! The eleventh level of consciousness develops over a period of time. The actor is conscious from the very first time he steps on the stage, and he must be so. As his knowledge of craft grows and he becomes more facile with the process, he will push that level of consciousness further back until it reaches the "eleventh" level.

When programming the unconscious for a specific role, the actor must start with a healthy and well-developed eleventh level of consciousness. He must know from the outset what he is doing and why he is doing it. When we are daydreaming, we may get very deeply involved with the fantasy, really carried away by it; we may enjoy it, be deeply affected by it, but at all times during and after it, we are aware that we are daydreaming. This awareness does not interfere with our involvement or the pleasure it affords. It may seem like a contradiction to say that you can become totally involved in an emotional state and even be carried away with unconscious impulses and still retain an awareness and an ability to control the situation, but it really isn't! It is the eleventh level of consciousness that allows you to enjoy even a dreadful experience on stage. It is that part of you that relishes what true experiential acting is all about.

When I was at the Actors Studio, I heard Lee Strasberg caution actors not to use painful or traumatic experiences as choices for Affective Memory explorations unless the events had occurred more than a year before. His reasoning was that if the experience was too fresh or too painful, it would not be effectively recallable because of the natural function of the instrument to protect us from the memory of pain. His rationale was also that it took the fun out of acting! All of that is probably true. With the absence of fun no one would look forward to the acting experience. However, with a well-developed eleventh level of consciousness, the actor always has a buffer between the experience and his awareness of why he is having it.

There is a wide chasm between what we have become accustomed to accepting as conventional acting, and experiential acting. An actor who imposes behavior, presents or represents it without really experiencing the true emotional life that he is expressing, is considered a representational actor. That kind of actor depends on various techniques to manifest the emotional life of the character, without having the experience of what that character is really feeling. There are actors who have elevated their ability to do this to a high degree of excellence. They imitate emotions with such facility that they are even considered good actors, and in a sense they are good *actors!* However, they are not even mediocre *experiencers.* The actor who has dedicated himself to becoming an experiencer really experiences totally what the character does, from his own frame of reference—meaning that he uses his own life to produce the reality of the character's emotions. The reason for what seems to be a prejudiced digression is to make a very important point: The "actor," the one who facilitates the representation of emotion, is always aware of what he is doing and how he is doing it. So his state of consciousness probably falls far below the eleventh level, while the *experiencer* definitely needs to have a well-developed eleventh level of consciousness in order to be able to trust that his experiencing of the emotional life of the character is safe to commit to.

THE ELEVENTH LEVEL OF CONSCIOUSNESS—DON'T LEAVE HOME WITHOUT IT!

DEPROGRAMMING THE UNCONSCIOUS

The process of deprogramming the unconscious should take place after you are finished doing a role, but it must start at the beginning, possibly even with the first reading of the play. You must set out with a knowledge of what you are going to do and why you are going to do it, and must objectify the experience in relation to your real life: "I am going to ask my unconscious to support my journey in the exploration of this character. I want to create a life parallel to his, and I am going to enlist the help of the unconscious to provide thoughts, impulses, and feelings that will make the experience a greater reality for me and subsequently for the audience." Encourage your eleventh level of consciousness to participate in the journey, then do "spot checks" all along the way, making sure that you are always solidly aware of the process and its results.

Remember that from the very beginning you must keep a record of the programming process in your programming journal and take scrupulous notes detailing your comments as well as your techniques. At the beginning of the journey, you will most likely create a number of parallel experiences with most of the other characters in the piece. These imaging improvisations will relate to events that do not take place in the play. Their purpose is to establish a history of relationships with the other characters—which you hope to carry into the action of the written material. Each of those imaging parallels, whether based on real personal experiences or on fantasy, should be specifically detailed in your notes. You will be returning to those notes after the play is over. To deprogram, you must have the specific details of your imaging process, including the entries from your programming and dream journals.

These journal entries should detail each programming involvement. Even daydreams that occur impulsively should be entered. The actor can do as much of the subtextual work as he feels is necessary, and he should record all of his techniques specifically. When he feels ready to parallel the written material, he should make the same kind of journal entries. Each scene and each parallel should be recorded, replete with the content of the scene, the imaging parallel, and the imaging techniques used. The actor's comments should be very specific, and the results of the parallels should be clear. If he used any additional techniques, such as Selective Emphasis or Creative Manipulation, he should detail them in his entry.

Earlier in this chapter, I gave examples of six scenes from *The Glass Menagerie* and of the actor's journal entries. I explained the approaches he used in the different scenes, gave specific reasons why he was doing what he was doing, and described some of the dreams he had. As I said before, all the work he did on the play would be included in his programming journal.

Here again I want to restate the responsibilities that the actor has if he is going to take the programming journey:

1. He must make clear to himself at the very outset that he knows what he will be doing and why he will be doing it.

2. He must make a strong decision to maintain his awareness at all times, exercising the eleventh level of consciousness all the way through.

3. He must also make a strong commitment to allowing himself to be affected by his process and to open the gates for the unconscious to enter and support his realities. It is very much like pretending when we were children. We believed in the imaginary circumstances to a point where our hearts beat faster and we felt fear, excitement, anger, or joy in their fullest form. We knew, however, that we were playing a pretend game, but that did not in any way inhibit us or make the experience less real!

4. When the actor is ready to start the deprogramming process, and before he addresses the first entry, he might try a *mantra,* repeating it many times throughout the deprogramming process:

"I worked on this character, Tom, from *The Glass Menagerie,* inviting myself to believe that I was like him. I suggested things to my unconscious and worked for choices that made me feel and think the way the character does. I did this because I am a professional experiencer and a creative artist. My motives were positive. I am not like the character Tom. I am very different. My relationships are different and much healthier, and I feel I am succeeding in my life."

If you are thinking that this is somewhat unnecessary and a little corny, you are wrong! If he repeats this mantra many times during and even after the deprogramming process, the actor will be feeding it into his unconscious, and with sincerity and repetition the unconscious will accept the truth. It is somewhat like reprogramming a computer. He is downloading new information and creating a new condition for his unconscious to process.

5. He should then begin with the first entry in his journal, which may be his first reading of the play, and deal with each of the entries in the order in which they were recorded. He should go over all of the information and all the things he did and identify and remember the content of each of his imaging parallels as they occurred.

Using the first journal entry given in the section on the programming journal earlier in the chapter, for example, the actor begins by reading it to himself aloud and remembering the images he created. In this case, he was working to establish some subtextual background for the events and action of the play. He imaged various evenings at home, with his mother and little brother involved in a variety of activities over a period of time. At a point when he remembers the thrust of his imaging involvement, as well as any fantasy contributions, he should set the record straight by going over each element and differentiating what is real in his life from what was created and manipulated.

6. He may do a reverse imaging process for every image he created and for every entry, until he has totally returned to reality.

> ### Example of the Deprogramming Process

The actor attempts to visualize his images as well as he can and says to himself: "My home is much nicer than the one in my image!...My little brother has a few learning problems, but he is much sharper and self-dependent than he appeared in most of my images...We have an automatic dishwasher, and I have never seen my mother wash dishes... Actually, I spent very little time at home with the family. I was usually out working or socializing with my friends...My real mother, in spite of her issues or problems, doesn't feel sorry for herself and has quite an active social life..." and so forth and so on.

All of this commentary should come as a result of the images the actor created, images of his real home, of his real brother as he looks and behaves, of his mother and his true relationship with her. All of the antidotal images should be as detailed as the original parallels he created to address the play.

The actor should work on every issue that existed in the imaging parallels, objectifying the reality. He might want to go over each one several times over an entire week. If he feels the need to, he can use the imaging process to re-create the images of his *true* reality, thereby implanting new and opposite images into his unconscious. Whenever he used components from his reality, he will leave them as they are and may even want to emphasize them and juxtapose them to his distortions. The entire deprogramming process is dependent on his objectifying his images and carrying them into what is real. He must do this process for each entry in his programming record. At some point he will know that he is free of the impact of his programming process. If it hangs on longer than he would like it to, he can re-image those parallels that he feels still need work. When he creates those alternate images, he must be sure that they mirror the reality of his life. There are two sides to every approach: He may need or want to reverse the process by implanting opposite information into his hypnagogic state or by encouraging dreams that antidote the original programming.

The deprogramming process actually starts with the first programming involvement. It is extremely important that the actor know every step of the programming process so that he can use his reality to reverse the impact of all of the information, images, and dreams he may have implanted in his unconscious. Working with the unconscious is like communicating with someone whom you cannot see, hear, or feel, but who you know is there! Having a conscious experience that emanates from the unconscious is an undeniable event. For the actor it is exciting, dimensionalizing, and impacting.

If you follow the steps involved in deprogramming, you will have no problem removing any suggestions that you made to elicit the support of the unconscious in addressing a role. I am sure that you will have some fear or trepidation when you first approach the programming process, since it is not something that is being taught to actors anywhere. You will, however, gain confidence and momentum as you work with the techniques, and I promise you that you are in for the ride of your life!

The body has a phenomenon known as *homeostasis,* which has to do with its natural intelligence. It knows what it needs and craves, and if you are at all tuned into it, it will in some way communicate its requirements. For example, pregnant women are known to have cravings at various times during their pregnancy, which have to do with the messages their body is sending to their brain or vice versa. Since we *must not* separate the body from the mind, we can assume that some of that communication emanates from the unconscious, which I believe has its own homeostatic function. In other words, the unconscious too will always seek to adjust to organic reality. So we must somehow trust that the genius of the unconscious will cooperate with us in our little acting games but that when the fun is over, its homeostatic function will return it to reality.

Psychology and medicine have been exploring the unconscious for decades, studying REM sleep, interrupting dreams, and using sleep deprivation, chemicals, hypnosis, mind control, brainwashing, and so on. Somehow, almost all of their "guinea pigs" have returned to normal after the experiments were over. On the other hand, some of the effects of torture or wartime brainwashing are long lasting; but I can assure you that there will be no torture or brainwashing involved in any part of this process, so you may proceed with the confidence that it is you who are in the driver's seat. IF AT ANY TIME DURING THE PROGRAMMING PROCESS IT DOESN'T FEEL RIGHT, STOP WORKING AND ADJUST YOUR APPROACH UNTIL YOU BECOME MORE COMFORTABLE WITH IT! The creative process should be inspiring, exciting, and fulfilling. If it isn't, there is something wrong! Go back to the drawing board, find out what that is, and fix it!

The truth is the truth is the truth! And on some very deep and meaningful level we all know it and retain it. It is my contention that no matter how we relate to the unconscious and what we lead ourselves to believe, we know what is really the truth at our core. It has been my experience that no matter what you implant in the unconscious, in a very short time it will return to reality. The unconscious is truly unconscious, but it is also brilliant! Whenever I have used dreams or images to pique unconscious life and whatever the impetus, I was always able to return to the authentic reality automatically. It is like having a nightmare that stays with you for a whole day after but slowly dissipates with the passage of time.

I know that there are people out there who will read this section and say, He is nuts! This is dangerous! You don't have to go through all this to act! It's too complicated, too much work. We shouldn't be playing around with things like that! It could damage a person for life! Well, to those comments I say, What about hypnosis? Any qualified hypnotist will tell you that a person will not do anything under hypnosis that he wouldn't do if he were conscious. There are entire groups of people, Native American tribes, who have used peyote to elevate their consciousness. As part of spiritual and religious practice, people attend retreats where they meditate and experience the consciousness-altering "sweat lodges." The Senoi tribe structure their lives on the meaning of their dreams. They sit at the breakfast table and everyone in the whole family shares the previous night's dreams. They interpret those dreams and adjust their lives accordingly. There are numerous organizations all around this country that were created to explore dreams and dreaming. There are literally hundreds of books, pamphlets, and videotapes about exploring, understanding, and using our dreams to enhance our lives. Many are dedicated to understanding and communicating with the unconscious through dreams. Jung spent his entire life exploring, writing about, and working with dreams and the unconscious. This is definitely not a new field! To my knowledge, however, it has never been explored or experimented with in relation to acting, until now! It is my sincere belief and fervent hope that the techniques contained in this book will enrich the art of acting and elevate it to important new heights.

This is the work of the future! Accessing the unconscious and programming it to support the creative process is the *new frontier* of acting. At present, it is avant-garde and experimental, but twenty years down the line it may be the conventional approach to create and dimensionalize reality. In the thirties, forties, and fifties, acting was far less real or believable than it is today. Actors were representational, obvious, and unconvincing. We accepted it because that was where we were in our evolution. We were naïve, unsophisticated, attached to the age of innocence, and ignorant of many truths. As our society has matured, grown, become more sophisticated and technologically aware, we have become much more cynical and demanding of the truth. With the advent of television, mass communication, and the flood of instant information, our children are more informed, sophisticated, and aware than we were when we became adults. Society is moving with the speed of light into the new millenium, and with that growth we will become even more demanding of reality and truth. What is considered good acting today will be laughed at in thirty or forty years. Organic reality, however, will never be laughable. What is true behavior today will also be true thirty years from now! Our priorities will change. What we consider important today will be less important then, and even our truths may become the truths of our historical period, but remember that what a person really feels will be real always! The deeper we dig and the more we include the forces of the unconscious in our acting, the more impacting and important will be our work as actors!

BIBLIOGRAPHY

About Imaging

Achterberg, Jeanne. *Imagery in Healing: Shamanism and Modern Medicine*. Boston: New Science Library, 1985.

Bandler, Richard. *Using Your Brain for a Change*. Moab, UT: Real People Press, 1985.

Chopra, Deepak, M.D. *Quantum Healing: Exploring the Frontier of Mind/Body Medicine*. New York: Bantam, 1989.

Gawain, Shakti. *Creative Visualization*. Mill Valley, CA: Whatever Publishing, 1978.

Middlekoop, Pieter. *The Wise Old Man: Healing through Inner Images*. Translated by Adrienne Dixon. Boston: Shambhala Publications, 1989.

Miller, Emmett E., M.D., with Deborah Lueth. *Self-Imagery: Creating Your Own Good Health*. New ed. Berkeley, CA: Celestial Arts, 1986.

Norris, Patricia A., and Garrett Porter. *I Choose Life: The Dynamics of Visualization & Biofeedback*. Walpole, NH: Stillpoint Publishing, 1987.

Ryan, Regina S., and John W. Travis, M.D. *The Wellness Workbook*. Berkeley, CA: Ten Speed Press, 1981.

Serinus, Jason, ed. *Psychoimmunity & the Healing Process: A Holistic Approach to Immunity & AIDS*. Berkeley, CA: Celestial Arts, 1986.

Shorr, Joseph. *Go See the Movie in your Head: Imagery: The Key to Awareness*. 2d ed. Santa Barbara: Ross-Erikson Publishers, 1983.

Shuman, Sandra G. *Source Imagery: Releasing the Power of Your Creativity*. New York: Doubleday, 1989.

Simonton, O. Carl, M.D., Stephanie Matthews-Simonton, and James Creighton. *Getting Well Again*. New York: Bantam, 1980.

About Dreams

C.G. Jung Institute of Los Angeles. *Psychological Perspectives* 33. (Spring 1996). *Dreaming*. Los Angeles: C.G. Jung Institute, 1996.

Fay, Marie. *The Dream Guide*. Los Angeles: Center for the Healing Arts, 1978.

Garfield, Patricia L. *Creative Dreaming: Plan and Control Your Dreams to Develop Creativity, Overcome Fear, Solve Problems and Create a Better Self*. New York: Fireside, 1995.

Shahan, Elizabeth. *The Language of Dreams*. Video Series. Pacoima, CA: DreamWeavers, 1995.

Watkins, Mary. *Waking Dreams*. Dallas, TX: Spring Publications, 1984.

About Subpersonalities

Stone, Hal and Sidra Winkelman. *Embracing Ourselves: The Voice Dialogue Manual*. San Rafael, CA: New World Library, 1989.

——————. *Embracing Each Other: Relationship as Teacher, Healer & Guide*. Mill Valley, CA: Nataraj Publishing, 1989.

——————. *Embracing the Inner Critic*. San Francisco: Harper Collins, 1993.

Plays

Nash, N. Richard. *The Rainmaker*. New York: Samuel French, Inc., 1983.

John Gassner, ed. *A Treasury of the Theatre*. "The Glass Menagerie." New York:Simon and Schuster, 1950.

INDEX

J

If you found the information in this book valuable, you'll be interested to know that cassette tapes by Eric Morris are also available. These audio tapes were recorded live at actual workshops and seminars conducted by Mr. Morris and are ideal for use in conjunction with his books. They are offered in three series: *The Craft of Acting, The Meg-Approaches,* and *Imaging for Acting.* This last and newest one, *Imaging for Acting,* is a perfect companion to this book.

To receive the first tape in *The Craft of Acting* series plus a full information brochure, send your check for $9.95 plus $1.00 for postage and handling to:

Ermor Enterprises
8004 Fareholm Drive
Los Angeles, CA 90046

Money refunded if not satisfied.